HENRY VIII'S LAST VICTIM

HENRY VIII'S LAST VICTIM

*The Life and Times
of Henry Howard,
Earl of Surrey*

JESSIE CHILDS

JONATHAN CAPE
LONDON

First published in Great Britain in 2006 by
Jonathan Cape
Random House, 20 Vauxhall Bridge Road,
London SW1V 2SA

Random House Australia (Pty) Limited
20 Alfred Street, Milsons Point, Sydney,
New South Wales 2061, Australia

Random House New Zealand Limited
18 Poland Road, Glenfield,
Auckland 10, New Zealand

Random House South Africa (Pty) Limited
Isle of Houghton, Corner of Boundary Road & Carse O'Gowrie,
Houghton 2198, South Africa

Random House Publishers India Private Limited
301 World Trade Tower, Hotel Intercontinental Grand Complex,
Barakhamba Lane, New Delhi 110 001, India

The Random House Group Limited Reg. No. 954009
www.randomhouse.co.uk

A CIP catalogue record for this book is available from the British Library

ISBN 978 0-224-06325-8 (from Jan 2007)
ISBN 0-224-6325-1

FSC

Mixed Sources
Product group from well-managed
forests and other controlled sources

Cert no. TT-COC-2139
www.fsc.org
©1996 Forest Stewardship Council

Typeset by Palimpsest Book Production Limited, Grangemouth, Stirlingshire

Printed and bound in Great Britain by William Clowes Ltd, Beccles, Suffolk

O what a noble mind is here o'erthrown!
The courtier's, soldier's, scholar's, eye, tongue, sword,
Th'expectancy and rose of the fair state,
The glass of fashion and the mould of form,
Th'observed of all observers, quite, quite, down!

Hamlet, Act 3, scene 1, lines 153–7

CONTENTS

LIST OF ILLUSTRATIONS

12. Anne Boleyn, artist unknown. (National Portrait Gallery, London)

13. Thomas Cromwell (slightly cropped) after Hans Holbein the Younger. (National Portrait Gallery, London)

14. Henry VII and Henry VIII, cartoon for the *Whitehall Mural* by Hans Holbein the Younger. (National Portrait Gallery, London)

15. Henry Howard, Earl of Surrey by Hans Holbein the Younger. (The Royal Collection © 2006 Her Majesty Queen Elizabeth II)

16. Thomas Wyatt by Hans Holbein the Younger. (The Royal Collection © 2006 Her Majesty Queen Elizabeth II)

17. The first two stanzas of Surrey's poem 'O happy dames', inscribed by his sister Mary into the Devonshire Manuscript. (Permission British Library, Add. MS 17492, fo. 55r)

18. Mary, Duchess of Richmond by Hans Holbein the Younger. (The Royal Collection © 2006 Her Majesty Queen Elizabeth II)

19. Title-page of *The fourth boke of Virgill . . . by Henrye late Earle of Surrey*, published by John Day, 1554. (Harry Ransom Humanities Research Center, The University of Texas at Austin, Pforzheimer Collection: PFORZ 510)

20. Henry Howard, Earl of Surrey by Hans Holbein the Younger. (Museu de Arte de São Paulo, Assis Chateaubriand, São Paulo, Brazil)

21. Henry Howard, Earl of Surrey, artist unknown. (The Royal Collection © 2006 Her Majesty Queen Elizabeth II)

22. Henry Howard, Earl of Surrey by William Scrots. (National Portrait Gallery, London)

23. Henry Howard, Earl of Surrey, artist unknown. (Pierpont Morgan Library, New York)

24. Henry VIII jousting before Catherine of Aragon in 1511, from *The Great Tournament Roll of Westminster*, artist unknown. (College of Arms, London)

25. *The Siege of Boulogne* engraved by James Basire from the Cowdray House mural. (The Royal Collection © 2006 Her Majesty Queen Elizabeth II)

26. Henry Howard, Earl of Surrey. Arundel Portrait after William Scrots. (National Portrait Gallery, London)

27. Henry VIII by Cornelis Matsys. (The Royal Collection © 2006 Her Majesty Queen Elizabeth II)

28. William Paget (slightly cropped) attributed to the Master of the Stätthalterin Madonna. (National Portrait Gallery, London)

29. Thomas Wriothesley, artist unknown. (Reproduced by kind permission of Lord Montagu of Beaulieu)

30. Edward Seymour, artist unknown. (Reproduced by kind permission of the Marquess of Bath, Longleat House)

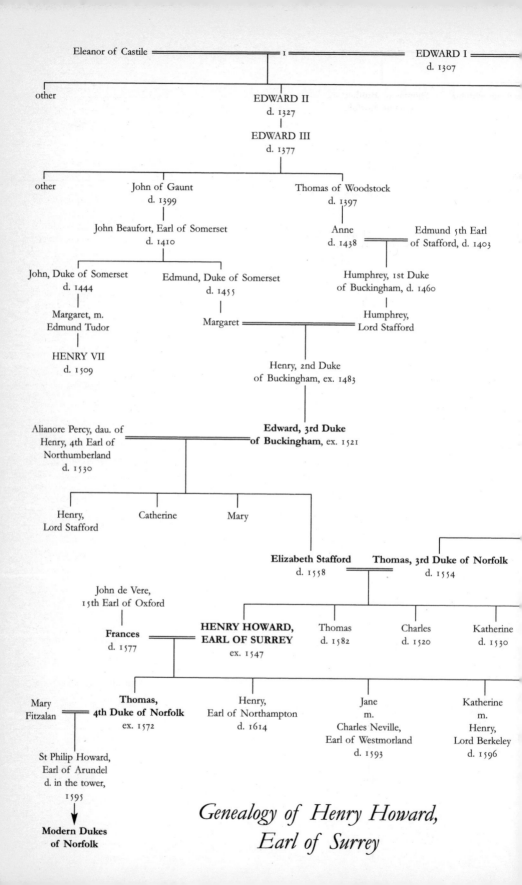

Eleanor of Castile ══════════ I ══════════ EDWARD I ══════════
d. 1307

other

EDWARD II
d. 1327

EDWARD III
d. 1377

other

John of Gaunt
d. 1399

Thomas of Woodstock
d. 1397

John Beaufort, Earl of Somerset
d. 1410

Anne
d. 1438 ══════════ Edmund 5th Earl
of Stafford, d. 1403

John, Duke of Somerset
d. 1444

Edmund, Duke of Somerset
d. 1455

Humphrey, 1st Duke
of Buckingham, d. 1460

Margaret, m.
Edmund Tudor

Margaret ══════════ Humphrey,
Lord Stafford

HENRY VII
d. 1509

Henry, 2nd Duke
of Buckingham, ex. 1483

Alianore Percy, dau. of
Henry, 4th Earl of
Northumberland
d. 1530 ══════════ Edward, 3rd Duke
of Buckingham, ex. 1521

Henry,
Lord Stafford

Catherine

Mary

Elizabeth Stafford
d. 1558 ══════════ Thomas, 3rd Duke of Norfolk
d. 1554

John de Vere,
15th Earl of Oxford

Frances ══════════ HENRY HOWARD,
d. 1577   EARL OF SURREY
ex. 1547

Thomas
d. 1582

Charles
d. 1520

Katherine
d. 1530

Mary
Fitzalan ══════════ Thomas,
4th Duke of Norfolk
ex. 1572

Henry,
Earl of Northampton
d. 1614

Jane
m.
Charles Neville,
Earl of Westmorland
d. 1593

Katherine
m.
Henry,
Lord Berkeley
d. 1596

St Philip Howard,
Earl of Arundel
d. in the tower,
1595

↓

**Modern Dukes
of Norfolk**

*Genealogy of Henry Howard,
Earl of Surrey*

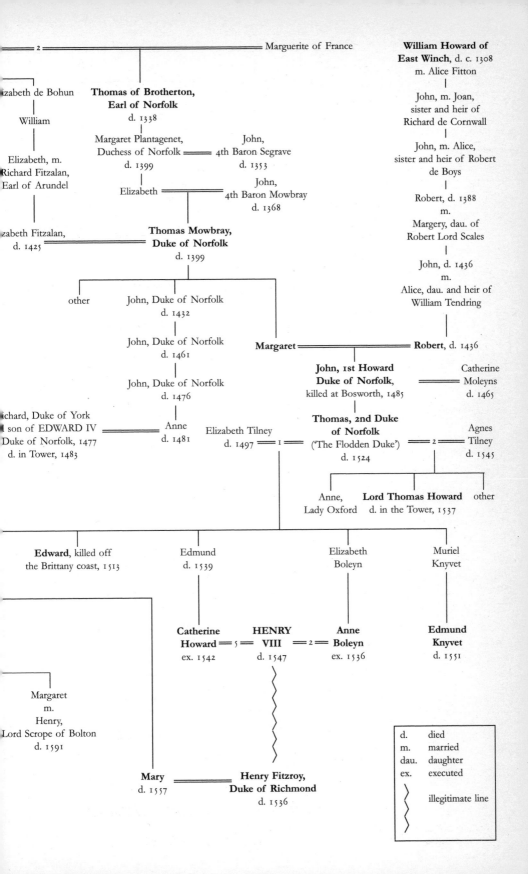

══ 2 ══ Marguerite of France

William Howard of East Winch, d. c. 1308
m. Alice Fitton

izabeth de Bohun

William

Thomas of Brotherton, Earl of Norfolk
d. 1338

John, m. Joan, sister and heir of Richard de Cornwall

Margaret Plantagenet, Duchess of Norfolk ══ John, 4th Baron Segrave
d. 1399 — d. 1353

John, m. Alice, sister and heir of Robert de Boys

Elizabeth, m. Richard Fitzalan, Earl of Arundel

John, 4th Baron Mowbray
Elizabeth ══ d. 1368

Robert, d. 1388
m.
Margery, dau. of Robert Lord Scales

zabeth Fitzalan, d. 1425

Thomas Mowbray, Duke of Norfolk
d. 1399

John, d. 1436
m.
Alice, dau. and heir of William Tendring

other · John, Duke of Norfolk d. 1432

Margaret ══ Robert, d. 1436

John, Duke of Norfolk d. 1461

John, 1st Howard Duke of Norfolk, killed at Bosworth, 1485
Catherine ══ Moleyns d. 1465

John, Duke of Norfolk d. 1476

ichard, Duke of York son of EDWARD IV Duke of Norfolk, 1477 d. in Tower, 1483 ══ Anne d. 1481

Elizabeth Tilney d. 1497 ══ 1 ══

Thomas, 2nd Duke of Norfolk ('The Flodden Duke') d. 1524 ══ 2 ══
Agnes Tilney d. 1545

Anne, Lady Oxford · **Lord Thomas Howard** d. in the Tower, 1537 · other

Edward, killed off the Brittany coast, 1513

Edmund d. 1539

Elizabeth Boleyn

Muriel Knyvet

Catherine Howard ══ 5 ══ **HENRY VIII** ══ 2 ══ **Anne Boleyn**
ex. 1542 — d. 1547 — ex. 1536

Edmund Knyvet d. 1551

Margaret
m.
Henry,
Lord Scrope of Bolton
d. 1591

Mary d. 1557 ═══ **Henry Fitzroy, Duke of Richmond** d. 1536

d.	died
m.	married
dau.	daughter
ex.	executed
⌇	illegitimate line

ACKNOWLEDGEMENTS

I am not the first nor, I hope, the last to write about the Earl of Surrey and I would like to take this opportunity to acknowledge the biographers and scholars that have gone before me. Deserved of particular recognition are George Frederick Nott, whose work of 1815 remains, despite some romantic conclusions, an outstanding body of work, and William A. Sessions, whose literary analysis, in particular, is unrivalled. Even the most cursory of glances at my notes will reveal the enormous obligation and gratitude I owe them.

My profound thanks go to His Grace the Duke of Norfolk for allowing me to read and cite his manuscripts at Arundel Castle. It was a privilege to work there and I am immensely grateful to Dr John Martin Robinson, Librarian to the Duke of Norfolk, Mrs Sara Rodger, Assistant Librarian, Mrs Heather Warne and Miss Pamela Taylor, Archivists, for making it such an enjoyable experience. The Marquess of Bath graciously permitted me to cite materials from his archives at Longleat House, for which I am most grateful. Henry Bedingfeld welcomed me warmly to his home at Oxburgh Hall and allowed me to read his manuscripts there. Delving into his trunk of rarely seen manuscripts was one of the most exciting moments of my research and I would also like to extend my thanks to Mrs Bedingfeld for her hospitality and fortifying cups of tea and biscuits. I am very grateful to Dr Anthony Smith of the Historical Manuscripts Commission for kindly putting me in touch with them in the first place.

I was continually heartened by the altruism of the libraries and institutions that I encountered during my research and would like to thank the archivists and staff of the British Library, the National Archives, the Bodleian Library, Cambridge University Library, Pembroke College, Cambridge, the Corporation of London Record Office, the College of Arms, the House of Lords Record Office, the Norfolk Record Office, the Institute of Historical Research and the Bancroft Library, University of California, Berkeley.

I have profited greatly from the advice of Brett Dolman, Curator, Historic Royal Palaces, who graciously answered all my queries about the Earl of Surrey's possible escape attempt from the Tower of London. Robin Self, Chairman of the Friends of St Michael's Church, Framlingham, was a genial guide to the church and Nicholas Nottidge was kind enough to share his expertise on the magnificent tombs there. Thanks too to Mrs John Brown for welcoming me to her home at Kenninghall and allowing me to take photographs.

I am enormously grateful to Matthew Fletcher MS FRCS, Medical Director and Consultant Urologist, Brighton and Sussex University Hospital Trust, for reading the Duke of Norfolk's exhaustive medical complaints and advising on the state of his health. I also wish to thank him and his wife Sue more personally for their support and encouragement.

Richard Carter, Nicola Fletcher and John Holland (Quintus' Latin Translations) provided invaluable services in translation, while Sarah Stewart-Richardson generously advised on the practicalities of picture research. I am immensely grateful to Johanna McDonald, Richard Morton Jack, James and Nicola Fletcher, Jane Childs and Anna and Mark Richards, who read my typescript, offered constructive criticism and saved me from numerous errors and infelicities of speech. Those that remain are entirely my own responsibility.

I am fortunate to have a wonderful agent in Andrew Lownie and I owe him much for his sound advice, hard work and unstinting support. It has also been a pleasure to work closely with Will Sulkin, who not only commissioned and edited the book, but also offered words of encouragement when they were most needed and forbore my numerous pleas for deadline extensions with remarkable tolerance. Thank you! I salute Rosalind Porter at Jonathan Cape, who assisted with every aspect of the book and, along with Jo North, Pendleton Campbell, Alan Rutter, Matt Broughton, Neil Bradford and Laura Hassan, helped to bring it to fruition.

My heartfelt thanks go to all the friends and family, who have endured my obsession with patience and good humour for over four years. In particular I would like to thank Anna for having in me the kind of faith that only a sister can. My love and thanks go to my fiancé James for providing strength, advice, tenderness and laughter. Finally, I wish to express my profound admiration and love for my mother Jane Childs. From the beginning, when I announced that I was giving up my sensible job to write a book, to the very end, she has selflessly supported and encouraged me. My father, the late Derek Childs, inspired and still inspires me in so many ways and it is to him that I dedicate this book.

AUTHOR'S NOTE

Dates are given in the Old Style Julian Calendar, but the year is assumed to have begun on 1 January rather than on Lady Day (25 March), which was taken as the first day of the English calendar year until 1752.

Money appears in the predecimal form used until 1971. There were twelve pence to a shilling and twenty shillings to one pound sterling. The mark was worth two-thirds of a pound.

The effects of inflation and the changing relative values of commodities throughout the ages render modern equivalents misleading. One sheep, for example, cost less than a pound of cinnamon in Tudor England, but often five times more than the daily wage of a footman in Henry VIII's army, who received just sixpence a day. In 1527 the royal tailor could charge seven shillings for a yard of black satin, while the suit of armour that the Earl of Surrey purchased in the mid-1540s cost him £8. A building labourer earned less than £4 a year, while the average assessed income from lands per annum for the peerage was £801 in 1523, £921 in 1534 and £873 in 1545.

Spelling and punctuation have been modernised throughout, except in the titles of printed sources and in poems where a change would have interfered with the rhythm.

PROLOGUE

On the night of Sunday, 21 January 1543 the prostitutes of Bankside, a red-light district in Southwark, were out in force. A new session of Parliament was due to open the following day and, as the prostitutes were forbidden from working 'after the sun is gone to rest' while Parliament was sitting, this was their last legal night of trade for quite some time. Hordes of women dressed in gaudy concoctions of silk and taffeta clustered round the Boar's Head, the Unicorn and the other 'bawdy houses' of the suburb, a tumult of colour against the buildings, which were painted white to distinguish them from more reputable establishments. As the night progressed, many went inside to seek refuge by the hearth, but some were prepared to brave the harsh riverine draughts and work the route along the South Bank of the Thames.

Soon after midnight it seemed as though their forbearance might be rewarded as a few specks of candlelight were spied edging across the river. At this time of night, long past the London curfew, it could mean only one thing. As the boats drew closer, it became apparent that about half a dozen restless young men were on board. But they had no intention of alighting. Instead they took out their stonebows* and began to fire at their targets on the bank. The women rapidly dispersed and soon the gang grew bored and rowed back to the steps north of the river. It had been a busy night. Earlier on they had rampaged through the streets and alleys of London, shouting obscenities at anyone foolish enough to outstay the curfew and smashing the windows of smart

---

* Light crossbows that shot stones

merchant dwellings and even some churches. Back on dry land after their whorebashing, the vandals continued to terrorise the neighbour-hood until two o'clock, when they returned to their lodging, the inn of one Mistress Milicent Arundel in St Lawrence Lane, Cheapside.

The following morning there was 'a great clamour' in the City and a strong civic determination to hunt down the vandals and bring them to justice. Many suspected they were members of the ubiquitous vagabond community; others thought they were apprentices, tight on cheap ale. But few were prepared for the name that emerged. For the ringleader, it transpired, was no apprentice and certainly no vagabond, but an earl, and not only an earl, but the heir to England's premier peer, a Knight of the Most Noble Order of the Garter and, so it was thought, a sensitive and refined poet.

Back in Mistress Arundel's inn, Henry Howard, Earl of Surrey, was beginning to regret his night of hell raising. He was, he told his friend George Blagge, 'very sorry' and wished for 'all the good in the world it were undone'. Maybe twenty years ago Henry VIII would have smiled benignly at Surrey's antics, but age and infirmity had made him capri-cious and cruel. The prospect of him finding out was not one that Surrey relished. 'But,' he concluded with a smirk, 'we will have a madding time in our youth.'[1]

INTRODUCTION

Henry Howard, Earl of Surrey, was born into one of the most powerful families in England. He was the son and heir of the third Duke of Norfolk and the first cousin to two queens: Anne Boleyn and Catherine Howard. By the age of thirteen his precocious talents had earned him a place of honour in the household of Henry VIII's illegitimate son. While still in his teens he spent a year in France as a guarantor for Henry VIII's friendship with Francis I. At twenty-four Surrey was installed as a Knight of the Garter. He served as the King's cupbearer, as a Steward for the Duchy of Lancaster, as joint Steward of Cambridge University and, in the country, as a Justice of the Peace. While still only twenty-eight he became Henry VIII's supreme military commander. Just over a year later he was dead.

Despite having had his portrait painted more often than any other Tudor courtier, the Earl of Surrey is today an unfamiliar figure. To the extent that he is recognised at all, it is usually for one of two reasons: as an innovative poet who created several new verse forms in English – most notably blank verse and the 'English' or 'Shakespearian' sonnet – and as the last person to be executed for treason in Henry VIII's reign.

I first came across him at university while studying a paper on the literature and politics of early modern England. The course covered all the great writers of the time: More and Wyatt, Sidney and Spenser, Shakespeare, Marlowe and Milton, but it was the rawness of Surrey's voice that most struck me and it was to his poems that I found myself returning. They revealed a witty, passionate man who dared to write about 'aged kings, wedded to will, that work without advice'. At a time when it was said that 'for fear no man durst either speak or wink', Surrey defied convention. Cromwell was a 'foul churl', Paget a 'mean creature' and the problems that beset Henry VIII's realm were, Surrey hinted, 'the bitter fruit of false concupiscence'.[1] For his candour alone he warrants attention.

Surrey witnessed and was inextricably caught up in all the major events of Henry VIII's reign: the Break with Rome, the Reformation, the Pilgrimage of Grace, the wars against Scotland and France, and the brutal power struggle at the end of the reign to which he fell victim. Biographies can offer thicker descriptions than general histories and provide new perspectives. Through Surrey it is possible to glimpse the rarefied world of the noble household and experience both the headiness of the Court and the violent antipathies that underlay it. We can sit in with Surrey at the trial of Anne Boleyn, hurtle through the streets of Tudor London and march across the battlefields of France. And we can find out what it was like to feel the favour of a king like Henry VIII and, ultimately, also his wrath.

By the time of his death Surrey was as accustomed to the 'pestilent airs' of prison as he was to the opulence of palace life. He was imprisoned four times, twice for violent behaviour towards fellow courtiers, once for his rampage through London and once, the last time, for treason. Ever ready to defend the privileges of high birth, Surrey was equally quick to resist its pressures. A man of intriguing contradictions, he was both law enforcer and law breaker, political conservative and religious reformer. He was nostalgic for the 'rude age', but eager to imbibe the culture of the Renaissance. He scorned courtiers of 'vile birth', but some of his best lyrics express his love for men of inferior lineage. Praised by many, including the Holy Roman Emperor, for his gentility and grace, Surrey was branded by one contemporary as 'the most foolish proud boy that is in England'.[2]

Later generations put their own stamp on Surrey's reputation. For the Elizabethans he was a pioneer of the English Renaissance:

> More heavenly were those gifts he had, than earthly was his form;
> His corpse too worthy for the grave, his flesh no meat for worm.
> An Earl of birth; a God of sprite, a Tully* for his tongue,
> Me think of right the world should shake, when half his praise were
>   rung.[3]

---

* *Tully*: Cicero.

The Victorians, inspired by Surrey's romantic editor, George Frederick Nott, saw him as a noble hero. In the last century he has been described as 'a thoroughbred courser let loose among the shire horses', 'a picturesque anomaly in a world that had no time for him', an 'infinitely gifted juvenile delinquent' and as the visionary 'poet Earl who revolutionised in his own texts and in his own life concepts of honour and nobility'.[4] I see a sensitive and sentimental young man who acted more on impulse than design. His haughty exterior confirmed objectionable pride, but also masked loneliness and insecurity.

In 1841 Isaac D'Israeli wrote:

> Could the life or what we have of late called the psychological history of this poetic Earl of Surrey be now written, it would assuredly open a vivid display of fine genius, high passions and romantic enthusiasm. Little is known save a few public events but the print of the footsteps show their dimension. We trace the excellence while we know but little of the person.[5]

The biography of a nobleman born nearly five centuries ago cannot possibly aspire to the intimacy of a modern portrait. Nevertheless, it is true to say that much more is known about Surrey since the time of D'Israeli's tribute. The Herculean task of cataloguing and abstracting all the major documents of Henry VIII's reign was completed in 1932 in a work comprising over twenty volumes. Also in print are letters, ambassadorial dispatches, church records, inventories, hunting accounts, treatises and little-known chronicles, like that of Elis Gruffydd, a Welsh soldier whose vivid impressions of the warfront were published in a series of articles in the mid-twentieth century. Our understanding of the Henrician period is continually being challenged and enriched by fresh scholarship and new discoveries. Surrey's most recent and most successful biographer, W. A. Sessions, unearthed several new finds, including long-forgotten portraits and information about Surrey's mansion in Norwich. My own research, most memorably among the Bedingfeld manuscripts at Oxburgh Hall, has, I hope, also borne fruit.

Tracing Surrey's footsteps in not an easy task. His poems are full of images of restlessness, of a questing, a striving: for recognition, contentment, love, lasting friendship, faith and, above all, for a true sense of self. It may be impossible ever to catch up with him, but in researching and writing this book, I hope I have come closer to the man who made those footsteps and the ground over which he trod.

PART ONE

YOUTH

ONLY VIRTUE UNCONQUERED

It is a spur in brave and good spirits to bear in mind those things which their ancestors have nobly achieved.

It transferreth itself unto posterity and, as for the most part, we see the children of noble personages to bear the lineaments and resemblance of their parents, so in like manner, for the most part, their virtues and noble dispositions, which even in their tenderest years will bud forth and discover itself.

Henry Peacham, *The Complete Gentleman*

'These new erected men,' Henry Howard once wailed in an attack upon the arrivistes of the Court, 'would by their wills leave no nobleman on life!'[1] He was proud of his ancestry and jealous of his honour. All around him, engraved on tableware, carved in the furniture, sewn into tapestries and stained onto glass, coats of arms boasted of his descent from the blood of kings.

Yet the Howards had been 'new erected' once too, and not, perhaps, as long ago as they might have wished. The first Howard of any note was William Howard, a talented lawyer who purchased a manor and lands in East Winch, a small village in north Norfolk near King's Lynn. He was knighted by Edward I and, in 1297, became Chief Justice of the Common Pleas. The next few generations saw more lawyers and a smattering of fine public servants and military captains. They married well and gradually the Howard patrimony grew, but it was only when Sir William's great-great-great grandson, Robert, married Lady

Margaret Mowbray around 1420 that the family can really be said to have arrived.

She was the elder daughter of Thomas Mowbray, Duke of Norfolk and Earl Marshal of England. From his side of the family, Margaret descended from Edward I through Thomas of Brotherton, King Edward's son by his second marriage to Marguerite of France. From her mother (Elizabeth, daughter of Richard Fitzalan, Earl of Arundel, and Elizabeth de Bohun), Margaret could also trace her descent to Edward I, this time through his first marriage to Eleanor of Castile. The Howard–Mowbray marriage thus linked a gentry family of modest proportions to three royal houses and a wealth of English Baronies. Robert and Margaret's son John (and all his descendants, including his great-grandson, Henry Howard) had the blood of Plantagenet, Capet, Mowbray, Bigod, Warenne, de Bohun, Segrave, Percy and Fitzalan in his veins.

John Howard pinned his colours firmly to the Yorkist mast, fighting for Edward IV in the Wars of the Roses and earning himself a Barony in the late 1460s – one of only eight men to be raised from the gentry in Edward IV's reign.[2] Following the death of the King, John supported the usurpation of Richard III. His loyalty was richly rewarded: on 28 June 1483 he was created Duke of Norfolk and Earl Marshal of England; he received half the Mowbray estate and his heir, Thomas, was elevated to the Earldom of Surrey.* A month later the first Howard Duke of Norfolk was appointed Steward for the Duchy of Lancaster and Lord Admiral of England, Ireland and Aquitaine.

Thus the fortunes of the Howards were attained by the same means as those of the new men that Henry Howard so abhorred: advanta-

---

* These grants led some later commentators to suspect that John Howard may have been complicit in the murders of Richard, Duke of York, and his elder brother, Edward V – the 'Princes in the Tower'.

Following the extinction of the male Mowbray line of descent in 1476, the Dukedom of Norfolk fell into abeyance (though other Mowbray titles and estates were inherited by the heiress, Lady Anne Mowbray). Edward IV granted the Dukedom to his son Richard, Duke of York, who had married Lady Anne. The King also passed an Act of Parliament giving his son the enjoyment of the Mowbray estates for life even if his wife predeceased him. Anne died in 1481, leaving the Mowbray co-heirs, John Howard (by virtue of his mother, Lady Margaret Mowbray) and William Berkeley, blocked from their inheritance for the duration of Richard's life. With Richard out of the way, the chief obstacle to Howard's inheritance was removed and the Dukedom of Norfolk lay in the gift of the new King, Richard III, almost certainly the murderer of his nephews. However, no contemporary accused Howard of complicity in the murders and the evidence presented against him is circumstantial at best. Anne Crawford, who provides the best analysis of this, concludes: 'That Howard had any hand in that son's death is inherently unlikely' (Crawford, 'John Howard, Duke of Norfolk: A Possible Murderer of the Princes?', in *Richard III: Crown and People*, ed. J. Petre, 1985).

geous marriage and loyal service. But to Henry there was a difference. Not for nothing was the family motto *Sola Virtus Invicta* – Only Virtue Unconquered. While the upstarts at Court were 'mean creatures', well versed in the machiavellian arts of dissimulation and betrayal, the Howards, so Henry grew up to believe, embodied a unique nobility of spirit. They upheld a chivalric code that placed loyalty and trust above all else; 'the friendship sworn, each promise kept so just', as the poet Earl would later put it.[3]

Such a promise was duly kept by John Howard, Duke of Norfolk, to his King, Richard III, at Bosworth Field on 22 August 1485. The Wars of the Roses – the thirty years of intermittent fighting for the Crown of England – pitted Yorkist against Lancastrian, the White Rose against the Red. With the extinction of the main Lancastrian line in 1471, Henry Tudor, Earl of Richmond, became the chief claimant.* He was a little-known Welshman who had spent many years exiled in Brittany, but his pledge to unify the two Houses appealed to many war-weary Englishmen. The extreme unpopularity of Richard III – Shakespeare's 'poisonous bunch-backed toad'[4] – also aided Henry Tudor's cause. The Stanleys and the Percys were carefully won over. Lancastrian agents attempted to lure Norfolk too, sending blandishments and threats. It is said that on the night before he left to join the King's forces, Norfolk found nailed to his gates the warning:

Jack of Norfolk be not too bold
For Dickon thy master is bought and sold.[5]

The Duke could not be turned. As promised, he led the vanguard into a battle that he must have known he could not win. He charged into the mêlée and fought on as his men were hacked to pieces around him. Soon he was face-to-face with his cousin, the Earl of Oxford. One blow threw off Norfolk's visor. An instant later an arrow punctured his skull. It was an honourable death according to the Tudor chronicler, Edward Hall:

---

* Henry Tudor's claim was not beyond dispute. His mother, Lady Margaret Beaufort, descended from Edward III through a son of John of Gaunt (third son of Edward III) and his mistress (later his third wife) Catherine Swinford. The son had been born out of wedlock and, although he and his Beaufort siblings were subsequently legitimised, they were expressly forbidden from inheriting the throne.

He regarded more his oath, his honour and promise made to King Richard; like a gentleman and a faithful subject to his Prince [he] absented not himself from his master but, as he faithfully lived under him, so he manfully died with him to his great fame and laud.[6]

King Richard was also slain, but while his corpse was stripped with 'not so much as a clout to cover his privy members' and trussed up 'like a hog', no such degradation befell John Howard. His body was rescued from the field and carried, unharmed, to Thetford Priory in Norfolk, where it was solemnly buried alongside his Mowbray ancestors.

His son Thomas Howard, Earl of Surrey, had fought bravely alongside his father's corpse – 'Young Howard, single, with an army fights'[7] – but he too had been felled. Injured but not dead, he had begged Sir Gilbert Talbot to inflict the final blow so that he might die by the hand of a nobleman. This honour was refused and he was carried from the field and dispatched to the Tower of London. The seventeenth-century poet Sir John Beaumont later gave a flowery rendering to Howard's justification for fighting for Richard III:

> I never will my luckless choice repent,
> Nor can it stain mine honour or descent;
> Set England's royal wreath upon a stake,
> There will I fight, and not the place forsake.
> And if the will of God hath so disposed,
> That Richmond's brow be with the Crown enclosed,
> That duty in my thoughts, not faction, shines.[8]

The first Parliament of the new reign passed an act of attainder against Howard. Not only did it declare him a high traitor (with all his lands, titles and possessions forfeited to the Crown), but it also tainted his blood and that of all his progeny. He was, in effect, legally dead and remained thus for nearly three-and-a-half years. But Henry VII was shrewd enough to realise the potential of the Howards. In 1489 he had the attainder reversed and Thomas Howard became Earl of Surrey once again, though most of his estates were withheld. He was released from the Tower and sent to the North to protect the borders. His children (including Henry Howard's father, also called Thomas, then only sixteen) were brought to Court as surety. The King need not have worried. Time and again, Howard proved his loyalty and worth. In 1501 he was appointed Lord Treasurer, one of the three principal offices of state, and in 1509 Henry VII, on his deathbed, restored his entire patrimony.

The accession of Henry VIII signalled new opportunities for the Howards. Hale and hearty and bursting with hubris, Henry VIII was itching to prove his mettle against the French as his hero, Henry V, had done. By 1512 England was at war with France and the younger Howards, whom the King knew well from their time at Court, were given key positions. Thomas' second son, Edward, a special favourite of the King, was appointed Lord Admiral. His encounter the following year with the French fleet off the coast of Brittany secured his place for ever in the affections of his friend and King; it also cost him his life.

After his brother-in-law, Sir Thomas Knyvet, had burnt to death in an engagement with a French carrack, Edward swore that he would 'never see the King in the face' until he had avenged Knyvet's death.[9] Consequently, when Edward espied the enemy fleet sheltering in Brest harbour, he swept towards it and boarded the command galley 'with great courage', we are told, and little regard for his personal safety.[10] The French threw off the grappling irons, cutting Edward off from most of his men. Realising there could only be one outcome, Edward tore his golden whistle, the badge of the Lord Admiral, from his breast and flung it into the sea. Seconds later he was stabbed to death and dumped overboard.

Once again a Howard had died honourably in action and once again the bards were inspired:

His life not ended foul nor dishonestly,
In bed nor tavern his lusts to maintain,
But like as beseemed a noble captain,
In sturdy harness he died for the right,
From death's danger no man may flee certain,
But such death is meetest unto so noble a knight.

But death it to call me think it unright,
Sith his worthy name shall last perpetual,
To all his nation example and clear light,
But to his progeny most specially of all,
His soul is in pleasure of glory eternal . . .[11]

One more battle ensured the Howards' rise from the ashes of Bosworth. While Henry VIII set off for France in June 1513 in search of his own Agincourt, Thomas Howard, Earl of Surrey, now in his seventies, and his son Lord Thomas Howard – Henry Howard's grandfather and father respectively – were left behind to guard the northern borders. It was a painful duty. They felt they had earned the right to fight alongside their King and, as the English army prepared to cross the Channel, 'the Earl could scantly speak', so great was his frustration. 'My Lord,' warned the King, 'I trust not the Scots; therefore I pray you to be not negligent.'[12]

The King's fears proved well founded. James IV of Scotland, in honour of the 'auld alliance' with the French, took advantage of the English exodus and invaded from the North. By the end of August about forty thousand Scots were encamped on Flodden Hill, six miles inside the English border. While Catherine of Aragon busied herself with the sewing of standards and banners, the Howards prepared to do battle. The Scots outnumbered the English by about two to one; they were well fed and supplied, rested and ready for battle. The English had arrived only days before and were already down to their last rations. The Scots also held the strategic advantage, encamped upon a five hundred-foot hill with the English in full view below. But they had not counted on the Howards.

As dawn broke on 9 September 1513, the English columns marched away from Flodden towards the north. By the afternoon, they had regrouped at Branxton. The Scots, fearful lest their baggage supplies be cut off and thirsty for English blood, abandoned Flodden for Branxton Hill and, at around four o'clock, thundered down on the English. After initial setbacks, the English re-formed and counterattacked. The battleground became a quagmire and many soldiers removed their boots to gain better footing. Soon it became clear that the long German pikes wielded by the Scots were too heavy and cumbersome for hand-to-hand fighting. With their swords and bills (hand weapons tipped with a bladed hook), Surrey's men cut the Scots dead in their tracks. James IV perished in the battle along with the flower of his nobility. Surrey's autobiographical epitaph, composed ten years later, claimed that the Scottish King was slain 'in plain battle directly before his own standard'.[13] According to this account, the Scots lost seventeen thousand men, though a figure of ten thousand is more realistic. The English lost fewer than fifteen hundred.

It was a spectacular triumph, far more impressive than the 'ungracious dogholes' Henry VIII had wrested from the French.[14] Surrey dispatched James IV's bloodied surcoat to Queen Catherine, who promptly forwarded it on to her husband in France, 'sending for your banners a king's coat'. 'I thought to send himself unto you,' she added with gleeful bloodlust, 'but our Englishmen's hearts would not suffer it.'[15] The poets and broadsiders drew, like a sixteenth-century press pack, to the scent of freshly spilt blood. While the Scots mourned

The flowers of the forest that fought aye the foremost,
The prime of our land lie cold in the clay,[16]

the English Poet Laureate, John Skelton, could not resist a cruel taunt:

King Jamy, Jemmy, Jocky my jo,
Ye summoned our King, why did ye so?[17]

Flodden marked the complete rehabilitation of the Howards. The blood of one battle had washed away the stain of another. In a lavish ceremony held at Lambeth Palace on Candlemas Day 1514, Thomas Howard senior was granted the Dukedom of Norfolk and appointed Earl Marshal of England, while his son, Thomas Howard junior, was elevated to the Earldom of Surrey for life. As a further reward, Norfolk 'and his heirs forever' received an augmentation to their coat of arms: the upper half of a lion 'pierced in the mouth with an arrow, and coloured according to the arms of Scotland, as borne by the said King of Scots.'[18]

Such was the legacy Henry Howard inherited. He grew up listening to stories of Howard gallantry – stories, if his grandfather's epitaph is anything to go by, that would have lost nothing in the re-telling. By the time of Henry's birth four years after Flodden, his father was Earl of Surrey and Lord Admiral of England. His grandfather was the Duke of Norfolk, Earl Marshal and Lord High Treasurer. With a fortune equal to their rank, they were two of the most powerful magnates in England.

But Howard gains had not come easily. Their past was turbulent and bloody and their future by no means assured. Nothing could be taken for granted, especially with a capricious king like Henry VIII on the throne. One false move and the foundations of their house – the lands, the titles, the offices – could be removed again. Had Henry Howard been more sensitive to the fragility of his family's greatness, his fate might have been very different.

2

HENRY HOWARD

Henry Howard was probably born in 1517.* In an age when people looked to the weather – and much else besides – for providential signs, the year did not augur well. The winter was so harsh that it claimed almost four hundred deer from his grandfather's park at Framlingham and caused the Thames to freeze over, so that 'men with horse and carts might pass betwixt Westminster and Lambeth'.[1] A very hot summer followed in which the sweating sickness, a virulent and highly contagious form of influenza, broke out in London. 'The patients experience nothing but a profuse sweat, which dissolves the frame,' the Venetian ambassador observed, while one Italian traveller recorded a daily death toll of five hundred.[2]

The Earl and Countess of Surrey hardly needed further incentive to have their baby boy baptised as quickly as possible. Child mortality was a severe problem in the sixteenth century, with up to forty per cent of children dying before they reached their fifteenth year. The Howard chapel at St Mary's, Lambeth, the family's London parish,† contained

---

* The date of his birth is not known. Before the introduction of parish registers in 1538, births were recorded arbitrarily. We only know Thomas More's birthday, for example, because his father scribbled it into his copy of Geoffrey of Monmouth's *Historia Regum Britanniae*. The year of Henry's birth is debatable, the only real clue being an inscription on a portrait of him, which reads: 'ANNO DNI. 1546. AETATIS SUE 29'. Despite much searching in the archives for a reference to his birth or christening, I have been unable to illuminate the matter, though I am unconvinced by W. A. Sessions' argument for 1516 based on his belief that Henry seemed older than his two years in the household account of 1519 (Sessions, 1999, pp. 46–7). Henry's age is impossible to ascertain from this source. For the sake of uniformity, I have adhered to the common assumption that the year was 1517.

† The present church is a nineteenth-century restoration. It was deconsecrated in 1972 and is now the site of the Museum of Garden History.

the little bodies of Thomas Howard's four children by his first wife, Anne Plantagenet, the daughter of Edward IV. Two of them, Henry and Thomas, had been baptised before their deaths, but there had not been time for the others.[3] According to the beliefs of the Catholic Church, they had died in a state of original sin and were consigned to limbo, forever denied the vision of God. Following Anne's death in 1512, Thomas Howard – with indecent haste, some felt – married Elizabeth Stafford, daughter of the Duke of Buckingham. She had provided him with one surviving daughter, Katherine, but not, until now, the longed-for son.

This boy was therefore a very special child. Finally his father had an heir. And to this special child was given a special name: as the priest immersed the baby three times in holy water, the word on his lips was not John or Thomas, the traditional names for Howard heirs, but Henry, the name of the King of England.* He would represent the next phase of Howard greatness, offered up at the baptismal font as a symbol of the family's loyalty to the Tudor regime.

While all available steps were taken for the preservation of Henry Howard's health, his parents were not expected to care for him on a daily basis. The routine tasks necessary for nurturing an infant were considered menial, not at all suitable for a countess whose priorities were to be a good wife and householder. Her chief duty was to produce as many children as possible and for the next three years she was almost constantly pregnant. Anything that would have affected her fertility, such as breastfeeding, was ruled out.† So Henry was handed over to a wet-nurse, and the nursery, peopled by gentlewomen, nurses and a laundress, became the centre of his world.

Strict criteria governed the choice of Henry's wet-nurse. She should be 'of no servile condition or vice notable,' wrote Sir Thomas Elyot,

---

* Henry VIII may well have been his godfather, though there are no extant records to confirm this. Perhaps the presence of Thomas Wolsey, the King's chief minister, at the Howard castle of Framlingham in the summer of 1517 points to his acting as the King's proxy at the baptism. ('The Framlingham Park Game Roll', in J. Cummins, *The Hound and the Hawk: The Art of Medieval Hunting*, 2001, p. 264.) However, Wolsey had other reasons for being in the county at the time and may only have been paying his respects to its chief landowner.

† The connection between lactation and infertility was understood at the time. Furthermore, breastfeeding would have delayed the resumption of sexual relations as intercourse with a nursing woman was taboo (B. J. Harris, 'Property, Power and Personal Relations: Elite Mothers and Sons in Yorkist and Early Tudor England', *Signs*, 15/3, 1990, p. 613).

for, as some ancient writers do suppose, often times the child sucketh the vice of his nurse with the milk of her pap. And also observe that she be of mature or ripe age, not under twenty years or above thirty, her body also being clean from all sickness or deformity, and having her complexion most of the right and pure sanguine, forasmuch as the milk thereof coming excelleth all other both in sweetness and substance.[4]

Infants were acutely vulnerable to disease at a time when medicine was not far advanced. One doctor accused his colleagues of 'everywhere and continually . . . feeling their way with unseeing eyes'.[5] *The Boke of Chyldren*, a guide to paediatrics published in 1544, listed some of the ailments to which the early modern child was prone. They included 'a postume of the brain, swelling of the head . . . terrible dreams, the falling evil, the palsy, cramp, stiffness of limbs, bloodshot eyes . . . scabbiness and itch, diseases in the ears, neasing [sneezing] out of measure, breeding of teeth . . . colic and rumbling in the guts . . . worms, swelling of the navel, the stone, pissing in bed . . . consumption, leanness and goggle eyes.' Remedies were prescribed for each condition, but their efficacy is questionable. Stiff limbs, for example, were to be rubbed with an unguent of goat's urine and dung, while a child suffering from earache was to be treated with a snakeskin 'boiled in oil and dropped into the ears'.[6]

By the end of 1519 Henry had been joined by another sister, Mary, and a brother, Thomas, while a second brother, who was baptised Charles, died in infancy in 1520.[7] Their main home was Tendring Hall in Stoke by Nayland, a small cloth-producing town on the Essex–Suffolk border. The Stour Valley provided a scenic playground for Henry and his siblings just as it did for John Constable more than two centuries later. 'The scene of my childhood,' he wrote, 'made me a painter.'

Its gentle declivities, its luxuriant meadow-flats, sprinkled with flocks and herds, its well cultivated uplands, its woods and rivers, with numerous scattered villages and churches, farms and picturesque cottages, all impart to this delightful county an amenity and an elegance hardly anywhere else to be found.[8]

Many of Henry's earliest memories would have been of travelling between his father's various estates. Much time was spent at Kenninghall, a medieval manor house twenty miles from Norwich. According to an account book detailing the family's expenditure there between 1519 and 1520, the children were given sweets, silks and shoes, while in the summer of 1519 a blue ribbon was bought just for Henry. Occasionally, too, their parents took them to London where they stayed in a house in Lambeth that was just a quick ferry ride across the Thames to the Court.[9] Up until Henry's eighth birthday, the family tended to winter at Hunsdon Hall in Hertfordshire, an impressive moated manor that boasted a brick tower one hundred feet high. In 1525 the King bought it from the Howards and took 'great pleasure to resort [there] for the health, comfort & preservation of his most royal person'.*[10]

Moving from one estate to another was an irksome affair. Carriages were needed not only for the household personnel, but also for the furniture, hangings, tableware, cooking utensils and chapel plate. Even the beds were removed, and not just the lord and lady's beds, but those of their children, the ushers, grooms, cooks, bakers and the rest of the travelling household. A contemporary book belonging to the fifth Earl of Northumberland gives a set of verbose instructions on how 'to assign the said carriages, how they shall be occupied and how the said carriages shall be appointed and what they be that shall be appointed to every carriage and what carriages shall be appointed for every cause.'[11] Roads were often poorly maintained and those, like the Howards, who regularly travelled through Suffolk, had to contend with 'the foulness of the ways, which in the clay woodland soil is ever increased especially in winter season'.[12]

The logistics of moving house resembled those of an army on the move. Advance parties rode out to scout the route and arrange checkpoints. Others went ahead to hang tapestries, light fires, check food stores and generally ensure that the house was ready for habitation. Then, in one long caravan, the family and household departed, leaving only a skeleton staff behind. A record of one of the Howards' sixty-mile treks from Tendring Hall to Hunsdon has survived. The six-year-old Henry set off with his mother, siblings and 'all the household' at daybreak on 29 October 1523. After twenty miles south-west, they reached Easterford (now Kelvedon) in Essex, where they were allowed a brief respite for breakfast. Travelling west, they passed through

---

* The Tudor mansions of Tendring Hall and Hunsdon Hall have not survived. The latter, which Henry VIII transformed into a royal palace, can be glimpsed in the background of a portrait of Edward VI thought to have been painted in 1546. Kenninghall was demolished around 1650. Today only one part of one wing survives as a farmhouse.

Dunmow, where they had a light lunch, entered Hertfordshire, crossed the River Stort and finally reached Hunsdon in time for a hearty supper.[13]

When Henry was three his father was appointed Lord Lieutenant of Ireland. English kings had claimed overlordship of the island ever since a dubious papal grant in the twelfth century, but most had shown little interest in the 'wild Irish' and since the beginning of his reign Henry VIII had deputed the governance of the country to the Anglo-Irish Earls of Kildare. In 1520 though, he decided upon a change in policy. Complaints had reached him that Gerald Fitzgerald, ninth Earl of Kildare, and deputy since 1513, had been abusing his power. Through extortion and terror, he was treating Ireland as if it was his own private fiefdom, with scant regard for English interests. Henry VIII promptly discharged him and appointed Thomas Howard to head a new strategy for the establishment of English suzerainty. The King was told that, if managed properly, Ireland could become 'a very Paradise' and a useful source of revenue. Howard was ordered to set up Court in Dublin and, to give credibility and a sense of permanence to his mission, his family and household were expected to relocate with him.

The news cannot have been met with much enthusiasm by Elizabeth Howard. As the daughter of the Duke of Buckingham, she had been brought up in what was generally considered the most magnificent noble household of the age. Marriage to an earl had led to a reduced standard of living. That had been a bearable inconvenience, but how was she to cope with the wilderness of Ireland where, in many places, so it was rumoured, 'they care not for pot, pan, kettle, nor for mattress, feather bed, nor such implements of household'?[14] Surely it was no place to take small children. One Greek envoy, describing English impressions of Ireland, wrote: 'They fabulously tell that Hades and the gates of Hades are there, imagining that they hear the groans of men undergoing punishment; and they add, moreover, that various spectres and adverse powers are seen.' While such tales were dismissed by the envoy, the rest of what he was told 'appeared to me to be true, and susceptible of sober consideration':

Such . . . as live in forests and bogs are entirely wild and savage; and there remains only the human form, whereby they may be distinguished to be men . . . And towards their own females they conduct themselves with too great simplicity, inasmuch as sometimes they have sexual intercourse with them in public; neither does this appear to themselves shameful. They feed on everything, and gorge themselves to excess with flesh.[15]

The Countess and her children were to be based in the more civilised area around Dublin, known as the Pale, where it was conceded that the inhabitants were 'meetly well mannered, using the English tongue'. But even here the Irish were considered a challenge: 'Naturally they be testy, specially if they be vexed.'[16]

On 23 May 1520 the Howards, their household and some five hundred troops arrived in Dublin, having crossed the Irish Sea on two galleasses, *Katherine* and *Rose*. From the outset, the situation was intolerable. While the English army faced resistance and rebellion from the Irish chieftains, the Howard household struggled with food shortages and dysentery. Sir John Bulmer, who arrived in Ireland not long after the Howards, claimed that in all his time there he never experienced even one day of good health.[17] With the summer came the plague. 'Undoubtedly no thing is so troublous to me here,' Howard wrote from Dublin at the end of July, 'as the universal infection of great sickness, which daily increaseth in this town.' By early August it was inciting mass hysteria. In one infected area the villagers had forsaken their houses for the woods but even there the plague had found them and now, Howard informed Cardinal Wolsey, 'the bodies lie dead, like swine unburied'. Howard's main concern, though, was closer to home:

> Three of my household folks hath sickened in my house, and died in the town, within seven days last past; notwithstanding I am fain to keep my wife and children here still, for I know no place in this country where to send them in clean air. Wherefore most humbly I beseech Your Grace to give me leave to send my wife and children into Wales or Lancashire, to remain near the seaside, unto the time it shall please God to cease this death here. And I shall take such fortune as God will send, for whilst I live fear of death, nor other thing, shall cause me to forbear to serve my Master, where it shall be his pleasure to command me.[18]

This simple request was apparently refused for the Archbishop of Armagh reported from Dublin almost two months later that Howard's wife and children were still there despite 'the great plague of sickness which now here reigneth and remaineth and hath remained still to his and their great jeopardy.'[19] Not only did Elizabeth Howard have to cope with the very real threat of death, but she also had to reckon with a household full of soldiers. Scarcity had driven up prices and reduced the value of the men's wages to such an extent that they could no longer afford food or lodging. They made 'so pitiful complaint,' Howard wrote, 'that I am enforced to take them into my house', so the corridors reverberated with the clatter of armour and the carpets were trampled by heavy boots.[20]

The Howards remained in Ireland for the rest of the year and most of the next. A stronger military presence was clearly needed to subdue the population, but Henry VIII deflected Howard's petitions for reinforcements, advising instead, with breathtaking disregard for the situation, 'sober ways, politic drifts and amiable persuasions'.[21] In June 1521, disillusioned and fed up, Howard asked to be recalled. He was ignored. On 16 September he renewed his plea with more urgency:

> I have continued now here one year and a half, to Your Grace's great costs and charges, and to mine undoing, for I have spent all that I might make. The country is so much disposed to flux of the body, with which disease I have of late been so sore vexed, and yet am, that I fear, if Your Grace should command me to remain this winter coming, I should be in right great danger of my life. There is dead of the same disease here, of Your Grace's retinue, above sixty, and of the great sickness a more number.[22]

Four long months passed until the Howards were finally allowed to go home. Despite his obvious distaste for Irish affairs, Thomas Howard's humane treatment of her people won him their hearts. One Irish chronicle told how

> he had such grace that there was neither poor, neither rich, but lamented his departure as though all goodness were from them ravished. He was so careful for the poor, so upright amongst the higher powers, that he was rather to be *alter Salmon** called than a private minister. He never sought no man's blood; he never coveted nothing of any that was other men's; he was never malicious to any. To be short, without many frivolous words to multiply, it was thought by diverse that he never offended within the compass of the seven deadly sins all the while he was in Ireland. What shall I say of his Lordship more?[23]

---

* *alter Salmon*: another Solomon.

The English also appreciated his efforts at statecraft. 'Hard it will be to find any other English captain to do more, or as much, as he hath done in that room,' Wolsey informed the King.[24] Ireland continued to be problematic for the rest of Henry VIII's reign and Thomas Howard's advice was constantly sought. This he was happy to give, but his reaction to a suggestion mooted in 1534 that he return to Ireland is telling: 'If the King really wishes to send me to Ireland, he must first construct a bridge over the sea for me to return freely to England whenever I like.'[25]

In the Howards' absence a family tragedy had played out at Court. On 17 May 1521 Elizabeth's father, the Duke of Buckingham, was executed for treason. Few things aroused Henry VIII's finely tuned sense of suspicion more than a recalcitrant nobleman. Edward Stafford, Duke of Buckingham, was debonair, flamboyant and highly provocative. He exuded magnificence and thought nothing of putting on a banquet for over four hundred people. The Holy Roman Emperor Charles V, demonstrating an unfortunate aptitude for weak puns, called him 'the finest buck in England'.[26]

At Court Buckingham was outspoken in his criticism of the King's policies. He dismissed the Field of the Cloth of Gold – the Anglo-French extravaganza of 1520 at which Henry VIII had attempted, at considerable expense, to outshine his French counterpart – as 'a conference of trivialities'. Once ordered to attend, however, he had made sure that he was the best dressed there. Above all, he derided the King's chief minister, Cardinal Wolsey, and his carnificial background, labelling him a 'Butcher's Cur'.[27]

Henry VIII attempted to keep the nobility in line by following his father's policy of containment. He needed their vast resources in order to wage wars, maintain law and order and project magnificence at Court, but he subjected them to strict regulation. The distribution of livery was limited, the retaining of followers licensed and 'recognisances' were imposed. These were bonds designed to ensure good behaviour on the part of the nobleman. If the King ruled that the bond had been broken, he could exact a monetary penalty. The Howards fell into line. Buckingham did not. In November 1520 he enraged the King by poaching one of his servants. When, in the same month, he requested permission to lead several hundred armed retainers into Wales, ostensibly to quell disorder there, it was suspected he might be planning his own rebellion. When a servant, who had just been dismissed by Buckingham, stepped forward with information concerning the Duke's treasonous muttering – notably that he threatened to stab and depose the King – his testimony was taken at face value.

Buckingham was charged with the treason of intending to assassinate the King, but the threat he had posed to Henry VIII had been less to his person than to the future of his dynasty. In 1521, after twelve years on the throne, the King still had no legitimate male heir. The Wars of the Roses were not so long ago that people had forgotten the havoc an insecure succession could wreak. Buckingham, a descendant of Edward III through both Thomas of Woodstock and John of Gaunt, was Henry VIII's nearest living male relative in the Lancastrian line. For some time it had been whispered that 'were the King to die without heirs male, he might easily obtain the Crown'.[28] Buckingham's real crime lay in stoking these flames when he should have sought by all means possible to quench them. He was executed on the morning of Friday, 17 May 1521. From the scaffold, he warned his fellow noblemen to take heed of his fate. Then the axe was wielded and, in three clumsy strokes, his head was severed from his body.[29]

Elizabeth Howard was devastated by her father's death, made all the more painful because she had been marooned in Ireland at the time. She may also have felt betrayed by her husband's family. In November Buckingham had written to the Duke and Duchess of Norfolk (Elizabeth's parents-in-law), seeking guidance and support because 'we have as great trust in them as any child they have'. But it had been Norfolk, as Lord Steward, who, with tears in his eyes, had pronounced the death sentence at Buckingham's trial.[30] It is likely, too, that Elizabeth blamed her husband. Buckingham himself certainly did. From the bar of the courtroom, he had launched a devastating attack on his son-in-law, stating, as Thomas Howard later recalled, 'that of all men living he hated me most, thinking I was the man that had hurt him most to the King's Majesty'.[31] It is hard to conceive how Thomas could have done much in Ireland to affect events in London, but he certainly would have had little inclination to help the man who so detested him. Elizabeth grieved alone, then, in the wilds of Ireland. When, the following year, both her father-in-law and her husband received a substantial portion of her father's estate, it must have seemed as if they were dancing on his grave.[32]

Upon the execution of Buckingham, Elizabeth lost not only a father but also a powerful protector. Consequently she had no one to fight for her when her marriage later disintegrated. The breakdown of the Howard marriage would become public only in 1534 when Thomas threw Elizabeth out of the house. Thenceforth the couple exchanged a devastating volley of insults. She accused him of sustained physical and mental abuse; he retorted that she was a hysterical fantasist. Amid all the accusations and counter-accusations, it is very difficult to ascertain the truth. Up until 1526, when Norfolk began to flout a mistress in front of his wife, there is no evidence of marital breakdown. Henry's parents ate, travelled and appeared in public together. Towards the end of 1524, following a lengthy posting for Thomas in the North, both husband and wife wrote to Wolsey expressing their agitation at the prolonged separation.[33] From the outside, then, it seemed as though the Howards had a perfectly conventional marriage. From within, however, it is possible that there had been tension from the outset.

Elizabeth had only been fifteen when she was courted by the recently widowed Thomas Howard. And she was in love with another. Ralph Neville, Earl of Westmorland, was one of her father's wards. 'He and I had loved together two years,' she later claimed, and had it not been for Thomas sniffing about, 'I [would have] been married afore Christmas to my Lord of Westmorland.' Buckingham had tried to lure Thomas away from Elizabeth using his other daughters as bait, but Thomas 'would have none of my sisters, but only me'.[34] His persistence eventually paid off and in 1512 Elizabeth forsook her sweetheart and married her suitor.

Thomas' relentless pursuit of Elizabeth had convinced her that 'he chose me for love'.[35] Despite the considerable age gap – at thirty-nine, he was older than her own father – she fully expected romance to blossom. Elizabeth was passably pretty, with soft features, light colouring and a distinguished forehead. Thomas may well have taken a fancy to her, but for him her chief assets lay elsewhere. Union with the Duke of Buckingham's eldest daughter (her sisters being too young for childbirth) brought Howard wealth, power and prestige. That is why he married her and why, possibly even before the mistress came on the scene, Elizabeth felt cheated.

None of this was explained to their son Henry. Sixteenth-century children, especially aristocratic children, were not expected to ask intrusive personal questions, and certainly not of their parents. When they were both at home, Henry would join them for meals in his father's chamber. Sitting in obedient silence, he learnt how to gauge the mood from a subtle vocal inflection, a raised eyebrow, furrowed brow or frozen smile. As an adult Henry was hypersensitive both to his environment and the people within it. This trait could manifest itself creatively, as it did in his lyrics, but it also incurred self-destructive side-effects: he could be introspective (often seen as self-absorption) and frequently overreacted to perceived slights.

For vast tracts of his childhood, though, Henry's parents were away from home. As Lord Admiral, Thomas Howard spent much of 1522 harrying the French coastline and between 1523 and 1524 he served against the Scots as the King's Lieutenant in the North.[36] One surviving household account, revealing all the comings and goings of the Howards from April 1523 to January 1524, shows that in that nine-month period, Henry's father was home for only twenty-three days.[37] His mother could boast a better record, but she too was absent for almost three months. As lady-in-waiting to Queen Catherine, she was frequently required at Court and, as Countess of Surrey, she had local duties to fulfil. On Saturday, 8 August 1523, for example, she 'rode after breakfast' from Tendring Hall, and returned in time for supper the following Tuesday. On such trips, she usually visited neighbouring estates, joined hunting parties or went on pilgrimages to East Anglia's famous shrines.[38]

When his mother was home, Henry had daily contact with her, the two of them taking their breakfast together in her chamber. She was only twenty in 1523, but the lessons of life – notably, marriage to a man more than twice her age, the hardship of Ireland and the execution of her father – had forged a worldliness beyond her years. Like her father, she was high-minded and independent, sometimes recklessly so, but these were not traits that she wished to see in her children. A letter from Elizabeth to her brother, written in the 1540s, tells us something of her approach to parenting. In response to his request that one of his daughters be brought up in her household, Elizabeth replied:

I pray you to send me my niece Dorothy, for I am well acquainted with her conditions already, and so I am not with the others; and she is the youngest too; and if she be changed, therefore, she is better to break as concerning her youth.[39]

A strict disciplinarian, then, who believed in the suppression of wilfulness from an early age, but also someone committed to child rearing, who wanted to be 'well acquainted' with their 'conditions'. Thus, although Elizabeth's duties at Court and in the county often precluded regular interaction with her children, this does not mean that she was not devoted to them. Years later, following the children's decision to side with their father in the marriage dispute, Elizabeth complained of their 'unnatural' behaviour towards her.[40] Her choice of word implies the prior existence of an innate bond that, for her part, she claimed always to have upheld.

Elizabeth's approach to discipline was entirely in keeping with the age. God-fearing parents believed that wilfulness in children was a sign of the devil and that measures should be taken to lead them away from temptation. Parents were warned not to 'let your children go whither they will, but know whither they go, in what company, and what they have done, good or evil'. They were discouraged from showing 'much familiarity' and were advised to 'labour how to make them love and dread you, as well for love as for fear'. The Lord's Commandments were drummed in from a very early age, none more so than the Fourth: 'Honour thy father and thy mother'. When his parents were home, Henry would fall to his knees every morning and ask for their blessing. Only once they had made the sign of the cross – 'In the name of the Father, Son and Holy Ghost, Amen' – would he be permitted to rise.[41]

The Howard household was linked by chains of hierarchy. Just as Henry had a duty of obedience to his parents, so did the servants to him. A gentleman usher – the sixteenth-century equivalent of a valet – slept on a pallet-bed outside Henry's door and was ready to jump to attention when called. In one contemporary manual for servants, there is an entry on 'How to order your master's chamber':

When your master intendeth to bedward, see that you have fire and candle sufficient. Ye must have clean water at night and in the morning. If your master lie in fresh sheets, dry off the moistness at the fire . . . In the morning, if it be cold, make a fire, and have ready clean water, bring him his petti-coat warm, with his doublet and all his apparel clean brushed, and his shoes made clean, and help to array him, truss his points,* strike up his hosen, and see all thing cleanly about him.[42]

---

* *points*: the laces that tied the breeches or 'hosen' to the doublet.

Henry barely had to lift a finger. Not only did his servants dress him, they also combed his hair, prepared his pew twice daily for Mass and Evensong ('beads and book, forget not that'), and maintained his lavatory:

> See the privy-house for easement be fair, soot,* and clean;
> And that the boards thereupon be covered with cloth fair and green;
> And the hole himself, look there no board be seen;
> Thereon a fair cushion, the ordure no man to teen[†]
> Look there be blanket, cotton or linen to wipe the nether end,
> And even he clepith,[‡] wait ready and entende,
> Basin and ewer, and on your shoulder a towel.[43]

There was no privacy at bath time. Henry would sit in a tub as his usher lathered him in soap and then sponged him down with rose water.[44] But bathing was a rare occurrence, as it was regarded by many as a risky activity. Andrew Boorde, a doctor who was sometimes consulted by Henry's father and who dedicated his *Dyetary of Helth* to him, pronounced that bathing 'allowed the venomous airs to enter and destroyeth the lively spirits in man and enfeebleth the body'. Somewhat paradoxically, medicinal baths were sometimes prescribed, which were as hot as possible and mixed with various herbs including hollyhock, St John's Wort, wildflax and camomile.[45] Servants were to be well presented at all times and strict regulations governed their behaviour. Those drawn up by John Harington of Stepney ordered 'that no servant be absent from prayer, at morning or evening, without a lawful excuse', 'that no man make water within either of the courts', 'that no man teach any of the children any unhonest speech or bawdy word or oath' and 'that none toy with the maids'. However, the imposition of fines for each offence shows that whatever the ideal, the reality must have been somewhat different.[46]

Meals were taken three times a day: breakfast at six, dinner between ten and twelve and supper around six in the evening. In the Howard household, where guests were frequently entertained, the ritual associated with the serving of food was the fullest expression of a nobleman's

---

* *soot*: sweet.
† *teen*: annoy.
‡ *clepith*: calls.

status. On a normal day around twenty servants were involved. Before the guests were seated, the table was laid with exactitude and the salt cellar set in its correct position to the left of the principal diner. During the meal a team of cupbearers, carvers and waiters attended. Once the customary two courses had been consumed, bowls of water were produced and the servants ceremonially washed the diners' hands. The table was then cleared with as much ritual as it had been laid and the leftovers were gathered up and distributed amongst the poor.

Apart from the Grace, meals were usually conducted in silence and bad manners were not brooked. One contemporary book of etiquette forbade coughing, retching, hiccuping, belching and scratching – 'put not your hands in your hosen your codware for to claw'. Another directed:

> Scratch not thy head with thy fingers
> when thou art at thy meat;
> nor spit you over the table board;
> see thou doest not this forget.
> Pick not thy teeth with thy knife
> nor with thy finger's end,
> but take a stick, or some clean thing,
> then do you not offend.
> If that your teeth be putrefied,
> me think it is no right
> to touch the meat other should eat;
> it is no cleanly sight.
> . . . .
> Blow not your nose on the napkin
> where you should wipe your hand
> but cleanse it in your handkercher,
> then pass you not your hand.[47]

Henry had evidently learnt all this by the age of six when he was expected to host formal meals in his parents' absence. On 16 September 1523, for example, the Earl of Essex called at Tendring Hall with four servants. He was given dinner in the Great Chamber with little Henry, dressed in his finest clothes, perched at the head of the table.[48]

Early Tudor aristocrats consumed about 4,500 calories a day, around three-quarters of which was meat.[49] Foreigners often baulked at such a heavy diet, but as one Englishman explained to an enquiring Italian, 'as the subtle air of Italy doth not allow you to feed grossly, so the gross air of England doth not allow us to feed subtly'.[50] Contemporaries were just as diligent as we are today in their search for a healthy diet. The *Dyetary of Helth* recommended garlic to destroy bacteria and almonds to ease digestion. Mandrake was said to be an effective aid to conception; effective that is, until one of its other properties kicked in: 'it doth provoke men to sleep'.[51]

The Howard household books contain detailed entries for all Henry's meals. For breakfast he either had chicken or mutton while dinner and supper regularly consisted of an assortment of beef, lamb, pig (including the head and trotters), chicken, veal, venison, goose, rabbit, capon, duck, pheasant, pigeon, crane and swan, all washed down with weak beer, water being considered unsafe. Although the family did not have pudding in the sense of a separate course, they did occasionally treat themselves to custards, nuts, jellies, gingerbread, apples, pears and pomegranates. On Fridays and Saturdays, during Lent and on Rogation days, Henry ate only fish and dairy products, though he was exempted from his mother's stricter abstentions from meat on Wednesdays and from breakfast and supper on the holy days.[52] In addition to the more common types of fish, the Howards were able to obtain fresh oysters, crayfish and caviar from Colchester, Yarmouth and Norwich.

If Lent was a time of abstinence, then Christmas was indisputably a time for indulgence. Then, as now, the birth of Christ was celebrated with much merriment and was a time for families and friends to gather and rejoice. In December 1523, as the halls of Hunsdon were decked with holly and ivy, one can imagine the mounting excitement of the six-year-old Henry. But on 22 December he could only wave as his parents rode away to celebrate Christmas with the King. The return of 'my Lord's yeomen' from Windsor on Christmas Eve can hardly have eased Henry's sense of abandonment. He spent the whole of Christmas Day in the nursery, taking all his meals there, the only concession to the occasion being 'ten great birds' for dinner. Once the servants had attended to him, they rushed down to the Hall, where the rest of the household was celebrating what was, no doubt, a livelier affair. The Howards could usually expect at least one or two visitors on a normal day, far more at Christmas. On this day, however, there were none at all.

On Boxing Day the local parson dropped in, perhaps to check on the Howard children. The following day five 'players' or actors called at Hunsdon and performed to an audience of Henry, his siblings and servants, the parson, two men of the county, and three men of the town.[53] Perhaps the parson had taken pity on the children, alone at Christmas, and arranged some local entertainment. Perhaps the players were an itinerant troupe of actors touring the county or, most likely, Thomas and Elizabeth Howard had made provision for some interludes for their children's edification. These were short, dramatic pieces, based on the Scriptures and considering the date of their performance – the eve of the Feast of the Holy Innocents – it is possible that they included a re-enactment of King Herod's slaughter of the infants at Bethlehem.

Thomas and Elizabeth returned to Hunsdon two days after Twelfth Night and a week later Thomas left again for the North. While it would be unwise to overemphasise Henry's sense of abandonment in an age when aristocratic parents regularly left their children at home for prolonged periods, the extent of his father's absences was extreme even by the standards of the day. Henry was acutely aware that he was his father's heir and that great things were expected of him. Believing, perhaps, that he had not done enough to satisfy him, Henry became desperately anxious to please, ever hopeful of his father's approval.

But Thomas Howard, as Holbein's famous portrait of him (plate 1) illustrates, was not an easy man to please. The work confirms contemporary descriptions that he was short and spare. His gaunt face is dominated by a great beak of a nose, arched brows, heavy lids and thin, pursed lips. The artist has also managed to capture something of the discontentment that pervades his sitter, as if, at any moment, Thomas might let out a weary sigh as was 'his wonted fashion'.[54] Although he is decked out in ermined finery, with the chain of St George around his neck, the Earl Marshal's gold baton in his right hand and the Lord Treasurer's white staff in his left, he seems distinctly unimpressed by the symbols of his status. Indeed, the ermine weighs him down, the chain constricts him and his hands are bound by the staves of office. He is consumed by politics. Only his eyes are free to warn the viewer of the heavy burden of unlimited ambition.

Having grown up in the aftermath of Bosworth, when his father was in the Tower and the Howard name disgraced, Thomas Howard lived in dread that it could happen again. His one goal in life was to secure Howard pre-eminence at Court. By turns he could be charming, ruthless, bluff, obsequious, affable and cruel. The many conflicting accounts of him are testament to his mastery of dissimulation. He 'is esteemed very resolute,' one French ambassador noted, 'and not easily moved to show by his face what his heart conceives.'[55] As a father he could be protective and affectionate, but his children never quite knew if this concern was genuinely for them or for their status as Howard assets. When one of his servants later wrote to Henry: 'I heard my Lord say that he had rather bury you and the rest of his children before he should give his consent to the ruin of this realm',[56] it was no empty threat. He was merely outlining the reality with which they had all learnt to live: that Thomas Howard was a politician first and a father second.

On 21 May 1524 Henry's grandfather, the second Duke of Norfolk, died at the age of eighty. Popularly known as the Flodden Duke, his victory over the Scots, as well as his sheer longevity, accorded him legendary status. Henry had last seen his grandfather only a few months before, when he had stayed for two days at Tendring Hall,[57] and it is likely that the Duke, a consummate storyteller, would have delighted his grandson with tales from his colourful past.

Four hundred and forty yards of black funerary cloth were needed to adorn the state chambers, the chapel, the Great Court and the gates of Framlingham Castle, the ducal seat in East Suffolk.* For a month the Duke's body lay in state in the chapel, surrounded by nineteen kneeling mourners. Every day three Masses were sung and every night twenty-eight servants kept vigil. On 22 June incense infused the summer air as the coffin was placed in a chariot and taken off on its two-day journey to Thetford Priory, the traditional burial place of the Dukes of Norfolk. Henry, dressed in a hooded black gown, rode behind his father at the head of a nine hundred-strong procession of heralds, churchmen, lords, knights, gentlemen, servants and torch bearers. Along the road they were accompanied by the ringing of bells and every church they passed was presented with escutcheons of the Howard arms and a purse of six shillings and eightpence.

Having arrived at Thetford after a night's stopover at Diss, Henry and the rest of the mourners rose early and processed to the priory. The

---

* Built by Roger Bigod in the late twelfth or early thirteenth century, Framlingham Castle later became the seat of the Mowbray and Howard Dukes of Norfolk. Although little more than the shell of the castle now survives, its thick stone walls, crenellated towers and ornate Tudor chimneys tell of its former glory. Since 1984 it has been managed by English Heritage. The wall-walk affords wonderful views of the town and the Mere.

Duke's catafalque, fringed with a valance of black silk and Venice gold and surrounded by one hundred wax effigies, lay under the flicker of seven hundred candles. After three Masses, Henry sat transfixed in his pew as an elaborate spectacle unfolded. First the late Duke's coat of arms was offered by the principal herald, Garter King of Arms, to the Bishop of Ely. The Bishop then delivered it to the Duke's heir, Thomas Howard, symbolically investing him with his father's honours. Thomas then returned the coat to Garter, who carried it to the altar. Next, Clarenceux King of Arms offered the late Duke's shield to the Bishop, who in turn delivered it to Thomas, who then handed it back to Clarenceux, who took it to the altar. This process was repeated for the Duke's sword and helmet, with a different herald officiating each time. Finally, Carlisle Herald went to the priory door and conducted a mounted knight, clad in the late Duke's armour, down the aisle and up to the offering. The knight dismounted and delivered the Duke's battleaxe, head down, to Carlisle who, having presented it to the Bishop, received it back in turn and took up his place alongside his fellow heralds at the altar. An hour-long sermon followed on the theme of Revelations, 5: 'Behold the Lion of the Tribe of Judah Triumphs'. It reportedly whipped up 'so violent a fear' among the congregation that many 'ran out with haste'. Next, the burial vault was consecrated and the Duke's chief servants broke their staves of office and threw them in. Finally, slowly, the coffin of Henry's grandfather was lowered into the vault.*

That evening a magnificent banquet was laid on for around two thousand diners. In all, the funeral had cost the staggering sum of £1,340. It had been a celebration of the life of the Flodden Duke and an appreciation of his role as a secular and spiritual leader of East Anglia. It was also a display of Howard power and regeneration. The yards and yards of black cloth that were draped throughout Framlingham Castle were decorated with the Howard arms. The horses that had drawn the chariot were similarly caparisoned and practically every square foot of Thetford Priory was covered in a patchwork of Howard symbolism.[58] It conveyed a powerful message, but the role of the royal heralds in the obsequies conveyed an even stronger one: that the strength and continuity of the Howard dynasty was facilitated by, and ultimately depended upon, the authority of the King.

* Following the dissolution of Thetford Priory in 1540, the Duke's body was reburied in the parish church of St Mary's, Lambeth. The remains of the brick vault are still visible amidst the sad ruins of Thetford Priory.

3

EARL OF SURREY

On the death of the Flodden Duke, Henry's father became the third Duke of Norfolk and Henry himself, at the age of seven, was styled Earl of Surrey. This was only a courtesy title, the Earldom having previously been invested in his father alone for life, but such technical niceties did not seem to matter in 1524 and from thenceforth everybody, including the King, referred to Henry as the Earl of Surrey.

His father now enjoyed a gross annual income of between £3,500 and £4,000. This was a massive sum at a time when the average taxable income of the peerage was £801.[1] With the inheritance came an extensive network of the old Duke's followers and additional responsibilities in local administration, religion, politics and law. The effects were keenly felt at Tendring Hall. The household, previously comprising around sixty people, swelled to nearly a hundred as Norfolk took on many of his father's retinue. Another addition was Surrey's half-aunt, Anne, Lady Oxford, who sought refuge with the Howards in 1526 after she was forcibly expelled from her lands by her late husband's successor, the fifteenth Earl of Oxford, Surrey's future father-in-law.

Now that theirs was a ducal household, the Howards had a responsibility to entertain greater numbers, and on a more lavish scale, than before. The household book of 1526–7 reveals a steady stream of visitors flowing through their gates. Many were neighbouring gentlemen coming to cement their ties or form new ones, but others came from all walks of life. A random selection, all of whom were given hospitality, includes the goldsmith of Ipswich, a priest of Oxford, the bailiff of the town, a man of Lynn, a friar of Ipswich, a pursuivant of the King, a scholar of Cambridge and a 'a strange* priest'.² Lower down the social scale, the Norfolks upheld their Christian duty to bestow charity on the poor. Hermits and gypsies were as welcome at their table as lords and ladies, Norfolk having reportedly said 'that he would eat grasses and drink water rather than he would be at a banquet with the heavy heart and curse of the poor'. An Irish chronicle reported that during the Howard sojourn there, he 'commanded his officers that no man should depart from his gates without meat and drink, in so much the poor and simple people thought he was the King's son.'³ Not everyone agreed with this assessment. Norfolk was one of the few landlords to retain villeinage on some of his estates and there were complaints from his bondmen that he treated them with 'much more extremity than his ancestors did'.⁴

The Christmas season of 1526–7 could not have been more different for Surrey than the drab affair of three years before. Now, in a grand gesture of magnificence, the gates were flung open and hundreds of people were fed and entertained in an orgy of conspicuous consumption.⁵ Tendring Hall soon groaned under the pressure of so many people and parties and the Duke of Norfolk took steps to transfer the household to Kenninghall. Situated in the heart of East Anglia, only twenty miles from Norwich, and set amid seven hundred acres of parkland, Kenninghall was the ideal site for the ducal headquarters. Having pulled down the original medieval manor house, Norfolk enlisted an army of builders, carpenters, joiners, plasterers and glaziers to turn his ambitious construction programme into reality. The result was a spectacular H-shaped red-brick palace, built in the latest style of Bridewell or Hampton Court, where the lodgings were arranged vertically rather than horizontally.⁶

There was much in the seventy-odd rooms at Kenninghall for a small boy to explore. In the Great Chamber, Surrey could feast his eyes upon a splendid set of eight tapestries depicting the feats of Hercules. In the Long Gallery, he was met by a vast painting of the recent siege of Pavia, where Imperialist troops had inflicted a crushing defeat on the French and captured King Francis I himself. On the second floor of the Ewery Court were Surrey's lodgings: one outer chamber, dominated by a huge fireplace, and an inner chamber where he slept. Then there was the Armoury, a treasure trove of weapons and helmets and 'diverse pieces

---

* *strange*: foreign.

of broken harness'. Here Surrey could run his fingers along the cool steel and escape into a world of chivalric fantasy. If he climbed right up to the garret in the turret, Surrey's efforts were rewarded by the wholesome image of grazing cattle, deer parks and the farmers toiling on his father's land. At nearby Shelfhanger Farm were the kennels and the stables, where nearly every horse was named after a Howard affiliate. There were fish ponds there too, a real tennis court and a slaughter house, the stench from which competed with the fumes of burning tallow billowing out of the Candle Yard.[7]

The spring of 1528 should have been a happy time for the Howards settling into their new home, but the atmosphere was soured by the Duke of Norfolk's ill-health. Throughout his later life (he was fifty-five in 1528), he was plagued by an ailment that was never properly diagnosed. The Imperial ambassador, Eustace Chapuys, thought that it had something to do with the Duke's liver, but Norfolk himself only ever made vague references to 'my disease of the lax'.* He was more forthcoming on its effects, frequently describing his bowel movements to the King and his ministers. 'It is scant credible,' Norfolk remarked after one session, 'that any man should have avoided [sic] that I did on Friday, from six at night unto ten o'clock in the morning. But now, thanked be Almighty God, I am stopped.' On another occasion, he complained that 'my flesh on my body, arms and legs doth so [di]minish that I am not a little afraid my time shall not be long in this world.'[8] Both loss of muscle and diarrhoea are compatible with liver disease, but they are also symptomatic of many other medical conditions including chronic pancreatitis. Ultimately, there are not enough specific details for any firm conclusions to be drawn, though it is unlikely that Norfolk's condition was as severe as he made out.† It is probable that he also suffered from a good dose of hypochondria. Frequently, he would complain about the 'choler and agony' of his condition, only to saddle up for the hunt or continue with his business a few hours later. He had good reason to exaggerate his infirmity; most of his complaints (especially when he was writing from the North of England) were followed by

---

* Deriving from the Latin *laxus* (loose), 'the lax' was commonly used to denote a looseness of the bowels.

† I am much indebted to Matthew Fletcher MS FRCS, Medical Director and Consultant Urologist, Brighton and Sussex University Hospital Trust, for reading Norfolk's exhaustive complaints and giving me his views. As he points out, the fact that Norfolk survived to the age of eighty-one suggests that his condition could not have been that severe. Certainly any serious liver or bowel disease would have carried him off long before then.

requests to come to Court where, he argued, the weather was more temperate and he could be treated by London's 'cunning men' – but where, of course, he would also have access to the King.

Norfolk's attack in May 1528 was serious enough, though, for Henry VIII to send his prized physician Dr Butts to East Anglia. Without the doctor's treatment, Norfolk wrote in a letter of thanks to Wolsey on 17 May, 'I think I should not have recovered'.[9] Two weeks later the Duke reported that 'I am now, thanked be God, something in better case than I was, and may endure to ride a soft pace, but in no wise to walk on foot, the fume doth so arise in my head.' Every week, he continued,

> I have not failed to have one sore fit, nor by no means can have good digestion, nor do not eat in three days so much as I was wont to do at one meal. Wherefore, if it may stand with the Kings Highness' pleasure, and Your Grace's, I intend to ride towards London before the beginning of the next term, fearing that I shall not recover perfect health nor bring my stomach again in good order without better advice than can be had in these parts.[10]

But Norfolk could not ride to London as planned, for in June there was an outbreak of sweating sickness. According to all reports, it was even worse than that of 1517. Thousands succumbed in London where, the French ambassador quipped, 'the priests have a better time of it than the doctors'. The Duke of Norfolk, only just out of his sickbed, immediately began to suffer from the telltale 'shaking fits'.* He was sent back to bed and warned not to stir, for 'if a man only put his hand out of bed during twenty-four hours, it becomes as stiff as a pane of glass.'[11] The first day was critical; during those hours Norfolk would either rally or die.

As Surrey paced the corridors waiting for news, he could be forgiven for allowing his thoughts to stray towards his own future. If his father were to die, Surrey, at eleven, would become the fourth Duke of Norfolk. As the final hours drew near, and then passed, it became clear that the chaplain twitching nervously at Norfolk's bedside would not have to

---

* The quotation comes from Surrey's poem, 'If care do cause men cry' (*Poems*, 17). The following couplet suggests that he had witnessed the effects of the disease:
  And in those cares so cold I force myself a heat,
  As sick men in their shaking fits procure them self to sweat.

administer the last rites. The Duke had survived. Others in his household were not so fortunate.

In August Norfolk's stepmother Agnes, the Dowager Duchess of Norfolk, wrote to Cardinal Wolsey detailing her success in combating the disease. 'I have had the experience daily in my house of all manner of sorts, both good and bad; and, thanked be God, there is none miscarried, neither in my house nor within the parish that I am in. For if they that be in danger perceive themselves very sick, they send for such of my house as hath had it and knoweth the experience, whereby, thanked be God, they do escape.' Clearly rather pleased with herself, Agnes proceeded to give Wolsey the benefit of her sage advice:

> If they be sick at the heart, I give them treacle and water imperial, the which doth drive it from the heart . . . And the best remedy that I do know in it is to take little or no sustenance or drink, until sixteen hours be past . . . Vinegar, wormwood, rosewater, and crumbs of brown bread is very good and comfortable to put in a linen cloth, to smell unto your nose, so that it touch not your visage.

Having informed Wolsey of Norfolk's recent scare, Agnes divulged that 'diverse in his house are dead' and added rather smugly that she thought it was 'through default of keeping'.[12]

This is the only surviving record of the tragedy that befell Kenninghall in the summer of 1528. Agnes does not give details. The Howard servants meant little to her. But if any of the casualties had been members of Surrey's immediate retinue, then their deaths would have cut him deeply. The proximity of Surrey to his servants, both during the day when they dressed and washed him, and at night when they slept outside his bedchamber, forged an intimate bond. Although hierarchy was observed and, at least in public, due deference paid, beneath the surface there was jocularity and friendship. 'Ay me!' Surrey would exclaim on the death of one of his squires in 1545, 'while life did last that league was tender.'[13] Surrey may have grown up alongside his siblings and his father's wards,* but it was to his servants that he would later turn for

---

* Wards were minor heirs (girls under fourteen; boys under twenty-one). By buying their wardships, the Duke of Norfolk assumed control of their estates during their minority. In return, he became their guardian and supervised their upbringing. Norfolk's wards included William Temperley, George Blount and Elizabeth Marney, eldest daughter of Lord Marney. Norfolk also had the right to arrange his wards' marriages and, in 1533, he married Elizabeth Marney to his second son Thomas.

companionship. And, in the last instance, when his final fate drew near, it was his servants, not his family, who would stay true to him.

Had Surrey been plunged into a premature inheritance in 1528, he could at least have been confident that he was well trained for it. From the moment of his birth, he had been groomed for the eventuality of succeeding his father and serving his King. Up until the age of seven, this largely entailed the inculcation of good manners along with rudimentary instruction in reading and writing. From thenceforth – and this coincided neatly with his becoming Earl – Surrey benefited from the more holistic, regimented curriculum expounded by the humanists.

Humanism was a movement pioneered by scholars like Desiderus Erasmus, Thomas More and John Colet, who sought to rejuvenate the moral, religious and political values of society by drawing on the wisdom of the ancients. Most humanists agreed that high birth was not an automatic qualification for public office, but they did acknowledge that noble men and women possessed a natural propensity to virtue, the *sine qua non* of honourable service. Such fertile soil had to be carefully cultivated. 'A family tree is nothing,' wrote Henry Peacham in the dedication of *The Complete Gentleman*, 'unless you furnish the mind with good manners and take pains by your studies to make yourself worthy of your high birth.'[14]

Surrey's education focused on the liberal arts considered most likely to instil the correct moral and political virtues. He studied rhetoric – the art of eloquent speaking – ostensibly to encourage his King to virtue and dissuade him from bad counsel. By translating Cicero and other Latin authors, both into English and then back again into the original, and by producing his own literary compositions in imitation of the ancients, Surrey developed a thorough grasp of the language and grammar of Latin, through which, it was believed, the noblest thoughts of mankind were articulated. Moral philosophy taught Surrey the principles of virtuous conduct, while history, literature (Virgil and Martial being his favourites) and the Scriptures furnished him with examples of its application or abuse.[15]

Surrey's studies also aimed at fashioning him into the perfect courtier. In many ways, the Howard household was a court in miniature and much of what other Tudor children had to study – manners, graceful carriage, social polish, heraldry, the importance of hierarchy and precedence – Surrey simply absorbed as a way of life. However, he did have to learn French, Italian and Spanish, so that he would be able to converse freely with foreign rulers and ambassadors. He was also taught the various dances of the Tudor Court, including the stately *pavane* and more energetic *galliard*, and he learnt how to carry them off gracefully, without the 'unclean motions of countenances' that the humanist Thomas Elyot believed would 'irritate the minds of the dancers to venereal lusts'.[16] A measured singing voice and an ability to play the lute and virginals* were also valued at Court. Surrey's poems, some of which were later set to music, testify to an innate grasp of rhythm and harmony.

Curiously, none of the names of any of Surrey's schoolmasters has survived. There is only one entry to 'm. Scole m.' in the household book of 1526–7 and it provides no clue as to his identity apart from the fact that he dined with 'my Lord Surrey's servants in my Lord Surrey's chamber', his status not being great enough for him to eat with the family.[17] Thomas Elyot advised in his book *The Governor* (1531) that the ideal schoolmaster 'should be an ancient and worshipful man, in whom is approved to be much gentleness, mixed with gravity, and, as nigh as can be, such one as the child by imitation following may grow to be excellent'. But having outlined a long list of requirements – including a mastery of languages, poetry, music, astronomy and philosophy – Elyot admitted that the reality often fell far short. 'Behold,' he lamented, 'how few grammarians after this description be in this realm.'[18]

It is likely, though, that Surrey's tutor or tutors would have fulfilled at least some of Elyot's criteria. The Howards were generous patrons of literature and learned men. Works dedicated to Surrey's father and grandfather include Alexander Barclay's French grammar, John Harding's *Chronicle*, and Andrew Boorde's *Dyetary of Helth*. Surrey himself would later receive a romance, a devotional work and a medical treatise. Hovering in and out of the Howard orbit was an eclectic group of writers and scholars: men like the antiquarian John Leland, the humanist John Palsgrave, the Poet Laureate John Skelton, and Nicolas Bourbon, Anne Boleyn's French protégé. Through their extensive network of blood and marital relations, the Howards could claim as kin Lord Berners, the famed translator of Froissart, and Henry Parker, Lord Morley, the first man to render Petrarch's *Trionfi* into English verse.

---

* The lute was a plucked stringed instrument with a curved back; the virginals, a keyed instrument resembling a spinet and set in a box.

Some of Surrey's past biographers have suggested that he was tutored by the Catholic writer John Clerke, who later served as the Duke of Norfolk's secretary. This is on the basis of a book entitled *L'Amant Mal Traité de Sa Mie*, translated by Clerke in the spring of 1543 and dedicated by him to Surrey. In the dedication, he writes:

> Knowing by long experience not only the great wisdom and singular judgement wherewith God, the disposer of all things, hath most abundantly endowed you, but also the exceeding great pains and travails sustained by yourself in traductions [translations], as well out of the Latin, Italian as the Spanish, and French, whereby your Lordship surmounteth many others not only in knowledge but also in laud and commendation . . . I humbly beseech your Lordship to take these my little labours and great good will in acceptable part and as the monument of my poor hearty affection always borne to the same.[19]

It is possible that 'the exceeding great pains and travails' taken by Surrey in his translations could have been observed by Clerke in the classroom, but it is far more likely that Clerke was referring to Surrey's more adult translations and the imitations that shaped much of his poetry. At no time did Clerke refer, as one might expect in a dedication of this sort, to a master–student relationship between himself and Surrey, nor is there any evidence to suggest that Clerke served in the Howard household before 1538. By the time of his dedication in 1543, five years had passed. This could easily account for the 'long experience' that Clerke felt he had gained of Surrey's skills. One thing is certain: if Clerke ever had played a part in Surrey's education, by the time of his own somewhat torturous translation in 1543, the pupil's talents far outstripped those of the master.

Surrey was a precocious child. Even Norfolk was impressed by his Latin compositions and took to gloating over them at Court. Despite his obvious talents, or perhaps because of them, Surrey was occasionally beaten. The favoured tool of punishment was a sturdy branch of birchwood that branded a stinging welt across the backside. 'My buttocks doth sweat a bloody sweat,' one young victim cried, while in London's markets the instruments were hawked with the words: 'Buy my fine Jemmies! Buy my London Tartars!'[20] Surrey's beatings were probably occasioned by insolence or minor rebellions against his tutor. He rarely responded well to authority imposed by someone of inferior rank and he could behave quite appallingly if he sensed that his honour had been touched. It is possible that Surrey's behaviour was also brought on by sheer boredom. If, as is likely, Surrey studied alongside his brother and his father's wards, then his budding genius would have been held back by their more pedestrian efforts. Learning was too easy and the lessons too tedious to hold Surrey's attention for long.

Yet it would be quite wrong to assume that his life had become monotonous. The Duke of Norfolk frequently hired minstrels and players to give musical and dramatic performances. On holy days a bear warden would sometimes come and delight his audience by baiting his bears into 'dancing' on their hind legs or fighting with savage dogs. At Thetford Priory, where the Flodden Duke was buried, there were two recorded appearances of 'the man with the camel' and it is quite possible that Surrey may have seen this strange hump-backed creature on one of these occasions.[21] A boy of Surrey's imagination would have had little difficulty in filling his spare time. In order to revive the practice of archery, a law had been passed in 1512 ensuring that every boy over the age of seven had his own bow and arrow.[22] Surrey could have fashioned other weapons from wood or bone and staged re-enactments of the Battle of Flodden around the grounds of Kenninghall. The poet Alexander Barclay, who was close to the Flodden Duke, observed that when pigs were slaughtered in the winter, children would stuff the bladders and use them for various ball games. The slaughter house at Shelfhanger Farm could have proved useful in this respect, as it might also have done after a heavy frost when the lakes and ponds around Kenninghall iced over; from as early as the twelfth century, it had been noted that children 'slid, and skated on the legbones of some animal, punting themselves along with an iron-shod pole, and charging one another'.[23] Surrey also had the run of the family tennis court and, in the Dining Chamber, there was a little board where he could play chess[24] – a game whose parallels to the politics of the Tudor Court were not lost on contemporaries.

He was happiest outside where he could escape from the stultifying regimens of the household. Although a sociable person – so much so that his father claimed to have summoned him to the North in 1537 for the purpose of entertaining his servants there – Surrey could also be solitary. His lyrics reveal an almost masochistic preoccupation with his sense of aloneness. The following sonnet is an example of this, but also reveals Surrey's sensitivity to nature. Like Chaucer, whose influence is evident, Surrey possessed an inspired eye for nature's movements: for animal behaviour, plant growth and the transformative effects of the seasons. He based his poem on Petrarch's sonnet, 'Zefiro torna', but his observations are peculiarly English:

> The soote season, that bud and bloom forth brings,
> With green hath clad the hill and eke the vale;
> The nightingale with feathers new she sings;
> The turtle to her make hath told her tale.
> Summer is come, for every spray now springs;
> The hart hath hung his old head on the pale;
> The buck in brake his winter coat he flings;
> The fishes float with new repaired scale;
> The adder all her slough away she slings;
> The swift swallow pursueth the flies smale;
> The busy bee her honey now she mings;
> Winter is worn that was the flowers' bale.
>   And thus I see among these pleasant things
>   Each care decays, and yet my sorrow springs.*[25]

If anything could be relied upon to rouse Surrey from his moments of despondency, it was the cry of the hounds. He loved to hunt. As an adult he would exasperate his father by arranging costly meets that reduced Kenninghall's deer population to dangerously low levels. Fortunately hunting with the hawk and the hound was seen as an honourable sport and a good grounding for war. 'Surely this manner of hunting,' wrote Thomas Elyot,

> may be called a necessary solace and pastime, for therein is the very imitation of battle; for not only it doth show the courage and strength as well of the horse as of him that rideth – traversing over mountains and valleys, encountering and overthrowing great and mighty beasts – but also it increaseth in them both agility and quickness; also sleight and policy to find

* line 1: *soote*: sweet.
  line 2: *eke*: also.
  line 4: *turtle*: turtle-dove; *make*: mate.
  line 10: *smale*: small (I have kept the original spelling to preserve Surrey's rhyme scheme).
  line 11: *mings*: remembers.

such passages and straits, where they may prevent or entrap their enemies. Also by continuance therein they shall easily sustain travail in wars, hunger and thirst, cold and heat.[26]

Hunting presented a further attraction to Surrey: it allowed him to spend quality time with his father. On 16 September 1526 the Duke of Norfolk, 'in a cheerful, jolly mood', took Surrey and his younger brother Thomas to a hunting party at Scuttegrove Wood in East Suffolk. Having spent the night at nearby Butley Priory, they rose early the next morning and chased the fox all day, through the fading light, until ten o'clock at night. The next day Surrey and Thomas accompanied their father as he went about his ducal business, surveying Staverton Park and ordering the desalination of the salt marshes at Hollesley. Three years later, on 23 July 1529, Norfolk returned to the area, this time taking only Surrey and his servants with him and, again, they stayed the night at Butley Priory.[27] On such occasions – and there must have been many more for which no records have survived – Norfolk prepared his heir for his future responsibilities.

If Surrey's childhood resembled, to some extent, a gilded cage, it also produced many of his fondest memories. In a poem that dwells on the mutability of life and the nature of man to be forever dissatisfied with his lot, Surrey's speaker lies on his bed and reflects on the various ages of man:

> I saw the little boy, in thought how oft that he
> Did wish of God to scape the rod, a tall young man to be.

The young man is himself desperate to race towards old age, where he hopes to find ease and contentment. But suddenly, he is stricken by a vision of his future self in 'withered skin' with 'toothless chaps' and 'white and hoarish hairs' and he realises that he will never be able to resurrect the blissful ignorance of youth:

> Where at I sight,* and said: Farewell, my wonted joy;
> Truss up thy pack, and trudge from me to every little boy,
> And tell them thus from me, their time most happy is,
> If, to their time, they reason had to know the truth of this.[28]

---

* *sight*: sighed.

Just after midnight, one day early in December 1529, the Duke of Norfolk escorted the Imperial ambassador, Eustace Chapuys, to his London lodging. Earlier in the evening, the Duke had hosted a supper and shown the ambassador an epistle that the twelve-year-old Surrey had composed. It was 'in very good Latin,' Chapuys recalled, and Norfolk 'was much pleased with the youth's proficiency and advancement in letters'. But Norfolk had no desire to encourage his son's literary talents. His sole interest lay in Surrey's potential as a Howard asset. Now, as he accompanied the ambassador through the streets of London, Norfolk revived the conversation. 'I told you that I was on many accounts delighted to see my son making so much progress in his studies and following the path of virtue.' His next sentence reveals why:

> The King has entrusted to me the education of his bastard son, the Duke of Richmond, of whom my own son may become in time preceptor and tutor, that he may attain both knowledge and virtue, so that a friendship thus cemented promises fair to be very strong and firm.[29]

It was time for Surrey to put his training to good use.

4

WITH A KING'S SON

Norfolk had been in high spirits at that supper. Only a few weeks earlier he had celebrated the fall from grace of his chief rival, Thomas Wolsey. For well over a decade Norfolk had been fighting, and losing, the battle for pre-eminence at Court. Wolsey may have been an 'upstart from the dung-cart', as the Poet Laureate John Skelton had put it,[1] but he had proved a wily politician and an administrative genius. Crucially, he had also been able to gain the trust of Henry VIII, something that Norfolk, even at the height of his power, was never quite able to achieve. Wolsey's success had lain quite simply in giving the King exactly what he wanted. No obstacle had seemed too great, no command too absurd. 'He was,' his gentleman usher recalled, 'most earnest and readiest among all the Council to advance the King's only will and pleasure without any respect to the case.'[2] But when Henry VIII called on Wolsey to put on his cardinal's hat and secure the annulment of his marriage to Catherine of Aragon, it proved a bridge too far.

Henry VIII's doubts about the validity of his marriage to Catherine of Aragon had, by 1529, hardened into firm resolution. They had married twenty years earlier, two months after the death of Henry VII. An affinity already existed between Catherine and Henry – she was the widow of his elder brother Arthur – but that had been a minor impediment, easily swatted by a papal dispensation. Two weeks later, on Midsummer Day 1509, with Henry VIII only four days shy of his eighteenth birthday, the couple was jointly crowned at Westminster amid great fanfare and jubilation. Thomas More's coronation poem captured the mood of English men and women everywhere: 'They rejoice, they exult, they leap for joy and celebrate their having such a king.' Lord Mountjoy, writing to Erasmus, echoed these sentiments in his own inimitable style: 'Heaven smiles, earth rejoices; all is milk and honey and nectar.'[3]

It was not long before this divine confection began to curdle. Despite becoming pregnant around seven times, Catherine could only manage one surviving heir for the Tudor dynasty, a daughter, Mary. Miscarriage, stillbirth and infant mortality had claimed the rest, while the early onset of menopause put paid to the possibility of any more. Henry did not doubt his virility; he had sired an illegitimate son – Henry Fitzroy, soon to be Surrey's new companion – in 1519 by his mistress Bessie Blount. If God could bless this sinful union with a healthy son, then surely, Henry reasoned, his marriage to Catherine must be even viler, even more deserving of God's punishment, than adultery. He turned to the Bible for confirmation. According to Leviticus 20:21, 'If a man shall take his brother's wife, it is an unclean thing; he hath uncovered his brother's nakedness; they shall be childless.' Advised by the Hebraist Robert Wakefield that 'childless' should be read as 'sonless', Henry became convinced that his marriage was cursed.

But there was another, perhaps even stronger reason why Henry VIII wished to dispense with Catherine.[4] Anne Boleyn was Surrey's first cousin, the daughter of Norfolk's sister Elizabeth and Thomas Boleyn. She was, according to one of her favourite clerics, 'competement belle' rather than beautiful. Her looks were unconventional; she was a brunette rather than the preferred blonde and had a dark – some said 'swarthy' – complexion that did not conform to the English rose stereotype so admired at Court. However, her glossy hair, delicate bone structure and long, graceful neck contrasted favourably with the features of Catherine of Aragon, who had lost her lustre and her figure through successive pregnancies. Anne was well aware of her sexuality and having spent her formative years at the libidinous French Court, she had mastered the art of seduction. One admirer described her in action. She had, he noted,

> eyes, always most attractive
> Which she knew well how to use with effect,
> Sometimes leaving them at rest,
> And at others, sending a message
> To carry the secret witness of the heart.
> And, truth to tell, such was their power
> That many surrendered to their obedience.[5]

By the end of 1526 so had Henry VIII. But Anne, unlike the other ladies of the Court, who had willingly serviced Henry's carnal appetite, refused to be bedded. She maintained her resistance the following year, even after Henry asked her to marry him. Only when they were officially man and wife, Anne vowed, would she surrender her body as well as her heart. Henry's letters to Anne have survived and now rest, rather inappositely, in the Vatican archives. They testify to the simple, deep-seated love that he bore her; they also provide details of his frustrated lust – 'wishing myself (specially an evening) in my sweetheart's arms, whose pretty dukkys* I trust shortly to cusse†.'[6] Divorce from Catherine had become a matter of great urgency.

But the 'Great Matter', as the annulment campaign‡ came to be known, was not running smoothly. Henry VIII had fully expected Wolsey to work his usual magic. He was, after all, not only a cardinal but also, as legate *a latere*, a papal emissary of the highest rank. In May 1527 Wolsey convened a secret court to try the marriage, but it soon became tangled in some very determined briers. For one thing, there was a passage in Deuteronomy (25:5–6) that could be set up in contradiction to Leviticus, for it stated that a man was duty bound to marry his brother's widow, the resultant children being necessary for the continuance of the family line. Then there was the issue of jurisdiction. Henry argued, provocatively, that divine law worked in his favour, that it overrode canon law and that the original Pope had acted *ultra vires* in dispensing with it. The Vatican's present incumbent, Pope Clement VII, did not take kindly to an English King questioning the judgement of his predecessor. Only the institution of the Papacy, Clement argued, had the right to interpret and, ultimately, arbitrate upon God's Word. Betwixt and between these opposing standpoints was a myriad of complex legal and theological issues, the consideration of which ultimately engaged over a hundred and fifty contemporary scholars.[7]

Henry never wavered. He was adamant that his marriage was invalid in the eyes of God. 'If an angel was to descend from heaven,' the papal legate Cardinal Campeggio wrote, 'he would not be able to persuade him to the contrary.'[8] Catherine, for her part, was equally convinced of the sanctity of the marriage and the legitimacy of her daughter. She

* *dukkys*: breasts.
† *cusse*: kiss.
‡ Technically Henry VIII was seeking an annulment to his marriage, rather than a divorce, the latter word not being recognised by medieval canon law. However, both words were used interchangeably at the time (MacCulloch, *Thomas Cranmer*, p. 42, note 4).

rose to the challenge magnificently. Impervious to bribes or threats, she refused to co-operate or compromise in any way. She won the battle for hearts and minds hands down, playing the part of the wronged wife to perfection, while Anne was cast as a scheming temptress. Indeed, feelings ran so high against Anne in London that the Venetian ambassador reported a story about a mob of seven to eight thousand women, and men disguised as women, who had apparently tried to lynch her at a Thames-side villa. It was said that she only just managed to escape by crossing the river in a small boat. This is the only account of this strange incident and it is probably apocryphal, but the fact that the Venetian ambassador thought it worth reporting suggests that he for one deemed it plausible.[9]

In addition to the groundswell of popular support, Catherine also had influential allies. In England these included Sir Thomas More, Nicholas Carew, John Fisher, Bishop of Rochester and Surrey's mother, the Duchess of Norfolk, who refused to toe the family line against her mistress and friend. On the Continent Catherine had the powerful backing of her nephew, Charles V. He was the Holy Roman Emperor, the King of Spain and the Duke of Burgundy. His empire stretched from Mexico to Naples and encompassed much of present-day Germany, Belgium, Holland, Austria, Hungary and Spain. At war with France over the control of Northern Italy, Charles had so far only been able to support his aunt from afar. But on 6 May 1527 his hungry, mutinous troops entered Rome and rampaged through the city. 'Right pitiful were the cryings and lamentations of the women of Rome,' wrote the chronicler Raphael Holinshed,

> and no less worthy of compassion, the calamity of nuns and virgins professed, whom the soldiers ravished . . . No age, no sex, no dignity or calling was free from the violation of soldiers, in whom it was doubtful whether bare [which bore] more rule: the humour of cruelty to kill, or the appetite of lust to deflower, or lastly, the rage of covetousness to rob and spoil.[10]

The 'Sack of Rome', as it became known, was a shocking affair and Charles immediately condemned it, but he and Catherine did welcome one unexpected outcome: languishing under house arrest in the Castel Sant' Angelo was Pope Clement VII. Although Charles allowed Clement to 'escape' in December, he maintained his grip on the Papacy and any hopes that the French might be able to loosen it were dashed on 21

June 1529, when they were routed by the Imperial army at the Battle of Landriano. It was these unfavourable winds that blew their way towards London, and into the court of Blackfriars, just as the second phase of the divorce proceedings reached their dénouement.

Summoned to present her case to Wolsey and the Pope's emissary Cardinal Campeggio, Catherine walked calmly across the courtroom towards Henry VIII. Then she threw herself at his feet and begged him to consider her honour, his own honour and the honour of their child. Still kneeling in front of her squirming husband, Catherine questioned the impartiality of the court and called for the case to be tried in Rome. Then she rose to her feet, curtsied to the King and strode out of the court. The crier repeatedly tried to recall her, but to the jubilation of the public gallery, he was defiantly ignored. It was a winning performance. On 16 July a committee of cardinals authorised by the Pope upheld Catherine's appeal and 'advoked' the case to Rome. A fortnight later Cardinal Campeggio adjourned the Blackfriars trial.

Henry VIII was apoplectic with rage. He had been publicly humiliated by Catherine and played for a fool by Clement and Charles. The past two years had been a complete waste of time; he was no closer to resolving his Great Matter than he had been from the outset. Anne, far from assuaging Henry's wounds, poured salt into them, accusing him of being too soft on Catherine: 'I have been waiting long,' she harped, 'and might in the meanwhile have contracted some advantageous marriage, out of which I might have had issue, which is the greatest consolation in the world. But, alas! Farewell to my time and youth spent to no purpose at all.'[11] Henry needed a scapegoat and Wolsey, who had staked everything on a papal solution, was the obvious candidate. On 9 October 1529 he was indicted for *praemunire* – the illegal application of papal authority to matters under English jurisdiction. The Duke of Norfolk, having bided his time against his old enemy, now revelled in his distress. Indeed, such was the power that Wolsey had once exerted, and so great was the fear of a possible comeback, that Norfolk, Anne and their allies eventually hounded him to his death.*

* Henry VIII was persuaded that Wolsey had been in the pocket of the Pope, that he had deliberately set out to sabotage the divorce and that since his indictment for *praemunire* he had been intriguing with the King's enemies. On 4 November 1530 Wolsey was arrested for high treason. He died twenty-five days later on his way to the Tower of London. Broken in body and spirit, he had just enough strength to utter his famous last words: 'If I had served God as diligently as I have done the King, he would not have given me over in my grey hairs' (*Two Early Tudor Lives*, p. 183).

His fall left a power vacuum at Court that Norfolk was initially tipped to fill. The Imperial ambassador documented the Duke's rising star. On 25 October 1529 he noted that 'the whole government of this country was fast falling into the hands of the Duke of Norfolk.' Two weeks later: 'the Duke of Norfolk is now the personage who enjoys most credit and favour with the King', and on 13 December 1529: 'the Duke of Norfolk's influence and power are daily increasing.'[12] His triumph would prove short-lived. While he was an expert handler of people – be they friends or foe – Norfolk possessed neither the intellect nor the imagination to break the impasse with Rome. Very soon, Henry VIII would look elsewhere for solutions to his Great Matter. But in the meantime Norfolk had created for himself a window of opportunity through which he was able to obtain control over the education of the King's illegitimate son. Thus it was, in the spring of 1530, that the Earl of Surrey found himself on the road to Windsor, sent by his father to become the best friend to a boy he had never before met.[13]

Henry Fitzroy was eleven in 1530, two years younger than Surrey. He was the product of a dalliance between the King and his erstwhile mistress, Bessie Blount, 'a fair damsel' of the Court.[14] Despite his bastardy, Henry Fitzroy was, as his name suggests, a source of pride for his father – as well as welcome proof of his virility. Indeed Henry VIII was inordinately fond of his son. He showered him with gifts, not only on New Year's Day, when it was conventional to give ostentatiously, but also at random times throughout the year. On one occasion he paid his fletcher twenty shillings for arrows to supply Fitzroy's bow; in 1531 he bought him a lute; another time saw Fitzroy being presented with a gold collar, enamelled with white roses, 'sent from the King's Highness for a token'.[15] Fitzroy was Henry VIII's 'worldly jewel', and the King loved him, so the Venetian ambassador observed, 'like his own soul'.[16]

On 18 June 1525 Henry VIII had bestowed on his then six-year-old son the Dukedoms of Richmond and Somerset and the Earldom of Nottingham. It was the first time since the twelfth century that a king of England had raised his illegitimate son to the peerage and it precipitated a whispering campaign that he might one day name him as heir. The rumours were fanned seven days later when the new Duke of Richmond was installed as a Knight of the Garter, and even more so

WITH A KING'S SON

the following month, when Henry VIII made him Warden General of the Scottish Marches and Lord High Admiral of England. Soon after these investitures, Richmond was sent to the North as the nominal head of its regional government. He was furnished with £88 worth of new clothes, his own Council and a princely household that included Henry VIII's physician Doctor Butts.[17] Whatever the King's plans for the succession in 1525, it is clear that he envisaged a role for his son at the highest level of public office.*

The Duke of Norfolk was well aware of this and had planned accordingly. If, as he hoped, Surrey could 'cement' a 'strong and firm' friendship with Richmond, then the rewards could be very great. In order to consolidate this Howard–Richmond association, Surrey's younger sister Mary was roped in as Richmond's future bride. This latter coup owed much to the influence of Anne Boleyn, who, Surrey's mother later wrote, 'got the marriage clear for my lord, my husband'.[18] Had Richmond married any one of a number of foreign princesses that were mooted for him – an impressive list that included Catherine de' Medici – then he would have been in a stronger position to threaten Anne's future children's claims to the succession. But married to Mary Howard, Richmond would effectively be assimilated into Anne's family and his threat neutralised. That Anne managed to persuade the King to allow his son to be betrothed to Mary Howard, without any kind of dowry payment, shows how strong her influence was at this time.

Richmond was clearly his father's son. Not only did he bear a striking resemblance to Henry VIII, but he also shared his passion for outdoor pursuits. By the age of six Richmond had already killed his first buck and, as he travelled north in the same year, he eschewed the horse litter that had been laid on for him at considerable expense, preferring instead to ride his own pony.[19] Two years later he wrote to Henry VIII asking for a suit of harness 'for my exercise in arms according to my learning in Julius Caesar' – a crafty request that downplayed his priorities only to justify them in the end.[20]

In 1525 the Archdeacon of Durham wrote that 'my Lord of

---

* Richmond had been Henry VII's title before Bosworth while the Somerset title was even more significant to those who looked for signs of an imminent change in the succession. John Beaufort, Henry VIII's great-great-grandfather, had been created Earl of Somerset in 1397. He had been born a bastard, but was subsequently legitimised. However, Henry VIII was always guarded about matters relating to the succession. At the same time that Richmond was sent north, Henry arranged for his daughter Mary to head up her own, even larger, establishment in Wales – the traditional training ground for heirs to the throne.

Richmond is a child of excellent wisdom and towardness; and, for his good and quick capacity, retentive memory, virtuous inclination to all honour, humanity and goodness, I think hard it would be to find any creature living, of twice his age, able or worthy to be compared to him.'[21] More often than not, though, Richmond neglected his studies in favour of his sport. He was encouraged in this by a phalanx of servants, who consistently sought to undermine the authority of his schoolmasters. Their first victim was the eminent humanist, John Palsgrave, who had previously taught Henry VIII's sister, Mary. He was impressed by Richmond's wit, but soon grew exasperated by the contemptuous treatment meted out to him. He lasted six months.

His successor, Richard Croke, a Greek scholar who had taught at the universities of Louvain, Cologne, Leipzig and Cambridge, fared little better. On 26 May 1527 he wrote a long Latin letter to Wolsey complaining of 'the frenzy of those men who every day endeavour to drive the hearts of my Prince and his young classmates to a hatred equally of study and the clergy by means of some exceedingly cunning deceits.' The ringleader, Croke explained, was George Cotton, Richmond's gentleman usher. Not only did Cotton cancel Richmond's early morning and late evening classes, but he also encouraged truancy, enjoining Richmond and his fellow students to indulge instead in archery and hunting. 'Yet this fellow,' Croke continued, 'who is so diligent in keeping the Prince's teacher away, happily allows clowns and players to be admitted, to warble ditties fit for a brothel before the Prince in his own private chamber.' Where Cotton led, his sidekick, a boy named Scrope, was eager to follow:

> In the presence of the other boys he vilifies the Latin language and literature to an amazing degree and stirs the boys against me so that they are uncooperative. He says terrible things about me behind my back; in church last Trinity Sunday, he clung to the Prince's awning and abused me and then boasted that he had done so in such a manner. For in a loud voice, which betrayed a sort of uneducated vindictiveness, he called me a bastard, a good-for-nothing, a villain, a hypochondriac, and a thousand other names of that kind.

The effects of these malign influences were so wholly detrimental to Richmond that Croke feared for his future:

For what will he refrain from doing as an adult when, even now, he is being taught to say to me in jest, 'Teacher, if you beat me, I shall beat you'. And why should he not think that he may say these things with impunity when he hears his classmates, who are socially far inferior to him, not only slandering me behind my back, while the servants of his own private chamber laugh at me and encourage them, but also abusing me to my face. When the boys come to me for a beating they are pulled from my hands by the grooms, who threaten me and, in the presence of the Prince, noisily assert, 'Why are you baring the buttocks of the boys in the presence of so great a Prince?'

Croke found himself powerless in the face of such mockery: 'I have often objected,' he wrote, 'and often complained, but I have achieved nothing.' It was all the more lamentable, he continued, because of Richmond's potential:

Is it not remarkable that a boy of eight years of age can translate any passage of Caesar into English, and in so doing preserve the grammatical structure and art of the original? Yet impressive though this is, it is as nothing compared with the progress he would already have made in the Latin language without any difficulty, if he had not been obstructed by Cotton's treachery . . . The Prince's benefit is at stake; great hopes were entertained that within two years his knowledge of Latin and Greek would be such that he would be attracted to them by themselves and by a sort of affection for them. But now, unless Your Grace lends assistance, I clearly despair of benefiting him.[22]

Croke surrendered his charge in October 1527. Well might the Earl of Surrey have trembled, therefore, as he rode through the turreted gatehouse of Windsor Castle, Richmond's new home. But Surrey's role was entirely different to that of Palsgrave and Croke. He was too young to be a conventional schoolmaster – another man was retained for that – rather he was to act, as the Duke of Norfolk had put it, as Richmond's *précepteur ou incitateur*.[23] Both words can be translated as 'tutor', but the latter, deriving from the Latin *incitare* (to incite), is distinctive and unique. Surrey would, it was hoped, provide an example that Richmond would seek to emulate. Part study companion, part mentor, he was expected to impress, induce and stimulate Richmond so 'that he may attain both knowledge and virtue'.[24]

Surrey was an inspired choice for this difficult role. Similar in age and station to Richmond, his upbringing allowed him to identify with his charge in a way that few else could. Both had grown up under the double-edged sword of high birth, surrounded by privilege, but also immured by the concomitant pressures. Richmond's motto – 'duty binds me' – could just as easily have been Surrey's. Both were in awe of their powerful fathers and desperate to fulfil their great expectations. Both grew up showered with attention, but without the anchor provided by permanent parental presence. They were the stars of the future, but also outsiders, set apart by their elevated status from the rest of their generation.

In character as well as circumstance, Surrey and Richmond were kindred spirits. They were bright, energetic boys with a low boredom threshold and a clear preference for outdoor activities. Both were hotheaded and highly competitive, constantly striving to better them-selves and eager, too, to test the limits of toleration. Both were jealous of their honour and tended to display arrogance and haughtiness towards their social inferiors. In this they were in danger of crossing the fine line between maintaining one's reputation and station in life (an admirable and essential quality) and displaying pride (a cardinal sin). In many ways, though, Surrey and Richmond were just typical adolescents, doing what all adolescents do: testing boundaries, devel-oping their identities and adapting to the changing needs of their bodies and minds. And, like growing boys the world over, Surrey and Richmond bonded over their two shared passions: women and sport.

Although Richmond was formally betrothed to Surrey's sister Mary, he would only marry her in 1533. Until then he was free to admire with Surrey the ladies of the Court. In a beautiful poem about their time together at Windsor, Surrey described his and Richmond's pubescent longing for 'the ladies bright of hue' and their clumsy attempts to impress. Loitering around the 'large green courts', that afforded a good view of the 'maidens' tower', Surrey and Richmond would steal surreptitious glances at the objects of their desire. Often they played real tennis and, if there were ladies in the spectators' gallery, the boys would strip to their waists and indulge in horseplay: 'with dazed eyes oft we by gleams of love / have missed the ball and got sight of our dame'. In the evenings, they would take advantage of the courtly dances, 'where each of us did plead the other's right'. Despite frequent knock-backs and 'looks that tigers could but rue', their persistence occasionally paid off, for later these two partners in crime would retreat to 'the secret groves', and compare notes with boyish bravado, 'recording soft what grace each one had found'.[25]

Surrey and Richmond were on a surer footing with their second love, sport. They were now of an age to begin their martial education and Windsor Castle provided the perfect training ground. Originally a motte-and-bailey fortress erected by William the Conqueror, Windsor Castle had been radically transformed in the mid-fourteenth century into a vast Gothic palace, designed to celebrate Edward III's triumphs against the French. Windsor's new aesthetic projected Edward's passion for the cult of chivalry and it became the home to his new foundation, the Order of the Garter, a confraternity of knights that embodied the ethos of King Arthur's Round Table. Within Surrey and Richmond's own chambers, tapestries and hangings continued the chivalric theme. There was 'a piece of the Lady Pleasance, accompanied with many Virtues and assaulted with diverse Vices', while another depicted the story of Paris and Helen.[26]

It was imbued with the spirit of this glorified world, this fusion of mythology and reality, that Surrey chose to interpret his own relationship with Richmond. It was in:

> . . . proud Windsor, where I in lust and joy
> With a king's son my childish years did pass,
> In greater feast than Priam's sons of Troy.

Surrey employs the word 'childish' here not in the modern sense, but with the traditional meaning in mind, signifying that these were the years when he and Richmond had begun their military apprenticeship, but had not yet attained knighthood.[27] They were brothers-in-arms as well as future brothers-in-law, striving towards their destiny as chivalric warriors. They hunted as often as possible and, in the tiltyard, practised their jousting skills, either by running at the ring, when they had to spear a hoop suspended in the air, or at the quintain, a pivoted target against which they had to shatter their lances. They were taught the cut and thrust of swordsmanship, both on foot and on horseback, and grew accustomed to the weight and constriction of armour. Each activity fostered a fierce but friendly rivalry:

The gravelled ground, with sleeves tied on the helm,
On foaming horse, with swords and friendly hearts,
With cheer as though the one should overwhelm,
Where we have fought and chased oft with darts.

With silver drops the meads yet spread for ruth,
In active games of nimbleness and strength
Where we did strain, trailed by swarms of youth,
Our tender limbs, that yet shot up in length.

. . . .

The wild forest, the clothed holts with green,
With reins availed and swift y'breathed horse,
With cry of hounds and merry blasts between,
Where we did chase the fearful hart a force.

At night, exhausted, they would hang up their spurs and retire to
their shared chamber, where they would talk together frankly and freely:

The secret thoughts imparted with such trust,
The wanton talk, the diverse change of play,
The friendship sworn, each promise kept so just,
Wherewith we passed the winter nights away.[28]

It is hard to imagine a more intimate evocation of friendship in any
period, let alone the Tudor age, when such glimpses are rarely afforded.

Surrey composed his poem at a later, uncertain time, when Windsor
had become a 'cruel prison' and Richmond had been tragically taken
from him. He wrote with the conviction that the core values that defined
his and Richmond's sense of honour were being undermined by the
arrivistes of the Court. Surrey's poem is an elegy, whereby the Windsor
of his 'childish years' is viewed through a rosy gauze as an idyll, a
'place of bliss', a haven 'where all my freedom grew'. His recollections
are idealistic and selective. He provides us with no scenes from the
classroom. We hear nothing of the sudden death from the plague of
his elder sister Katherine.[29] Nor does he mention the frequent visits of
Henry VIII and his Court, or the day in August 1531 when Catherine
of Aragon, who was staying at Windsor with her daughter Princess

Mary, received a brutal message from the King ordering her out of the castle. Henry VIII was arriving there shortly with Anne Boleyn and Catherine, the message demanded, was to depart forthwith to The More while Mary was to ride to Richmond.[30] Catherine would never see her daughter again. Surrey would have been a witness to her distress, but there is no sign of this dark cloud in his Windsor poem. Instead, all is wonderful and playful, innocent and brilliant. In Surrey and Richmond's Windsor even complaints are 'pleasant' and sighs 'easy'. It is as if they were living in a parallel universe, where nothing and no one could touch them.

But is it too good to be true? How much of the actuality of life has Surrey rendered in his art? Has he portrayed real events as he remembered them, or has he, as his nineteenth-century French biographer, Edmond Bapst, believed, composed 'un tableau tout imaginaire'?[31] Poetry cannot be examined with the forensic tools that can be applied to other historical sources. We can affirm that Surrey and Richmond both loved hunting and military training, that they were at Windsor together (though Surrey occasionally returned to Kenninghall and Richmond sometimes travelled to his father's other residences) and that there were ladies at Windsor who the pubescent boys would have seen. But we cannot verify Surrey's memories with precision. We might speculate that they could have happened as he described them, give or take a few rhetorical flourishes, or we may conclude that they are too epic in scale and too sentimental to belong to the realm of fact.

But therein lies the beauty of Surrey's art. The moment it is subjected to cross-reference, broken down and scrutinised, the essence of that beauty is undermined. Surrey's tableau, *tout imaginaire* or not, is how he chose to remember his time at Windsor. It represents, if not the truth, then a distillation of a certain kind of truth, a poetic truth: a truth about the speaker. It reveals Surrey's tastes and values, his aspirations and ideals. He was reviving the past in an attempt to distract himself from the present. Just as in the poem cited in the previous chapter, where Surrey's speaker wants to trudge to every little boy and tell them that their childhood is their happiest time, so here Surrey marvels with hindsight at the innocence and vitality of youth. It is intentionally idealistic, a reaction to the cynicism and pragmatism of the Court, a defence of an ideology that he held, and still holds, dear.

It has been suggested that Surrey's elegy can also be read as a love poem.[32] He adopts romantic language and applies Chaucerian subtexts

in order to convey the strength of his feelings for Richmond. He wants
to express the power of their 'sweet accord' and emphasise the unique-
ness of a relationship that transcended all others. This sentiment is
extremely powerful and very real. Surrey longed for close companionship and a friendship based on trust and mutual attraction, not kinship
or service. His exultation at finding a soulmate, an alter ego, is
contrasted with his isolation and pain at his subsequent separation from
Richmond – 'Give me account where is my noble fere* . . . To other
lief,† but unto me most dear.' Surrey defined himself in terms of his
relationship with Richmond; together they were Priam's sons whose
destiny was intertwined and even in his last portrait, Surrey chose to
depict his friend alongside him. His poetry, here and elsewhere, provides
us with one more dialectic of the past and in many ways it tells us
more about him, and with greater authenticity, than a letter or a
chronicle or an ambassador's observation ever could.

In the late spring of 1532 Surrey, now fifteen, sat to the great Court
portraitist Hans Holbein. The final oil painting has not survived, but
the preparatory drawing has and now forms part of the Royal Collection at Windsor (plate 4). Surrey is sketched on pink paper in coloured
chalks, reinforced by pen and ink. His face, framed by a high-necked
lace collar, is the same oval shape as his father's, but he has inherited
the lighter colouring of his mother. Under his plumed hat, Surrey's fine,
auburn hair is cut into a very correct pudding-bowl style. He is an
attractive, almost cherubic boy, with hazel eyes and full, pink lips, but
he appears awkward and apprehensive. And well he might, for it is
likely that this drawing was the preliminary study for a portrait intended
to commemorate a very special event: the wedding of the Earl of Surrey
to Lady Frances de Vere.[33]

After Richmond had become engaged to Mary Howard, Surrey inherited the mantle of England's most eligible bachelor. His marriage was
big business and, true to form, the Duke of Norfolk determined to
make as much political and financial capital out of it as possible. At
first he angled for the greatest catch of them all, Princess Mary, Henry
VIII's only legitimate child. As with his daughter's marriage, Norfolk
was assisted and guided by the hand of Anne Boleyn, who saw Surrey
as a way of absorbing the threat posed by Mary Tudor to herself and

* *fere*: companion.
† *lief*: beloved.

her future children. 'I have just heard from a very good source,' Eustace Chapuys revealed to Emperor Charles V on 8 October 1529, 'that this King is so blindly and passionately fond of his Anne that he has, at her persuasion, consented to treat of a marriage between the Princess Mary his daughter, and the son of the Duke of Norfolk.'[34]

A couple of months later, though, Anne changed her mind. Under no circumstance, she now resolved, should Surrey be permitted to marry Mary. Her volte-face probably stemmed from her distrust of Norfolk. She realised that her wily uncle would only support her for as long as she offered the most attractive path to Howard advancement. If Surrey married Mary, then Norfolk would have a very strong incentive to uphold the Princess' legitimacy and defend Henry VIII's marriage to Catherine of Aragon. Her suspicions were well founded. On 13 December 1529 Chapuys confided in Charles V that he had 'no doubt' that Norfolk could be won over to Catherine's side 'by means of some promise of help and assistance in the marriage of his son to Princess Mary'. The match, Chapuys continued, 'is so much spoken of here that I consider myself perfectly justified to urge it on by pointing out the mutual advantages to be derived from it, as well as the troubles and anxieties it would remove.'[35]

The following month Chapuys was more blunt. 'I told him plainly,' he wrote, that a future marriage between Henry VIII and Anne Boleyn would be 'more detrimental to him than to anyone else, for it was generally reported that the King wished to marry the Princess to his eldest son, who would then, for want of male issue, become the heir to the throne.' By now, though, Norfolk had bowed to Anne's wishes. He was well aware of his niece's influence over the King and the fate of his father-in-law had taught him the folly of venturing too close to the throne. So he backtracked, protesting to Chapuys that the rumours of his son's marriage to Mary Tudor were 'pure invention'. 'Such a thought,' he added, 'had never entered his mind and he would much prefer to see his son drowned than to have him in such a position.'[36] Anne was not content with mere denials. On 13 February 1532, in order 'to remove all suspicion of his aiming at a marriage between his son and the Princess', Norfolk affianced Surrey to Lady Frances de Vere.[37]

Chapuys was not at all impressed with Norfolk's choice of daughter-in-law: 'The Duke must have had very urgent reasons for acting thus . . . the Lady is neither rich nor a very desirable alliance otherwise.'[38]

In fact Lady Frances de Vere had impeccable credentials. She was the daughter of John, fifteenth Earl of Oxford, by his second wife Elizabeth Trussel. Oxford, 'a man of valour and authority', came from ancient noble stock; he had a strong landed interest and, as hereditary Lord Great Chamberlain of England, he held considerable sway at Court.[39] On 13 February 1532 the deal was struck. According to sixteenth-century custom, the bride's father had to provide her with a marriage portion, or dowry, which she would surrender to the groom. In return, his family would bestow on the couple a landed settlement, customarily ten per cent of the total dowry, the income from which would form the bride's 'jointure' or living should she survive her husband. A thousand marks (just over £666) was considered a generous dowry in this period for the daughter of a nobleman.[40] Frances was endowed with four times that sum, two hundred marks to be paid on the day of the marriage, and the rest in regular instalments. In return, Norfolk promised to settle on the couple lands that yielded a yearly rent of £300. The stakes were high. This was not a marriage that could be allowed to fail.[41]

Nevertheless Norfolk was at pains to assure Chapuys that, had his hand had not been forced, he would not have betrothed his son to Frances 'even had she thirty thousand crowns more revenue than she actually had'.[42] The Howards and the de Veres had a long and chequered past and, although there was a tradition of mutual dependence and intermarriage between them, there was also a history of conflict. They had fought on opposing sides during the Wars of the Roses and it had been John de Vere, the thirteenth Earl of Oxford, who had slain Surrey's great-grandfather at Bosworth. Norfolk's half-sister, Anne, had been married to the fourteenth Earl of Oxford, but he had treated her so appallingly that in 1524 Wolsey had ordered him to handle her 'lovingly, familiarly and kindly'.[43] On the Earl's death two years later his cousin, Surrey's future father-in-law, became the fifteenth Earl and immediately broke the terms of Anne's jointure. With a mob of five hundred armed retainers, Oxford had rampaged through her lands and slaughtered over a hundred of her deer. After a week of escalating intimidation, she had written to Wolsey in despair: he 'hath broken up my house, and beaten my servants, and taken all my goods.'[44] Expelled from her lands, Anne had sought refuge at Tendring Hall, where she became a permanent, if rather forlorn feature of the Howard household.

Norfolk and Oxford also clashed over religion. While Norfolk, the

foremost Catholic peer in the country, was committed to the defence
of traditionalism, Oxford fully embraced the beliefs that were flooding
in from the Continent. He patronised several evangelical writers and
his personal troupe of actors regularly performed plays designed to
popularise the reformers' programme.[45]

Surrey and Frances had little say in the matter of their marriage.
Their paths had probably crossed before – the de Veres had attended
the Flodden Duke's funeral and the Howard household books reveal
occasional visits from de Vere family members – but it is unlikely that
the two children would have made more than a passing acquaintance.
Not that it mattered. Love and mutual attraction were luxuries that
few aristocratic families could afford. With luck, such feelings would
develop but, as one contemporary put it, the tradition was to 'marry
first, and love after by leisure'.[46]

When Surrey caught his first glimpse of Frances in her bridal attire
(probably a colourful gown, the 'white wedding' being an eighteenth-
century innovation), with her hair covered in jewels and flowers and
hanging loose to symbolise her virginity, he may have mused that he
could have done far worse. The Holbein drawing of Frances (plate 5),
almost certainly produced at the same time as that of Surrey, reveals
an attractive young lady. She was the same age as her groom and had
lovely brown eyes with long lashes and a sweet, snub nose. But her
clenched jaw and clasped hands betray her anxiety and her nervous,
somewhat dazed, expression is very similar to Surrey's own.

The wedding took place on the feast of Pentecost 1532, and was
attended by various representatives of the nobility.[47] Much of the ceremony took place outside the church door, where Surrey stood at Frances'
right hand, signifying that Eve was formed from one of Adam's left
ribs. The banns were read and the vows exchanged, with Frances
promising to be 'bonair [courteous] and buxom [obliging] in bed and
at board'. Then the ring was blessed and Surrey, in accordance with
the Sarum rite, placed it

upon the thumb of the bride, saying *In the name of the Father*; then upon
the second finger, saying *and of the Son*; then upon the third finger, saying
and of the Holy Ghost; then upon the fourth finger, saying *Amen*, and there
let him leave it . . . because in that finger there is a certain vein, which runs
from thence as far as the heart.[48]

The couple then led the congregation into the church and knelt at the altar under a bridal canopy of fine linen. Further prayers and blessings were followed by the Mass. Then the couple rose and Surrey, having received the pax from the priest, conveyed it to his bride, 'kissing her', as instructed by the Sarum Missal, which added that 'neither the bridegroom nor the bride are to kiss anyone else'.[49]

It was probably with great relief, if their wedding portraits are anything to go by, that the couple went their separate ways after the ceremony. Although they had both reached the official age of consent – fourteen for boys, twelve for girls – Surrey and Frances were nevertheless deemed too young to have sexual relations and it would be three more years until the marriage was consummated. So Surrey returned to Windsor Castle, where the Court soon flocked with its usual fanfare. The record of Henry VIII's privy purse payments at this time reveal that he indulged his love of hunting, while on one occasion fifteen shillings were given to 'two poor folk that the King's grace healed of their disease'.[50] This miraculous ability to cure the sick simply by placing a hand on them was known as 'The King's Touch' and was one of the many facets of majesty believed to be ordained by God.

This was not the only divine right of kingship that Henry VIII had been exercising lately. Ever since the summer of 1530, when the germ of the idea of the Royal Supremacy – that is, the supreme jurisdiction of the King of England over the Church in England – was first planted in his mind, Henry had been testing the waters of acceptance and attempting, through Parliament and the efforts of his new favourite Thomas Cromwell, to browbeat the English clergy into acknowledging his spiritual dominance. On 15 May 1532 he scored his first major triumph with the 'Submission of the Clergy', whereby Convocation was forced to accept Henry's arbitration over all matters relating to the English Church. The next day the Lord Chancellor, Sir Thomas More, resigned in disgust.

In the country, Anne's unpopularity showed no sign of abating. Throughout the summer progress of 1532, she encountered a barrage of 'hooting and hissing' from the crowd.[51] But she had invested too much to be put off by a few insults. The phrase embroidered on the coats of her liveried servants summarised her position: *Ainsi sera, groigne qui groigne* – It will be thus, whoever grudges it. Despite Anne's confidence, the Great Matter continued to be a complex and fragile affair. Foreign policy was crucial and Henry's friendship with Francis

I of France, his only worthwhile ally against the might of the Empire, needed careful nurturing. Despite his protestations to the contrary, Henry had not entirely given up on the Pope, but only the backing of Francis I would enable him to exert sufficient pressure on Clement VII.

On Sunday, 1 September 1532, at a lavish investiture ceremony held at Windsor Castle, Henry VIII created Anne Marchioness of Pembroke. Surrey's mother was supposed to have borne Anne's train during the ceremony. The Duke of Norfolk had even arranged for her to have a robe of crimson velvet made for the occasion.[52] But the Duchess refused to betray her Queen by honouring Anne, so Surrey's sister Mary stepped in. Anne was dressed resplendently, 'completely covered with the most costly jewels',[53] and along with the new title she received lands worth £1,000 a year.

At the same time, the Treaty of Mutual Aid with France, previously agreed on 23 June, was ratified and an interview between the two kings was formally confirmed. Anne's investiture was no frivolous gesture of affection, but a deliberate move to raise her status and improve her respectability in advance of the French meeting. Months of meticulous planning had gone into the summit, which was to be conducted in two stages – the first at French Boulogne and the second at English Calais. Henry VIII demanded the attendance of his nobility, and Richmond and Surrey duly received their summons. Although they probably did not yet know it, their role in the ensuing events would be even more crucial than that of their peers. Once again, Surrey's future became caught up in someone else's plans.

5

A FRENCHMAN AT HEART

They set sail before dawn on Friday, 11 October 1532. Surrey, the first named earl in the official list, was allowed twenty-four servants in his train; his father and Richmond, both dukes, each had forty. In all, the party that accompanied Henry VIII and Anne Boleyn to France included almost three thousand noblemen, knights, esquires, bishops, heralds, courtiers, minstrels and servants.[1] The Channel crossing from Dover to Calais was notoriously unpredictable, 'specially in October,' the chronicler Edward Hall noted, 'when the seas be rough'.[2] If, as is often supposed, an anonymous painting at Hampton Court entitled *The Embarkation of Henry VIII at Dover* (plate 10) can be attributed to the journey of 1532, then the seas were indeed choppy on the day that Surrey sailed away from the white cliffs.[3] Fortunately, though, his first Channel crossing proceeded without incident and within five hours the battlements of Calais, the last English outpost in France, came into view.

The original plan had been for Henry and Anne to be entertained on French soil for the first leg of the interview, but it was soon apparent that there was no French lady of suitable rank willing to receive Anne. Eleanor, Queen of France, had been ruled out as she was Catherine of Aragon's niece, but it was hoped that Francis' sister, Marguerite of Navarre, would perform the honour. At the last minute, though, she pulled out, pleading ill-health, and Francis' alternative proposal – that his own mistress greet Anne – was politely, but firmly, rejected. Thus it was as part of an all-male party that Surrey rode to Boulogne on Monday, 21 October. The next four days comprised one long jamboree. 'As for the great cheer that was there,' recorded one English guest, 'no man can express it', for the King's Grace was there entertained all at the French King's costs and charges. And every day noblemen of France desired our nobles and gentlemen home to their lodgings, where they found their houses richly hanged, great cupboards of plate, sumptuous fare, with singing and playing of all kinds of music. And also there was sent unto our lodgings great fare with all manner of wines for our servants; and our horses' meat was paid for; and all at their charges . . . And this continued with as great cheer and familiarity as might be.[4]

On Friday, 25 October Surrey and the rest of the Englishmen escorted Francis and his train to Calais for the second phase of the summit. As they processed through the various towns of the Calais Pale, three thousand shot were discharged from the English guns, whereas at Boulogne, the English crowed, the salute had 'passed not two hundred shot'.[5] This was the first of many attempts made by Henry VIII in the next few days to outshine his French counterpart.

Ever since New Year's Day 1515, when Francis, duc de Valois, became King of France, a title to which Henry VIII also laid ancient claim, an intense rivalry had characterised the two kings' relationship. 'Is he as tall as I am?' Henry had quizzed the Venetian ambassador in May 1515, to which he received the reply that there was little difference. 'Is he as stout?' The Venetian assured him that Francis was not, but Henry continued to fish for compliments:

'What sort of legs has he?'
    I replied, 'Spare'.
    Whereupon he opened the front of his doublet, and placing his hand on his thigh, said 'Look here! and I have also a good calf to my leg.'[6]

Four years later another Venetian ambassador noted that Henry VIII was 'a great deal handsomer than the King of France', but it is telling that 'on hearing that Francis I wore a beard, he allowed his own to grow'.[7]

The interviews in October 1532 brought back memories of the celebrated Field of the Cloth of Gold of 1520, when Henry and Francis had shone in magnificence. Both kings had spent enormous sums, but Henry's extravagance had appeared obvious and gaudy in comparison to Francis' easy style. Worse for Henry had been his defeat at Francis' hands in a very public wrestling match, an ignominy not to be repeated in 1532, when Henry wisely employed a team of Cornish wrestlers to represent him.

The interviews at Boulogne and Calais were not meant to be as ostentatious as they had been twelve years earlier. The levels of display and the numbers of attendants were limited according to strict protocol and only the kings and the ladies were permitted to wear cloth of gold and silver.[8] But Henry's competitive spirit was not easily subdued. The French had already snubbed Anne; they would not, under any circumstance, be allowed to show Henry up again. 'If the French King made good cheer to the King of England and his train at Boulogne,' chronicled Hall, 'I assure you he and his train were requited at Calais, for the plenty of wild foul, venison, fish and all other things which were there, it was marvel to see, for the King's Officers of England had made preparation in every place, so that the Frenchmen were served with such multitude of diverse fishes this Friday and Saturday that the masters of the French King's household much wondered at the provision.'[9]

In all, Henry spent around £6,000 on the Calais interview. On Sunday, 27 October there was bull and bear baiting, followed by a banquet in a specially prepared chamber. 'To tell the riches of the cloths of estates, the basins and other vessels which was there occupied, I assure you my wit is insufficient, for there was nothing occupied that night, but all of gold.'[10] After three courses, the first of forty dishes, the second of sixty and the third of seventy, Anne Boleyn finally made her entrance accompanied by seven of her ladies, all 'gorgeously apparelled, with visors on their faces'.[11] Anne danced with Francis a while until Henry could contain his excitement no longer and tore off her mask to reveal to the French King and all the onlookers the identity of his dancing partner. Then, as the guests returned to the dance, Anne and Francis retired to a quiet corner to talk.

The festivities came to an end on 29 October, when the two kings took their leave of each other. The Venetian ambassador to France, furious at being omitted from the guest list, dismissed the interview as 'a superfluous expenditure – entertainments and pageants and nothing else'.[12] But behind the showmanship lay serious issues. A treaty of alliance was signed against the 'Infidel' Turk and, more importantly, Francis pledged his support for Henry's Great Matter. Two French cardinals set off at once for Rome with instructions to promote Henry's campaign and request a meeting between Francis and the Pope. They were also given the authority to propose a marriage between Francis' second son, Henri, and Clement VII's niece, Catherine de' Medici. If all went to plan, so Francis promised, then he would invite English representatives, perhaps even Henry VIII himself, to the meeting, where they could present a united front to the Pope.

It was a firm espousal of Henry's cause. Seven years earlier, when Charles V had defeated Francis I at the Battle of Pavia, the French King had been taken hostage and only released in exchange for his two elder sons. On St Peter's Day, 1530 the French princes were finally ransomed. Their liberation had owed much to the mediation and money of Henry VIII. Now, as a sign of his gratitude for Francis' support of the divorce, Henry vowed to write off the entire debt that the French owed him. In order to guarantee this pledge in particular, and for the greater security of the treaty as a whole, it was agreed that the Duke of Richmond and the Earl of Surrey would stay behind in France as guests of Francis I and his Court.[13]

Although there had been talks both before and during the summit about a possible French exchange involving Surrey and Richmond on the one hand and either of Francis' younger sons on the other,[14] it is unlikely that the English boys were made aware of their fate until the very end of the Calais interview. Only then did it become clear that the princes would remain at the French Court and that Surrey and Richmond would join them there for an indefinite period. On the eve of their departure, Richmond was busy making last-minute provision for the servants he had left behind in England. Evidently he had not anticipated a lengthy stay.[15]

Just before Surrey and Richmond departed, the weather, so obliging for the summit, took a turn for the worse. A north-westerly gale prevented Henry VIII and his entourage from sailing to England for a fortnight and on 8 November 1532 there 'rose such a wind, tempest and thunder that no man could conveniently stir in the streets of Calais'.[16] It was during this time that Surrey contracted a fever that was to plague him for the next month. Although it was serious enough to warrant mention in a dispatch to England, it was not bad enough to preclude travel. A few days later Surrey, Richmond and sixty attendants rode out of Calais towards the French Court. In their retinue was Richmond's almoner, Richard Tate, who wrote back to England with encouraging news of their progress: 'My Lord of Richmond and my Lord of Surrey in all their journey toward the French Court hath been very well welcomed and in all places have had presents of wines with other gentle offers.'[17]

By the end of November they had caught up with the Court at Chantilly on the outskirts of Paris. There, at the château of Anne de Montmorency, *grand maître* of France, Surrey and Richmond received a hearty welcome. As one would expect, it was Francis' treatment of his English rival's son that received the most interest. 'The King,' Tate reported, 'at the first meeting of my Lord, embracing him, made him great cheer, saying that he thought himself now to have four sons and esteemed him no less and likewise the Dauphin and his two brethren with all other noblemen after embraced my Lord.'[18] A few days later the Court travelled through a bitter frost to Paris. Upon arrival, both Richmond and Surrey were housed 'at very great expense and very honourably' within the Dauphin's lodgings at the Louvre.[19] A letter from Montmorency of 8 December made it clear that Surrey was to be 'nurtured' with the French princes just as much as Richmond, and by 11 December Tate could report that all was well. Surrey's fever had subsided and, although Tate was not entirely happy with the 'setting forward of my Lord's train', he found the French both 'tractable' and 'willing'.[20]

The whole of the winter was spent in Paris, where Surrey and Richmond dined and supped daily with the French princes. Less than three years had passed since the release of the two elder brothers, François and Henri, from their captivity in Spain and they still bore the emotional scars of their four-and-a-half-year ordeal. The Dauphin François, aged fourteen, only ever wore sombre clothes and was reportedly 'cold, temperate and staid'.[21] Henri, Duke of Orléans was thirteen and prone to severe melancholy, but he was more spirited than his elder brother. He had refused to submit to his imprisonment, attempting escape more than once, and when, on his release, one of his captors had sought his forgiveness, Henri had turned his back on him and farted.[22]

Francis I was insensitive to his sons' subsequent mood swings, declaring that he did not care for 'dreamy, sullen, sleepy children'.[23] Instead he showered attention on his youngest son Charles, Duke of Angoulême, who was ten and already a hotheaded extrovert. He would eventually meet his death at the age of twenty-three after entering a house infected with the plague. Slashing the pillows and beds, Charles shouted through the billowing feathers, 'never yet hath a son of France died of the plague'. Three days later he succumbed.[24] But all three boys were active sportsmen who loved nothing more than a game of tennis or a spot of hunting; indeed François himself would allegedly die from over-exertion on the tennis court and Henri from a jousting accident. Surrey and Richmond certainly seem to have endeared themselves to their new chamber companions; even eight years after their sojourn, the English ambassador to France wrote that the princes remembered their English friends with great fondness.[25]

French culture was a curious amalgam of coarseness and sophistication. One Neapolitan traveller appreciated the generous hospitality, the pretty ladies who danced 'with supreme grace' and the banquets, where delicate food and exquisite wines were served. But he was appalled by the French eschewal of chamber pots: 'For want of any alternative one has to urinate on the fire. They do this everywhere, by night and day; and indeed the greater the nobleman or lord, the more readily and openly will he do it.'[26] French customs took some getting used to: men kept their hats on at the table, even in the presence of the King, and it was considered the height of manners to chew with one's mouth open.[27]

Then there were the bizarre pagan ceremonies peculiar to Paris. One such event, which Surrey would have witnessed on 26 December, was held in celebration of the winter solstice. Within the square of the Place de Grève, the town council erected an enormous bonfire comprising a sixty-foot tree stacked with wood and straw. On the top was placed a barrel, a wheel, flowers and garlands and affixed to the tree was a basket containing two dozen cats and a fox to be burned alive 'for the King's pleasure'. Trumpets blared as Francis stepped up and sparked the conflagration with a wax torch wrapped in red velvet. An impressive demonstration of fireworks ensued and then Francis and his Court proceeded to the Hôtel de Ville, where they were treated to a confection of dried fruits, scented sweets, tarts and other sugared delicacies.[28]

At Court, Francis' lascivious inclinations were given free rein. His marriage to Charles V's sister, Eleanor, was purely political. She bore the unfortunate Habsburg trait of a large, jutting chin and frankly repulsed her husband. In a moment of indiscretion during the summer of 1533, Francis' sister Marguerite divulged to the Duke of Norfolk that the King and Queen had not lain together for seven months. 'Why?' Norfolk had enquired innocently. Because, Marguerite replied, Eleanor would not allow Francis to sleep: 'she is very hot in bed and desireth to be too much embraced.'[29]

Francis made up for his lack of action in the marital bed elsewhere. He was, according to one traveller, 'a great womaniser and readily breaks into others' gardens and drinks at many sources'.[30] An annual allowance, paid out of the royal coffers, ensured the upkeep of the 'filles de joie suivant la court'. Although many of the scabrous stories concerning Francis' libido cannot be verified, it is almost certainly true that he contracted syphilis, 'the French disease', in 1524 and, according to one of his biographers, 'the King's philandering appears to have got worse with age.'[31] By the time of Surrey and Richmond's internship, the King's eye had focused on Anne d'Heilly, whom he later made Duchess d'Étampes. Her political influence over the King was not lost on Surrey, who later encouraged his sister to strive for a similar role at the English Court.

Francis indulged in a boisterous lifestyle and the French annals abound with anecdotes of high jinks and low deeds. He was, ostensibly at least, more accessible and easy going than his English counterpart. He staged mock battles that regularly got out of hand, his own face bearing a scar from one such event, and in 1546 one of his favourites would die when a linen chest was dropped on his head during a snowball fight.[32]

Abusing the underclasses seems to have been a favourite pastime of the French. In a satire on the English habit of copying all things French, Sir Thomas More lampooned one English courtier who

> pays [his] servant nothing like a Frenchman; he clothes him in worn-out rags in the French manner; he feeds him little and that little poor, as the French do; he works him hard like the French; he strikes him often like a Frenchman; at social gatherings and on the street and in the market place and in public, he quarrels with him and abuses him always in the French fashion.[33]

In 1519 a group of Henry VIII's favourite young courtiers, his 'minions', had run riot through the streets of Paris, encouraged, according to Edward Hall, by Francis I himself: 'They, with the French King, rode daily disguised through Paris, throwing eggs, stones and other foolish trifles at the people.'[34]

Surrey and Richmond did not escape these influences. Ten years after his return from France, Surrey rampaged through the streets of London just as the minions had done. This act of vandalism earned him the dubious honour of being branded 'a Frenchman at heart'.[35] When the life of Richmond's page, Nicholas Throckmorton, was put to verse, his time in service was portrayed thus:

> By parents' hest, I served as a page
> To Richmond's Duke and waited, still at hand,
> For fear of blows, which happened in his rage.
> In France with him I lived most carelessly,
> And learned the tongue, though nothing readily.[36]

But if the more unsavoury aspects of the French Court rubbed off on its English guests, so too did some of its polish. Francis and many of his Italian courtiers featured in Baldassare Castiglione's *Il Libro del Cortegiano* [*The Book of the Courtier*], which ever since its publication in 1528 had become the handbook for all Renaissance Courts.[37] Francis' nonchalant manner and effortless style seemed the very embodiment of *sprezzatura*, the essential quality espoused by Castiglione. In England many believed that it was Anne Boleyn's apprenticeship at the French Court that had enabled her to captivate Henry VIII: 'For behaviour, manners, attire and tongue, she excelled them all for she had been brought up in France.'[38]

Surrey also benefited from the superior intellectual climate in France. At the beginning of the sixteenth century the number of London's printing presses could be counted on the fingers of one hand. Paris, on the other hand, could boast no less than eighty-five presses all clanking out exciting new texts.[39] Francis revelled in his role as *père des lettres* and by the end of his reign he had built up one of the finest libraries in Europe. He was a generous patron to many eminent humanists, including Guillaume Budé, who encouraged him to found four royal lectureships, two in Greek and two in Hebrew. These formed the origins of the Collège de France.

France's frequent wars in the Italian peninsula had brought her into close contact with Renaissance culture and when the Republic of Florence fell in 1530, refugees like the poet Luigi Alamanni found a second home at the French Court. There Surrey and Richmond found themselves absorbed into an extraordinarily sophisticated milieu of writers and poets, men like the reformed Christian Clément Marot and the Dauphin's almoner Mellin de Saint-Gelais, who introduced the sonnet to France. Francis I even composed his own poetry, and during meals the *lecteur de roi* would stimulate King and Court with readings from innovative works.

Surrey was also exposed to Renaissance art and sculpture, the likes of which he had never before seen. Francis fancied himself as a connoisseur. He employed a team of agents to source pieces from all over the Continent and his collection included works by Michelangelo, Raphael and Leonardo da Vinci. Dotted throughout the Loire valley and the Île de France were testaments to French Renaissance architecture. Old Gothic châteaux were refashioned along classical lines and new ones were erected to project the imperial magnificence of the French King. None was more impressive than Fontainebleau, forty miles south-east of Paris, which the French Court visited in the spring of 1533.

Ever since 1528, when Francis I had announced that he wanted to spend more time in the region, workers had begun to rebuild the original medieval castle. By the end of Francis' reign, although still not complete, Fontainebleau had become a sumptuous Renaissance palace. The pièce de résistance, completed in 1539, was the Galerie François Premier. Francis treasured his gallery and kept the keys to its door safely on his person. The walls were horizontally divided, the lower part containing carved wainscoting, and the upper part a combination of frescoed panels and high-relief stucco that projected a complex iconographical schema. Its chief designer was Giovanni Battista Rosso, a Florentine artist whose distinctive Mannerist style, also reflected in Francesco Primaticcio's decorative work in the royal apartments, became the defining component of a new school of art, L'École de Fontainebleau. Below the gallery there would be baths and saunas, and in the courtyard, atop a fountain designed by Primaticcio, would stand Michelangelo's marble sculpture of Hercules. In time Fontainebleau became, according to Vasari, 'a kind of new Rome'. Tourists flocked there to gaze in wonder at Francis I's new aesthetic. 'All this house,' wrote the Englishman Sir Thomas Cheyney in July 1546, is 'to me a thing incredible, unless I had seen it myself.'[40]

Fontainebleau, like Paris, broadened Surrey's horizons. It taught him that the Italian Renaissance could be assimilated into other cultures and it revealed the awesome power of visual spectacle. However, it would be unwise to overemphasise Fontainebleau's influence on the young Earl. While Surrey was there it was little more than a building site. The gallery, cluttered with internal scaffolding and board cloths, was probably out of bounds and there is no record of any painting being done there until August 1533, that is, after Surrey had moved on. In the early 1530s Francis did not yet have a unified vision for Fontainebleau. It evolved piecemeal, according to the changing needs of the royal family and Court.[41]

In fact Surrey spent less than a week at Fontainebleau[42] and he would have enjoyed a good part of it in the neighbouring forest, hunting red deer and wild boar. Perhaps one of his strongest memories of the place, more reminiscent of medieval England than Renaissance Italy, was the ceremony held on 23 April in celebration of the Order of the Garter. Francis had been made a Companion of the Order by Henry VIII in 1527, but St George's Day was not usually a high point in his calendar. On this occasion, however, in honour of his English guests and in particular his fellow Companion, the Duke of Richmond, the feast day was conducted 'with much ceremony'.[43]

The next day the Court packed up and began a long, leisurely journey towards Provence, where Francis planned to meet the Pope at the end of July and celebrate the marriage of Prince Henri to Catherine de' Medici. This gave Francis three months, enough time to visit the most important towns along the route. As each was approached, King and Court were trumpeted at the gates by the citizens, who then escorted them in procession through newly gravelled streets. Gifts and pledges of faith were exchanged and banquets and pageants laid on for the Court's delectation. From Fontainebleau they travelled to Montargis, from Montargis to Gien, then through Bourges and Issoudun and on to Moulins, where the *entrée* was staged 'with all possible honour', and Francis was presented with a silver mill worth one thousand crowns.[44]

By the end of May they had reached Lyons, where Francis received word that Clement VII had postponed their meeting until autumn. Francis decided to stay in the town over June and then conduct a tour of the Auvergne and Languedoc. Lyons was a thriving commercial centre whose proximity to France's borders lent it a truly cosmopolitan flavour. Its women were reportedly among the most beautiful in France. It was vibrant and licentious, opulent and alluring – the kind of town, so it was said, where kings forgot their duties. According to Clément Marot:

C'est un grand cas voir le mont Pélion,
Ou d'avoir veu les ruines de Troye:
Mais qui ne voit la ville de Lyon,
Aucun plaisir à ses yeux il n'octroye.*[45]

Unfortunately, Lyons was also overpopulated and cramped. It soon became apparent that it would not be able to cater for the needs of the thousands who made up Francis' travelling Court. 'This town,' the Venetian ambassador groused, 'cannot accommodate so many men and horses.' There was a scarcity of lodging and stabling and the bread, which was 'very coarse and bad', had trebled in price. 'Should the Court remain here some days longer,' he moaned, 'the cost will become unbearable.'[46] The Court therefore split. Queen Eleanor and the French princes departed south to Nîmes; Surrey and Richmond stayed behind with Francis. Any sadness Surrey might have felt about bidding farewell to the boys with whom he had lived at close quarters for the past six months was soon lifted by the news that he would shortly see his father.

Much had happened in England during Surrey's absence. Not long after the Calais interview, Anne Boleyn had finally relented to Henry VIII's incessant appeals for sex. To his joy, she fell pregnant almost immediately. The Great Matter, so he now felt, was vindicated in the eyes of God. Matters assumed a new urgency – the child could not be born out of wedlock – and in two secret ceremonies, one in November 1532 and the second the following January, Henry committed bigamy and married Anne. In March her brother Lord Rochford sailed to France to deliver the news. He returned with messages of congratulations and a wedding present of 'a most beautiful and costly' horse litter.[47]

Parliament continued to pass Acts that bolstered the King's authority vis-à-vis the Pope. The most revolutionary so far was the Act in Restraint of Appeals, entered into the statute book just before prorogation on 7 April 1533. Taking away the right of Henry's subjects – including, of course, Catherine of Aragon – to make judicial appeals to Rome, the Act provided the clearest declaration so far of the supremacy of the Crown over the English Church. 'By diverse sundry old authentic histories and chronicles,' the preamble stated, 'it is manifestly declared and expressed that this realm of England is an Empire . . . governed

---

* 'It is a great thing to see Mount Pelion, / or to have seen the ruins of Troy: / but he who does not see the city of Lyons / bestows no pleasure upon his eyes.'

1, 2. Surrey's parents, Thomas and Elizabeth Howard, third Duke and Duchess of Norfolk. 'He can speak fair as well to his enemy as to his friend,' Elizabeth once noted of her husband.

3. The only surviving wing of Kenninghall, the Howard seat in Norfolk. In Surrey's time it had over seventy rooms and seven hundred acres of parkland.

Thomas Earl of Surry.

4, 5. Holbein's drawings of Surrey and (*opposite*) Frances around the time of their marriage in 1532. The inscription 'Thomas Earl of Surry' is erroneous.

The Lady Surry.

'With a king's son my childish years did pass,
In greater feast than Priam's sons of Troy.'

6. Henry VIII's illegitimate son,
Henry Fitzroy, Duke of Richmond.

7, 8, 9. 'Active games of nimbleness and strength': (*above right*) hunting, (*below*) real tennis
and (*bottom*) knights-in-training learning to joust.

10. *The Embarkation of Henry VIII at Dover*, 1532 (?)

11. The French Court. Antoine Macault reads his translation of Diodorus Siculus to Francis I, his three sons (on his right), pet monkey, dog and assembled courtiers.

12, 13. Politics in the 1530s. Howard stock rose when Surrey's cousin Anne Boleyn (*above*) became Queen, but fell after her execution engineered by the Howards' inveterate enemy, Thomas Cromwell (*below*).

14. Fragment of the cartoon for the mural on the Privy Chamber wall at Whitehall by Holbein, 1537.

15, 16. Holbein's drawings of Surrey and (*right*) Sir Thomas Wyatt. For the Elizabethan George Puttenham, they were 'the two chief lanterns of light to all others that have since employed their pens upon English poesy'.

o happy dames that may enbrace braces
the frute of yo deseyt
helpe to bewaile the woefulle case
e eke the hevy plyte
off me that routede to rejoyes.
the fortune off my pleasante daryes
god ladies helpe to ffelle my mordemeuge

en aspere framagle it remeberanes
off wordes e pleassures paste
he ffaylles that haryst en governimes
my losse whyle et mage lape
to freedange ffewleth ffer winde off wylde
fintenge his loye that is his ffaylle
to warde me the fiwele parte off seb amaelle

17, 18. The first
two stanzas of
Surrey's poem
'O happy dames',
inscribed by his sister
Mary, Duchess of
Richmond (*below left*),
into the courtly
anthology known
as the Devonshire
Manuscript.

The Lady of Richmond.

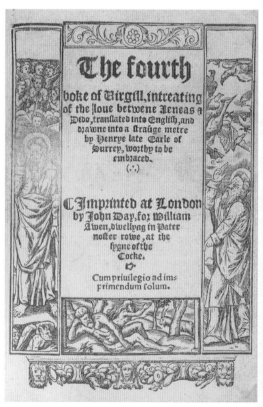

The fourth
boke of Uirgill, intreating
of the loue betwene Aeneas &
Dido, translated into English, and
drawne into a strauge metre
by Henrye late Earle of
Surrey, worthy to be
embraced.
(∴)

¶Imprinted at London
by John Day, for William
Owen, dwellyng in Pater
noster rowe, at the
sygne of the
Cocke.
☞
Cum priuilegio ad im-
primendum solum.

19. The title-page of Surrey's innovative
translation of Book IV of the *Aeneid*,
published posthumously in 1554.

by one Supreme Head and King.' God had invested Henry VIII 'with plenary, whole and entire power, pre-eminence, authority, prerogative and jurisdiction' to govern his subjects, without interference from 'any foreign princes or potentates'.[48] Thenceforth the King, not the Pope, was the de facto head of the English Church.

On 23 May 1533 the new Archbishop of Canterbury, Thomas Cranmer, pronounced from a courtroom in Dunstable Priory that the marriage between Henry VIII and Catherine of Aragon was 'against the law of God'.[49] Five days later he validated Henry's marriage to Anne Boleyn and on 1 June, two days after the Duke of Norfolk landed in Calais, a heavily pregnant Anne was crowned Queen of England at Westminster. Pope Clement VII now began to make ominous noises about excommunication. Although Henry had flagrantly defied Clement, he was keen to avoid public censure and was fearful of invasion: something the Vatican had the power to license. It was out of the question for Henry to join Francis at his meeting with Clement. Indeed the English King was now uneasy about the whole enterprise. He needed his French ally more than ever and it would not augur well for the security of England if Clement and Francis were seen to be cosying up together.

Thus Henry had dispatched the Duke of Norfolk to France with strict instructions. Norfolk had to remind Francis of his English alliance and convince him that Clement was still under the Emperor's sway. He was to appeal to Francis' sense of pride by encouraging his indignation at Clement's postponement of their meeting. 'We be not a little troubled, and moved in our heart,' Henry VIII wrote, 'to see our said good brother and us, being such Princes of Christendom, to be so handled with the Pope, so much to our dishonours, and to the Pope's and the Emperor's advancement.' Henry's concern was less for his own personal matter, so Norfolk would have to convince Francis, than for the French King's divine rights. Popes had no right 'to play and dally with kings and princes; whose honour ye may say is above all thing, and more dear to us, in the person of our good brother, than is any piece of our cause at the Pope's hand.' By these and other insinuations, which Norfolk was to 'often times repeat and inculk', Francis should be persuaded to cancel the interview. If Francis remained intractable, then Norfolk should at least 'devise for the certainty of our aid at his hand'.[50]

Replying to this letter nine days later from Brière, Norfolk confirmed suspicions that 'the interview is clearly determined to take effect', and conveyed his fears that 'it shall be very difficult to dissuade the French King therefrom'.[51] Despite optimism in some quarters that the Franco-papal meeting could be frustrated, Norfolk's mission was little more than damage limitation. And yet, according to the Imperial ambassador in London, he had been remarkably buoyant at the prospect of going to France: 'I cannot say whether he will come back in such high spirits, but he certainly appears very desirous and even impatient of setting out on his journey.'[52] Once in France, Norfolk outpaced his younger colleagues on the ride south. Peter Vannes noted that the sixty-year-old 'excels us all in sustaining the labours of the journey and the heat'.[53] Could it be that this dour old Duke was looking forward to seeing his son? Surrey, for his part, was genuinely enthused. Having received word on the morning of 10 July that his father was approaching the French Court at Riom, Surrey, with Richmond at his side, galloped out of the town to greet him, outstripping the official French welcoming party by half a mile.[54]

Sir William Paulet, one of the ambassadors in Norfolk's train, claimed that the French welcomed them 'in the best and most friendly manner'. This is confirmed by the Imperial ambassador to Rome, who was uneasy about the 'splendid and flattering reception' given to Norfolk and his party.[55] But while Francis was only too happy to play the gallant host, he made it clear that he would not cancel his meeting unless Clement 'innovated' against Henry VIII in the meantime.[56]

Having delivered his message, Francis resumed his progress through the blistering heat towards Provence with Surrey and Richmond still in tow. Norfolk and his embassy planned to rest in Lyons for a few days and then proceed to Nice for the interview. But events soon overtook them as news broke that, on 11 July, the Pope had pronounced in Consistory that Henry VIII must renounce Anne Boleyn and take back Catherine of Aragon on pain of excommunication. According to one French onlooker, 'the poor Duke was so astonished that he nearly fainted.'[57] This was undoubtedly an 'innovation' by the Pope against Henry, but Francis reneged on his promise and remained determined to meet Clement.

Back in London, the Imperialists received the news from France with schadenfreude. The originators of Norfolk's embassy, Chapuys crowed, 'must now feel ashamed of themselves for all their presentiments have led to nothing else but disappointment and confusion, being now the laughing stock for all parties.'[58] Henry VIII flew into one of his notorious rages. Norfolk, he fumed, must return to England at once and bring Surrey and Richmond back with him. Although Norfolk diplomatically claimed that the boys' removal from the French Court was due to the fact that Richmond was now of age to contract his marriage to Surrey's sister, no one was fooled.[59] Recent events had rendered these two symbols of the Anglo-French alliance obsolete.

Surrey and Richmond's farewells must have been somewhat strained. Norfolk rode ahead of them post-haste, averaging over sixty miles a day.[60] On 24 August 1533 he was at Moulins, four days later Amiens, and on 29 August he arrived in Calais and immediately sailed for England. He made it to Court in time for the birth of Henry VIII's longed-for heir. It was a girl, Elizabeth. The celebratory joust was cancelled and the word 'Prince', so confidently inscribed in the pre-prepared document announcing the birth, was hastily altered to accommodate the new heir's unfortunate gender. Surrey and Richmond assumed a more leisurely pace homewards, only arriving in Calais on 25 September.[61] Two months later Surrey attended the marriage of his sister to his friend at Hampton Court. It changed the dynamics of his relationship with Richmond, for the Duke no longer required an *incitateur*. Although their paths would continue to cross at various intervals, the days of daily interaction and chamber companionship were over.

Nothing has survived to reveal exactly what the two boys thought of France, but within a year of their return Richmond, having heard that Henry VIII was soon to cross the Channel, was vigorously petitioning Cromwell for a place in the party.[62] Surrey's experience seems to have influenced him in a number of ways. Although Richmond's page stated that he himself had 'learned the tongue, though nothing readily', the presence of French idioms in Surrey's lyrics reveals an easy familiarity with the language. His later experiments with Italian and classical verse forms were surely encouraged by the spirit of imitation and adaptation alive in France, and portraits reveal him to be a dedicated follower of continental fashion.

Whether or not Surrey had become 'a Frenchman at heart', as the Imperial ambassador supposed, is a matter of opinion. Certainly when the time would come to take up arms against France, Surrey's patriotism was never in doubt. Yet when he was forced to explain how the whole back line of an army under his command could desert the field of battle, Surrey tellingly referred to 'a humour that sometime reigneth in Englishmen'.[63] According to his cousin Sir Edmund Knyvet, Surrey 'loved to converse with strangers [foreigners] and to conform his behaviour to them'.[64] This was not intended as a compliment. Indeed Knyvet's words have only survived because they formed part of a deposition taken down by the Council after Surrey's arrest for treason.

If Surrey did return from France with new airs and graces, it is likely he would have faced the sharp edge of a few barbs. As Knyvet's testimony illustrates, Englishmen were suspicious of anyone who betrayed a fondness for foreign customs. This was particularly the case if those customs happened to be French. When Henry VIII's egg-hurling minions had arrived home from their frolics in 1519, they were disparaged by contemporaries as 'all French in eating, drinking and apparel, yea, and in French vices and brags'.[65] Shakespeare and Fletcher brilliantly capture the attitude of their countrymen towards the French in King Henry the Eighth. Act One, Scene Three, finds the Lord Chamberlain and Lord Sands in an antechamber of the palace, railing against Henry VIII's minions:

CHAMBERLAIN:
Is't possible the spells of France should juggle
Men into such strange mysteries?

SANDS: New customs,
Though they be never so ridiculous –
Nay, let 'em be unmanly – yet are followed.

CHAMBERLAIN:
As far as I see, all the good our English
Have got by the late voyage is but merely
A fit or two o'th' face. But they are shrewd ones,
For when they hold 'em you would swear directly
Their very noses had been counsellors
To Pépin or Clotharius, they keep state so.

Sir Thomas Lovell soon enters and announces the introduction of a new proclamation:

CHAMBERLAIN: What is't for?

LOVELL:
The reformation of our travelled gallants
That fill the Court with quarrels, talk and tailors.

CHAMBERLAIN:
I'm glad 'tis there. Now I would pray our *messieurs*
To think an English courtier may be wise
And never see the Louvre.

LOVELL: They must either,
For so run the conditions, leave those remnants
Of fool and feather that they got in France,
With all their honourable points of ignorance
Pertaining thereunto – as fights and fireworks,
Abusing better men than they can be
Out of a foreign wisdom, renouncing clean
The faith they have in tennis and tall stockings,
Short blistered breeches, and those types of travel –
And understand again like honest men,
Or pack to their old playfellows. There, I take it,
They may, *cum privilegio, oui* away
The lag end of their lewdness and be laughed at.

SANDS:
'Tis time to give 'em physic, their diseases
Are grown so catching.[66]

Sands' final comment neatly encapsulates the paradox: while
Englishmen were ostensibly contemptuous of French frivolities and
fashions, they inwardly yearned for a measure of Gallic sophistication
and for the *sprezzatura* that Francis I so confidently displayed. 'I have
much wondered,' mused Henry Peacham in *The Truth of Our Times*,
'why our English above other nations should so much dote upon new
fashions, but more I wonder at our want of wit that we cannot invent
them ourselves, but, when one is grown stale, run presently over into
France to seek a new, making that noble and flourishing Kingdom the
magazine of our fooleries.'[67] Perhaps Surrey's silence about France is

an indication that he absorbed her culture almost osmotically. Everybody in England was striving to ape French customs. Surrey, like Anne Boleyn before him, never had to try.[68]

Seventeen years after Surrey's sojourn in France, the two surviving French princes, Henri and Charles, praised him 'as well for his wisdom and soberness, as also good learning'. Henry VIII also seemed impressed by Surrey's performance in France, for in the New Year of 1534 he presented him with a silver ewer. The Duke of Norfolk deemed his heir's internship so successful that he was 'determined' to send his second son Thomas there 'for one year at the least'.[69] Evidently the Earl of Surrey was showing all the signs of being a dutiful heir and subject.

When Surrey had been in Paris, Richmond's physician, David Edwardes, had dedicated an anatomical treatise to him as a New Year's gift. Bound with this work under a common title-page was a treatise on medical prognostication, which Edwardes had dedicated to Richmond – an indication of the two boys' close association. The author's address to Surrey is revealing, not only in its praise of the fifteen-year-old, but also in highlighting the pressures that he faced as heir to the Howard dynasty. Having extolled 'the honourable achievements' in peace and at war of Surrey's grandfather and father, Edwardes continued:

I cannot sufficiently admire your family, but not so much for those reasons as because I see you established above what can be said for many other young men in this age, and turning your mind so seriously to those things which will render it better.

I am by no means certain whether I ought to ascribe this to the benefit of that stock from which you have been brought forth to us, whether to the gods, who through you smile upon and favour us English. However it may be, let us hope what has occurred will be to the advantage of our commonwealth and that the more so since you have pursued worthwhile things for so long a time. Thus you will approach the next age better prepared and good habits will meanwhile strengthen your mind so that later you will not easily fall into worse. But the more you may be strengthened by counsel and prudence, with confidence placed in your family, so much the better guidance will Norfolk have when you succeed as heir to your father's estates. Meanwhile how much more useful you will be to your people as Earl of Surrey, and finally so much the more will all Englishmen desire you to undertake the affairs of the commonwealth. There is no doubt that you can achieve all these things, which will be to the increase of your honours and to the honour of your family.

As your talent and gravity of character promise, so we have great hope that you will be like your father and grandfather. I wish you both the greatest successes and the most fruitful increase of all the best things.[70]

By contrast, Edwardes' dedication to Richmond is neither personal nor expressive in its praise; it is merely the vehicle for a diatribe against contemporary doctors. Also curious is the nature of the two works. Richmond's treatise follows medieval tradition on symptoms and prognostication and is of little import, whereas Surrey's is an original, avant-garde study. It employs the new humanistic nomenclature; it contains the first reference to a human dissection in England; it is the first work published in England to be devoted solely to anatomy. One might have expected Edwardes to dedicate the more exciting work to his patron Richmond, who also, of course, outranked Surrey. But it is the Earl who receives the honour and the eulogy, and it is tempting to speculate that the author's decision may reflect his views on the comparative qualities of his two dedicatees. Whatever the reason for Edwardes' decision, it is clear that Surrey had distinguished himself as a young man with a bright future.

PART TWO

POLITICS

6

BLOODY DAYS

Surrey returned to an England that had a new Queen, a new heir and a new Church, over which Henry VIII now reigned as Supreme Head. Thomas Cranmer, a man of minor gentry stock with evangelical inclinations, now held the Archbishopric of Canterbury and Thomas Cromwell, the son of a Putney tradesman, was the King's new favourite.

Even greater change confronted Surrey on the domestic front. Returning to Kenninghall, he discovered that his father's mistress, Bess Holland, had effectively displaced his mother as lady of the house. Although Elizabeth denigrated Bess as 'a churl's daughter', a 'washer of my nursery', a 'drab', a 'quean'* and a 'harlot', she was in fact the daughter of John Holland, Norfolk's chief steward, a position unlikely to have been acquired without a degree of gentility.[1] Bess had caught Norfolk's eye in 1526 and he had lavished love and clothes and jewellery on her ever since.[2] This was not particularly shocking. Aristocratic male adultery was relatively common and, despite the Church's official censure, tacitly accepted.[3] What really scandalised polite society was the Duchess' response. Instead of biting her lip and turning a blind eye as other wives had learned to do, Elizabeth chose to fight.

Like her father before her, and her son after, Elizabeth was proud, self-righteous and outspoken. Once it had dawned on her that her husband had not, as she had assumed, married her for love, Elizabeth unleashed her fury. She quarrelled with Norfolk over Surrey and Mary's marriages, both of which she disapproved, mainly on account of Anne Boleyn's meddling.[4] At Court, in open defiance of her husband and

* *drab* and *quean* are both sixteenth-century terms for a prostitute.

King, she sided with Catherine of Aragon. Elizabeth held a strong affection for her Queen, whom she had served as a lady-in-waiting for over sixteen years and, as a spurned wife herself, she identified with Catherine's cause, especially as her nemesis, Bess, supported Anne.

From 1530 Elizabeth had begun to spy on her husband, turning over any useful information regarding the Great Matter to Catherine. On one occasion she had even sent her secret communications from the papal emissary hidden in an orange. On 30 January 1531, she reportedly 'sent a message to the Queen to say that those of the opposite party were trying hard to win her over to their opinion, but if the whole world were to set about it they would not make her change. She was and would continue to be one of her party.' Elizabeth was true to her word. Four months later ambassador Chapuys informed the Emperor that, in order to 'please' Anne Boleyn, Elizabeth had been banished from Court 'owing to her speaking too freely and having declared in favour of the Queen much more openly than these people like.'[5]

If Anne and her supporters had intended to teach Elizabeth a lesson in humility, then they had quite underestimated her. If anything, she felt empowered by her exile and, on her return, she redoubled her opposition to the divorce. She refused to bear Anne's train at her investiture as Marchioness of Pembroke; she ignored the summons to the French interviews of 1532; she absented herself from Anne's coronation the following summer and took no part in the christening of Princess Elizabeth. All the while she persisted in her excoriation of Norfolk and Bess. Elizabeth was proving not just an embarrassment to her husband, but a dangerous liability.

By the spring of 1533 Norfolk had had enough. He wanted Elizabeth out of his house and wrote several letters to her brother, Henry Stafford, asking him to take her in. Stafford's reply on 13 May made it quite clear that he wanted nothing to do with his sister: 'Her accustomed wild language . . . lieth not in my power to stop, whereby so great danger might ensue to me and all mine though I never deserved it.' All Stafford would do, he wrote, was pray that God would 'send my Lady a better mind'. With that, he signed off.[6]

While Surrey had no doubt been conscious from an early age of the frost in his parents' marriage, he would not have grasped the full extent of their estrangement. The last time he had been at home for any length of time was over three years ago. Now he returned from France to find conditions arctic. A few months later he probably witnessed the final straw. On Tuesday of Passion Week, 1534, the Duke of Norfolk rode home from Court. He was in a foul mood, having failed in his mission to coerce Mary Tudor into acknowledging her illegitimacy.[7] Consequently his relationship with Anne Boleyn, already sour, had deteriorated further. After 'riding all night' to Kenninghall, the weary Duke arrived to find Elizabeth in a frenzied rage, slandering his mistress and her cronies. He 'can lay nothing to my charge,' Elizabeth later insisted, 'but for because I would not be contented to suffer the bawd and the harlots.' It was enough. According to Elizabeth, Norfolk promptly 'locked me up in a chamber, and took away all my jewels and all my apparel'.[8]

Elizabeth was banished to Redbourne, a manor in Hertfordshire that Norfolk rented from the Crown. Although she was permitted twenty servants and an allowance of three hundred marks (£200) a year, she found the conditions unbearable: 'I am a gentlewoman born, and hath been brought up daintily and not to live so barely as I do.'[9] Elizabeth effectively lived under house arrest. Time and again she referred to her 'imprisonment'. She was not allowed to 'come abroad and see my friends', nor was anyone permitted to visit her 'but such as he appointeth'.[10] Twice she attempted reconciliation. Twice she was rebuffed. In the summer of 1535 she rode to Dunstable where the King was holding Court. Henry VIII, who had little sympathy for her, commanded her to write a third 'gentle' letter to Norfolk and when this was reciprocated with 'cruel messages and threatenings', Elizabeth's resolve hardened: 'From this day forward, I will never sue to the King, nor to none other, to desire my Lord, my husband, to take me again; for I have made much suit to him and nothing regarded and I made him no fault, but in declaring of his shameful handling of me.'[11]

'Shameful' or not, Norfolk had been quite within his rights to handle Elizabeth as he did. Sixteenth-century wives were legally subordinate to, and financially dependent upon, their husbands. 'As it is a part of your penance, ye women, to travail in bearing your children,' Hugh Latimer bellowed from the pulpit, 'so it is a part of your penance to be subjects unto your husband; ye are underlings, underlings, and must be obedient.'[12] Norfolk enjoyed almost complete physical power over Elizabeth. He could control her movements and her contacts and was allowed to limit her resources and restrict her lifestyle as much as he saw fit. The law even permitted him to punish her physically and it seems he was only too happy to exercise his rights.

Strewn amidst Elizabeth's impassioned appeals for support in the many letters with which she bombarded Thomas Cromwell are accusations of abuse. Four times she referred to an incident when Norfolk 'set his women to bind me till blood come out at my fingers' ends, and pinnacled me, and sat on my breast till I spat blood'. Ever since, she claimed, 'I am sick at the fall of the leaf and at the spring of the year'. Repeating these allegations in another letter, Elizabeth concluded 'that if I should come home again I should be poisoned for the love that he beareth to that harlot Bess Holland'.[13]

Norfolk retaliated by denouncing Elizabeth as a vengeful shrew of questionable sanity, who dealt in 'false and abominable lies'.[14] When she accused him of having assaulted her as early as 1519 during the birth of Surrey's sister Mary, now Duchess of Richmond, he fired off an angry rebuttal to Cromwell:

> She hath untruly slandered me in writing and saying that when she had been in childbed of my daughter of Richmond two nights and a day, I should draw her out of her bed by the hair of her head about the house and with my dagger give her a wound in the head. My good Lord, if I prove not by witness, and that with many honest persons, that she had the scar in her head fifteen months before she was delivered of my said daughter and that the same was cut by a surgeon of London for a swelling she had in her head, of drawing of two teeth, never trust my word after; reporting me to your good Lordship whether I shall play the fool or no, to put me in her danger, that so falsely will slander me, and so wilfully stick thereby. Surely I think there is no man on live [living] that would handle a woman in childbed of that sort, nor for my part would not so have done for all that I am worth.[15]

Even if here, as seems likely, Elizabeth had been caught out in a lie, it is instructive that Norfolk's indignation stemmed not from the alleged abuse itself, but from its circumstances. He would not strike his wife when pregnant; he would not jeopardise the life of his unborn child.

There can be no doubt that Norfolk was prone to flashes of temper. His treasurer in Ireland, John Stile, complained that his master 'was sometimes more hasty than needeth', and during Wolsey's fall from grace, Norfolk had threatened to 'tear' the Cardinal 'with my teeth'. The Tudor historian, Polydore Vergil, noted that the Duke could be quick with his fists, and perhaps this is borne out by Norfolk's own threat at the end of his letter of spluttering denial: if Elizabeth was ever to come into his company again, he warned, she 'might give me occasion to handle her otherwise than I have done yet'.[16] Elizabeth took the threat seriously: 'I know well, if I should come home again, my life should be but short.'[17]

Ultimately, though, one can only speculate on the veracity of Elizabeth's accusations. It was her word against his, and the law was on his side. Had her formidable father not been executed in 1521, Elizabeth may not have been so isolated.[18] But she did still have one power. Norfolk needed her consent for a 'divorce'.* This Elizabeth would not grant, not even when Norfolk attempted to bribe her with 'all my jewels and all my apparel and a great part of his plate and of his stuff of household'. Norfolk resorted to threats, but Elizabeth vowed never to relent 'neither for less living nor for imprisonment, for I have been used to both'.[19]

Elizabeth's stand was championed by another discarded wife, the self-proclaimed prophetess, Mistress Amadas. After her husband, the King's goldsmith Robert Amadas, abandoned her, she directed her energies towards foretelling the destruction of Henry VIII and Anne Boleyn. Among her many pronouncements was the claim 'that there was never a good married woman in England except Prince Arthur's dowager [Catherine of Aragon], the Duchess of Norfolk and herself'.[20] However, the rest of society was horrified by Elizabeth's behaviour and readily acquiesced in her ostracism. Her children also sided with their father. For Surrey, brought up on a diet of Howard honour and duty, his mother's subordination of her family's interests to those of her own may have appeared selfish. It was bad enough that his parents' marriage had been exposed as a sham, but for his mother to have confided in the one man whom his father detested more than any other was surely the ultimate betrayal.

'Notwithstanding all their efforts to dissemble', the mutual antipathy

---

* Harris, 'Marriage Sixteenth-Century Style', note 55: 'Divorce in the [modern] sense – i.e. the end of a marriage and right of each party to remarry – did not exist in Tudor England. The term referred to the separation of a couple – "of bed and board" in the contemporary phrase. The separation left the husband free to do virtually everything but remarry. The wife received an allowance for her support. It is not clear why the Duke of Norfolk was willing to pay his wife for a divorce of this type since they were, in fact, living in this situation de facto. He may have wanted a legal separation to clarify and limit Duchess Elizabeth's financial claims on him. There is an outside chance he sought an annulment of the type Henry VIII secured against Catherine of Aragon, but this is unlikely since it would have illegitimized his children.'

between the lowborn Cromwell and the Duke of Norfolk was an open secret at Court.[21] Each sought the other's downfall and Cromwell, it seems, had used his position as Elizabeth's confidant to probe her for incriminating information. 'My Lord,' Cromwell later admitted to Norfolk, 'ye are a happy man that your wife knoweth no hurt by you, for if she did, she would undo you.'[22] Had Norfolk been 'undone', his children would have been also.

Nevertheless, Surrey may have had some sympathy for his mother. He certainly seemed to resent his father's mistress. Bess herself claimed that 'the Earl of Surrey loved her not' and once, when he was short of cash and petitioned his father's treasurer for funds, the reply came back that Norfolk was 'so straight girt that there will be gotten nothing of him . . . except it be by Mrs Holland, whom I think ye will not trouble for the matter'.[23] Whatever Surrey's sentiments, there was little that he could have done. His father held the purse strings tightly and, according to a letter that Surrey sent around this time to the Prior of Bury St Edmunds, he could ill afford to lose his chief source of income:

> My Lord, notwithstanding that aforetime I have borrowed off you to the sum of 30 *li*. pound sterling, having not yet repaid it, yet by very need & extreme necessity I am again constrained, my known good Lord, at this present affectuously to desire you to show yourself so much my cordial friend as to lend some over & above 20 *li*. pounds in such haste as I may have it here tomorrow by 8 of the clock for such is my present need . . . ye might & may it well believe my Lord my father will not so see your hearty kindness uncontented . . . Displease you not so though my Lord [Norfolk] being out of the country in this my necessity I rather attempt to assay you his ancient friend than other farther off.[24]

So Surrey, to his mother's evident distress, tolerated Norfolk's *maîtresse en titre*. Although his younger brother Thomas is not mentioned in the correspondence, Surrey's sister Mary also supported her father and, in fact, formed a firm friendship with Bess. 'I may say,' Elizabeth wailed, 'I was born in an unhappy hour to be matched with such an ungracious husband and so ungracious a son and a daughter.' Showing scant regard for her children's predicament, Elizabeth branded them 'unnatural' and, in one heartbreaking sentence that reveals the full extent of her eventual alienation from Surrey and Mary, she referred to them as *his* children. She did later admit that 'I have always love unto them', but there is no evidence to suggest that Surrey or Mary ever saw or communicated with their mother again.[25]

Some time in 1535, as Bess settled into the palatial lodgings, replete with Turkish carpets, tapestries and silk curtains, that Norfolk had established for her at Kenninghall, the Countess of Surrey moved in. Since their marriage three years earlier, Surrey had seen very little of Frances and one can only guess at the awkward nature of their first few months together. The unhappy precedent set by Surrey's parents can have done little to assuage their anxiety. But they were both eighteen, healthy and active, and conjugal relations were soon established. It was not long, though, before their domesticity was interrupted by the affairs of the realm.

At the end of January 1536 Frances was summoned to Peterborough Abbey to serve as one of the chief mourners at the funeral of Catherine of Aragon.[26] Even as the cancer that eventually claimed her ravished Catherine's body, she had continued to fight for her cause. Although Henry VIII had commanded that she only be known as the Dowager Princess of Wales, many persisted in regarding her as their rightful Queen and Anne, as one Suffolk spinster memorably put it, as a 'goggle-eyed whore'.[27] On 23 August 1533 two London women, one 'big with child', had been stripped to the waist and nailed by their ears to the Standard at Cheapside where they had been soundly thrashed. Their crime: 'they said Queen Catherine was the true Queen of England, & not Queen Anne.'[28]

Catherine's death may have eased the pressure on the King from the Papacy and the Empire, but it produced a further wave of revulsion towards Anne. People recalled her spite in seizing Catherine's jewels for the French interviews and in appropriating and defacing Catherine's barge for her coronation. They remembered her violent language – Anne had once shrieked 'that she wished all Spaniards were at the bottom of the sea'[29] – and they were appalled when they heard that Henry and Anne had celebrated Catherine's death by wearing yellow and dancing the night away. It was Anne, many now believed, who had, directly or indirectly, caused Catherine's death. And it was Anne who was blamed for the latest wave of draconian legislation that made even words spoken against her union with Henry treason and ordered Englishmen to swear an oath renouncing the Pope and endorsing their marriage.[30]

Three monks of the London Charterhouse, one of whom had once served as a Howard chaplain, were among the first to be sacrificed on the altar of Anne's ambition. For refusing to acknowledge the King's supremacy over the English Church, they were dragged on hurdles from the Tower to Tyburn. There they were hanged from the gallows and cut down before they lost consciousness. They were stripped of their habits, and their bowels and private parts were ripped from their bodies and burnt before their eyes. Then their heads were cut off and their bodies were hacked into quarters. The severed limbs were parboiled in a cauldron and stuck on spikes throughout London. The Dukes of Norfolk and Richmond both witnessed the butchery, reportedly displaying themselves 'openly and quite close to the victims'.[31]

Catherine's elderly stalwart, John Fisher, Bishop of Rochester, was next. Once his head was off, Henry VIII ordered that it be placed in a small iron cage and displayed on London Bridge, a gruesome show-case to the might of the King.[32] 'What must we feel,' the new Pope, Paul III, wrote to Francis I on hearing the news, 'when the Church of Christ is thus lacerated!'[33] Then it was the turn of Thomas More, Saint Thomas More, the man with whom Henry had once chosen to stroll, arm in arm, through his garden discussing astronomy and geometry and mathematics. 'The wrath of the King is death', Norfolk had warned. 'Is that all, my Lord?' More had replied. 'Then in good faith is there no more difference between your grace and me, but that I shall die today and you tomorrow.'[34]

Anne was also blamed for infecting the Court with heresy and giving sustenance to a nest of Lutherans. As long as there had been an official religion in England, there had been dissent. But the first few decades of the sixteenth century witnessed a change. Throughout Western Europe, an intense 'spirit of enquiry' that engendered and was, in turn, stimulated by the Renaissance and the discovery of new worlds and peoples spread, inevitability, to religion. The humanists had let out a clarion call for a return *ad fontes* and fertile minds soon thought they had found, in the pristine Christian texts, the key to revelation. Adherents to the Reformation, as it became known, were convinced that true Christianity could only be taught by the Word of God as revealed in its purest form by the Scriptures, not by the muddying edicts of Rome. They emphasised the overriding importance of a living, unifying relationship with God. Papal indulgences, pilgrimages, prayers for the dead, fasting, the veneration of saints and the whole panoply of Roman

Catholic custom could not, the reformers preached, atone for sin. Christ's work, not man's, had earned salvation and only by faith in his merits and in God's charity could a man receive grace. *Sola Fide, Sola Scriptura*: this was the bedrock of the reformers' message.

But the European Reformation was a protean beast, constantly evolving, dividing, reforming and adapting to the peculiarities of circumstance and country. There was no one leader and there was no single, unifying creed. Nor could there be. The Reformation, by its very nature, opposed the imposition of any authority other than God's Word. There were spokesmen who tried to clarify the main points of the Scriptures, but men and women had a responsibility to read and interpret them themselves until they discovered their faith. From studying the same source, some people emerged with extreme new views on transubstantiation, the sacraments, predestination and much, much more. Other, no less committed, evangelicals abhorred the radicalism of their contemporaries. Second, third and subsequent readings of the Scriptures might crystallise beliefs or fundamentally alter them. Nor was it unusual for people to flirt with reform only to revert to their original orientation. Faith was fluid and there were no clear lines of demarcation. France, during the middle years of Francis I's reign, is said to have experienced a period of 'magnificent religious anarchy'.[35] So too did England under Henry VIII.

That is why confessional labels can be anachronistic and misleading. The term 'Protestant', so often bandied about, did not exist until 1529 and thereafter Surrey's generation saw it as a term peculiar to the German states. Enemies to reform regarded all their opponents as heretics and tended to lump them into one uniform category, 'Lutheran' being the preferred pejorative. Reformist groupings did form, especially at the Henrician Court, and while they were eclectic and heterogeneous, they shared similar orientations (towards the Gospel) and aspirations (the dissemination of the Word and the reform of the Church). In the interests of clarity, a point of reference is necessary and so, following the lead of many Tudor historians today, the term 'evangelical' shall henceforth be used to describe the outlook of these reformers.

Although Anne Boleyn was by no means the first to take up strands of the new faith, she had the highest profile and she took her role very seriously. Leaning towards the form of French evangelism sponsored by Francis I's sister, Marguerite of Navarre, Anne launched herself into the Scriptures and especially the Epistles of St Paul. Her piety was intentionally conspicuous. She encouraged scriptural debate at her table, kept an open Bible at her desk and provided her ladies with prayer books to hang from their girdles. She protected and patronised like-minded reformers and defied the law by importing reformist literature from overseas. She even dared to recommend some of these works to Henry VIII. On completing William Tyndale's *Obedience of a Christian Man*, the King reportedly declared that 'this book is for me and all kings to read'.[36]

Henry VIII's beliefs are almost impossible to pin down. They tended to fluctuate according to his inconsistent cogitations and in response to domestic and foreign circumstances. In 1521 he had written a diatribe against Martin Luther, the *Assertio Septem Sacramentorum*, to which the grateful Pope had responded by bestowing upon Henry the title 'Defender of the Faith'.* But, as the King pursued his Great Matter, he tended to embrace proposals, even the more controversial ones, that put pressure on the Pope. In November 1533, for example, the French ambassador reported that Henry had 'made up his mind to a final and complete revolt from the Holy See. He says that he will have the Holy Word of God preached throughout the country.'[37] Whether or not the King meant this, his mood was seized upon by evangelicals like Cromwell and Cranmer, who saw the annulment campaign as a heaven-sent opportunity for spreading the Gospel throughout the realm.

As Supreme Head of the Church of England, Henry had the sole right to decide the religion of his people. His actions were therefore subjected to close scrutiny. In January 1535 he appointed Cromwell Vice-Gerent in Spirituals, a post that effectively made the minister Henry VIII's deputy in all matters of the Church. In the summer Henry and Anne staged a progress through the West Country and showed open favour to the evangelicals based there. The following autumn Henry sent an embassy to the Lutheran Princes of the Holy Roman Empire and even made noises about joining their League. A stream of evangelical propaganda was issued in February 1536 to coincide with the opening of the last session of the Reformation Parliament and, the following month, an act for the dissolution of England's smaller monasteries was passed.

To conservative stalwarts like the Duke of Norfolk and Stephen Gardiner, Bishop of Winchester, these developments were sinister indeed.

---

* Henry felt no need to relinquish this title when he broke with Rome and the initials *F.D.* for *Fidei Defensor* can still be seen on English coins today.

They considered the 'New Learning' anathema and dangerous – a threat not only to centuries-old customs, but to the very foundations of Church and State. Particularly alarming to more *politique* conservatives like Norfolk was the evangelical challenge to the Church hierarchy based on Luther's tenet that the faithful belonged to the 'priesthood of all believers'. In some parts of the Holy Roman Empire this had been misinterpreted as an argument for emancipation, and was used to justify the Peasants' War of 1525. Who was to say that disgruntled members of the underclass might not enact a similar revolt in England? What then for the nobility? For others, like Thomas More, John Fisher and the Carthusian monks, the traditional faith had been worth dying for. Although some people invariably used religion for their own political ends, the battle between the conservatives and reformers was not just petty factionalism. People thought they were fighting for God against the devil. Souls were at stake. The ultimate prize was salvation; failure meant damnation. It was a holy war.

It was into this savage, frenetic environment that the Earl of Surrey was summoned in the spring of 1536. He had experienced the Court before, but mainly on ceremonial occasions such as the French interviews or during the merry days at Windsor. Then, safely cocooned within Richmond's circle, he had watched with detached amusement the fawning and frenzied competition that surrounded the King. Now Howard stock was falling, Norfolk's relationship with Anne Boleyn was at breaking point and the reformers were gaining ground. Surrey was going to have to learn for himself the art of advancement at Court.

The Henrician Court was the political, social and cultural heart of England. It was the 'great theatre', where men and women swarmed for power and patronage, gossip and entertainment, reputation, riches and revenge. There, basking in the limelight, at least for now, was Thomas Cromwell. His late father Walter, described variously as an innkeeper, a tanner and a blacksmith, had been a petty criminal with convictions for fraud, drunkenness and assault. The resourcefulness and steely determination that Thomas Cromwell had needed to escape the shadows of his childhood were put to good use at Court, where he ascended the slippery pole with alacrity. It was Cromwell who had made Henry VIII's divorce from Catherine and marriage to Anne a reality and, within three-and-a-half years, the grateful King had made him Master of the King's Jewels, Chancellor of the Exchequer, Principal

Secretary, Master of the Rolls, Vice-Gerent and Vicar General. He was the King's chief minister in affairs both temporal and spiritual. A self-made man, Cromwell was no friend to the nobility. Dynamic, erudite, personable but inscrutable, nothing escaped his gimlet eye.

Scurrying about nearby in a flurry of archiepiscopal robes was Thomas Cranmer, another beneficiary of the Break with Rome: earnest, seemingly sincere, but to the conservatives a dangerous man with dangerous aspirations, who had vowed at his consecration 'to prosecute and reform matters wheresoever they seem to me to be for the reform of the English Church'.[38] Never far away was the Seymour clan, a Wiltshire gentry family, the rising stars of the Tudor Court. Surrey knew the eldest son Edward, who had been Richmond's Master of the Horse. Just recently he had been made a Gentleman of the Privy Chamber. At his side was his attractive but pretentious wife Anne, his amorous brother Thomas, and Jane, the demure little sister.

Shuffling after his master with his pet monkey perched upon his hunchback was Will Somers, Henry VIII's fool, the only man to get away with calling Anne Boleyn a 'ribald'. Another colourful character was Sir Francis Bryan, a Howard ally, who had lost an eye in a jousting accident; his reputation for drinking, gambling and whoring had earned him the sobriquet 'Vicar of Hell'. Surrey would have recognised a large contingent from East Anglia: the Knyvets, the Cleres, the Sheltons and the Southwells, all members of the sprawling Howard affinity. Then there was a host of extras: young ladies, old nobles, heralds splendid in their tabards, churchmen murderously divided, astrologers, doctors, minstrels, artists and hangers-on. Keeping out the ubiquitous vagabonds was a phalanx of halberdiers – 'By God,' one Venetian had exclaimed 'they were all as big as giants!'[39] Loitering in the wings were the ambassadors: watching, whispering, colluding, ever poised, quill at hand, for the latest scoop. Behind the scenes, making it all happen, was an army of cooks, bakers, barbers, chandlers, tailors, launderers, carpenters, blacksmiths, goldsmiths, messengers, stableboys and scantily clad scullions. It was only in 1526 that they had been made to wear clothes at all.

Centre stage was the 'majestic awing presence' of King Henry VIII.[40] In the first two decades of his reign, Venetian diplomats had exalted Henry's physical beauty. According to Hironimo Moriano, there was no man in the world 'handsomer, more elegant and better proportioned' than Henry. Indeed, he concluded, 'nature, in producing this Prince,

did her utmost to create a perfect model of manly beauty in these times.'
While Piero Pasqualigo was impressed by Henry's accoutrements – the
diamond pendant on his gold collar was 'the size of the largest walnut
I ever saw' and his fingers were 'one mass of jewelled rings' – Sebastian
Giustinian observed that it was the King himself that dazzled. His
auburn beard shone like gold while, on the tennis court, 'it is the
prettiest thing in the world to see him play, his fair skin glowing through
a shirt of the finest texture'.[41]

By the mid-1530s, though, some of Henry's lustre had faded. His
left leg was afflicted by an ulcer, either the result of varicose veins or
an infection of the bone. It caused severe discomfort and, when it
swelled, fevers and acute pain. The King's once youthful physique now
bore an overcoat of fat. If his waist had not yet ballooned to the fifty-
four inches measured for a suit of armour in 1545, it had certainly
expanded well beyond the thirty-two inches of 1512.[42] On 24 January
1536, while running in the lists at Greenwich, he was thrown from his
horse. Clattering to the ground in his armour, he was knocked uncon-
scious for two hours. Thereafter, his ulcer became chronic and another
soon developed on his right leg.[43]

The pressures of state also bore down on Henry. His jousting accident had made him all too aware of his own mortality and the fact
that he still had no male heir was an open sore that tormented him as
relentlessly as his ulcers. The Break with Rome had spawned powerful
enemies. Machiavelli had argued that it was better for rulers to be
feared than loved, and Henry, like his father before him, was beginning to favour the security of fear. As Supreme Head of the Church of
England, he also had a responsibility to project the appropriate level
of spiritual dignity. This meant less levity, flamboyance and familiarity,
and more gravity, solemnity and distance.

The new image required a new iconography, a manifestation of which
was the Whitehall mural produced by Holbein in 1537 for the entrance
to the King's Privy Chamber. Here a full-length Henry VIII stood in
the foreground, a larger, mightier presence than his father Henry VII,
whose image shrivelled into the background. The sheer proportion of
Henry VIII's frame in contrast to the mural's other figures, his aggressive stance – legs astride, one hand on hip, the other edging towards
his dagger – the broad shoulders, enormous codpiece and direct,
penetrating stare, brows raised as if in interrogation, combined to
overawe the onlooker, just as the King himself was supposed to do in

person. Visitors, we are told, now stood before Henry 'astonished and abashed, so trembling and quaking, utterly in a manner mute, as if they had been taken with the palsy, such is the majesty of the Prince.'[44]

When Surrey came to Court in the spring of 1536, he was nineteen years old to Henry's forty-four. The King still enjoyed the company of exuberant young men and in Surrey's restless energy, aggressive sense of honour and political naivety, he may have found a tonic. It has been suggested that Surrey reminded Henry of his own once-youthful self.[45] Despite the King's increasingly fearsome temper, he seems to have treated the young Earl with avuncular indulgence. But Surrey would have done well to learn that even Henry's greatest favourites were expendable. 'If my head could win him a castle in France,' Thomas More once said, 'it should not fail to go.'[46]

There was still fun to be had at Court and ample opportunity for 'pastime with good company'. There were tennis courts and tilting yards, bowling alleys and dicing tables. In the evenings, troupes of minstrels swept merrily through the Hall and a constant round of masques and dances entertained all comers. According to the poet Sir Thomas Wyatt, courtiers worshipped 'Venus and Bacchus all their life long'.[47] The febrile 'press' of so many young people at Court created an atmosphere that was highly charged. Tokens of love and pledges of faith were given and received. High-minded poetry mingled with bawdy doggerel and the games of courtly love sometimes, inevitably, gave way to less innocent pleasures.

Yet lurking beneath the surface frivolity was an undercurrent of menace. One contemporary described the Court as a 'queasy' and 'unstable' place where 'every man here is for himself'.[48] The mercurial personality of Henry VIII dictated the rules of the game. His favour was often instantaneous, reactive to a problem solved or a joke shared. Courtiers could be raised higher than in their wildest dreams, but if they slipped up or Henry's suspicions were aroused, they could be dispatched to oblivion or the executioner's block just as swiftly. The glint in Henry's eye revealed instability and unpredictability. 'You often boast to me that you have the King's ear,' Thomas More once wrote in a satirical epigram to a courtier, 'and often have fun with him, freely and according to your whims. This is like having fun with tamed lions – often it is harmless, but just as often there is the fear of harm. Often he roars in rage for no known reason, and suddenly the fun becomes fatal.'[49]

This was no place for weakness or naivety. The more experienced courtiers had sharpened instincts, finely tuned to the blustery winds of the King's will. Often they had no choice but to be swept along with them, but sometimes they could subtly alter their path. To dissuade the King from bad policy by providing good counsel was, in theory, the duty of every courtier. But to challenge the royal will was treason. It was a fine line and, if crossed, the penalty was death. Access to the King was crucial and competition fierce. Rivals had to be ousted and friends advanced. In this seamy environment factions flourished and, with the increase in religious controversy, they operated with a savagery previously unknown. Only fools were sure of their friends. Alliances were fluid and easily betrayed and everyone, it seemed, wore a mask. As John Husee warned his master Lord Lisle, there were men at Court 'which beareth your Lordship fair face and a double dissembling heart'.[50]

The collective noun for courtiers was a 'threat'. According to the 'Vicar of Hell', Sir Francis Bryan, 'many there be that will do off their bonnet to you that gladly would see your heads off by the shoulders; and such there be that makes reverence unto you that would have his leg broken to see you dead and carried to your grave.'[51] The Howards, as figureheads of the old aristocracy and traditional religion, were more vulnerable than most. Throughout his long career, the Duke of Norfolk faced constant attempts to undermine him or destroy him altogether. He had learned to play the game well. But nothing in Surrey's upbringing in East Anglia or at Windsor or France had fully prepared him for the Court. He had been taught the chivalric values of honesty and fidelity. The Court encouraged dissimulation and betrayal. In order to survive, Sir Thomas Wyatt observed in his satire on the Court, one had to 'use virtue as it goeth nowadays / in word alone to make thy language sweet'.[52]

In one of Surrey's many undated poems, written to sympathise with a young man whose nobility has been 'devoured' by a fickle lady, Surrey reveals his own distaste for the false environment in which she operates:

Too dearly had I bought my green and youthful years,
If in mine age I could not find when craft for love appears;
And seldom though I come in Court among the rest,
Yet can I judge in colours dim as deep as can the best.[53]

Unfortunately for Surrey his ability to spot 'colours dim' – that is, dark deceits or false practices – was never as assured as he supposed.

Surrey had not been summoned to Court just for the experience. At the beginning of March 1536 a meeting was mooted between Henry VIII and James V of Scotland. It was to take place at York and, once an alliance was brokered, Surrey, Richmond and the eldest son of the Marquis of Dorset were to remain behind as surety. It would be France mark two, only colder and less glamorous. All was arranged by 10 March and it was agreed that the English would go north straight after Easter.[54] But the plans soon fell through and before he had time to pack for home, Surrey was called to attend an even more important event – the trial of his cousin, and Queen, Anne Boleyn.[55]

The feisty, wilful spirit that Henry VIII had found so thrilling in Anne when she was his mistress soon proved galling and overbearing once she was Queen. Henry had sacrificed much for her: he had broken with Rome, incurred the enmity of Charles V, executed dear friends and transformed his public image. In return, he expected gratitude and subservience, and did not take kindly to Anne's jealous rages when his eye began to wander towards other ladies at the Court. Henry demanded a Queen who would reflect his majesty, not a tantrum-prone termagant. The passion was still there, but as the years progressed, it increasingly found expression in tempestuous quarrels and, after each angry scene, a little of Henry's fondness for Anne died. Her worst crime by far, though, was her failure to produce a male heir.

On 29 January 1536, only five days after Henry's near-fatal tumble from his horse, Anne suffered her second miscarriage. It would have been a boy. To a distraught Anne, crumpled in her bed, Henry showed no concern. Instead of soothing her grief, he spat out a few staccato words that must have stabbed at her heart: 'when you are up, I will come and speak to you.' To one of his principal courtiers Henry now murmured 'as if in confession' that his marriage was cursed, that he had been duped into it 'by means of sortileges and charms' and that he would relieve himself of God's displeasure by taking a third wife.[56]

Just days later Eustace Chapuys reported that Henry had 'une nouvelle amour'.[57] Jane Seymour, the daughter of Sir John of Wolf Hall, Wiltshire, was one of Anne Boleyn's waiting ladies. She could not have been more different from her mistress. Jane was meek, sweet-tempered and bashful. Her motto was 'bound to obey and serve'; her religion, orthodox. She also – and this would not have gone unnoticed by a king desperate for a male heir – hailed from a family with a high quota of male offspring. Sir Nicholas Carew, Henry Courtenay Marquis of Exeter, and a group of Court conservatives, who had supported Catherine of Aragon and remained true to Princess Mary, observed Henry's interest in Jane with mounting excitement. If Anne could be replaced by Jane, then the flood of reform might be dammed, an aristocratic Council established and Mary restored to the succession. But the King's fancies were notoriously fickle. For their campaign to succeed, the King's attraction for Jane would have to be made permanent. They therefore allied with the Seymours, and Carew began to instruct Jane in the art of ensnaring her King.

Anne Boleyn had already given the masterclass. All Jane had to do was follow her example. Carew told her to offer enough of herself out to Henry to keep him lusting after her, but not, under any circumstances, to surrender her body. Not until they were married. So, when Jane was presented by Henry's messenger with a purse full of sovereigns and a letter, she kissed the letter but did not open it. Instead, she returned it to the messenger and fell to her knees, begging him to entreat the King in her name that she was a gentlewoman born who trusted only to her honour, that she would not sacrifice it for a thousand deaths and that if the King wished to give her money in the future, she hoped it would be at such time as God would be pleased to send her some advantageous marriage.[58]

Henry's attraction to Jane was not just a matter of frustrated lust. It stemmed, too, from the fact that he was surrounded by toadying schemers. He had once told the French ambassador that as he himself spoke what he meant, he would have others speak plainly to him too.[59] The idea that people could be themselves with him, that they could see him as a man, as well as an omnipotent king was, when it suited Henry, rather charming. But Jane was not, of course, being herself and, after her well-choreographed performance, she had Henry, the Supreme Head of the Church of England, dancing to her, or rather her supporters', tune. Anne was queen bee no more and it became increasingly apparent that it might suit the King well if someone swatted her.

By the end of March 1536 Thomas Cromwell, ever the vigilant courtier, had noted these developments with alarm. Although his recent quarrels with Anne over religion and foreign policy had led to an increasingly strained relationship, he knew that he was still seen as one of her chief allies – in Chapuys' words, 'Anne's right hand'[60] – and he had no wish to be dragged down with her. When, on 2 April, Anne used the sermon of her almoner, John Skip, to voice her disapproval of Cromwell, he resolved to join the conservatives. But their aims were not his. He did not want to revive Mary's legitimacy or see an aristocratic caucus in power or allow his hard-fought reform programme to be derailed. He wanted Anne and all her supporters not just repudiated but destroyed altogether. That way there could be no comeback and no counter-attack and he would be free to deal with the conservatives on his own terms. He therefore hijacked the proceedings against Anne. Two months later he could boast that he 'had planned and brought about the whole affair'.[61]

Anne was to be accused of adultery, which might be construed as treason as it brought the succession into disrepute. On 24 April 1536 a commission of 'oyer and terminer' was set up 'to hear and determine' sundry offences in Middlesex and Kent. One of the men appointed to the commission was the Duke of Norfolk. It is not clear at what stage he joined the alliance against his niece, but by now he had good reason to despise her. On New Year's Day, 1535 Chapuys reported that one of his sources had told how Anne had 'used more insulting language' towards Norfolk 'than one would to a dog, such that he was obliged to leave the room'. In his fury Norfolk had issued a tirade against Anne, calling her, amongst other things, a 'great whore'. The following summer Chapuys, citing 'a reliable source', reported that Anne schemed 'day and night' to destroy her uncle.[62] As a religious and political traditionalist, Norfolk naturally inclined to the conservatives, but he had long since burned his bridges with their figurehead, Princess Mary. He had his own motives for conspiring against Anne. If Princess Elizabeth was declared a bastard, then Henry VIII would have three illegitimate children, only one of whom was a son: the Duke of Richmond, Surrey's best friend and Norfolk's son-in-law.

By the end of April Henry VIII was, if not entirely convinced of Anne's guilt, certainly suspicious. On the last day of the month her musician Mark Smeaton was arrested. The same day Anne cradled her daughter in her arms and pleaded with her husband for mercy. Two days later Henry sent his closest companion and groom of the stool, Henry Norris, to the Tower. Both Norris and Smeaton were accused of adultery with the Queen. Norris vigorously proclaimed his innocence,

but Smeaton confessed, probably under torture, to sleeping with Anne.
It was enough for the moment.

Anne herself did the rest. Although she denied all the charges at
Greenwich when interrogated by Norfolk, who was clearly enjoying
the reversal of power – '"tut, tut, tut"' he had said to her, 'shaking his
head three or four times'[63] – once she was a prisoner in the Tower of
London, she began to grow hysterical. Speculating as to what her
enemies could possibly have against her, she blurted out her own in-
coherent suggestions. She recalled her rash words to Norris following
his innocuous profession of courtly love: 'You look for dead men's
shoes, for if ought came to the King but good you would look to have
me.'[64] These details were duly passed on to Cromwell, who added
conspiracy to murder the King to Anne and Norris' charges. Very soon
Anne's remembrances – a spot of flirtation here, some innocent ribaldry
there – implicated others. Sir Francis Weston and William Brereton, a
former servant of Richmond whose family had strong links with the
Howards, were subsequently arrested for adultery, as was Anne's own
brother Lord Rochford, who had the darker stain of incest appended
to his charge.

On Friday, 12 May 1536 the four commoners, Smeaton, Norris,
Weston and Brereton, were tried for treason at Westminster Hall. All
but Smeaton protested their innocence. All were found guilty,
condemned, according to Chapuys, who had no reason to favour them,
'on mere presumption or on very slight grounds, without legal proof
or valid confession'.[65] The state trials of Anne Boleyn and Lord
Rochford were scheduled for the following Monday. They were to take
place back-to-back, Anne first and then her brother. As both the accused
were peers, they had to be tried by twenty-six lords of the realm under
a special tribunal. This was set up under the aegis of the Lord High
Steward, a ceremonial office filled for the day by the Duke of Norfolk.
The Earl Marshal of England had to preside too, but as Norfolk also
held this office, Surrey assumed the role for the day. Deputising for his
father would, under normal circumstances, have been a great honour.
On this occasion it presented Surrey with the unsavoury side to being
a Howard.

As the peers assembled in the Great Hall of the Tower of London,
Surrey, dressed in the Earl Marshal's robes and holding the golden staff
of office, took his seat at the feet of his father, who was enthroned
beneath the cloth of estate. Above them two thousand spectators jostled

for position in specially erected stands. Silence was demanded. Anne was called. An axe, the blade pointing forwards, was carried into the courtroom. Then Anne appeared with two of her ladies. The Constable and the Lieutenant of the Tower escorted her to the bar and she entered her plea: 'Not Guilty'.

Anne's case had already been prejudiced by the legal guilt of her 'lovers', but the actual evidence against her was sparse. Cromwell had the gossip of some of Anne's ladies, her own remembrances and Smeaton's confession, but it was all circumstantial. To get round this he had literally sexed up the charges into a sensational dossier that, he hoped, would shock the jury into a guilty verdict. The indictment stated that Anne,

> following daily her frail and carnal lust, did falsely and traitorously procure by base conversations and kisses, touchings, gifts and other infamous incitations, diverse of the King's daily and familiar servants to be her adulterers and concubines, so that several of the King's servants yielded to her vile provocations.[66]

As Surrey watched his cousin, he listened to a catalogue of sordid details. Anne, he was told, had 'procured and incited her own natural brother, George Boleyn . . . to violate her, alluring him with her tongue in the said George's mouth, and the said George's tongue in hers.' It was too much for Justice Spelman. 'All the evidence,' he stated, 'was of bawdry and lechery, so that there was no such whore in the realm.'[67] Once the jurors were convinced of Anne's sexual perversity, they found it easy to believe the other charges levelled against her: that she had conspired to assassinate the King, that she had promised to each of her lovers that she would marry him once Henry was dead, that she claimed never to have loved Henry, that she had poisoned Catherine of Aragon and planned to do the same to Princess Mary.

Anne defended herself with dignity. She admitted that she had occasionally presented her suitors with gifts in accordance with the convention of courtly love, but denied every other charge. According to one chronicler, 'she made so wise and discreet answers to all things laid against her, excusing herself with her words so clearly as though she had never been faulty to the same.'[68] Eustace Chapuys, the Imperial ambassador who had laboured so tirelessly for Catherine of Aragon, conceded that Anne answered the charges 'satisfactorily enough'. To him Anne had always been a 'concubine' and yet even he was doubtful of her guilt.[69]

Every peer in the jury knew his duty. One by one, beginning with the most junior and concluding with the most senior, each placed his hand on his heart and proclaimed Anne guilty. She was to be 'burned or beheaded as shall please the King,' announced the old crocodile, Norfolk, with tears streaming down his face.[70] Anne received her sentence with serenity. She was, she said, ready to die, but she was truly sorry that innocent and loyal men had to perish with her. Then she was led out of the courtroom with the axe borne before her, its blade now facing her in recognition of her fate. A minor commotion distracted Surrey for a moment. The Earl of Northumberland, the man who had once loved Anne dearly,* but who had just pronounced her guilty, collapsed under the strain and had to be carried out.

Lord Rochford was then marched to the bar. His sister's guilt presupposed his own, but as no witnesses had been called to testify, many wagered that he would get off. He raised a spirited defence and when one of the charges, too sensitive to be read in open court, was handed to him in writing, he stunned onlookers by reading it aloud. It revealed that Anne had branded Henry a flop in bed, possessing 'neither potency or force'.[71] This was a minor triumph that succeeded in raising official hackles, but it proved short-lived. Rochford was declared guilty by a unanimous verdict and, once again, Norfolk pronounced the death sentence.

On 17 May 1536 Smeaton, Norris, Weston, Brereton and Rochford went to the block. Across the river at Lambeth Palace, Archbishop Cranmer declared Princess Elizabeth illegitimate.† Two days later it was Anne's turn to die. She was dispatched not by a clumsy executioner with a rusty axe, but by an expert swordsman shipped in from Calais. We do not know if Surrey was there that May morning at Tower Green, but his father was and so was Richmond and, according to one source, a thousand others.[72]

Many suspected foul play; some even muttered darkly against the proceedings, but most were reputedly glad of the execution.[73] According

---

* Henry Percy (Earl of Northumberland from 1527) had been romantically linked to Anne in the early 1520s and, according to Wolsey's gentleman usher, an engagement had followed, only to be broken off at the King's behest.
† This was done by invalidating Henry VIII's marriage to Anne Boleyn on the basis of 'entirely just, true and lawful impediments'. Cranmer's pronouncement was patently absurd. Had Anne never been Henry's lawful wife, then she could not have committed adultery.

to Mary of Hungary, Regent of the Netherlands and sister of Emperor
Charles V, Anne suffered 'no great wrong'. The crimes may not have
fitted, but the punishment did as 'she is known to have been a worth-
less person'. And yet, Mary concluded with black humour, 'our sex
will not be too well satisfied if these practices come into vogue; and
though I have no fancy to expose myself to danger, yet being a woman
I will pray with the rest that God will have mercy on us.'[74]

Surrey's reaction to his cousin's judicial murder is nowhere recorded.
For his fellow poet Sir Thomas Wyatt, who had himself been briefly
imprisoned under suspicion of being one of Anne's lovers, the events
were unbearable. Having watched the executions through the grate of
his cell in the Bell Tower, he penned a prophetic warning:

> These bloody days have broken my heart.
> My lust, my youth did then depart,
> And blind desire of estate.
> Who hastes to climb seeks to revert.
> Of truth, circa Regna tonat.*[75]

---

* It thunders around thrones.

7

SO CRUEL PRISON

Less than a fortnight after the execution of his second wife, Henry VIII married his third. According to ambassador Chapuys, many likened his pre-nuptial excitement 'to the joy and pleasure a man feels in getting rid of a thin, old and vicious hack in the hope of getting soon a fine horse to ride'. On 3 June 1536 Sir John Russell wrote that Jane 'is as gentle a lady as ever I knew, and as fair a Queen as any in Christendom. The King hath come out of hell into heaven,' he added, 'for the gentleness in this, and the cursedness and the unhappines in the other.'[1]

Carew, Exeter and their faction revelled in their triumph, but their chief goal – the restitution of Mary Tudor to the succession – was thwarted by Cromwell. In a masterful demonstration of machiavellian deception, the King's minister now turned the tables on his former allies. According to the Act of Succession, Mary was a bastard and it was treason to declare otherwise. Despite relentless pressure to acknowledge her illegitimacy, Mary had always held out. But now, under the very real threat that her dear friends would otherwise go to the block for supporting her claim, Mary finally submitted and put her hand to the document that declared the invalidity of her parents' marriage and her own bastardy. The lives of Exeter, Carew and their allies were saved, if only temporarily, by Mary's sacrifice, but their political influence had been shot. Thomas Cromwell dominated both Court and Council. On 2 July he replaced Anne Boleyn's father as Lord Privy Seal; a week later he was raised to the peerage as Baron Cromwell and the following year his son Gregory married Queen Jane's sister Elizabeth.

The nobility attempted to close ranks on 3 July 1536 with a stupendous triple wedding that reinforced the ties between some of England's oldest families. Surrey's brother-in-law Lord John de Vere married Surrey's cousin Lady Dorothy Neville, the daughter of the Earl of Westmorland, who had been Surrey's mother's childhood sweetheart and had subsequently married her sister. Another of Westmorland's daughters, Lady Margaret Neville, wed Lord Henry Manners, heir to the Earl of Rutland, who had strong links with the Howards, while Rutland's daughter Lady Anne Manners married Westmorland's heir Lord Henry Neville. Surrey played his part in the ceremony as Lady Margaret's escort from the church to the reception at the Earl of Rutland's mansion in Shoreditch.

The hosts had prepared meticulously. The Rutland household accounts reveal payments for dozens of rushes to be spread over the floor, for sacks of coal and yards of black satin, velvet and cloth of silver. Money was also paid to dressmakers and to three separate barbers for the 'washing and trimming' and 'rounding' of Lord Henry Manners' hair. The reception included dancing, masquerading and a late-night banquet, and was an exclusive society event, attended by 'all the great estates of the realm'. Henry VIII even made the trip from Whitehall. Still in the first flushes of his new marriage, his *joie de vivre* seemed to have been resurrected for the night and he made a suitably stunning entrance dressed as a Turk.[2] The event was an impressive show of solidarity, but the real power lay at Court, where Cromwell's influence was pervasive. Just how much was made obvious by Norfolk's powerlessness in the face of his half-brother's arrest for treason just five days after the festivities.

Lord Thomas Howard, the son of the Flodden Duke by his second wife Agnes, had been a regular visitor at Tendring Hall and Kenninghall during Surrey's early years. Although he was Surrey's half-uncle, he was, in fact, only five years older than the Earl and it is likely that the two boys would have played together as children. When Surrey was at Court he sometimes joined his sister Mary, and Thomas, and their circle of lyricists and enthusiasts – a sort of mutual appreciation society whose members wrote down their favourite poems (including one ascribed to Surrey) in a courtly anthology that has survived to this day and is known as the Devonshire Manuscript. One contributor was Lady Margaret Douglas, the King's niece.* Some time in 1535 she and Lord

---

* She was the daughter of Henry VIII's elder sister Margaret (the widow of James IV of Scotland) by her second marriage to Archibald Douglas, Earl of Angus. Lady Margaret was born in England in 1515 and spent the next two years there before being taken to Scotland. She returned to England in 1528 and from 1530 lived 'like a queen's daughter' in the households of Princesses Mary and Elizabeth. Lady Margaret's son, Henry Darnley, would eventually marry Mary, Queen of Scots and father James I of England and VI of Scotland.

Thomas fell in love and over the Easter of 1536 they secretly plighted their troths.

Thomas had fallen for the wrong girl. As the King's niece, Lady Margaret was a protected asset. The fall of Anne Boleyn and the subsequent bastardisation of Elizabeth meant that Henry VIII was temporarily without an heir. A second Act of Succession, announcing Henry's right to nominate his own successor in case Jane Seymour could not give him an heir, was introduced to Parliament in June 1536. The Duke of Richmond was the name on everyone's lips,[3] but Lady Margaret, born and bought up in England, was a possible candidate.

Henry VIII was paranoid about anything that touched the succession, but the fact that Thomas Howard was a member of the family that had already placed Anne Boleyn in his bed and assimilated the Duke of Richmond into their ranks, made him doubly suspicious. To their friends, into whose manuscript the couple's love poems were inscribed, Margaret and Thomas' clandestine match was clearly a matter of the heart. To Henry VIII, it was evidence that Thomas aimed for the Crown. Henry once described Margaret as 'furnished with virtues and womanly demeanours after such sort that it would relent and mollify a heart of steel.'[4] On 8 July 1536 he had her and her lover imprisoned in the Tower of London.

Neither separation nor the physical hardship of their confinement could dampen the couple's ardour and they continued to pen lyrical love letters to each other:

Alas that ever prison strong
Should such two lovers separate!
Yet though our bodies sufferth wrong
Our hearts shall be of one estate.[5]

Margaret was too precious to be prosecuted, but on 18 July Thomas was charged with treason. Cromwell knew that a jury would be hardpressed to find him guilty. There was no evidence of malicious intent, nor was the 'crime' of an unauthorised marriage to the King's niece covered by the Treason Statute of 1352 or the 1534 Act of Succession, which had been formulated to deal with Henry's heirs by Anne Boleyn. The Second Succession Act stated that any word or deed that imperilled the succession was potentially treasonous, but a jury might object to its application in the case of Thomas and Margaret as the act had only been introduced to Parliament in June, that is, *after* the couple's Easter betrothal. Thomas was therefore condemned by an act of attainder – a particularly nasty instrument that declared him a traitor by statute rather than by trial.[6]

The preamble to the act stated that Thomas, 'being led and seduced by the Devil', had 'contemptuously and traitorously contracted himself by crafty fair and flattering words to and with the Lady Margaret Douglas', because, *'it is vehemently suspected and presumed'*, he 'maliciously and traitorously' intended 'to put division in this realm and to interrupt, impedite and let the said succession of the Crown'.[7] Writing from the sanctuary of Venice, Reginald Pole could observe the rank injustice of Thomas' conviction, 'condemned only on an *ex post facto* law'.[8] The death sentence against Thomas was not carried out, possibly because the marriage had never been consummated, but he was kept in the Tower, where he continued to dream of Margaret and hope for freedom:

My love truly shall not decay
For threatning nor for punishment;
For let them think and let them say
Toward you alone I am full bent:
Therefore I will be diligent
Our faithful love for to renew,
And still to keep me trusty and true.

Thus fare ye well my worldly treasure,
Desiring God that of his grace
To send us time his will and pleasure
And shortly to get us out of this place:
Then shall I be in as good case
As a hawk that gets out of his mew,
And straight doth seek his trust so true.[9]

It was not to be. At the end of October 1537 Thomas caught a fever and died. He was buried 'without pomp' at Thetford Priory.[10]

To Surrey, increasingly disillusioned by the goings on at the Tudor Court, his half-uncle had suffered a terrible injustice. In a later poem that trumpeted the spotless honour of the Howards, Surrey cited Lord Thomas as a manifestation of his family's values:

It is not long ago
since that for love one of the race did end his life in woe.
  In towre both strong and high, for his assured truth,
where as in tears he spent his breath, alas, the more the ruth.*
  This gentle beast likewise, who nothing could remove,
but willingly to seek his death for loss of his true love.[11]

On 18 July 1536, the same day that Lord Thomas Howard was attainted for treason, John Husee wrote to his master Lord Lisle: 'My Lord of Richmond [is] very sick. Jesu be his comfort.' Five days later, at St James's Palace, Surrey's best friend 'departed out of this transitory life'.[12]

Richmond's death was the cruellest blow in a year that had dealt many. He was only seventeen and relatively robust considering the age in which he lived. Indeed it had been Surrey, not Richmond, who had suffered from poor health when they had been together in France. Only a month before his death, Richmond had been well enough to attend the first session of the new Parliament, but thereafter he had fallen into 'a state of rapid consumption'.[13] He should have gone down in his armour to the hero's death that he and Surrey had enacted so many times in the tiltyard at Windsor. Instead he had succumbed, swollen and scabbed in his bedclothes, to an unworthy assailant. As if to drive Surrey's grief home, another link from his past was severed the following month when the Dauphin François died, probably of pleurisy, after gulping down a glass of freezing water following a vigorous game of tennis in the French sunshine.

Richmond was buried at the end of July by his adoptive family at Thetford Priory. Surrey rode along on his friend's jennet, Richmond's favourite horse, which had been delivered to him, along with its saddle and a harness of black velvet, from Richmond's stable.[14] The King, who, it seems, had wanted to keep Richmond's death quiet for as long as possible, had ordered that his son's body be wrapped in lead, covered with straw and 'conveyed secretly in a close cart unto Thetford', where he was to be buried without any pomp. After the event, though, he regretted his decision and, blind to his first order, blamed Norfolk for not according Richmond due honour – this despite the fact that Norfolk had actually buried Richmond with more ceremony than Henry VIII's instructions had originally allowed.

* *ruth*: pity.

When, on the night of 5 August 1536, rumours reached Norfolk that he was in disgrace and soon to be sent to the Tower of London, he penned an angry letter to Cromwell. 'When I shall deserve to be there, Tottenham shall turn French!' If only, he continued, he could challenge the man who had first slandered him to a duel, then all would see 'who should prove himself the more honest man'. Despite his bluster and the lateness of the hour, Norfolk set at once to the composition of his last will and testament. Already in poor health, 'full, full, full of choler and agony', the sixty-three-year-old Duke was perhaps mindful that a spell in the Tower could finish him. He had two copies drawn up, one for the King and the other for Cromwell. 'If I die, and when I shall die,' he wrote, 'I doubt not ye both will consider that to the one I have been a true poor servant and to the other a true faithful friend.'[15] Norfolk was under no illusion that it was Cromwell who had initiated the whispering campaign against him, but as the Duchess of Norfolk observed, 'he can speak fair as well to his enemy as to his friend'.[16]

The rumours about Norfolk's arrest proved unfounded, but the Howards remained deep in the King's disfavour. On 10 September 1536 Norfolk complained to Cromwell that, despite his many petitions, he had not received any spoils from the dissolution of the monasteries: 'the time of sowing is at hand, and every other nobleman hath already his portion.' Six days later he persisted in his suit: 'I know no nobleman but hath their desires, and if I shall now dance alone my back friends shall rejoice.'[17] He needed an opportunity to prove his loyalty to the King and on 2 October it arrived, when a revolt broke out in Lincolnshire and soon spread into Yorkshire and throughout the North of England. The rebels – largely peasants, artisans, tenants and churchmen – had risen spontaneously and then enjoined, sometimes forcibly, sympathetic lawyers and lords to lead them. As was to be expected from such an eclectic group, their grievances were disparate. Some complained about high taxes and swingeing rents; others called for the repeal of the Statute of Uses* and the Act of Treason; some wanted Princess Mary restored to the succession; still others bayed for the blood of Cromwell and his fellow upstarts. The Lincolnshire rebels had already lynched two of Cromwell's servants. The first they had hanged; the second they had wrapped in the hide of a newly killed calf

---

* The Statute of Uses (27 Hen. VIII, c. 10) was unpopular because it legislated against the common recourse to uses, or trusts, as a way of evading feudal obligations and the rules of primogeniture.

and thrown to a pack of dogs trained in bull baiting. Once the unfortunate man had been savaged to death, the rebels vowed to 'do as much for his master'.[18]

An aversion to the new religion and fear of further reform was the glue that held the rebels together. The past few months had seen monasteries that had adorned the landscape for centuries crumble as royal commissioners rampaged down the altars, defiling sacred objects, seizing gold plate and stripping the roofs of their lead. The nobility and gentry had few qualms about the dissolution as their coffers were fed in the ensuing 'sowing time', but to Robert Aske, the mouthpiece of the Yorkshire rebellion, the suppressions led 'greatly to the decay of the commonweal of the country'.[19] Monks and nuns were not isolated anomalies, but people's brothers and sisters who interacted with their community. They provided healthcare, education, hospitality and charity. They generated employment and financed local initiatives. They lent money, as Surrey had found to his relief when he had petitioned the Prior of Bury St Edmunds for a loan, and some, like Thetford Priory, provided the final resting-place for generations of families.

People now began to fear that the whole fabric of traditional religion would be rent. On 11 July 1536 the government had issued a doctrinal statement in an attempt to clarify matters, but the 'Ten Articles of Faith to Establish Christian Quietness' did nothing of the sort. The Articles tended towards evangelicalism. Prayers for the dead and the veneration of saints were demoted as permissible practices, but unnecessary for salvation, and only three sacraments (baptism, the Eucharist, penance) were sanctioned. But there were too many ambivalent clauses and compromise articles for a coherent message to be discerned. No further clarification was offered. The next day sermons were forbidden for two months and thereafter preachers were discouraged from interpreting the Articles 'after their fantastical appetites'. Instead the parish clergy were directed by a set of royal injunctions to preach four times a year against the usurped authority of the Bishop of Rome and to recite the Lord's Prayer, the Creed and the Ten Commandments in English, when previously they had only been rehearsed in Latin.[20]

Rumours soon abounded – that a tax would be levied on christenings, weddings and burials, that the remaining sacraments would be abolished, that churches would be amalgamated and their goods confiscated – and such was the state of confusion that many believed them. As each region rose in revolt, others were encouraged to do the same until, by mid-October, Henry VIII faced the largest English rebellion since the Peasants' Revolt of 1381.

Immediately denouncing the rebels as arrant traitors, Henry threatened to effect their 'total destruction and utter ruin by force and violence of the sword'.[21] He did not have a standing army and so had to rely almost entirely on the nobility for men and munitions. The Howards, with their extensive network of East Anglian clients, were essential, but the King still had his doubts about the Duke of Norfolk. Only after summoning him to Court and examining him very closely on his religion and his allegiance to the Tudor dynasty did Henry allow the Duke to go home and raise troops.[22] According to the Bishop of Carlisle, who dined with Norfolk before he set off for East Anglia on 7 October, the Duke was happier than he had ever seen him. Perhaps, Chapuys speculated, Norfolk's spirits had been raised by his recent reconciliation with the King. But perhaps too by 'the pleasure he feels at the present commotion', which might succeed in destroying Cromwell and arresting the cause of reform.[23] Chapuys was not the only one to doubt Norfolk's loyalty. Similar suggestions that he, and Surrey too, were rebel sympathisers would become a constant refrain over the next few months.

Back at home, Surrey helped his father with the musters. Despite a scarcity of uniforms and bows and arrows, father and son managed to raise, so Surrey bragged, 'a company of so able men and so goodly personage as I do think the like in such number upon so sudden warning assembled hath not been seen, as those here do judge which have seen many musters.'[24] The King's original plan was to send Surrey up in command of these troops, with Norfolk remaining in East Anglia 'to stay the country'. Norfolk vigorously protested; he could not, in all honour, 'sit still like a man of law'.[25] The Council acquiesced; Norfolk could go north, but would have to leave Surrey behind. On 11 October Norfolk begged that Surrey be allowed to join him, and by the night of the 25th, both father and son had crossed the Trent and lay at Welbeck, fourteen miles from Doncaster. At their disposal were around five thousand men. The Earl of Shrewsbury, encamped at Doncaster, commanded another seven thousand. The rebels had perhaps as many as forty thousand in position around Doncaster and Pontefract. At midnight, 'in bed and not asleep', Norfolk tacked up his horse and prepared to journey towards Doncaster with a party of just seven men that did not include Surrey.

Before he departed, he wrote a letter to the King. 'Sir, I trust the sending for me is meant to good purpose, and if it chance to me to miscarry, most noble and gracious master, be good to my sons and to my poor daughter.' Until he was joined by the rest of the royal forces, he warned that he might have to play for time by negotiating with the rebels: 'Sir, I most humbly beseech you to take in good part whatsoever promise I shall make unto the rebels (if any such I shall by the advice of others make), for surely I shall observe no part thereof . . . thinking and reputing that none oath nor promise made for policy to serve you, mine only master and sovereign, can disdain me, who shall rather be torn in a million of pieces than to show one point of cowardice or untruth to Your Majesty.' Henry VIII replied assuring Norfolk that he would trust to his strategy and promising to look after his children – 'your lively images' – in the event of the Duke's death.[26]

The next day Surrey caught up with his father at Doncaster, where they stayed in the house of a local friar. All around them the plague raged and ten to twelve houses were infected 'within two butts' lengths' of their host's dwelling.[27] On 27 October Norfolk and Surrey met the rebels' representatives on Doncaster Bridge.[28] Their cause, the rebels opined, was a pilgrimage, a Pilgrimage of Grace. They were loyal subjects of the King and wished only for him to hear and resolve their grievances. If he refused, then they would have no choice but to use force. Norfolk duly held out the prospect of a royal pardon and promised the rebels that, if they agreed to a truce, he would provide a safe escort for two of their representatives to come to Court and air their grievances to the King. They accepted and both armies dispersed.

At the beginning of December Norfolk, this time without Surrey, prepared to meet the rebels again. They had drawn up a more detailed set of demands, which they expected Norfolk, in the King's name, to accept. But Henry VIII was not willing to hear their grievances. In fact, he had listened only to Norfolk's 'back friends' at Court, who insinuated that the Duke was a rebel sympathiser. The pilgrims' articles, they suggested, particularly those calling for the restoration of the old religion and the expulsion of 'all villein's blood and evil counsellors', chimed with Norfolk's own goals.[29] He had exaggerated their threat. The rebels lacked numbers and commitment. Had Norfolk really wanted to suppress them, his enemies implied, he could have done so with ease.

On 2 December Henry VIII wrote to Norfolk accusing him of misinformation and inaction. 'It is much to our marvel,' he wrote, 'to receive

so many desperate letters from you, and in the same no remedies.'
Should the rebels, 'by your negligences', now march forward, Henry
warned, 'we should have just cause to think ourself evil served, and
our commandments less regarded than appertained.' With regard to
the upcoming meeting, Henry forbade Norfolk to address any of the
rebels' specific demands. Instead he was to lecture them on the sin of
rebellion. Only in the last resort, and after stalling them for at least
a week, would he be permitted to grant certain concessions. But Henry
was confident that the rebels were repentant and would willingly
disband.[30]

Yet Norfolk, on the ground, could see what Henry could not. He
had no army beyond his own retinue, while the rebels were in the field
with the majority of their original force. They were highly agitated and,
as Norfolk wrote in a series of increasingly desperate missives to both
Cromwell and the King, they had resolved that if no agreement could
be reached, they would proceed in their Pilgrimage and willingly die
for their cause.[31] Norfolk met them at Doncaster on 4 December 1536.
The only way that he could prevent a blood-bath and at the same time
avoid the discussion of specific grievances was by granting a universal
free pardon on the spot and promising the rebels that the next Parliament would be held in the North for the redress of their grievances.
In addition, Norfolk seems to have made other assurances, including
the coronation of Jane Seymour at York and the temporary restoration
of the dissolved monasteries. Confident of the word of such an
honourable nobleman – the man, after all, who had helped his father
save them from a Scottish invasion at Flodden – the pilgrims disbanded
and went home. The rebellion had been liquidated.

Norfolk was well aware that he had exceeded his brief and that the
concessions he had granted in the King's name would never be honoured.
When, early in 1537, a few trouble spots in Yorkshire and Cumberland
flared up, the Duke seized the opportunity to redeem himself and
declared Martial Law on the region – 'Now shall appear whether for
favour of these countrymen I forbore to fight with them at Doncaster.'[32]
Having rounded up more than two hundred former rebels, Norfolk
had them publicly hanged from the trees and steeples of their villages.
When grieving mothers and widows attempted to cut the bodies down
for burial, they too were punished.

Some time in March Norfolk summoned Surrey to help him subjugate
the region.[33] As the Earl rode through the villages, he would have seen

the mouldering bodies swaying gently in the spring breeze. The work was arduous and Surrey and his father rarely stayed in the same place for long. Stray rebels had to be ferreted out and executed, inquests held, monasteries suppressed, and border fortifications inspected and strengthened. By the end of the season, though, Norfolk could report that their work was done: 'These countries, thanked be God, be in such order that I trust never in our life no new commotions shall be attempted. And surely I see nothing here but too much fear, which His Majesty may remedy when it shall be His pleasure so to do.'[34]

Although Henry VIII declared himself thrilled with Norfolk's blood-lust – 'you have done unto us such thankful and acceptable service as we shall never put in oblivion'– the rumour mill continued to grind at Court. 'Here goeth so many lies and tales,' John Husee reported to Lord Lisle, 'that a man knoweth not whereunto to trust.'[35] As Norfolk had himself observed, few of his soldiers had believed in their mission and most had been reluctant to fight their countrymen. According to a report of 29 November, many of Norfolk's men did in fact defect to the rebel camp. John Fowberry, a servant of Surrey, had taken part in the first insurrection, though he later redeemed himself by informing on the rebels' plan to take Hull. More worrying was a report claiming that Surrey himself had twice listened to a song in support of the Pilgrimage and had refrained from punishing the singer. The Howards also had known links with some of the rebel leaders. Dr Mackeral, the Abbot of Barlings, who was executed for his part in the Lincolnshire uprising, had preached at the Flodden Duke's funeral and Lords Darcy and Hussey, who were implicated in the rebellions in Yorkshire and Lincolnshire respectively, had discussed the possibility of a rising as early as 1534 and had suggested then that Norfolk might be willing to join them.[36]

One man in particular, Thomas Pope, a follower of Cromwell well known for his mendacity, now determined to hound Norfolk out of favour.[37] John Freeman, Pope's colleague in the Court of Augmentations, who had witnessed Norfolk's first meeting with the rebels, told Pope that the Duke had sympathised with their grievances and had told two or three hundred of them that he supported their opposition to the Statute of Uses. Pope ordered Freeman to write everything down and, though he could find no other signatories, presented the charges to Lord Chancellor Audley.

Norfolk immediately sent long letters of denial to Cromwell and the

King: 'Fie, fie on them that so falsely will report a true gentleman.' Pope's charge was ludicrous, he argued. Never had he seen even as many as a hundred rebels together, 'and I doubt not all that were there will testify they never heard like words pass my mouth'. Another allegation, levelled by 'some false malicious men', charged Norfolk with having denounced the Papacy and the monasteries 'with so heavy cheer and countenance' that he appeared to mean quite the opposite to what he had said. On the contrary, Norfolk countered, everyone who had heard him champion the King's religious policies had been impressed by his vehemence and frankness. Indeed, he wrote, 'they think my words did more good than the sermons of any six bishops of your realm should have done.'[38]

Another charge concerned Surrey. Why, people asked, had Surrey joined Norfolk in the North without the King's permission or even knowledge? The common rumour, as Norfolk heard it, was 'that I sent for him to the intent I might bring him up here with me to be trained in the affairs of these parts that I might depart hence and leave him to occupy here as my deputy.' 'Sir,' Norfolk protested to the King, 'on the troth I owe to God and you my Sovereign Lord, I never had such thought.'[39] Yet there was substance to this charge. On 7 March Norfolk had suggested that the wild borderers would not respect the governance of 'mean men', but that 'some man of great nobility should have the rule'. But whenever a nobleman was suggested, he had raised doubts about his suitability.[40] Governance of the North was something of a Howard rite of passage; both Norfolk and his father had cut their teeth there and it is likely that Norfolk desired a similar experience for his son.

Once confronted, Norfolk protested with his usual bluster. 'On my faith,' he spluttered, no such thought had crossed his mind. He was, he argued, hoping shortly to come to Court but doubted his servants would remain in the North without him 'unless my said son had tarried here with them until my return'.

Another cause was that of truth I am very affectionate unto him and love him better than all my children and would have gladly had him here with me, both to have kept me company in hunting, hawking, playing at cards, shooting & other pastimes, and also to have entertained my servants to the intent they should have been the less desirous to ask leave to go home to their wives and friends.

And if I minded any other thing in sending for him than these, and specially if ever I thought the other false surmises matter, God let me shortly die the most shameful death that ever man did.[41]

How much Norfolk actually meant this is difficult to tell. He had never been so affectionate towards his son before, nor would he be again, and it is perhaps sad to conclude that a certain amount of policy dictated his love for Surrey on this occasion. On the other hand, Surrey's personal magnetism must have been powerful enough for Norfolk to deem it a convincing excuse. In his reply, Henry declared himself satisfied that Surrey would not have been sent 'for any purpose than should not be to our good contentment. Nevertheless,' he continued, 'we marvelled that without our knowledge you would send for him into those parts whereby you may perceive what occasion you ministered to men to divine evil of it.' The King concluded by assuring Norfolk of his trust in him and advising him against crediting 'such light tales' in the future.[42]

The following month more weighty accusations were hurled at the Howards when Lord Darcy, the nobleman implicated in the Yorkshire rebellion, began to squawk from within the Tower of London. Norfolk, he claimed, had favoured many of the rebels' articles at his first meeting with them. Darcy had every reason to hate Norfolk. It was the Duke who had gathered evidence against him and who had branded him 'the most arrant traitor that ever was living', and the two had exchanged harsh words on Doncaster Bridge, when Darcy had refused to defect to the royal forces. According to Norfolk, once again forced to defend his honour, Robert Aske, before his execution at York, had warned him that Darcy bore him 'ill will' and 'was pricked to say against me'.[43] Not only did Darcy accuse Norfolk of complicity with the rebels, but he also made a 'false surmise' against Surrey. The specific allegation was not recorded but it was serious enough to compel Norfolk to seek Cromwell's intervention. On Sunday, 8 July 1537 Norfolk followed this up with an obsequious message of thanks 'for your most loving fashion so friendly showed at this time in trying out of my troth and my son's'.[44]

Even if one takes into account the number of men at Court who would have willingly perjured themselves in order to destroy the Howards, the accumulation of charges against them does imply that something must have been said in favour of the rebels at the time of the first meeting on Doncaster Bridge. Considering the delicate nature of the negotiations, this is hardly surprising. Norfolk had had to placate the representatives of forty thousand angry men. He had to convince them that he, and the King, thought their grievances worthy of consideration. Norfolk had warned as much in his letter to the King of 25 October. But whatever sympathy Norfolk or Surrey may have expressed for the rebels' ends, they had shown by their actions that they abhorred the means. Henry VIII was satisfied and no action was taken against either father or son.

The summer of 1537 saw Surrey back at Kenninghall, where he grew 'very weak, his nature running from him abundantly'. According to Norfolk, he had been in the same state 'a great part of the last year' whenever he 'thought of my Lord of Richmond'.[45] His friend's death had hit Surrey hard, but excessive grief was considered unnatural and subversive. A period of mourning was permissible, but anything beyond that was thought to challenge God's ordinance. The sixteenth-century attitude to mourning is best illustrated by a letter of 'consolation' written by Catherine Parr (later Henry VIII's sixth wife) to Lady Wriothesley on the death of her only son:

> What is excess sorrow but a plain evidence against you that your inward mind doth repine against God's doings and a declaration that you are not contented that God hath put your son by nature, but his by adoption, in possession of the heavenly Kingdom? . . . If you lament your son's death, you do him great wrong, and show yourself to sorrow for the happiest thing there ever came to him, being in the hands of his best Father. If you are sorry for your own commodity, you show yourself to live to yourself . . . Wherefore, good my Lady Wriothesley, put away all immoderate and unjust heaviness.[46]

Surrey was too sensitive and passionate a person to be able to turn off his grief according to convention. Norfolk found this incomprehensible. He promptly sent for the King's physician to diagnose Surrey's 'disease' and then petitioned for him to be summoned to the North, presumably in the hope that some virile service might banish his weak, effeminate behaviour. His son, Norfolk mused, couldn't possibly still be mourning Richmond; his condition must have returned 'by some other thought'. Maybe it had. The last few months had certainly given Surrey much to worry about. But perhaps Norfolk was missing the point. Surrey became withdrawn in July. Richmond had died the previous July. What Surrey was experiencing may well have been an 'anniversary reaction' exacerbated by the strain of recent events.[47]

Unsurprisingly, Norfolk's petition was refused, but Surrey did try to keep up appearances and, much to his father's chagrin, hosted a series of costly parties at Kenninghall. 'His being there,' Norfolk complained from York, 'doth not only cause many to resort to him to my charge, but also doth cause my deer not to be spared.'[48] Some time at the end of July or beginning of August 1537 Surrey ventured to Court. There, at Hampton Court, he heard for himself the charges levelled against him and his father. He saw his father's enemies whispering in corners and then raising their voices as he passed and he observed the smug delight on their faces as they revelled in his discomfort. Norfolk had vowed to 'adventure my poor body' in defence of his reputation against the 'false caitiffs', who were 'loath to show their faces'.[49] Surrey, having now seen them, was ready to honour his father's pledge.

One day, within the confines of the Court, someone said something that offended Surrey. Unwinding like a tightly coiled spring, he struck the man in the face. Despite a persistent and groundless tradition that the recipient of Surrey's blow was Queen Jane's brother, Edward Seymour, the only reference that so much as hints at his identity comes from Surrey's sister Mary. She later claimed that ever since this incident, Surrey harboured a mortal grudge against 'all' the 'new men' of the Court.[50] This hardly narrows the field. In Surrey's opinion anyone who lacked noble blood was a new man. But he did reserve special venom for Cromwell and his cronies, the newest of the new men, and it is possible that the victim of Surrey's assault came from that camp. If one is looking for candidates, then Thomas Pope seems the most likely. He had taken his allegation of misconduct against Norfolk right up to the Lord Chancellor and, even when it was dismissed, he refused to give it up. Ten years later he would repeat the same charge.[51]

Whoever it was that provoked Surrey, he could be satisfied that his taunt had elicited the desired response. Shedding blood within the confines of the Court disturbed the King's Peace and was punishable by the loss of the right hand. A team of ten men was required for the operation and it had to be administered according to strict protocol:

First, the sergeant surgeon with his instrument appertaining to his office; the sergeant of the woodyard with the mallet and a block whereupon the hand should lie; the master-cook for the King, with the knife; the sergeant of the larder, to set the knife right on the joint; the sergeant ferrer with his searing irons to sear the veins; the sergeant of the poultry, with a cock, which cock should have his head smitten off upon the same block and with the same knife; the yeoman of the chandry, with sear cloths; the yeoman of the scullery, with a pan of fire to heat the irons, a chafer of water to cool the ends of the irons, and two formes* for all officers to set their stuff on; the sergeant of the cellar, with wine, ale and beer; the [sergeant] of the ewery . . . with basin, ewer and towels. Thus every man in his office ready to do the execution.[52]

It was a sentence designed to mete out pain and shame in equal measure, for a man was no use to anyone if he could not hold his sword. On 8 August 1537 Norfolk wrote to Cromwell from the North about 'the multitude of pricks of agony that are in my heart', the chief being the thought of Surrey being 'maimed of his right arm'.[53] He begged Cromwell to show his letter to the King and to plead for his case. Norfolk's tone was sufficiently subservient. Surrey did not go under the knife. Instead he was banished to Windsor Castle, where he was left to ruminate over the folly of his deed.

It was during this rustication that Surrey is thought to have composed two elegiac poems. Both expose the ephemerality of life by contrasting the present Windsor of 1537 to the earlier Windsor of his 'childish years' with Richmond. Then, as we have seen, it was the scene of adolescent delight, the setting for a constant round of tennis, jousting, hunting, dancing and flirting, all invested with 'lust and joy'. Above all, it was the site of an intimate bond forged in accordance with the code of chivalry: 'the friendship sworn, each promise kept so just'. Now Surrey surveys the 'large green courts', the 'gravelled ground', the 'secret groves' and the 'wild forest' and 'each sweet place returns a taste full sour'. Windsor has become a 'cruel prison'; its 'void walls' loom over him. The memory of his fellowship with Richmond haunts him until 'the blood forsakes my face / the tears berayne my cheek of deadly hue'. Finally, the poet Earl can restrain his awkward grief no more. In an anguished apostrophe, he cries out,

> O place of bliss, renewer of my woes,
> Give me account where is my noble fere,†

---

* *formes*: tables.
† *fere*: companion.

Whom in thy walls thou didst each night enclose,
To other lief,* but unto me most dear.

Only the walls are listening and they amplify Surrey's grief:

Each stone, alas, that doth my sorrow rue,
Returns thereto a hollow sound of plaint.
Thus I alone, where all my freedom grew,
In prison pine with bondage and restraint.

And with remembrance of the greater grief,
To banish the less I find my chief relief.[54]

But there can be no relief. The lyrical Richmond created by Surrey transcended time, defining both past and present. Richmond alive embodied Surrey's happiness, his innocence and his 'freedom', literally in the sense of liberty, but also according to the early definition of the term: nobility. Richmond dead personified Surrey's sorrow, his disenchantment and his 'bondage', both as a prisoner within Windsor and as a nobleman whose sense of honour – his 'freedom' – was steadily being constricted. Surrey now lives in a world where his kinsmen are persecuted by a paranoid king, a world where his father has to sacrifice his word – the most precious asset of any aristocrat – in order to dupe a crowd of rebels, a world where noblemen crouch and fawn to base-born upstarts. This is a world turned upside down, where it is possible for a tradesman's son to become a Knight of the Most Noble Order of the Garter. Thomas Cromwell's installation took place at Windsor on 26 August 1537 and it is perfectly possible that Surrey witnessed the procession to St George's Chapel from his window.[55] 'Remembrance of the greater grief' of Richmond's death, then, only intensified Surrey's sense of thraldom within Windsor and within society at large.

The 'Windsor Elegy', as it is known, is commonly regarded as Surrey's first poem. Described as 'the first great elegy in modern English',[56] it is wrought in a new verse form – the heroic quatrain. Each stanza of four pentameter lines, rhyming *abab*, *cdcd* etc., lends the poem an epic quality that succeeds in restoring to Richmond some of the dignity of

* *lief*: beloved.

which his wretched death and hurried burial had deprived him. At the same time Surrey injects his verse with a note of pathos and subjectivity never previously realised by an English elegy.

In a second poem, also thought to date from his confinement, Surrey furnishes the sonnet, recently imported from Italy by Sir Thomas Wyatt, with a new rhyme scheme – *ababcdcdefefgg*. This form, so suited to English with its comparative scarcity of collective rhyming words, was subsequently adopted by Shakespeare and so masterful was his handling of it that it is often referred to as the 'Shakespearian sonnet'. But it was the twenty-year-old Surrey's creation.

The scene opens with the poet leaning over the castle parapet in a conventional melancholic pose. As the speaker surveys the view, he observes the natural harmony of the landscape until a dramatic break in the sixth line forces his thoughts inward. Fond memories of his 'rakehell life' with Richmond stir pain within his heart. He tries to suppress his grief in conformity with society's attitude to mourning, but emotion breaks out 'against my will'. Yet it is only in the last, abrupt line that the reader is presented with the full extent of the poet's torment:

When Windsor walls sustained my wearied arm,
My hand my chin, to ease my restless head,
Each pleasant plot revested green with warm,
The blossomed boughs with lusty Ver*y'spread,
The flowered meads, the wedded birds so late
Mine eyes discovered. Then did to mind resort
The jolly woes, the hateless short debate,
The rakehell life that longs to love's disport.
Wherewith, alas, mine heavy charge of care
Heaped in my breast brake forth against my will,
And smoky sighs that overcast the air.
My vapoured eyes such dreary tears distil
   The tender spring to quicken where they fall,
   And I half bent to throw me down withal.[57]

* Ver: Spring.

8

EN FAMILLE

Fortunately for the House of Howard, for Surrey's friends and admirers and for the future of English poetry, Surrey did not leap to his death from the parapet of Windsor Castle. His exile was over by 6 October 1537, when Norfolk wrote to Cromwell requesting permission for himself and Surrey, whom he had arranged to meet at Ware, to come to Court.[1] Queen Jane was due to give birth and Norfolk wanted to make sure that both he and Surrey would be close to the King for the happy event. On 12 October two thousand salvoes were fired from the Tower of London, a High Mass was sung at St Paul's, bonfires were lit throughout the city and wine and ale flowed freely in the streets. Jane had given birth to a boy.

Three days later the new heir was christened Edward in the King's Chapel at Hampton Court. The ceremony was attended by all the great estates of the realm and the Duke of Norfolk stood at the font as the Prince's godfather.[2] But Surrey was conspicuously absent, his presence at Hampton Court probably deemed inappropriate on account of his recent disgrace there. Within a fortnight the nation's celebrations turned to mourning as the Queen succumbed to a fever and died in her birthing chamber. On Monday, 12 November Surrey was called to attend her funeral as one of 'the six assistants about the corpse and chair'.[3] Thereafter he returned to East Anglia.

The next few years of Surrey's life are as frustrating for his biographer as they must have been for him. He pops up from time to time in the chronicles, usually in reference to some local administration or Court ceremonial, but more often than not, the records are silent as to his activities. Surrey was in thrall to his family's fortunes. When the Howards were in favour, so was he. When they were not, he was underemployed and unwelcome at Court. Thomas Cromwell remained very much in the ascendant and, according to the French ambassador, succeeded in blocking the Duke of Norfolk's access to the King until the spring of 1538.[4]

Surrey kept his head down for most of this year. He was in London in November 1538, when he dined on four separate occasions at Beauchamplace, the Seymour residence on the Strand,* but on the whole he remained in the country, where he was engaged, as a Commissioner of the Sewers, in the maintenance of the watercourses in Norfolk. Occasionally he assisted his father in his ducal business. On 20 September, for example, he oversaw the surrender of the house, church, lands and possessions of the Grey Friars of Norwich.[5]

During this period – indeed all his life – Surrey was short of ready money. As the son of the richest nobleman in England, he had a duty to display magnificence, but he seems to have used this as justification for reckless extravagance. He spent vast sums on the maintenance of his image, be it on hunting parties, portraits by the King's artists or, later, on the gorgeous tapestries and furniture that adorned his new home in Norwich. An inventory of his possessions taken on his death reveals a substantial wardrobe, including 'a hat of crimson satin and crimson velvet with a white feather', 'a pair of hose of black velvet laid on with threads of Venice gold', 'a doublet of orange velvet embroidered with white satin and silver' and 'a gown of cloth of gold furred and faced with sables'.[6] Evidently this last item raised eyebrows; in a cryptic list of memoranda drawn up at the time of Surrey's fall, there is one entry concerning 'my Lord of Surrey's pride and his gown of gold'.[7]

Surrey also fraternised with London's high-rolling gambling set and was probably, like his father, 'a great player'.[8] One can imagine Norfolk's restraint, his steady head and inscrutable countenance proving useful at the dicing and carding tables. Surrey's impulsiveness and inability to dissemble, on the other hand, could hardly have served him well. He could be generous to a fault. When Sir Edward Wotton's son showed an interest in one of his horses, Surrey immediately handed it over and

---

* Following his elevation to the Dukedom of Somerset in 1547, Edward Seymour rebuilt Beauchamplace along classical lines and renamed it Somerset House. It survived the Great Fire of London, but fell into disrepair in the eighteenth century and was demolished in 1775. Construction of the building we see today began the following year and was completed at the turn of the century.

promised to send a better one shortly. When he later commanded the King's army in France, Surrey used his own purse to augment the meagre wages of some of the soldiers and, when one of his servants died, the man's will revealed that he owed the Earl £200.[9] This was money Surrey could ill afford. Despite a sizeable income from his marriage settlement and an allowance from his father, he was almost constantly in debt and had to rely on loans from local dignitaries and even his own servants.[10] It was surely for this reason that Surrey and his wife Frances continued to reside at Kenninghall. It was hardly an ideal situation. Not only was his father's mistress, Bess Holland, ensconced as the lady of the house, but Surrey's sister Mary was also there.

The death of the Duke of Richmond in 1536 had left Mary a young widow. According to her marriage contract, she was entitled to a jointure, but her royal father-in-law was proving slippery in this respect. Henry VIII argued that because Mary and Richmond had never consummated their marriage, he did not owe her a penny. Norfolk did his best to defend Mary's suit; he consulted a field of experts – 'all learned men do say that I speak with: there is no doubt of her right'[11] – and sent streams of letters, but he was wary of falling foul of the King. Mary, who seems to have inherited her mother's fiery nature, was less than satisfied with her father's efforts and resolved to go to Court to pursue her suit in person. 'My daughter of Richmond,' Norfolk grumbled on 6 April 1538, 'doth continually with weeping and wailing cry out on me to have me give her licence to ride to London to sue for her cause, thinking that I have not effectually followed the same.'[12] Mary's persistence eventually paid off; in 1539 she began to receive payments from the King and the following year she was granted a generous income.[13] Norfolk's attitude to Mary's independence is typical of the patriarchal age in which they lived. 'In all my life,' he admitted to Cromwell, 'I never communed with her in any serious cause ere now, and would not have thought she had been such as I find her, which, as I think, is but too wise for a woman.'[14]

No records survive about Surrey's relationship with his younger brother Thomas, who would become Viscount Howard of Bindon in the reign of Elizabeth I, but there is much to suggest that his relationship with Mary was volatile. Born within two years of each other, they had many of the same friends as well as a shared appreciation of literature. It was Mary who inscribed one of Surrey's poems into the anthology known as the Devonshire Manuscript. She was reputedly a great beauty and Surrey, like most brothers, was protective of her. According to a Spanish chronicler, he once rebuked her for being 'too free with her favours'; on another occasion he advised her to temper her zeal for religious reform.[15] But Surrey could no more subdue his sister's passions than he could his own and the effects of their clashes reverberated throughout the household.

Surrey's relationship with his wife is the hardest of all to gauge, in part because it has been blurred by his posthumous reputation as a romantic hero. This arose from a sonnet he penned in praise of a lady called Geraldine. There are enough biographical clues in the poem to identify her as Lady Elizabeth Fitzgerald, the daughter of Gerald Fitzgerald, ninth Earl of Kildare by his second wife, Elizabeth Grey. Elizabeth Fitzgerald, who served as a lady-in-waiting at the English Court, was some eleven years younger than Surrey and still only a teenager when he died in 1547:

> From Tuscan came my lady's worthy race;
> Fair Florence was sometime her ancient seat;
> The western isle, whose pleasant shore doth face
> Wild Chambar's cliffs, did give her lively heat.
> Fostered she was with milk of Irish breast;
> Her sire an earl; her dame of princes blood;
> From tender years in Britain she doth rest,
> With a king's child, where she tastes ghostly food.
> Hunsdon did first present her to mine eyen:
> Bright is her hue, and Geraldine she hight;
> Hampton me taught to wish her first for mine,
> And Windsor, alas, doth chase me from her sight.
>   Beauty of kind, her virtues from above;
>   Happy is he that may obtain her love.*[16]

What are we to make of this? The Elizabethans had no doubt that it was a sincere profession of love from Surrey to his mistress. Surrey's first editor furnished it with his own title – 'Description and praise of his love Geraldine' – and, in a subsequent edition, replaced the word 'lady' in

* line 1: *Tuscan*: Tuscany.
line 4: *Chambar's*: Cambria's (Wales's).
line 8: *where she tastes ghostly food*: where she partakes in Holy Communion.
line 9: *eyen*: eye.
line 10: *hight*: is called.

another of Surrey's poems with 'Garret', a corruption of the Fitzgerald name that was sometimes used by the family.[17] By 1594 the 'romance' between Surrey and Geraldine had gained enough currency for Thomas Nashe to send it up in his novel, *The Unfortunate Traveller*. Here Surrey travels to Florence and visits the house where Geraldine was born. 'When he came to the chamber,' Nashe's protagonist narrates,

> where his Geraldine's clear sunbeams first thrust themselves into this cloud of flesh and acquainted mortality with the purity of angels, then did his mouth overthrow with magnificats; his tongue thrust the stars out of heaven, and eclipsed the sun and moon with comparisons.[18]

Fired by his passion, Nashe's Surrey fights in a tournament where he successfully defends Geraldine's beauty against all comers and 'so great was his glory that day as Geraldine was thereby eternally glorified'.[19]

Although Nashe's account is a fictitious parody of Petrarchan romance – Surrey never even set foot in Italy – his contemporaries received it with apparent credulity. Between 1598 and 1599 Michael Drayton composed a pair of elaborate verse epistles. The first he attributed to Surrey pining in Florence; the second was Geraldine's breathless reply. In his introductory 'Argument' and endnotes, Drayton lent an air of authenticity to Nashe's fiction and claimed that Surrey wrote 'many excellent poems' in praise of Geraldine.[20] By the time of Alexander Pope's *Windsor Forest* of 1713, the idealisation of Surrey as a romantic hero was firmly established:

> Matchless his pen, victorious was his Lance,
> Bold in the Lists, and graceful in the Dance:
> In the same Shades the Cupids tuned his Lyre,
> To the same Notes of Love, and soft Desire:
> Fair Geraldine, bright Object of his Vow,
> Then filled the Groves . . .[21]

Into the next century the popularity of the story showed no signs of abating. In the hands of Sir Walter Scott (*Lay of the Last Minstrel*, 1805), it was injected with eroticism. As Scott's Surrey gazes upon a mirror, the image reflected is not of himself but of 'the slender form' of a lady reclining on a silken bed in a room 'party lighted by a lamp with silver beam' and partly 'hid in gloom':

O'er her white bosom strayed her hazel hair,
   Pale her dear cheek, as if for love she pined;
All in her nightrobe loose she lay reclined,
   And pensive, read from tablet eburnine*,
Some strain that seemed her inmost soul to find:-
   That favoured strain was Surrey's raptured line,
That fair and lovely form, the Lady Geraldine.[22]

Following Drayton, Scott appended an authorial note to his work claiming that it was founded on the historical incidents of Surrey's life.[23]

The Fair Geraldine myth reached its apogee in 1815, when Surrey's romantic editor, George Frederick Nott, announced that no less than nineteen of Surrey's poems were inspired by his love for her. Lyrics where Geraldine is nowhere mentioned and where the lady seems little more than a poetic conceit were given titles such as: 'Surrey complains of the malice of fortune in separating him from the Fair Geraldine; but assures her that absence shall not diminish his love'; 'He praises the exceeding beauty of the Fair Geraldine'; 'He reproaches the Fair Geraldine for her fickleness and insincerity'; 'He sends the Fair Geraldine a tender assurance of his constancy, and tells her that however rewarded, he will love her and serve her faithfully'. And so on and so forth ad nauseam.[24]

It is a tribute to the imagination of the Elizabethans and their romantic descendants that such a legend could be inspired by a single sonnet; a sonnet, moreover, where the speaker's sentiments do not stray from established courtly convention. It is, of course, possible that Surrey took a fancy to the young Elizabeth Fitzgerald and decided to proclaim his devotion to her by composing a poem in her honour, but it is more likely that he had another motive. Lady Elizabeth Fitzgerald was in a precarious position at the English Court. In 1534 her father, a suspected traitor, had died in the Tower of London and three years later her half-brother was hanged at Tyburn for leading a rebellion against Henry VIII in Ireland. The disgrace of her family had impoverished Elizabeth and drastically impaired her chances of marriage. It has been convincingly argued that Surrey aimed to boost her prospects by 'advertising her marriageability' in verse.[25] Surrey's speaker, struck more by awe than love, trumpets Elizabeth's credentials – her Tuscan descent (this was semi-mythical but the speaker does not doubt its veracity), her Irish heritage, her pious upbringing 'in Britain', her service to the Tudor

---

* *eburnine*: ivory.

dynasty, her beauty and her heavenly virtues. It concludes on an aspi-rational note intended to reel in the eligible bachelors of the Tudor Court: 'Happy is he that may obtain her love'. If this was Surrey's strategy, it worked. In December 1542 Lady Elizabeth Fitzgerald wed Sir Anthony Browne, a Howard ally and Henry VIII's Master of the Horse.

Whatever Surrey's motive for his sonnet, it reveals nothing about his feelings for his wife. Indeed there is very little extant about their marriage at all. Of Frances, few comments were made, no portraits apart from the early marriage sketch survive, and nothing at all exists in her own hand. Back in the summer of 1537, when Norfolk was concerned about Surrey's poor health and his prolonged grief for Richmond, he commented that 'he is there with his wife, which is an ill medicine for that purpose'.[26] Maddeningly, he did not elaborate. It should be remem-bered that Norfolk was never particularly keen on the marriage, having preferred Mary Tudor for his son, and that Frances' father and he were not friendly. He may, therefore, have been prejudiced against Frances and regarded her as an unfit wife for his son. On the other hand, it could be argued that Norfolk was against Surrey being with Frances at this time because she was too caring, too considerate, too gentle. According to Norfolk, what was needed to rouse his son from his melan-choly was some kind of masculine activity, preferably martial service in the North, not inactivity and feminine indulgence.

On 10 March 1538 Frances gave birth to a son.[27] He was the Surreys' second child, a daughter, Jane, having been born some time between the end of spring 1536 and the beginning of summer 1537.[28] The baby boy was over a month premature. He had been expected 'after Palm Sunday', which in 1538 fell on 14 April. Despite this, and the onset of plague in the area, the Duke of Norfolk was able to report on 14 March that 'the child is as lusty a boy as needeth to be of that age'. He was named Thomas, the traditional name for Howard heirs. 'I intended to have asked to the King's Highness to have beseeched him to have had it christened in his name,' Norfolk told Cromwell, 'and in likewise to your good Lord-ship to have been another godfather, but because she was so long deliv-ered before her reckoning, the women here would not suffer me to let the child be so long unchristened.'[29] Even in the sixteenth century there were some areas of the household where the oppressed sex held sway.

Surrey was now in his twenties, but Norfolk's letter shows how much control he still wielded over his son. It was Norfolk who had preselected the godfathers and it was Norfolk who immediately began to plan his grandson's future. In the same letter, he told Cromwell how overjoyed he was that Surrey and his other son Thomas both now had sons of around the same age as Henry VIII's heir, Prince Edward,

> trusting that when time convenient shall be, the King's Majesty will be content they shall be of the first sort that shall be appointed to await upon him, which to see shall be more to my comfort than I can with my pen express.

Surrey and Frances had three more children in the next five years: Katherine in 1539, Henry the following February and Margaret at the beginning of 1543.[30]

Biographers have frequently searched for allusions to Frances in Surrey's lyrics. A number of poems have been proffered, but only one specifically concerns her. Both internal and external evidence suggests that it was composed between 1544 and 1546, when Surrey was on military service in France. We know that he missed Frances when he was away, as he petitioned the Council more than once for permission to send for her. The poem takes the form of a song performed by a lady lamenting the absence of her lover overseas. She prays for his safe return ('without which hope my life, alas, were shortly at an end') and then tells her audience, all women similarly abandoned, about

> The fearful dreams I have, oft times they grieve me so
> That then I wake, and stand in doubt if they be true or no.
>   Sometime the roaring seas, me seems, they grow so high,
> That my sweet lord in danger great, alas, doth often lie.
>   Another time, the same doth tell me he is come,
> And playing where I shall him find with T. his little son.
>   So forth I go apace, to see that lifesome sight,
> And with a kiss me thinks I say, 'Now welcome home, my knight;
>   Welcome, my sweet, alas, the stay of my welfare;
> Thy presence bringeth forth a truce betwixt me and my care'.
>   Then lively doth he look, and salvith me again,*
> And saith, 'My dear, how is it now that you have all this pain?'
>   Where with the heavy cares, that heaped are in my breast,
> Break forth, and me dischargeth clean of all my great unrest.
>   But when I me awake and find it but a dream,
> The anguish of my former woe beginneth more extreme.[31]

* *salvith me again*: kisses me back.

'T. his little son' is surely Thomas; the absent lover, Surrey; the singer, Frances. But it is not Frances' historical voice that is heard here, but Surrey's fictive representation of it. In Surrey's ventriloquism we may be no closer to the real Frances, but at least we can see how Surrey himself chose to view and hear her: pining for him dreadfully and dependent on him for her happiness. That Surrey saw himself as Frances' knight in shining armour is typical of him; far more remarkable is the intimacy of his imagined homecoming and the touching details that enliven it: Frances rushing towards the nursery, kissing him before she even speaks, his 'lively' look and soothing words and the shuddering sobs that over-come her. The scene is so vivid and natural that it seems entirely credible, just as it did to the dreaming lady herself.

According to the little evidence that remains, and by the standards of the day, Surrey was an attentive father. His children's education clearly mattered to him and he employed the eminent Dutch humanist, Hadrianus Junius, to teach them, paying him double the wage that the royal tutor, Roger Ascham, received from Henry VIII.*[32] Of the five children, Surrey was understandably most mindful of 'T. his little son' and heir. The picture of the two of them playing together in the above poem is one of its loveliest details and it is possible that Surrey addressed another poem to Thomas which counselled moderation in life, some-thing that Surrey himself could seldom achieve.

Henry, the younger son, was a month shy of his seventh birthday when Surrey was executed, but it was he who would be the most curious about his father and the circumstances of his fall. It was also Henry who eventually removed Surrey's remains from the churchyard near the Tower and buried them alongside Frances beneath a magnificent tomb in St Michael's Church, Framlingham.† All three daughters impressed contemporaries with their learning, especially Jane, who was named by her brother's secretary as one of the most learned ladies of the realm. 'Few men may compare with her,' he wrote, and 'all the world doth acknowledge her a worthy daughter of a most worthy father.'[33] But it

---

* Junius had studied at Harlem, Louvain and Bologna and was a celebrated polymath, variously admired as a physician, historian, poet, philologist and botanist. It was in the latter capacity that he discovered an eye-catching species of fungus, which was named *Phallus Hadriani* in his honour.

† St Michael's replaced Thetford Priory as the family mausoleum after the Dissolution. Surrey's tomb can still be seen there as can the earlier tombs of the third Duke of Norfolk and the Duke of Richmond, two of the finest examples of Renaissance monumental sculpture in England.

was Katherine, later Lady Berkeley, who more closely resembled her father. She was a tomboy who loved archery, hunting and hawking, the latter so much that she kept merlins in her chamber even though their droppings destroyed some of her finest gowns. She was profligate and constantly in debt. She adored poetry and music and often a horde of servants could be found pressing their ears against her chamber door in order to hear her singing. She had a certain star quality that prompted Queen Elizabeth to label her 'her golden lady'. Katherine could be haughty and was proud of her lineage, but she was also kind and considerate towards her servants.[34]

John Smyth, the steward of the Berkeley household, related a charming anecdote about Katherine in his history of the family. One day, not long after the teenaged Smyth had entered the household, he was ordered to deliver breakfast to her son. Rushing through the gallery with the covered dish in his hands, he encountered Katherine and only managed to present her 'with a running leg or curtsy' before speeding off. Katherine promptly recalled him and attempted to teach him how to curtsy properly,

> and such was her great nobleness to me therein (then a boy of no desert
> lately come from a country school and but newly entered into her service)
> that to show me the better how, she lifted up all her garments to the calf of
> her leg that I might the better observe the grace of drawing back the foot
> and bowing of the knee.[35]

Katherine inherited some of this easy charm from her father. Hadrianus Junius wrote in 1545 that 'the Earl of Surrey, my patron, shows enormous favour towards me; he congratulates me, feels for me, loves me.' According to Thomas Eynus, who had once served the Duke of Richmond and who Surrey helped find a place in Prince Edward's household, Surrey had a 'noble heart, naturally inclining to all humanity and gentleness'.[36] Thomas Churchyard, an Elizabethan poet who spent four years in Surrey's service, was so grateful to the Earl for taking the time to teach him the skills of verse and for building up his self-esteem that he wrote a poem in his honour:

> As told I have, this young man served, this master twice two year.
> And learned therein such fruitful skill, as long he held full dear.
> And used the pen as he was taught, and other gifts also,

Which made him hold the cap on head, where some do crouch full
  low.[37]

It should be remembered, moreover, that the Duke of Norfolk justified
his summoning of Surrey to the North after the Pilgrimage of Grace on
the grounds that his presence would raise the spirits of the servants there
and make them 'less desirous to ask leave to go home to their wives
and friends'.[38]

But all these positive reactions came from servants who presented no
threat to Surrey. At Court, on the other hand, where he perceived himself,
often with good reason, to be surrounded by men who bore him ill will,
Surrey put on an aggressive front and carried himself with an air of
superiority that frequently rankled. Whenever he sensed a challenge to
his honour, he lashed out, both verbally and physically. At his most
defensive he would refer to himself in the third person, a habit that
hardly endeared him to his colleagues. Even Junius – and he meant this
as a compliment – thought him 'a truly royal young man'.[39] Surrey's
abiding sin was his pride in his blood. He had been brought up on tales
of Howard heroism and his father, a stickler for etiquette, had taught
him the importance of deference. But the Duke of Norfolk also recognised the value in making the right friends at Court, whatever their
station in life.

The presence of arrivistes at the Court was hardly a novelty. English
kings had always had their favourites and noblemen had ever grumbled
about the curtailment of their rights. In the sixteenth century, though,
the reassertion of monarchical power was particularly pronounced.
Henry VIII and his father largely succeeded in checking the activities of
'overmighty subjects' like Surrey's maternal grandfather, the Duke of
Buckingham. The threat of attainder and bonds of recognisance, the
restriction in the number of personal followings and the expansion of
royal influence in local government encouraged interdependence with
the monarch rather than independence of him.

Increasingly, power depended on the King in Court and competition
for his favour was fierce. The development of the printing press, the rise
of literacy, the expansion of trade, law and government bureaucracy,
and the spread of humanist ideas about virtue and service meant that
more people were better educated and had more money and higher aspirations than ever before. In 1536 the Pilgrims of Grace had complained
that the King had excluded great men from his inner circle in favour of

'evil counsellors' like Cromwell. In response, the government propa-
gandist Richard Morison issued a treatise entitled *A Remedy for Sedition*.
'True nobility,' he wrote, 'is never but where virtue is.' The King, he
continued, should be thanked for 'giving offices, dignities and honour'
to those endowed with 'most qualities, most wit, most virtue'. 'In all
other things,' Morison concluded, 'it little availeth whose son a man
be.'[40] Noble birth still provided a stepping stone to high office, but it
could not guarantee automatic qualification.

Surrey was either unwilling or unable to accept the *modus operandi*.
Instead of reckoning with his own deficiencies, he whined about the
proliferation of 'mean creatures' in government. According to his sister,
he 'hated them all' and blamed them for his 1537 confinement at
Windsor. He was convinced that the lawyers and university men were
machiavellian intriguers, determined not only to usurp the nobility, but
to destroy them altogether. 'Those men,' Surrey groused, 'which are
made by the King's Majesty of vile birth, hath been the distraction of
all the nobility of this realm.' They 'loved no nobility,' he announced,
'and if God called away the King, they should smart for it.'[41] This was
fighting talk and it was not appreciated by all those 'new men' who had
worked hard to get to the top.

Surrey's comments earned him a less than favourable reputation at
Court. There the overriding impression was of an egotistical, obnox-
ious, haughty young man. After the Earl's death, Thomas Nashe
lampooned him in *The Unfortunate Traveller*. At one stage in the tale,
the protagonist Jack Wilton decides to impersonate Surrey on his travels
through Italy:

> Through all the cities passed I by no other name but the young Earl of
> Surrey; my pomp, my apparel, train and expense was nothing inferior to his;
> my looks were as lofty, my words as magnifical.[42]

Few, however, had the temerity to criticise Surrey to his face.[43] More
often than not his contemporaries brooded on their offended sensibilities.
Silent enemies proliferated and many would have been only too happy
to see the proud young aristocrat taught a lesson in humility.

9

CHEVALIER SANS REPROCHE

By the end of 1538 England faced a looming crisis. The previous June Francis I of France and the Emperor Charles V had, with the help of papal mediation, put aside their inveterate rivalry and signed a truce at Nice. In December Pope Paul III prepared to promulgate the bull of excommunication against Henry VIII that had been lying dormant in the Vatican since 1535. The final straw had been the desecration of the shrine of St Thomas Becket at Canterbury, the most shocking in a series of iconoclastic measures instituted by Cromwell that year. The bull pronounced Henry VIII a heretic and called on the Catholic rulers of Europe to depose him and return England to Christian obedience.

On 12 January 1539 Francis and Charles entered into a pact by which the one agreed not to ally with Henry VIII without the other's consent. By the end of February Charles V had ordered the detention of all English merchant ships landing in Flemish ports. He had also withdrawn his ambassador from Henry's Court and was rumoured to be gathering a great fleet at Antwerp. At the same time Francis I ordered his own ambassador to withdraw from London. Writing to Cromwell from Brussels on 3 March, Thomas Wriothesley reported that 'it is in every man's mouth that we shall have war'.[1]

Henry VIII's response was characteristically bullish. In November 1538 he ordered the arrests, and in December the executions, of the Marquis of Exeter and Lord Montagu, the cousin and brother respectively of the English renegade, Reginald Pole, who was campaigning

vigorously on the Continent for an invasion of England.* Having seized
all Imperial ships in English ports, Henry turned his attention towards
the defence of his realm. In every shire, the 'aptest and ablest gentlemen
to serve the King' were appointed and placed under the command of
'a person whom the King's Highness can best trust'. The Duke of
Norfolk was sent to the North to protect the borders against a Scottish
invasion and Surrey, at only twenty-two, was put in charge of the
Norfolk coastline.[2]

In addition to raising musters and gathering munitions, Surrey drew
up lists of all the ships and mariners in each port and surveyed and
fortified the seaboards, repairing beacons, digging trenches and erecting
bulwarks and forts wherever necessary. The same work was carried out
throughout the country and across the Channel at Calais and Guisnes.
Henry VIII toured the coastal defences and inspected his navy at
Portsmouth. 'Nothing left he undone,' observed the chronicler, Raphael
Holinshed, 'that tended to the foreseeing and preventing of a mischief
to ensue.' On 8 May 1539 a parade of over sixteen thousand troops
was held in London. It was, Holinshed wrote, 'a beautiful sight to
behold, for all the fields from Whitechapel to Mile End, and from
Bethnal Green to Radcliffe and Stepney, were all covered with armour,
men and weapons, and especially the battle [battalion] of pikes seemed
to be as it had been a great forest.'[3] Then, nothing. The Imperial fleet
at Antwerp began to disperse and the invasion threat, probably never
more than that, promptly died out.

Damp squib it may have been, but the prospect of his shores being

---

* Reginald Pole had been raised at Court alongside Henry VIII but had opposed the Break
with Rome and had been living in voluntary exile ever since. Evading Henry VIII's secret
assassins, Pole petitioned the powers of Catholic Europe to force England back to the papal
fold. Pole's opposition was especially threatening to Henry VIII because he was a descendant
of the House of York and a possible claimant to the throne. His mother Margaret, Countess
of Salisbury, was the niece of Edward IV. Both Margaret and Lord Montagu had recently
been in touch with Pole, while the Marquis of Exeter had been muttering for some time
against the current regime. Henry VIII, always paranoid about threats to the succession, more
so now that he had the interests of his baby son to protect and a potential invasion to
confront, was easily convinced that a conspiracy was afoot to depose him.

Montagu and Exeter were arrested in November 1538 and beheaded the following month.
Many of their associates including Sir Edward Neville and Sir Nicholas Carew were also
executed. Exeter's wife and his twelve-year-old son were imprisoned in the Tower as was
Montagu's young son who subsequently perished there. Two-and-a-half years later, Pole's
sixty-eight-year-old mother was executed by an inexperienced headsman who resorted to
hacking wildly at her writhing body. Pole remained in exile for the rest of Henry VIII's reign
and throughout the reign of his son. On the accession of Mary Tudor in 1553, he returned
to England and was appointed Archbishop of Canterbury. He was finally able to realise his
dream, the restoration of papal authority in England, but it would prove short-lived.

violated had been sufficiently alarming for Henry to introduce a number of important changes. Above all, he recognised the need to strengthen his realm internally. This meant religious concord and greater participation with the estates of the realm. The nobility had proved their value as agents of the Crown and Henry knew that he could not rule without their resources, just as they could not survive without his favour. In May 1539 Parliament passed the Act of Precedence. This established a defined hierarchy for the eleven 'great offices of state'. Of these, six were originally military or household positions and could only be held by peers of the realm. The remaining five offices were administrative, and in practice only the Principal Secretary was a commoner. Early the next year the holders of all eleven 'great offices' were made members of the Privy Council. There was nothing stopping Henry from raising commoners to the peerage, thus qualifying them for these posts. The act also displaced the previous order of precedence by ruling that those nobles who held the 'great offices' outranked those who did not, and this put some aristocratic noses out of joint (though not Norfolk's; he kept his position by virtue of his role as Lord Treasurer). Nevertheless the reforms conveyed the message that the nobility still mattered, and was in fact crucial, not only to the defence, but also to the governance of the commonwealth.[4]

Surrey was one of the beneficiaries of the King's reconciliatory mood. At the end of February 1539 he was appointed Master Forester of Ashdown Forest in Sussex. On 1 December he was granted, for the duration of his father's life, the reversion and rent of the house and certain lands formerly belonging to Wymondham Abbey in Norfolk. Five days later he was appointed Steward for the Duchy of Lancaster in Norfolk, Suffolk and Cambridgeshire.[5] Throughout 1539 Surrey was prominent at Court. He was frequently entertained at Beauchamplace, where he dined with the Seymours ten times in October alone.[6] On the weekend of 7 and 8 June he was an official mourner at the services held at St Paul's to commemorate Charles V's wife, the Empress Isabella, who had died in May. Once the obsequies were over, Surrey and the rest of the mourners went to Baynards Castle, 'where they dined and had a great dinner with many delicate meats and subtleties'.[7]

The memorial weekend, a conventional display of piety with dirges, requiem masses, bell-ringing, incense and images of the saints, was regarded by many as a sign of the King's new diplomatic and religious priorities. Yet only weeks later the royal artist Hans Holbein was dispatched to Düren with orders to produce a likeness of a lady called

Anne of Cleves. For some time the King's counsellors had been urging
him to remarry. Christina, Duchess of Milan, had been a favourite for
a while, but her representatives had proved obstructive and Christina
herself, mindful of the fates of Henry's previous wives, had been actively
opposed to the idea.[8] Several French ladies were then mooted, but
Henry VIII offended Gallic sensibilities by insisting that they parade
before him for inspection. They were not horses to be trotted out at a
fair, the French had sniffed. Castillon, Francis I's ambassador in London,
then rounded on Henry for his lack of courtesy and succeeded, as very
few could, in making the King blush. 'Your Majesty,' he said, 'would
perhaps like to try them all, one after the other, and keep the one that
suits you best. It was not thus, Sire, that the Knights of the Round
Table treated their ladies.'[9]

So it was that hopes eventually rested on Anne of Cleves, the sister
of Wilhelm, Duke of Cleves. The Duchy of Cleves was a strategically
important state located along the Rhine between the Low Countries
and the German Imperial territories. It had not joined the Lutheran
League of Schmalkalden against the Emperor, but was considered
progressive in religion and Wilhelm's brother-in-law, Duke Johann
Friedrich of Saxony, was one of the League's most vocal members. The
Cleves match was a controversial choice, therefore, and very much the
brainchild of Cromwell, who saw it as a vehicle for the advancement
of reform in England. Holbein soon returned with his portrait of Anne
and it pleased Henry VIII enough for him to authorise official negotiations with the Duchy.

The proceedings with Cleves and the commemoration of Empress
Isabella were typical of the mixed signals that Henry VIII was giving
out at this time. The year 1538 had been a triumphant one for reform.
The Observant friar, John Forest, had been burnt at the stake and a
Lutheran delegation had been officially welcomed in England. This was
also the year of Cromwell's Injunctions. Sacred images and shrines were
condemned as objects of false worship and destroyed. According to the
Injunctions, 'the King's Highness graciously tendering the weal of his
subjects' souls, hath in part already, and *more will hereafter*, travail for
the abolishing of such images as might be an occasion of so great an
offence to God, and so great a danger to the souls of his loving subjects.'[10]
Some of Henry's 'loving subjects' responded to the Injunctions with more
zeal than sense. The resultant iconoclasm, the invasion scare and the
return from a three-year embassy of Stephen Gardiner, the fiercely tradi-

tional Bishop of Winchester, all combined to stall the progress of reform. During Easter 1539 Henry VIII made a very public show of traditional piety. On Good Friday he crept to the cross, a custom which most reformers deemed superstitious. He also received the holy bread and water every Sunday in accordance with ancient custom and forbade, 'upon pain of death', the criticism of controversial ceremonies in London.[11] Then, in June, the Act of Six Articles was introduced.

Initially proposed as a way of resolving the chief points of difference between the two religious camps, the act, in its final form, bore the stamp of orthodoxy. The real presence of the body and blood of Christ in the Eucharist was asserted, priests were ordered to uphold their vows of celibacy and private masses were endorsed. Harsh penalties were prescribed for all those who dared to challenge these tenets. But the Act for the Abolishing of Diversity of Opinion, to use its official, wildly optimistic title, also contained clauses that could be read ambivalently. Auricular confession, for example, was described as 'necessary according to the law of God' in the original draft, but in the final wording of the act it was only considered 'expedient and necessary to be retained and continued, used and frequented in the Church of God', the implication being that it was not enjoined by the Scriptures.[12]

Nor could Henry's subjects be sure of the act's durability, for it was not easy to trust to the King's determination. He may have had his doubts about the existence of purgatory and the efficacy of many traditional customs, but he did not subscribe to the reforming principle of *Sola Fide* either. What this meant, in effect, was that the Supreme Head of the Church of England was unsure about how to attain salvation.[13] One moment he was sanctioning the dissolution of the remaining monasteries and labelling traditional practices as idolatrous, the next he was creeping to the cross and issuing proclamations against heresy; at one stage, priests were being ordered to display an English Bible in their churches and to 'expressly provoke, stir, and exhort every person to read the same'; at another, the King was drafting a proclamation against Bible-reading in public.[14] Little wonder, then, that at around this time Surrey began to question his own faith and respond positively to reform.

There was much about the new religion that was appealing. Whereas Roman Catholicism was full of uncertainties – how many good works were required to escape purgatory? How long would one's spell there be if the quota were not met? – the reformers could guarantee salvation through faith alone. The New Learning, as it was known, had also gained a reputation as a youthful, exciting religion, favoured by those who sought freedom from the constraints of the previous generation. In spite, or more likely because of the Duke of Norfolk's staunch traditionalism, Surrey's sister and brother embraced reform and Surrey may well have been attracted to the independence it seemed to offer. Whatever his reasons, by the summer of 1539 the reformist camp felt that he was ripe for the picking.

At the end of August two notable evangelicals, George Constantyne and John Barlow, rode together from Bristol to Slebech in South Wales. The journey was long and their conversation took many turns before it eventually rested on the negotiations with Cleves. 'I may tell you,' Constantyne confided, 'there is good hope yet that all shall be well enough if that marriage go forward, for the Duke of Cleves doth favour God's Word.'[15] By now, though, Henry VIII's reputation was such that Anne's people requested guarantors for her safety. 'If there should be any pledges sent into Cleves,' said Constantyne, 'in good faith I would the Earl of Surrey should be one of them.' Barlow, a dour redhead, who was 'very moderate in eating and drinking' and shunned the pleasures of the Court in his single-minded pursuit of reform, was taken aback:

'It is the most foolish proud boy that is in England!'

'What, man, he hath a wife and a child and ye call him boy?'

'By God's mercy me think he exceedeth.'

'What then? He is wise for all that, as I hear, and as for pride, experience will correct well enough. No marvel though a young man, so noble a man's son and heir apparent, be proud for we be too proud ourselves without those qualities. But I would wish that he should be one to be sent thither for that he should there be *fully instructed in God's Word* and of experience. For if the Duke of Norfolk were as fully persuaded in it as he is in the contrary, he should do much good, for he is an earnest man, a bold man and a witty [sic] in all his matters.'

'It is true,' Barlow conceded, 'and ye say well in that.'[16]

In the event, the English avoided having to send pledges to Cleves. The marriage treaty was signed on 6 October 1539 and within three months Anne had landed at Deal. Her reception was staged at Greenwich, where the streets had been newly gravelled. Surrey was one of the select group of lords chosen to ride before the King in an 'imposing and honourable' procession.[17] Henry VIII played the host with as much bonhomie as he could muster but inside he was seething. 'I see no such thing in her,' he confided in Lord Russell, 'as hath been showed me of her, and am ashamed that men have so praised her as they have done, and I like her not.'[18] Anne did not sing or play any musical instruments and she only spoke German. Her dark colouring and rough complexion were not to Henry's liking. Nor, he noted with disgust, was 'the hanging of her breasts, and the looseness of her flesh'.[19] But it was too late to back out. 'My Lord,' Henry growled at Cromwell before the solemnisation of the marriage on 6 January 1540, 'if it were not to satisfy the world and my realm, I would not do that I must do this day for none earthly thing.'[20] Henry could not bring himself to consummate the marriage. This was not, he assured his doctors, for want of ability. He had, after all, recently experienced 'duas pollutiones nocturnas in somne' (two wet dreams). Rather he found Anne's body 'in such a sort disordered and indisposed to excite and provoke any lust in him'.[21] Within days of the marriage, Henry was instructing his counsellors to find a way to liberate him from Anne. Cromwell had staked his reputation on the Cleves match; its failure marked the beginning of the end of his supremacy, his religious campaign and, ultimately, his life.

In the meantime, it was important to keep up appearances. In the early spring a proclamation was published throughout Europe. Under the licence of Henry VIII, six gentlemen of England – John Dudley, Thomas Seymour, Richard Cromwell, Thomas Poynings, George Carew and Anthony Kingston – challenged all comers to a tournament to be held at Westminster from the first day of May.[22] It was just the kind of enterprise Surrey relished and he immediately signed up.

Tournaments in the sixteenth century were not just a bit of sport before supper. They were magnificent theatrical productions, rich in drama and steeped in symbolism. This event, coming so soon after the royal marriage, would prove to the European Courts that Englishmen could, in fact, behave like Knights of the Round Table and that outward courtesy, at least, would be extended to the Queen that Henry VIII was so keen to dump. For Surrey the event was of great import. The rule of entry requiring combatants to prove their noble ancestry over a number of generations was no longer strictly applied, but to Surrey the tournament still belonged to the social élite. The tiltyard at Westminster would have evoked memories of 'the gravelled ground' at Windsor where he and Richmond had trained, 'with sleeves tied on the helm, /

on foaming horse, with swords and friendly hearts'.[23] This was no place
for Richard Cromwell, nephew of Thomas, and the other career
courtiers who had issued the challenge. Victory would validate Surrey's
own sense of nobility. Defeat, on the other hand, would imply dishonour
and disgrace.

The first day was scheduled for jousting. Competitors aimed to
shatter their lances on their opponents or, better still, to unhorse them;
he 'who striketh his fellow clean out of the saddle is best worth the
prize'.[24] As the illustration in the Great Tournament Roll of Westminster of Henry VIII jousting in 1511 reveals, the two contestants were
separated by a wooden barrier (plate 24). This had been introduced in
the 1420s in order to prevent collision. Each man wore full armour.
Not only did this restrict his mobility – jousting armour being far
heavier than field armour – but it also impaired his ventilation and
reduced his line of vision to a tiny slit in the visor. This was a necessary inconvenience. When Henry VIII forgot to close his visor for a
joust in March 1524, he received a helmet-full of splinters from a shat-
tered lance that only narrowly missed his eye. Francis I's son Henri,
whom Surrey had befriended in France, would not be so lucky. He died
in 1559 after a lance was drilled into his half-open visor and glided
through his eye and into his brain.

A successful jouster had to be an expert horseman, physically strong
and possessed of a fine sense of balance. It was hard enough to hold
out a long, heavy lance in one hand and a cumbersome shield in the
other, but to wield these objects on a galloping horse against an opponent hell-bent on destruction was a skilled undertaking indeed. Surrey
would have been extremely nervous, therefore, as he made his way into
the stadium at Westminster. As the highest ranked competitor he had
the honour – and the added pressure – of opening the proceedings. The
noise from the grandstands was deafening. Long pennons of arms,
including the Howard silver lion, flowed down from the royal tower
where Henry VIII and Anne of Cleves took their seats. Surrey led the
'Defendants' to the royal box, where they formally received permission
to compete. Then he took up his position at one end of the barrier.
His squire secured the fastenings on his armour, handed him his lance
and closed his visor. Waiting for Surrey at the opposite end, upon a
horse trapped in white velvet, was Sir John Dudley, Captain of the
Challengers. He was the son of Empson Dudley, arguably the most
despised minister of the previous reign. Over a decade older than Surrey,

John Dudley was tall, sturdy and battle hardened, having earned his spurs and a knighthood in the 1523 campaign against France. His prowess at the tilts was well known and he was famous, at home and abroad, for 'high courage'.[25] Surrey, at twenty-three years of age and with no battle experience to speak of, was making his debut at the public joust.

The trumpets sounded. Surrey dug his spurs into his horse and took off, thundering through the sand towards Dudley's charge. Just as the horses began to draw level, Surrey couched his lance and attempted to crunch it into Dudley's breastplate. Whether he succeeded, or Dudley beat him to it, is unknown. The scorecards have not survived, but the chroniclers did record every instance of unhorsing and neither Surrey nor Dudley managed to inflict that particular ignominy on the other.[26]

Surrey ran in the lists seven more times. Never once was he thrown off his horse, but nor did he succeed in unseating his opponent. After a day of rest on Sunday, he returned to the field for the tourney, where the Defendants and Challengers fought on horseback with blunted swords.* Once again Surrey was pitted against Dudley and the two men clashed with such ferocity that they lost their gauntlets.[27] The outcome was honourable as both men remained on their mounts for the duration of the contest. Surrey had done well – very well, in fact, considering his opponent was a man of greater age, bulk and experience. Whether he was satisfied with his performance is another matter. He certainly would have cast envious glances in the direction of Richard Cromwell, who had overthrown two of his opponents and was the undoubted star of the tournament. For the chroniclers, the displays of individual prowess were not as important as the chivalric values of courtesy and largesse that the tournament as a whole had engendered:

> After the said jousts were done, the said Challengers rode to Durham Place, where they kept open household; which said Place was richly behanged, and [there were] great cupboards of plate; where they feasted the King's Majesty, the Queen's Grace and her ladies, with all the Court, and for all other comers that would resort to their said place; where they had all delicious meats and drinks so plenteously as might be, and such melody of minstrelsy, and were served every meal with their own servants after the

---

* In the early days of the tourney, 'virtually no holds were barred (though the use of bolts and arrows seems to have been frowned on).' Keen, *Chivalry*, p. 85.

manner of war, their drum warning all the officers of household against every meal which was done to the great honour of this realm.[28]

Two months later Henry VIII divorced Anne of Cleves.*

Anne had enjoyed the May festivities seemingly unaware of her impending fate. One of her ladies-in-waiting was more knowing. Catherine Howard was the daughter of the Duke of Norfolk's younger brother Edmund, a wastrel who had squandered all his money by the time of his death in 1539. Catherine's mother had died in the late 1520s and, before she had reached her teens, Catherine had been packed off to live with her step-grandmother Agnes, the Dowager Duchess of Norfolk. Agnes owned two great mansions, one at Horsham in Sussex and the other at Lambeth, where Surrey and Norfolk tended to stay when they were in London.

Catherine first appeared at Court at the end of 1539, when her uncle, the Duke of Norfolk, secured a place for her in the Cleves household. Her pretty features and petite frame immediately attracted the King, who was said to have 'cast a fantasy' towards her the moment he saw her.[29] Norfolk realised that Catherine, like Anne Boleyn before her, could be used to revive Howard fortunes at Court. Her looks clearly appealed to the King and she had age on her side. She was naturally vivacious, devoid of guile and pliable in a way Anne Boleyn had never been. She also seemed to be the embodiment of virginal innocence, brought up away from the Court and, so it was thought, unsullied by its vices.

All was not left to chance. Henry VIII was invited to a series of 'feastings and entertainments' at Lambeth and at Stephen Gardiner's home in Southwark. Catherine was given new clothes and a tutorial in 'how to behave' and 'in what sort to entertain the King's Highness'. Henry was smitten and he didn't care who knew. In April 1540 he granted Catherine all the goods and chattels of two indicted criminals and, as the summer approached, the talk at Court was of little other than the prospect of a second Howard Queen.[30]

Norfolk was finally in a position to manoeuvre against Cromwell.

---

* The pretexts for the divorce were Anne's previous engagement to the Duke of Lorraine and her non-consummation with Henry. She raised no objection and her co-operation was rewarded with a generous settlement. She spent the rest of her life in the English countryside, occasionally returning to Court where she was welcomed as Henry VIII's 'beloved sister'. She died in July 1557 and is buried in Westminster Abbey.

Their rivalry was not just about policy; it was personal, it was deadly and it was dirty. Cromwell had tried on several occasions to engineer the destruction of the Howards, most dangerously during the Pilgrimage of Grace and most recently after the execution of the Marquis of Exeter in December 1538, when news had reached Norfolk that Cromwell had examined Exeter's wife 'more straitly of me than of all other men in the realm'.[31] Outwardly Norfolk bore the face of friendship. Indeed he was shamelessly unctuous, assuring his enemy in 1535 that 'you shall ever find me a faithful, assured friend, grudge who will', while in March 1539 he informed Cromwell that it was no longer necessary for him to address him as 'Your Grace' in his letters 'for surely it is not convenient that one of your sort should so do'.[32] All the while, though, Norfolk was biding his time.

Building on the King's keen sense of betrayal over the Cleves match and his suspicions over Cromwell's motives in promoting it, Norfolk and Stephen Gardiner (who hated Cromwell just as much, if not more, than the Duke) laid charges of religious radicalism at Cromwell's door. Had Cromwell's Injunctions, they enquired, not led to dangerous iconoclasm and radical preaching? Was not Cromwell protecting, nay patronising, heretics in Calais and at home? At first it seemed as though Cromwell would escape. On 18 April the King made him Earl of Essex and Lord Great Chamberlain. But the seeds of doubt had been planted in Henry's mind; Gardiner and Norfolk cultivated them with further poison and Catherine Howard did her part, mingling a little sweetness with the gall.

On 10 June 1540 Cromwell entered the Council Chamber for the last time. He was arrested by the Captain of the Guard. The Duke of Norfolk, who had been calmly awaiting Cromwell's arrival, rose from his seat, approached his foe and triumphantly ripped the badge of St George from his collar. Then the King's chief minister, his Vice-Gerent in Spirituals, Chancellor of the Exchequer, Lord Privy Seal and Lord Great Chamberlain, was bundled into a boat and swept off to the Tower. He was charged with the treason of threatening to take up arms in defence of his faith and of Sacramentarianism (the denial of the real presence in the Eucharist), a crime 'which is, if anything can be worse, more heinous than treason'.[33] Other accusations exposed the rank snobbery of the traditional nobility. Cromwell was accused of subverting the natural order by assuming a level of power inappropriate for one of 'very base and low degree'. He had then compounded that crime by treating his social superiors with 'great disdain' and was thus guilty of *scandalum magnatum*, the abuse of the nobility.[34]

Writing from the Tower with a 'heavy heart and trembling hand', Cromwell protested his innocence and begged the King for 'mercy, mercy, mercy'.[35] He did not even get a trial. Condemned by an act of attainder, the method of persecution that he himself had so favoured, Cromwell was executed at Tower Hill on 28 July 1540. Surrey refused to mask his jubilation: 'Now is that foul churl dead, so ambitious of other blood; now is he stricken with his own staff!' Rebuked by his cousin, Sir Edmund Knyvet, for speaking ill of the dead, Surrey retorted that 'new erected men' like Cromwell deserved no respect, for they 'would, by their wills, leave no nobleman on life'.[36]

The same day that Cromwell lost his head, Henry VIII married Catherine Howard. A frisky young filly had replaced the frumpy 'Flanders Mare', and Henry was said to be 'so amorous of her that he cannot treat her well enough and caresses her more than he did the others'. The French ambassador was stunned by the transformation in Henry: 'I, for one, have never seen the King in such good spirits or in so good a humour as he is at present.' There was a new spring in his step, he woke up earlier than usual and hunted every day. In the evenings there was singing and dancing and great feasts; 'nothing is talked of except rejoicings and amusements.'[37]

Catherine behaved, and was treated, like a spoilt child. 'The King,' it was said, 'had no wife who made him spend so much money in dresses and jewels as she did.' Every day Catherine had 'some fresh caprice' and every day Henry indulged it.[38] Nor did Catherine forget her family. Innocently scattered among her requests for clothes and jewels were petitions for treats and favours for her kin. Finally Surrey began to reap what he felt was a long-delayed harvest. On 21 July 1540 the King gave him a purple jacket and doublet, woven with gold and silver tinsel. On 8 September Surrey and his father were appointed conjointly to the stewardship of Cambridge University and in October, he was made a Justice of the Peace for Norfolk. The following spring Surrey was dubbed a Knight.[39] Soon afterwards an even greater distinction was bestowed upon the twenty-four-year-old Earl. On 23 April 1541 he was elected to the Order of the Garter.

Founded in 1348 by Edward III, the Order of the Garter embodied the chivalric ideals of King Arthur's Knights of the Round Table. It comprised twenty-five 'noble and valiant Knights' and the English sovereign. Their patron saint was St George and their motto, which was inscribed on the garter worn around the left leg, was 'Honi soit qui mal y pense' (evil be to him who evil thinks). Windsor Castle was the seat of the Order and in the quire of the Chapel of St George there were twenty-six stalls, thirteen on either side. Each bore the arms of its possessor and was hung with his banner, sword and helmet. To be a Knight of the Most Noble Order of the Garter meant being a 'chevalier sans reproche' and a 'friend, brother and companion' of the King. There was no greater honour in England.

Every year on St George's Day a Chapter of the Order was held and whenever there was a vacancy (by death or disgrace), each Knight proposed nine men for election. The candidate with the most nominations usually qualified for the empty stall, but the ultimate arbiter was the King, who 'shall pronounce him elected who is supported by the most votes *or* whom the sovereign himself shall judge more worthy, more honourable, more useful and more fit for his Kingdom and Crown'.[40] In Surrey's case, every single Knight nominated him and the King, no doubt encouraged by his wife and perhaps also mindful of Surrey's recent exploits at the May tournament, was only too happy to ratify the vote.[41]

Immediately after his election, Surrey was invested with the Garter. He gave a short speech of thanks, took the cross that was offered to him and kissed it. Then the Garter was buckled to his left leg with the words:

> Sir, the most friendly Companions of this Order denominated from the Garter have now admitted you their Friend, Brother and Companion, in faithful testimony of which, they impart and give you the Garter, which God grant that you deservedly receiving it, may rightly wear and use to the glory of God, the honour of the most famous Order and of your own.[42]

Before Surrey could become a fully fledged Knight Companion, he had to take possession of his stall at St George's Chapel. This involved an elaborate ceremony scheduled for 22 May. In the interim, 'for their pastime and disport', he and Sir Thomas Seymour were sent across the Channel to observe Sir William Fitzwilliam, Earl of Southampton, and Lord John Russell quell a border dispute.[43] Niggling squabbles between the French garrison at Ardres and the English garrison at Guisnes were commonplace, but on this occasion the 'taunts and bravadoes' between

the two camps threatened to get out of hand. It had flared up at the
end of 1540 when, according to one English chronicle, 'the French King
made a strong castle at Ardres, and also a bridge over into the English
Pale, which bridge the crew of Calais did beat down, and the Frenchmen
built it up again, but the Englishmen beat it down again.' Henry VIII
and Francis I both sent reinforcements and soon rumours abounded of
great armies arrayed throughout the region.[44]

Surrey and the English delegation arrived in Calais at four o'clock
on 5 May 1541. They immediately began to inspect the town's fortifications, raise musters and send men and munitions over to Guisnes.
Two days later they rode to Guisnes themselves and made a great show
of armed strength. Further inspections were made, the castle and town
were surveyed and a small military parade was held in the town 'in
two bands, with standards, drums and fifes'. Having shown that they
had no intention of shying from battle should the French so provoke
them, the English then made friendly overtures to the French governor,
Monsieur du Biez. Gifts of venison and bacon were exchanged, hunting
and dinner parties were arranged and, one evening, du Biez's servant
was treated to an impressive display of English wrestling. 'We wished
Your Majesty had been there to see them,' Southampton and Russell
wrote to Henry VIII; 'you should have seen one give another such a
hard thwack and fall to the ground that for the time the breath would
out of the body. And yet when he came to himself again, he was ready.'
Within days the status quo was restored. 'Where nothing but war was
talked of,' the French ambassador in London enthused, now 'there is
no mention but of wishing to live at peace.'[45]

On his return to England Surrey went shopping. For his formal installation into the Order of the Garter he needed a blue ceremonial robe
(the mantle), a black velvet cap with feathers, a gold chain of knots
and roses (the collar) and an image of St George designed to hang from
the collar. He also had to buy a helm, crest, surcoat and banner of his
arms to be set over his stall, a stall plate, and a cushion to lay his
mantle and collar upon. Surrey was determined to look good and,
despite his miserable finances, bought a collar that was suitably flamboyant. It weighed thirty-six ounces, six more than the maximum
prescribed by the Statutes of the Order, and the appendant George was
encrusted with ten diamonds.[46]

The day before the ceremony Surrey attended a dinner at Sheen. It
was hosted by Edward Seymour, who had been elected to the Order

earlier in the year. His guests included Surrey's fellow Knight Elect Sir John Gage, the King's deputy for the following day the Earl of Sussex, and the Earl of Rutland, who was charged with assisting Sussex. Over a meal of stockfish, ling, pike, sole, salmon, whiting, plaice and mackerel, Surrey was talked through the following day's proceedings.[47] After dinner they all rode to Windsor Castle.

The next day Surrey was led in procession to St George's Chapel. After the deputy's commission was read out, Surrey was conducted into the Chapter House, where his cloak was removed and replaced with a surcoat 'in token or sign of the most honourable Order you have received'. He was then girded with his sword and led, bareheaded, into the quire. Standing in the lower stalls and supported on either side by a Knight Companion, Surrey placed his right hand on the New Testament and took the oath of allegiance. He swore to 'help, keep, defend and sustain . . . the honour, quarrels, rights and dominions of the King' and to 'well and truly accomplish, and keep, and entertain all the statutes, points, articles and ordinances of the said Order'. This done, he ascended to his stall, which was the fifth on the sovereign's side. The supporting Knights received Surrey's mantle from the Garter herald and placed it over the Earl's shoulders. Then they took his collar and hung it over the mantle with the words:

> To the increase of your honour, and in token of the Honourable Order you have received, take this collar about your neck with the Image of the Holy Martyr and Christ's Knight, St George, by whose aid you, being defended, may pass through the prosperities and adversities of this world; that having here the Victory, as well of your ghostly as bodily enemies, you may not only receive the glory and renown of temporal Chivalry, but also at the last the endless and everlasting reward of Victory.

Finally, Surrey was handed the Book of Statutes and was allowed to put on his cap. He made a low bow to the altar, then to the King's stall, and was formally placed by his supporters into his own stall. The Earl of Surrey was now a full Knight of the Order of the Garter. All that remained was the great Feast of St George held later that day in the castle.[48]

During this period of advancement Surrey was also made cupbearer to the King.[49] He shared the post with Lord Hastings and Sir Francis

Bryan and they took it in turns to attend upon Henry at his meals, ensuring that his cup was always full. It was not a menial role, but a highly valued ceremonial position. Henry VIII was, after all, God's representative on Earth and Supreme Head of the Church of England. Attendance on his person, his 'sacred flesh', was seen as a privilege and an honour.[50] As a member of the King's dining service, Surrey was entitled to a wage and 'bouche of Court' – lodgings wherever the Court happened to be and a provision of candles, fuel, food and drink. Given his perennial lack of funds, this was a welcome perk, but even more valuable was the entrée it gave him to the Court. When previously he had had to rely on royal licence to come to Court, now he had regular access not only to the Court but also to the King and, hopefully, his ear.

Surrey was not the only Howard to be honoured. His sister Mary became a member of Catherine's household, receiving bouche of Court in her own right. Catherine's brother, Charles Howard, was made a gentleman of the King's Privy Chamber and the Duke of Norfolk's brother-in-law by marriage, Robert Radcliffe, Earl of Sussex, succeeded Cromwell as Lord Great Chamberlain. Norfolk himself was increasingly at the King's side, though the French ambassador overstated the case when he claimed that the Duke 'nowadays has the chief management of affairs'.[51] Henry VIII did not allow Norfolk to fill the vacuum left by Cromwell. He had resolved never again to allow one man to achieve the status of a Wolsey or a Cromwell. Instead he kept a much closer eye on the government of his realm. The Act of Precedence of 1539 and the conciliar reforms of 1540 may have increased the aristocratic composition of the Privy Council, but they also emphasised the nobility's reliance on royal favour and succeeded in harnessing noble power ever more tightly to that of the Crown. Thus the Howards were more than ever dependent on the favour of the King at a time when Henry was at his most volatile. On 18 January 1541 the French ambassador, Charles de Marillac, submitted a report to Francis I:

> I do not recollect having ever seen these people so crestfallen as they are at present, for they do not know whom to trust, and the King himself, having offended so many people, mistrusts everyone. There is still another unfortunate circumstance mixed up with the King's irresolution and despondency, which is that whenever he conceives the least suspicion he will go on dipping his hands in blood, from which no good can come in the end.[52]

The most extreme manifestation of this 'irresolution and despondency' had occurred only two days after Cromwell's beheading when three reformers and three conservatives were executed on the same day, the former for heresy, the latter for the treason of remaining faithful to the Pope. 'It was wonderful to see adherents to the two opposing parties dying at the same time,' Marillac wrote, 'and it gave offence to both . . . It is difficult to have a people entirely opposed to new errors which does not hold with the ancient authority of the Church and of the Holy See, or, on the other hand, hating the Pope, which does not share some opinions with the Germans. Yet the Government will not have either the one or the other but insists on their keeping what is commanded, which is so often altered that it is difficult to understand what it is.' According to Marillac, Henry was now so unpredictable that he was changing his mind from breakfast to dinner. He was even said to be blaming his councillors for the destruction of Cromwell, 'saying that, upon light pretexts, by false accusations, they made him put to death the most faithful servant he ever had'.[53]

All this was encouraging news for Cromwell's old followers. Their master may have gone, but the years he had spent packing the royal household ensured that a strong core survived his fall. These men were appalled by the thought of a Howard ascendancy. On 15 September 1540 John Lascelles met with two friends called Jonson and Maxey in the King's Great Chamber. All three were favourers of 'God's holy word' and together they lamented the loss of Cromwell, 'so noble a man which did love and favour it so well'. They discussed Norfolk and Stephen Gardiner's opposition to reform and Maxey exclaimed that the Duke 'was not ashamed to say that he never read of Scriptures nor never would read it and that it was merry in England afore the New Learning came up [and] that he would all things were as it hath been in times past'. Lascelles pondered the implications of these revelations for a while and then approached Mr Smithwick, a colleague who was impatient for reform. 'Be not too rash or quick in maintaining the Scripture,' Lascelles advised, 'for if we would let them [the conservatives] alone and suffer a little time, they would (I doubt not) overthrow themselves standing manifestly against God and their Prince as by manifest conjectures I might perceive.' Lascelles then filled Smithwick in on what Maxey had told him and added another story that he had heard about the Duke. Apparently Norfolk had rebuked a man in the Exchequer for having married a nun. 'My Lord,' the man had replied, 'I know no nuns nor religious folk in this realm nor no such bondage seeing God and the King have made them free.' Norfolk had reacted angrily. Clapping his hand to his heart, he reportedly spluttered: 'By God's body sacred, it will never out of my heart as long as I live!' The implication, as Lascelles and Smithwick took it, was that Norfolk had declared against the dissolution of the monasteries.

The following morning, as Lascelles had no doubt intended, Smithwick scurried to one 'Mr. Hare' and asked him if there might be a case for verbal treason against the Duke. Hare replied 'that it were meet and convenient to declare [Norfolk's words] to the King's Majesty's Council'. Then, as Lascelles later testified, Smithwick came to him 'forthwith' and said 'that if I would not declare them to the King's Council, he would'. Lascelles replied that 'I was as ready to do my duty of allegiance as he' and accordingly submitted his report.[54]

Nothing came of this attempt to destroy Norfolk. In getting Smithwick to do his dirty work, Lascelles had probably feared as much. But he continued to intrigue against the Duke and the conservatives and his conniving eventually paid off, for it was Lascelles who first triggered the enquiry into the behaviour of Catherine Howard.

Catherine had initially revelled in her status as Queen. The gifts, the clothes, the jewels, the new respect, the demands that were actually met, the sycophants, the adoration, the adulation – this was heady stuff for a girl just out of her teens. But with the privileges had come the duties, not least the sharing of the King's bed. Henry was fat, balding and lecherous and his body was in a state of decay. Catherine had to lie beneath this wheezing, sweating hulk as the foetid bandages, saturated with pus from his suppurating ulcers, sponged her legs. Nor was this all she had to endure. Henry's intense mood swings could be frightening. In the spring of 1541, following complications with his ulcers and a nasty fever, Henry fell into a black depression and took himself off to Hampton Court. Not even Catherine was granted access and the music and entertainments arranged for the Lenten festivities were cancelled.

The new season heralded a new disposition. Exhilarated by the prospect of a summer progress to the North of England, Henry became as jolly as he had been at the beginning of the marriage. Catherine, though, had already begun to stray. Throughout the progress she held clandestine meetings with Thomas Culpepper, a Gentleman of the Privy Chamber. Once the King was safely in his bed, Catherine's maid would usher Culpepper up the privy stairs and into her mistress' Chamber. One assignation was even conducted in that most intimate of places, the Stool Chamber, where the Queen's lavatory was housed. Catherine knew she was taking great risks; on one occasion she and Culpepper were almost discovered by the night-watchman. But she persisted with the trysts and even teased Culpepper that 'she had store of other lovers at other doors as well as he'.[55] That Catherine was so brazen may have had something to do with the fact that she had succeeded in deceiving Henry long before Culpepper came onto the scene. For unbeknownst to her husband, Catherine's past had been far from innocent.

Back in the household of the Dowager Duchess of Norfolk, she had enjoyed liaisons with her music teacher, Henry Manox, and a gentleman page, Francis Dereham. She had even welcomed the latter into the Maidens' Chamber, and 'such puffing and blowing' had emanated from her bed that few of her chamber-mates could sleep.[56] The ladies, many of whom experienced similar pleasures, had gossiped, and the men had regaled each other with details of their conquests. 'I know her well enough,' Manox had bragged, 'for I have had her by the cunt, and I know it among a hundred.'[57] But no one dared to spill these tales when Catherine was being courted by Henry. That fact probably led her to believe that no one would do so now she was Queen, and that the risks with Culpepper were worth taking.

Catherine was out of her depth in the murky waters and factional crosscurrents of Henry's Court. She cared not one jot for politics and seemingly thought little of religion either. Yet her position as Queen of England made her involved whether she liked it or not. There was a direct correlation between her royal status and the ascendancy of the Howards and their conservative allies. When John Lascelles heard from his sister about Catherine's activities in the Maidens' Chamber, he immediately informed Archbishop Cranmer, who then turned to Edward Seymour for advice. Both agreed to dig deeper. The royal couple returned from their progress at the end of October 1541. A few days later, on All Saints Day, the King gave a prayer of thanks 'for the good life he led and trusted to lead' with Catherine.[58] The following day he received a note from Cranmer. It told him about Manox and Dereham, but not yet about Culpepper.

Henry refused to give credence to the allegations and initiated a secret investigation to expose the slanderers. Catherine's old chamber-mates now fell over themselves to reveal the truth. Under interrogation,

Manox's bravado dissipated and he swore that while he had enjoyed many liberties with Catherine, he had never slept with her. Dereham, on the other hand, 'confessed that he had known her carnally many times, both in his doublet and hose between the sheets and in naked bed, alleging such witnesses of three sundry women one after another that had lien in the same bed with them when he did the acts'.[59] Even with the knowledge of Catherine's promiscuity, Henry was willing to spare her. The revelations were abhorrent, but they referred to events that had happened before the royal marriage. Then Culpepper's name came up. And that was it.

It is impossible to know whether Catherine and Culpepper had engaged in a full-blown affair. Both denied that it had gone beyond words. But the will was clearly there – 'if I had tarried still in the Maidens' Chamber,' Catherine had told Culpepper, 'I would have tried you' – and their nocturnal trysts pointed to a way.[60] As the investigation proceeded, a letter from Catherine to Culpepper was unearthed: 'I never longed so much for [a] thing as I do to see you and to speak with you . . . It makes my heart to die to think what fortune I have that I cannot be always in your company . . . I would you was with me now that you might see what pain I take in writing to you. Yours as long as life endures, Catherine.'[61] Even if she had not surrendered her body to Thomas, Catherine had clearly given him her heart. This was the bitterest pill for Henry. Cuckolded, betrayed and publicly humiliated, his wrath now knew no bounds.

On 1 December 1541 Dereham and Culpepper were tried and found guilty of treason. Nine days later they were executed at Tyburn and 'their heads set on London Bridge'.[62] The King then turned on the Howards. The Dowager Duchess of Norfolk, her daughter the Countess of Bridgewater, her son Lord William Howard, his wife Margaret and many others from the Duchess' household were tried for misprision (concealment) of treason. All were found guilty and sentenced to perpetual imprisonment and forfeiture of goods.

Norfolk and Surrey were vulnerable. From the moment he received news of his niece's disgrace, Norfolk had done everything possible to disentangle himself from her and prove his loyalty to the King. He had assisted Cranmer in the interrogation of Catherine and had recommended she be burnt alive. He had been one of the chief informers against the Dowager Duchess of Norfolk and had gone to Lambeth in person to ransack Dereham's coffers. Norfolk also officiated at the trial of Dereham and Culpepper and laughed throughout their examinations 'as if he had cause to rejoice'. The French ambassador, Marillac, was disgusted by Norfolk's demeanour and surprised too by Surrey's attendance at the trial and the behaviour of the brothers of Catherine and Culpepper, who paraded around London on their horses. 'Such is the custom of this land,' he informed Francis I, 'and it must be done to show that they do not share the crimes of their relatives and, more importantly, that they are faithful to the King, their sovereign.'[63]

Henry VIII still needed some convincing. In his report, Marillac noted that Norfolk had left Court for Kenninghall, 'which makes people think ill and at least that his influence is much diminished'. Of Norfolk's future, Marillac observed just over a week later, 'many presume ill and none good'.[64] It took a letter of abject grovelling, extreme even by the standards of Henry's Court, to extricate Norfolk from the King's suspicion. It reveals much about the Duke's character, his priorities and his instinct for self-preservation. The 'false and traitorous proceedings' of his imprisoned Howard relatives, Norfolk began, coupled with

the most abominable deeds done by two of my nieces against Your Highness hath brought me into the greatest perplexity that ever poor wretch was in; fearing that Your Majesty, having so often, and by so many of my kin, been thus falsely and traitorously handled, might not only conceive a displeasure in your heart against me and all other of that kin, but also, in manner, abhor to hear speak of any of the same.

Wherefore, most gracious Sovereign Lord, prostrate at your feet, most humbly I beseech Your Majesty to call to your remembrance that a great part of this matter is come to light by my declaration to Your Majesty, according to my bounden duty, of the words spoken to me by my mother-in-law when Your Highness sent me to Lambeth to search Dereham's coffers; without the which I think she had not be[en] further examined, nor consequently her ungracious children. Which my true proceedings towards Your Majesty considered, and also the small love my two false traitorous nieces and my mother-in-law have borne unto me, doth put me in some hope that Your Highness will not conceive any displeasure in your most gentle heart against me that, God knoweth, never did think thought which might be to your discontentation.

Wherefore, eftsoons, prostrate at your royal feet, most humbly I beseech Your Majesty that by such as it shall please you to command, I may be advertised plainly how Your Highness doth weigh your favour towards me;

assuring Your Highness that unless I may know Your Majesty to continue my good and gracious Lord, as ye were before their offences committed, I shall never desire to live in this world any longer, but shortly to finish this transitory life, as God knoweth, who send Your Majesty the accomplishments of your most noble heart's desires.

Scribbled at Kenninghall Lodge, the 15th day of December, with the hand of

Your most humble Servant
and Subject,
T. NORFOLK.[65]

Catherine had no one to protect her now. On 11 February 1542 she was found guilty of treason by an act of attainder. The following day she asked for the block to be delivered to her cell in the Tower. She spent the evening rehearsing her execution. The next morning, just after seven o'clock, she was led from the Tower to the scaffold. All the King's councillors were there apart from the Duke of Suffolk, who was unwell, and the Duke of Norfolk, who was skulking at Kenninghall. Surrey took his father's place and watched as his little cousin, to whom he owed all his recent promotions, placed her neck on the block for the last time.[66]

It is around this time that Surrey is thought to have composed one of his most vitriolic, and autobiographical, poems. Taking the form of a beast fable, it is a thinly veiled attack on the Seymours. They were the kind of recently ennobled family that Surrey resented. He did not regard them as social equals, but, as needs must at the Henrician Court, he had helped his father in soliciting their friendship at the time of Jane Seymour's marriage to Henry VIII and her brother Edward's elevation to the Earldom of Hertford. A marriage had even been proposed between Surrey's sister and Edward's younger brother in 1538 and, although nothing had come of it, cordial relations had been maintained and the two families had dined together frequently.

Edward Seymour had been one of the first to hear Lascelles' allegations against Catherine Howard and he had advised Cranmer to pursue them and reveal all to the King. He could hardly have done otherwise, but Surrey seems to have taken his actions to heart. Surrey's real venom, though, was directed at Seymour's wife Anne, the daughter of Sir Edward Stanhope. She was a beautiful but haughty woman whom

Surrey seems to have been attracted to and repulsed by in equal measure. Once, on 23 December 1539, they had enjoyed dinner *à deux* at Beauchamplace.[67] Surrey's poem reveals that Anne had recently snubbed him, perhaps, as Surrey's first editor suggested, on the dance floor. The poem begins with a narrator surveying the scene:

> A lion saw I there, as white as any snow,
>   which seemed well to lead the race, his port the same did show.
>   Upon this gentle beast to gaze it liked me
>   for still me thought it seemed me of noble blood to be;
>   And as he pranced before, still seeking for a make*
>   as who would say there is none here I trow† will me forsake.[68]

The lion can be identified as Surrey, whose family emblem was the silver or white lion. He 'seemed well to lead the race' – a reference to his position as the Howard heir – and his apparent gentility immediately distinguishes him as one of 'noble blood'. The lion's confident quest for a mate draws him towards a she-wolf:

> A fairer beast, a fresher hue beheld I never none,
>   Save that her looks were fierce and froward eke her grace.

The Stanhope emblem was the wolf and the Seymour country seat was called Wolf Hall. As Anne was twenty years older than Surrey, it may be that he is taking a swipe at her age in his reference to her fresh hue. Or it could be an allusion to the novelty of her husband's Earldom. Anne's 'fierce and froward' temperament was notorious.[69] The wolf rebuffs the lion's gracious advances 'with spite and great disdain'.

> Forthwith he beat his tail, his eyes begun to flame;
>   I might perceive his noble heart much moved by the same.
>   Yet saw I him refrain and eke his rage assuage
>   and unto her thus gan he say when he was past his rage:
>   'Crewell, you do me wrong to set me thus so light
>   Without desert for my good will to show me such despite.
>   How can you thus entreat a lion of the race
>   that with his paws a crowned king devoured in the place?'

* *make*: mate.
† *trow*: trust.

The final line is a reference to the Battle of Flodden in 1513, when Surrey's father and grandfather triumphed against James IV of Scotland. The lion then gives further examples of his race's innate sense of honour. He refers to Lord Thomas Howard, who died in the Tower 'for his assured truth' after his clandestine marriage to Lady Margaret Douglas. He was a 'gentle beast' who willingly sought death 'for loss of his true love'. 'Other there be,' the lion continues in what is surely a reference to the Howards imprisoned in the Tower for the misprision of Queen Catherine's treason, 'whose life to linger still in pain / against their will preserved is that would have died right fain.'

These lines bristle with aristocratic self-justification. Various family members may have been persecuted, the lion argues, but their deeds were honourable. 'But well I may perceive,' he tells the wolf, 'that nought it moved you / my good intent, my gentle heart, nor yet my kind so true.' The wolf lady cannot possibly understand the values of a Howard. She is a common interloper who represents the craven qualities of the Court:

> And thus behold my kind, how that we differ far;
> I seek my foes and you my friends do threaten still with war.
> I fawn where I am fed, you flee that seeks to you;
> I can devour no yielding prey, you kill where you subdue.
> My kind is to desire the honour of the field,
> and you, with blood to slake your thirst of such as to you yield.
> Wherefore I would you wist* that for your coy looks
> I am no man that will be trained nor tangled by such hooks.

The wolf is vicious and cunning. The lion, by contrast, is merciful and fair. He adheres to the ideology of 'noblesse of courage' proper to a Knight of the Garter: 'I will observe the law that nature gave to me / to conquer such as will resist and let the rest go free.'[70] The lion concludes his tirade by warning the wolf against crossing him again: 'And if to light on you my hap so good shall be / I shall be glad to feed on that that would have fed on me.' Then he dismisses her with contempt:

> Since that a lion's heart is for wolf no prey,
> with bloody mouth of simple sheep go slake your wrath I say.

---

* *wist*: knew.

Surrey's poem tells us what he wanted to say rather than what he did say and even then he writes 'with more despite and ire than I can now express'. But is he protesting a little too much? Two of his cousins had been officially condemned as harlots and the Howard name was bespattered with their blood. Many other Howards were languishing in the Tower. They would be pardoned the following year, but no thanks to Surrey's father, who had sold them out to save himself. Norfolk's letter to the King made him no better than the fawning, cowardly she-wolf that the lion savages. Surrey himself had attended the trials of Dereham and Culpepper and had watched the execution of his cousin without objection. His role in the affair was passive, but embarrassing nonetheless. Rewards even came his way in the aftermath of the scandal. Surrey retained his post as Henry VIII's cupbearer and his patent as a Norfolk JP was renewed. In December 1541 he even received a grant from the King for the rectory, manors and possessions of Rushworth College in Norfolk.[71] If the Seymours had drunk innocent blood, then the Howards had allowed them to do so.

In his allegory, Surrey seems to recognise this hypocrisy even as he fights against it. The lion prancing about with contrived chivalric mannerism is a parody. When he beats his tail and flashes his eyes at the wolf, the figure of litotes is employed to expose the pomposity of his reaction: 'I might perceive his noble heart much moved by the same.' The Howard heir, with his inflated ego and arrogant swagger, was in danger of becoming a preposterous figure at Court. Surrey was aware of this, but nevertheless cultivated the image in order to shield himself from his enemies. The poem might be seen as a kind of protective self-satire. The lion's outrage camouflages his insecurity. Attack becomes the best form of defence.

Under the cover of allegory, Surrey could flout convention and convey his malice towards the Seymours and his disgust at the mores of the Court. He could even champion his family's destruction of a crowned king, albeit a Scottish king. He had found, in poetry, a new and exciting form of expression.

POET WITHOUT PEER

Oh, it was a right noble lord, liberality itself, if in this iron age there
were any such creature as liberality left on the earth, a prince in content
because a poet without peer.

Jack Wilton, in mock-praise of the Earl of Surrey, in Thomas Nashe's
parody of Petrarchism, *The Unfortunate Traveller*, 1594

Poetry in the first half of the sixteenth century, as the opening line of
one of Henry VIII's own efforts reveals, was commonly regarded as a
form of 'pastime with good company'.[1] Every courtier worth his salt
was expected to have some skill in 'balet-making'. It was a sign of
refinement, a polite accomplishment, another arrow in the quiver
of courtly excellence. Lyrics were circulated freely – sometimes altered
or augmented in the process – and were often recited or sung, with
varying degrees of success, to a sophisticated coterie of lords and ladies.

Not that poetry was a frivolous exercise. The Court was the heart-
land of politics and society, and its literature was invariably shaped by
that context. Under a dynastic monarchy, especially one in which the
King would marry six times, public and private were inextricably linked.
Consequently the vocabulary employed to express attachment within
both spheres became fused. A suitor would pay court to his mistress,
desiring her favour and professing himself her faithful servant, just as
he would to his master for patronage. When Cardinal Wolsey petitioned
the King for access to the Court in 1527, he expressed himself in terms
that would not have seemed overwrought to his contemporaries: 'There

was never lover more desirous of the sight of his lady, than I am of your most noble and royal person.'² At the Tudor Court, where relationships were governed by 'the common infection of feigned friendship' and where increasingly repressive treason laws ensured that 'for fear no man durst either speak or wink', decorum and discretion were the rule.³ But courtiers found in this culture of 'linguistic borrowing'⁴ a useful way of circumventing, even subverting, the prevailing codes. In the hands of a skilled poet like Sir Thomas Wyatt, the language of love could be deployed to give voice to the tensions inherent in life at Court.

Wyatt's imitations of the works of Francesco Petrarch (1304–74) and his treatment of the theme of unrequited love had a particular resonance in this period, when the fickle favours of the King were constantly sought but seldom attained. In one famous example of Wyatt exploiting the Petrarchan antitheses of attraction and repulsion, hope and despair, power and impotence, his speaker, an honourable suitor, finds himself beguiled by his mistress, but humiliated by her 'strange fashion of forsaking'. He is contemptuous of her 'newfangleness', yet remains drawn to her in spite of himself. It has been suggested that the themes of this poem 'may displace wider frustrations and resentments arising from the contradictions, for male courtiers, inherent in courting itself, an activity perceived in the Henrician period as glamorous and shameful, its rewards both desirable and unstable'.⁵

As a pioneering poet, who introduced new styles and forms to English verse, Wyatt was greatly admired by his contemporaries and by none more than Surrey, who was fourteen years his junior and friends with his son. For Surrey, Wyatt possessed 'heavenly gifts'. He had

> A hand that taught what might be said in rhyme;
> That reft Chaucer the glory of his wit;
> A mark the which, unparfited for time,*
> Some may approach, but never none shall hit.⁶

Wyatt's poems provided lessons in technique and style. They also demonstrated *what might be said in rhyme*. They showed Surrey how to create façades and manipulate language in order to articulate feelings that he had hitherto been forced to suppress. In Surrey's tale of

---

* *unparfited for time*: unperfected for want of time.

the lion and the wolf, for example, the scornful wolf, like Wyatt's lady, represents a 'craven courtly power' that elicits paradoxical emotions of desire and revulsion from her noble suitor.[7] In another poem that draws on Ariosto and Petrarch and is wrought by Surrey in poulter's measure,* the speaker expresses his frustration with the 'wayward ways' of Love. 'Deceit is his delight,' Surrey writes, 'and to beguile and mock / the simple hearts which he doth strike with froward diverse stroke.' The speaker knows that he is entirely dependent on the omnipotent power of Love. In order to survive he has to seek Love's uncertain favour and adapt to his environment, where rivals will seek to undo him. The consequent pressures felt by the speaker are palpable:

> He lets me to pursue a conquest well near won,
> To follow where my pains were spilt or that my suit begun.
>   Lo, by these rules I know how soon a heart can turn
> From war to peace, from truce to strife, and so again return.
>   I know how to convert my will in others lust;
> Of little stuff unto my self to weave a web of trust;
>   And how to hide my harm with soft dissembled cheer,
> When in my face the painted thoughts would outwardly appear.
>   I know how that the blood forsakes the face for dread,
> And how by shame it stains again the cheek with flaming red.
>   I know under the green the serpent how he lurks;
> The hammer of the restless forge I know eke how it works.
>
>   . . . .
>
>   I know to seek the track of my desired foe,
> And fear to find that I do seek; but chiefly this I know:
>   That lovers must transform into the thing beloved,
> And live (alas, who could believe?) with spryte from life removed.
>   I know in hearty sighs and laughters of the spleen
> At once to change my state, my will, and eke my colour clean.
>   I know how to deceive myself withouten help,
> And how the lion chastised is by beating of the whelp.
>
>   . . . .
>
>   The hidden trains I know, and secret snares of love;
> How soon a look may print a thought that never will remove.

* A verse form characterised by alternate lines of twelve and fourteen syllables, so-called because the poulterer would often throw in a couple of extra eggs on the purchase of a second dozen.

That slipper state I know, those sudden turns from wealth,
That doubtful hope, that certain woe, and sure despair of health.[8]

Surrey's poem is ostensibly about love, but to his contemporaries, attuned to the language of the Court, a more political reading was possible. Surrey deliberately deploys the shared terminology of the private and public spheres. The lover pursues 'a conquest well near won'; a heart can turn 'from war to peace, from truce to strife'; the speaker presents his 'suit' just as a courtier would to the King, and he learns, in love as in politics, to hide his passions with 'dissembled cheer'. 'That slipper[y] state' derives from Petrarch, but is also an echo of Wyatt's translation of Seneca, beginning 'Stand whoso list upon the slipper top / of Court's estates', which advises against the 'brackish joys' of the Court and paints a grisly picture of warning for those who intend to run its gauntlet:

For him death grip'th right hard by the crop
That is much known of other, and of himself, alas,
Doth die unknown, dazed, with dreadful face.[9]

When Wyatt died eight months after the execution of Catherine Howard, Surrey composed his elegy and even allowed it to be published.* In the same heroic quatrains that he had used for Richmond's elegy, Surrey outlined Wyatt's inner virtues through a catalogue of his physical attributes. Wyatt's eye, he wrote, 'whose judgement none affect could blind', reflected 'a mind / with virtue fraught, reposed, void of guile.' Above all, Wyatt possessed 'a heart where dread was never so impressed / To hide the thought that might the truth advance.'[10]

---

* During this period much vernacular verse was deeply entrenched within an elitist culture. The dissemination of one's work among the masses was conventionally seen as otiose, undesirable, even shameful, as if the act of printing somehow undermined the virtues of the poem. That Surrey should compose an elegy on Wyatt, a man of a lower social status than he, and then allow it to be published, was a bold acknowledgement and celebration of Wyatt's achievement. W. A. Sessions sees the published elegy as part of Surrey's attempt to establish 'a new cultural hegemony' in which the role of the poet would be raised to an exalted plane. This perhaps overstates the case. Surrey's elegy was undeniably significant, but it was the only poem he allowed to be printed and it was done so anonymously. If he did envisage a revolution for the poet in society, it does not seem to have been a vision that he pursued with any vigour throughout the rest of his life. (See J. W. Saunders, 'The Stigma of Print. A Note on the Social Bases of Tudor Poetry', *Essays in Criticism*, 1/2 (1951); Sessions, 'Surrey's Wyatt: Autumn 1542 and the New Poet', in *Rethinking the Henrician Era*, ed. Herman; Burrow, *LRB*, p. 14.)

Yet Wyatt was always circumspect. A career diplomat and courtier, he knew the power of words and the ease with which they could be twisted. Having been imprisoned for treason in 1541, largely on the basis of words taken out of context, Wyatt was careful not to get burnt again. Even in his paraphrases of the seven penitential psalms,* which he dramatised through a series of narrative prologues, he operated covertly.[11] Wyatt's King David has to undergo a tortuous spiritual journey from confession to contrition and penitence before he can be reborn. He relives his sins; how he wrought destruction upon 'kingdoms and cities' by committing adultery with Bathsheba, and sending her husband Urias to his death. This was potentially risky. Following his Break with Rome Henry VIII favoured the image of David for himself, but as David the pious, David the sage, David the giant-slaying hero.[12] Wyatt had shown that David was also a sinner, and a lustful, murderous one at that. But nowhere did Wyatt identify this sinning David with his own King. His subject was David's spiritual progress; his concern was for issues of faith and salvation. He further distanced himself from any perceived judgement by drawing on a number of other people's biblical translations and by adapting his prologues from the work of the Italian, Pietro Aretino.

But if Wyatt covered his tracks, Surrey determinedly retraced them, leaving his own heavy prints with the kind of reckless abandon and lack of regard for consequences that characterised his whole life. In a sonnet in praise of Wyatt, Surrey claims to have known 'what harboured in that head'.[13] In another he explicitly states the parallels between Wyatt's David and present-day 'princes' and 'rulers'. It is in Wyatt's psalms, Surrey announces:

> Where rulers may see in a mirror clear
> The bitter fruit of false concupiscence,
> How Jewry bought Urias' death full dear.
>   In princes' hearts God's scourge yprinted deep
>   Might them awake out of their sinful sleep.[14]

There was a long classical tradition of associating poetry with prophecy and esteeming the divine character of the poetic gift. Virgil was popularly thought to have been a magician and Dante chose him

---

* Psalms 6, 32, 38, 51, 102, 130, 143 (Vulgate: 6, 31, 37, 50, 101, 129, 142).

as his guide to the mysteries of the afterlife in *The Divine Comedy*. 'Among the Romans,' wrote Sir Philip Sidney, 'a poet was called *vates*, which is as much as a diviner, foreseer, or prophet.'[15] It is the numinous wisdom of Wyatt's verse that Surrey celebrates and assumes for himself in the above poem. Just as the prophet Nathan admonished King David, so Surrey, through the agency of Wyatt's psalms, administers his own providential warning. And his message is dangerously clear. The whole of society pays for the sins of rulers, like David, who abuse their power by succumbing to 'false concupiscence'. Sinful leaders in Surrey's age must look into themselves, as David did, and learn from his penitential example before it is too late for them and for their people.

Tyranny was an issue that preoccupied many of Surrey's contemporaries. Humanists like Thomas More and Thomas Starkey thought long and hard about its nature and effect. Both writers, informed by classical ethics, regarded the salient feature of tyranny to be the subordination of public welfare to private pleasure, and pondered the argument that under such circumstances subjects had a right, even a duty, to depose the tyrant.[16] It is with this contemporary debate in mind that one should read Surrey's next sonnet, about Sardanapalus, the King of Assyria:

Th'Assyrians' King, in peace with foul desire
And filthy lust that stained his regal heart,
In war that should set princely hearts afire
Vanquished did yield for want of martial art.
The dent of swords from kisses seemed strange,
And harder than his lady's side his targe*;
From glutton feasts to soldier's fare a change,
His helmet far above a garland's charge.
Who scarce the name of manhood did retain,
Drenched in sloth and womanish delight,
Feeble of sprete,† unpatient of pain,
When he had lost his honour and his right,
  Proud time of wealth, in storms appalled with dread,
  Murdered himself to show some manful deed.[17]

Sardanapalus, a spineless, effeminate king, has betrayed the code of chivalry. Instead of conquering enemies in war, he allows his people to

* *targe*: shield.
† *sprete*: spirit.

perish while he revels in a corrupt Court. He is the very embodiment of tyranny and has sacrificed 'his honour and his right' to rule over his people. The historical Sardanapalus committed suicide. For Surrey's speaker, it was his only 'manful deed'.

Of course, Surrey is only referring to an ancient, eastern ruler and his sonnet, he could argue, is part of a long literary tradition. Previous writers, including Gower and Lydgate, had also cited Sardanapalus as an *exemplum* of degenerate kingship. But for them Sardanapalus was one in a long list of many; Surrey singles him out.[18] The Earl's use of language – 'foul desire', 'filthy lust', 'glutton feasts' – was risky considering his own King's carnal and culinary appetites. Nor, as we know from Surrey's previous sonnet, was he averse to drawing parallels between past and present rulers. But he stops short of doing so here. Any allusions that might be drawn, Surrey could have argued, between Sardanapalus and Henry VIII are coincidental. It is entirely up to the reader how he interprets the poem just as it was when it first circulated throughout the Tudor Court.

'A poet,' Percy Shelley would write three centuries after Surrey, 'is a nightingale, who sits in darkness and sings to cheer its own solitude with sweet sounds.'[19] Although one should always be wary of seeing self-revelation in poetic fiction, some themes are so prevalent and so intense that they surely point to the preoccupations of the poet.* Above all, as with Shelley's nightingale, is Surrey's sense of isolation. So many of his lyrics build up a picture of harmony and rest only for it to be disturbed by a refrain of alienation; all is well, 'but I', 'save I', 'not I'. Surrey's adoption of the Petrarchan method of contrasting external image with internal effect, allows him, as in the following poem, to convey this sense of loneliness:

---

* From the outset, however, it is necessary to insert a caveat. So much of Surrey's verse is ambiguous, and deliberately so, that interpretation can only be speculative and dependent as much on the reader as the poet. Indeed the nature of manuscript compilation and transmission in Surrey's time suggests that contemporaries could have collaborated in the composition of some lyrics or appropriated them for their own purposes. Furthermore, as many of Surrey's poems are translations or paraphrases of foreign, classical and biblical works, any search for authorial intention within them may invite charges of reductionism. Nevertheless, the choice of source and the way it was adapted by the poet is in itself revealing and themes emerge that suggest, to this reader at least, a degree of self-revelation in Surrey's work. Certainly there is no single way to read his poetry and the presentation of one reading by no means precludes the possibility of others.

If care do cause men cry, why do I not complain?
If each man do bewail his woe, why show I not my pain?
  Since that amongst them all, I dare well say is none
So far from weal, so full of woe, or hath more cause to moan.
  For all things having life sometime have quiet rest;
The bearing ass, the drawing ox and every other beast.
  The peasant and the post, that serve at all assayes,
The ship boy and the galley slave have time to take their ease,
  Save I, alas, whom care of force doth so constrain
To wail the day and wake the night continually in pain;
  From pensiveness to plaint, from plaint to bitter tears,
From tears to painful plaint again; and thus my life it wears.
  No thing under the sun that I can hear or see,
But moveth me for to bewail my cruel destiny.
  For where men do rejoice, since that I cannot so,
I take no pleasure in that place, it doubleth but my woe.
  And when I hear the sound of song or instrument,
Me think each tune there doleful is and helps me to lament.
  And if I see some have their most desired sight,
Alas, think I, each man hath weal save I most woeful wight.
  Then as the stricken deer withdraws himself alone,
So do I seek some secret place where I may make my moan.
  There do my flowing eyes show forth my melting heart,
So that the streams of those two wells right well declare my smart...[20]

The poem is about the speaker's longing for his absent lady – Surrey's wife Frances, some have suggested, though there is no way of knowing – and it concludes with a statement of constancy. Despite the anguish of separation, the speaker will stand fast to his lady, 'yea rather die a thousand times than once to false my faith'. He will serve her till his last breath and then 'bequeath my wearied ghost to serve her afterward'.

A sonnet of Surrey's beginning 'Set me whereas the sun doth parch the green', concludes with a similar resolution. Through a series of Petrarchan antitheses the speaker challenges his lady to test his fidelity. She can subject him to any extreme – of temperature, status, weather, age, health, 'in earth, in heaven, or yet in hell, / In hill, in dale, or in the foaming flood; / Thrall, or at large, alive whereso I dwell' – and he will stay true to her:

Yours will I be, and with that only thought
Comfort myself when that my hap is nought.[21]

The speaker's confidence in his own integrity, his inner virtue, consoles him in the face of life's cruel tests. Whatever happens, he will never change; he will always uphold the ideals of constancy and fidelity proper to the code of chivalry. Indeed it is these very values that have reduced him to such a febrile state. If he were more like others, more prone to slippage, then he would not suffer so. This is his 'cruel destiny'. Much of Surrey's poetry, like his self-styled public image, sets out to champion this solipsistic representation of the isolated but noble hero.[22]

All his life Surrey played a role: the son of the Duke of Norfolk, the Howard heir, the friend of the Duke of Richmond, the cousin of two Queens. He was expected to fulfil a pre-ordained plan created for him by others. Even his Christian name was a reminder that he existed for the sake of his family and King. The dedication sent to him when he was a fifteen-year-old in France had declared, 'we have great hope that you will be like your father and grandfather'.[23] Such high expectations invariably carried concomitant pressures. 'If a gentleman strays from the path of his forebears,' Castiglione had warned, 'he dishonours his family name and not only fails to achieve anything but loses what has already been achieved.'

> Noble birth is like a bright lamp that makes clear and visible both good deeds and bad, and inspires and incites to high performance as much as fear of dishonour or hope of praise; and since their deeds do not possess such noble brilliance, ordinary people lack both this stimulus and the fear of dishonour; nor do they believe that they are bound to surpass what was achieved by their forebears. Whereas to people of noble birth it seems reprehensible not to attain at least the standard set them by their ancestors.[24]

Surrey's vaunting of a noble identity, in life and in poetry, is, in part, his attempt to convey the requisite 'brilliance' and stave off the 'fear of dishonour'. But he struggled to uphold the image under the 'slippery' conditions of the Henrician Court and the constant restlessness that pervades his work may be a symptom of his search for a persona that will ease his anxiety, for a natural identity as opposed to a carefully crafted façade. In his extended dramatic soliloquy, 'The sun hath twice brought forth the tender green', Surrey's lover finds himself out of step with nature:

> . . . What cold again is able to restore
>   My fresh green years that wither thus and fade?
> Alas, I see nothing to hurt so sore
>   But time sometime reduceth a return;
>   Yet time my harm increaseth more and more,
> And seems to have my cure always in scorn.
>   Strange kind of death, in life that I do try:
>   At hand to melt, far off in flame to burn;
> And like as time list to my cure apply,
>   So doth each place my comfort clean refuse.
>   Each thing alive that sees the heaven with eye
> With cloak of night may cover and excuse
>   Himself from travail of the day's unrest,
>   Save I, alas, against all others use,
> That then stir up the torment of my breast
>   To curse each star as causer of my fate.
>   And when the sun hath eke the dark represt
> And brought the day, it doth nothing abate
>   The travail of my endless smart and pain.[25]

Surrey's speaker seems estranged not only from his lady, not only from society, but also from his own sense of self. He longs for the solitude of the night so that he can lament 'more covertly' and 'withdraw from every haunted place':

> And with my mind I measure pace by pace
>   To seek that place where I my self had lost.

This image of the tortured poet, losing his bearings in the landscape of his memory, is a far cry from the self-confident, brash young man that the majority of Surrey's contemporaries supposed him to be.

An outward manifestation of this conflict between self-assertion and self-doubt can be seen in Surrey's portraits. He sat more often than any other Tudor courtier.[26] In each sitting, he assumed a different guise: there is Surrey the pensive poet dressed in black; Surrey the military commander in his red sash; Surrey the bohemian artist with an unkempt beard; Surrey in profile, bare-headed like a Roman emperor; Surrey the urbane cosmopolitan, clad in Italian fashions, adorned with the insignia of the Garter and wrought in the Mannerist style of Fontainebleau. There is a natural flamboyance, even narcissism, to this role-playing, but there is also something sad about it, as if Surrey truly believed that if he reinvented himself enough times, he might yet be able to find himself.

Some of his most powerful lyrics are those that assume the voices of women abandoned by their lovers. He is extraordinarily adept at conveying their sense of loss and helplessness and it is possible that he found in this gender-swapping a cathartic outlet for his own suppressed feelings of vulnerability and passivity. Like sixteenth-century women, Surrey had to conform to a stereotype; his literary ventriloquism allowed him, if only momentarily, to alleviate the pressure of having to play the role of the aristocratic alpha male at Court. In other lyrics, he comes close to hinting that his high calling might be more of a curse than a privilege. In an inventive paraphrase of psalm 73, written towards the end of his life, Surrey's speaker, a member of God's 'elect', ultimately triumphs through faith, but only after he has suffered a profound crisis of faith, brought on by the prosperity of the wicked:

> For I am scourged still, that no offence have done,
> By wrath's children; and from my birth my chastening begun.
>   When I beheld their pride and slackness of thy hand,
> I gan bewail the woeful state wherein thy chosen stand.[27]

In another biblical translation, this time of the second chapter of Ecclesiastes, the speaker is wistful for 'the idle life / that never charged was with care, nor burdened with strife',[28] while in a beautiful sonnet translation of one of Martial's epigrams, the poet advocates the Golden Mean:

> . . . The happy life be these, I find:
> The riches left, not got with pain;
> The fruitful ground; the quiet mind;
> The equal friend; no grudge nor strife;
> No charge of rule nor governance;
> Without disease the healthful life;

The household of continuance;
The mean diet, no delicate fare;
Wisdom joined with simplicity;
The night discharged of all care . . .[29]

Other writers, most notably Wyatt, also sought 'the quiet mind', but it proved more elusive for Surrey with the light of nobility constantly shining upon him, always ready to illuminate his failings. His fellow courtier Ralph Vane recognised this in the postscript of a letter to Henry Knyvet in 1543, where he expressed his wish for 'honour, long life and quiet minds' to Lady Margaret Douglas, to Surrey's sister Mary, 'and no less to my Lord of Surrey'.[30]

Surrey's most celebrated literary achievement is his translation of Books II and IV of the *Aeneid*. Virgil's tale is epic, but at its heart is the very human story of one man's struggle to fulfil his destiny in a time of uncertainty. In his Windsor elegy Surrey saw himself, like Aeneas, as a 'son of Troy' and, like Aeneas, he found himself tested by extremes of fortune and conflicts of loyalty once his childhood idyll had been destroyed. In Book VIII, Aeneas shoulders the great shield upon which Vulcan has hammered the future deeds of Aeneas' descendants. It was a burden which the Howard heir would have recognised only too well.

It is interesting to speculate why Surrey only translated Books II and IV of the *Aeneid* (if, indeed, this is the case and the other books were not translated by him and subsequently lost). The former tells the story of the fall of Troy, the latter of Aeneas' desertion of Dido and her subsequent suicide. It is possible that Surrey was drawn to the idea of the noble but isolated hero and to the theme of female abandonment as he seems to have been in some of his other lyrics, but ultimately it can only ever be speculation. There are so many reasons why Surrey may have undertaken his translations. He may have wanted to honour his King as Virgil had honoured Emperor Augustus; he may have wanted to impress his peers by taking on the two best-known books of the greatest work of 'the King of Latin poets'.[31] He may have been specifically attracted by Virgil's classical hexameters and wanted to represent them in English; Books II and IV, the most intense sections of Virgil's work, certainly tested his artistry in this respect. On the other hand, Surrey had read Gavin Douglas' Scottish *Eneados*, a work on which he drew for his own version, and he may, as one critic has suggested,

have tackled the *Aeneid* as a way of bettering the Scots as his ancestors had done at Flodden.[32] In Book VI, Virgil wrote that poets of true
integrity 'civilised life by the skills they discovered'.[33] Whatever Surrey's
motives in translating Books II and IV of the *Aeneid*, he too discovered an extraordinary skill.

Surrey's translation technique had been well honed since his early
schooling at Kenninghall. *Imitatio* – the imitation of the Classics –
was one of the most valued aspects of the humanist curriculum. It
served a didactic purpose in teaching the moral truths of antiquity and
an artistic one in developing the rhetorical skills necessary for
eloquence. John Clerke, the Duke of Norfolk's secretary, dedicated one
of his own attempts at 'traduction' to Surrey in 1543. In his preface,
Clerke praises Surrey for keeping to the spirit of his sources and
announces that his own attempt will, 'according to your accustomed
fashion, regard and consider the witty devise of the thing, the manner
of locutions, the wise sentences and the subtle and discreet answers
made on both parties.'[34]

This organic approach is evident in Surrey's Virgilian translations,
where he attempts to communicate the effect of the *Aeneid* by
consciously imitating the author's form and style. Not only did Surrey
adopt Virgil's phrasal units and verse paragraphs, his syntax and many
of his rhetorical patterns, but he also strove to approximate Virgil's
diction and concision.[35] It was largely this fidelity to his author's means
as well as his meaning that prompted Thomas Warton in 1781 to hail
Surrey as 'the first English classical poet'.[36] It also led Surrey towards
a startling innovation. For in attempting to represent Virgil's classical
hexameters, and thereby his heroic style, Surrey introduced blank verse
to English poetry.[37]

The Italians and the French had previously experimented with
unrhymed verse (Surrey was certainly influenced by Italian *versi sciolti*
and had probably read Alamanni's *Opere Toscane*, which was published
during Surrey's sojourn in France), but poetry without rhyme or structural alliteration was alien in England. When Surrey's translation of
Book IV was first published seven years after his death, the printer
called it 'a strange metre', referring not only to its perceived oddness
but also to its foreign nature.[38] Yet Surrey's verse paragraphs of iambi-
cally patterned pentameters, enhanced as they are by a range of prosodic
variants and rhetorical devices, maintain rhythm without the need for

rhyme. Through plays of alliteration (rhetorical rather than structural), classical devices like *anastrophe* and *asyndeton*, the use of 'phonetic echoes' and differing levels of accent, and the occasional introduction of run-on lines, trochees and varied caesuras, Surrey captures much of the dignity, fluidity and momentum, if not quite the sonority, of Virgil's original.[39] Consider, for example, the following extract from Book IV. Aeneas has been forced to choose his duty over his love for Dido and has abandoned her on the shores of her native Carthage. Her despair drives her to suicide:

But trembling Dido all eagerly now bent
Upon her stern determination,
Her bloodshot eyes rolling within her head,
Her quivering cheeks flecked with deadly stain,
Both pale and wan, to think on death to come,
Into the inward wards of her palace
She rusheth in, and clam up as bestraught
The burial stack, and drew the Trojan sword
Her gift sometime, but meant to no such use.
Where when she saw his weed* and well knowen bed,
Weeping a while, in study gan she stay,
Fell on the bed, and these last words she said:
Sweet spoils, whiles God and destiny did permit,
Receive this spirit, and rid me of these cares.
I lived and ran the course fortune did grant,
And under earth my great ghost now shall wend.
A goodly town I built, and saw my walls,
Happy, alas too happy, if these coasts
The Trojan ships had never touched aye.
   This said, she laid her mouth close to the bed.
Why then (quoth she) unwroken† shall we die?
But let us die for thus, and in this sort
It liketh us to seek the shadows dark.
And from the seas the cruel Trojan eyes
Shall well discern this flame, and take with him
Eke these unlucky tokens of my death.
As she had said, her damsel might perceive

* *weed*: clothes.
* *unwroken*: unavenged.

Her with these words fall pierced on the sword,
The boiling blood with gore and hands imbrued.[40]

Surrey's translation is raw and unperfected, but there is much here
that anticipates the progress of later writers and it is a tribute to Surrey's
creative foresight that his 'strange metre' is now considered the staple
of the long English poem and much verse drama. It is the metre of
Shakespeare's *Hamlet*, Marlowe's *Doctor Faustus* and Milton's *Paradise
Lost*. It is the medium through which any shade of sentiment can be
expressed and sustained. Towards the end of the nineteenth century
J. A. Symonds wrote:

> English blank verse is, perhaps, more various and plastic than any other
> national metre. It is capable of being used for the most commonplace and
> the most sublime utterances; so that, without any alteration in the vehicle,
> we pass from merely colloquial dialogue to strains of impassioned soliloquy,
> from comic repartee to tragic eloquence, from terse epigrams to elaborate
> descriptions . . . There is no harmony of sound, no dignity of movement,
> no swiftness, no subtlety of languid sweetness, no brevity, no force of
> emphasis beyond its scope. In hearing good blank verse, we do not long
> for rhyme; our ears are satisfied without it; nor does our sense of order and
> proportion require the obvious and artificial recurrence of stanzas, when
> the sense creates for itself a melodious structure, and is not forced into the
> mould of any arbitrary form. So much can hardly be said for any other
> metre.[41]

Although his most famous, blank verse was not Surrey's only creation.
As we have seen, he invented the so-called 'Shakespearian' or 'English'
sonnet, as well as the innovative heroic quatrains that lent themselves
to a new genre of personal elegy. Surrey also experimented with other
forms, including unrhymed hexameters, poulter's measure, sapphics and
the *frottola, strambotto* and *capitolo* of Italy. He composed songs and
sonnets, elegies and epitaphs, orations, verse epistles, satires, epigrams,
biblical paraphrases and epic translations. As one would expect from
anything experimental, not all Surrey's attempts are successful. 'Of thy
life, Thomas', for example, an adaptation of Horace's ode on the Golden
Mean, has none of the fluidity of the classical epigram that Surrey
translated from Martial. Instead the imagery is petrified within a thicket
of Latinised inversions and mangled syntax.[42] H. A. Mason, who

regarded Surrey as a mere foil for Wyatt's 'isolated superiority', criticised Surrey's resort to 'the infernal jog-trot' of poulter's measure and
claimed that it led him 'away from the language of passion into an
artifice that makes only for banality and monotony'.[43] Other critics
dispraised Surrey's Virgilian translations for being too regular, too stiff,
and consequently too formal; 'It is Virgil in corsets,' C. S. Lewis memorably wrote.[44] Indeed for Lewis, none of Surrey's compositions, not
even his intensely vivid elegies, could save the period from being the
'Drab Age' of English poetry.

Yet the sense of order and proportion that Surrey brought to vernacular verse was seen as a necessary virtue in his time. By the beginning
of the Tudor period the English language had experienced monumental
phonological changes. Not only had the old inflectional system and the
syllabic final 'e' disappeared, but new words had been introduced, many
of which were of Latin origin or Anglicised versions of French, the
original language of the Court. Chaucer's Middle English, and with it
much of his prosody, fell into desuetude. Pronunciation grew chaotic,
versification unsettled, and much of the ensuing poetry was diffuse and
inelegant.[45] There was a need for the kind of dignity and measure that
was inherent in classical verse and had been developed along classical
lines on the Continent.

This Surrey appreciated perhaps better than any of his contemporaries, even Wyatt. By rejecting the 'aureate and mellifluate' in favour
of more moderate diction, he contributed to the evolution of a clearer,
more natural form of discourse.[46] In his smoother, steadier metres
(particularly his fourth syllable caesural pattern), he encouraged the
prosodic standards of the next generation. He was painstaking in his
method of composition. In Surrey's poems, George Turberville observed
in 1567, 'each word in place with such a sleight is couched, / Each
thing whereof he treats so firmly touched.' It was this precision, this
control of form and concern for context, balance and total effect that
was Surrey's peculiar strength.[47] Mason and Lewis may not have
approved, but many of Surrey's immediate beneficiaries did. 'What
should I speak in praise of Surrey's skill?' Turberville enquired,

Unless I had a thousand tongues at will;
No one is able to depaint at full,
The flowing fountain of his sacred skull.

. . . .

A mirror he the simple sort to train,
That ever beat his brain for Britain's gain.[48]

George Puttenham celebrated Surrey as a pioneer, who 'greatly polished our rude & homely manner of vulgar Poesie, from that it had been before'; John Cheke praised 'the happy head of wit, the tongue well set to speak / the skilful pen in hand to paint the wit's device'; while for Thomas Churchyard,

> More heavenly were those gifts he had, than earthly was his form;
> His corpse too worthy for the grave, his flesh no meat for worm.
> An Earl of birth; a God of sprite, a Tully* for his tongue,
> Me think of right the world should shake, when half his praise were
>   rung.[49]

Because Surrey was the heir to one of the noblest families in England, his legacy was magnified. He was, according to the antiquarian William Camden, 'first among the nobility of England [who] conjoined the honour of learning to the honour of high parentage'.[50] This combination proved irresistible to later editors. On 5 June 1557 Richard Tottel issued the first printed anthology of English verse. It contained 271 poems by various authors, only 40 of which were attributed to Surrey.[†] Nevertheless, Tottel gave Surrey top billing, entitling his anthology, *Songes and Sonettes, written by the ryght honorable Lorde Henry Haward late Earle of Surrey, and other*. In his preface, Tottel praised 'the honourable style of the noble Earl of Surrey' and exhorted his 'unlearned' readers 'to purge that swine-like grossness, that maketh the sweet majoram not to smell to their delight'.[51]

His strategy succeeded. The *Miscellany* was an instant best-seller, going through nine editions (with omissions and additions) in thirty years. It became the 'golden treasury' of English lyricism and inaugurated a blitz of anthologies, many with such extravagantly alliterated titles as *The Paradise of Dainty Devices* (1576), *A Gorgeous Gallery of Gallant Inventions* (1578) and *The Arbor of Amorous Devices* (1597). Shakespeare owned a copy of Tottel's *Songes and Sonettes* and incorporated one of the poems into the gravedigger's song in *Hamlet*.

---

* *Tully*: Cicero.

† Surrey wrote around 55–60 poems in total. The figure is imprecise because the authorship of some is uncertain.

In *The Merry Wives of Windsor*, Master Slender 'had rather than forty shillings I had my Book of *Songes and Sonettes* here'. According to the latest editor of Tottel's *Miscellany*, 'the beginning of modern English verse may be said to date from its publication in 1557.'[52]

Thus Surrey became the face of English poetry as marketed by Tottel and his followers. But this was a distinctly polite and romantic brand of poetry, one that can certainly be applied to Surrey's work, but not exclusively so. Not only did Tottel omit all Surrey's biblical and Virgilian translations in the *Songes and Sonettes*, but he also revised and 'polished' his poems and gave them artificial titles, fashioning an image of Surrey as a noble Petrarchan who penned lyrics to win the hearts of fair ladies.[53] It proved remarkably resilient and was reinforced countless times in the Elizabethan age, most notably by Thomas Sackville, Philip Sidney and George Puttenham. The latter even assumed in *The Arte of English Poesie* that Surrey had travelled to Petrarch's fatherland in order to acquire 'the sweet and stately measures and style of the Italian Poesie'.[54] The image was further conflated by Thomas Nashe in *The Unfortunate Traveller* (1594), where the incidents of Surrey's life were seized upon and mythologised. Surrey's prowess at the tournament in May 1540 gave enough truth behind the lie that he was the most skilled knight in Europe. The single sonnet to Lady Elizabeth Fitzgerald was developed into an epic love story. Nashe's novel was a burlesque; he was ridiculing the pedestal upon which Surrey had been placed and the romantic tradition he was thought to embody. But Nashe's successors took his account at face value. 'Who has not heard of Surrey's fame?' Sir Walter Scott enquired in his *Lay of the Last Minstrel* of 1805:

His was the hero's soul of fire,
And his the bard's immortal name,
And his was the love, exalted high
By all the glow of chivalry.[55]

It is not necessary to buy into the artificial branding of Surrey to appreciate his role in the development of English poetry. The beauty of his poems lies in the occasional nature of their composition and the plurality and ambiguity of their motives, not in one all-encompassing, Geraldine-worshipping impulse. He did indeed draw inspiration from Europe, but also from the native tradition; he penned conventional love lyrics, but also adopted female voices and celebrated male bonding. He could write with studied grace, but also produced sparks of unrestrained vitriol, class anger, religious zeal and political suggestiveness.

By experimenting with native forms and styles and by adapting classical and foreign ones to the vernacular, Surrey discovered new avenues through which he could articulate his conflicting emotions. In this way, he helped lay the groundwork for much of what was to follow. Shakespeare's sonnets and plays, for example, or the blank verse of Milton and Tennyson, or Gray's elegy of heroic quatrains, showed what could be achieved when Surrey's innovations were taken to the next level.

THE FURY OF RECKLESS YOUTH

Rightly to be great
Is not to stir without great argument,
But greatly to find quarrel in a straw
When honour's at the stake.

Hamlet, Act 4, scene 4, lines 53–6

If poetry prescribed a kind of therapy for Surrey, an outlet for his frustrations and a means of self-discipline, sometimes his emotions were just too powerful and spontaneous to be confined to literary form. In the summer of 1542, when Surrey was twenty-five, the 'foolish proud boy' in him resurfaced. On 13 July the Privy Council issued an order to the Warden of Fleet Prison 'to receive the Earl of Surrey to remain there prisoner during the King's pleasure, having two of his servants to attend upon him, and to suffer none to resort to banquet with him.'[1]

As with his first confinement, the exact circumstances leading up to Surrey's imprisonment are obscure. An entry in the Privy Council register reveals that it concerned a quarrel with one 'Jhon a Legh'. That Surrey's offence occasioned an imprisonment strongly suggests that he physically assaulted Legh or, as is sometimes assumed, challenged him to a duel within the environs of the Court. There are so many incidences and variants of the name Jhon a Legh in the official documents that it is impossible to uncover the identity of this man with absolute certainty. However, one likely candidate does emerge from the mass of index entries. John Leigh of Stockwell – whose surname was variously spelt

Lee, Legh, Leigh, a Lee, a Leghe, a Leigh, a Ligh and a Leyghe – was forty in 1542 and a half-brother of the late Queen Catherine Howard (their mother Jocasta married Edmund Howard after the death of her first husband Ralph Leigh).[2] The Leighs came from Stockwell in South London and belonged to the same Lambeth parish – St Mary's – as the Howards. Their respective family chapels were both founded in 1522 and faced each other on the north and south sides of the church.

John himself was an enigmatic fellow. He seems to have grown up at the English Court and served Cardinal Wolsey for a time. Following the Break with Rome he stayed loyal to the Pope and fled to Europe. According to his epitaph, he travelled widely and was 'to sundry countries known'.[3] In the first year of Edward VI's reign, Leigh would be committed to Fleet Prison and only released on the condition, upon pain of a £2,000 fine, that he remain in England. Interestingly, one of Leigh's guarantors was Thomas Pope, the same man who had accused the Duke of Norfolk of complicity with the Pilgrims of Grace in 1537.[4] Notwithstanding the conditions of his bond, Leigh resumed his travels and was imprisoned in the Tower on his return.[5] The accession of Queen Mary in 1553 heralded an upturn in his fortunes. He was, according to the French ambassador, a great favourite of the Queen and very familiar with her.[6] The day after Mary's coronation, Leigh was knighted, but when Mary was succeeded by her sister Elizabeth in 1558, he fled overseas once again.[7]

During his earlier travels in the 1530s Leigh had spent some time in Rome with Reginald Pole, Henry VIII's outlawed enemy.[8] On his return to England in May 1540, Leigh was sent to the Tower and interrogated by the Privy Council. A letter survives in the British Library in which Leigh gives a detailed account of the conversations he admitted to having had with Pole.[9] There is no mention of Surrey, nor of any Howard, but it is nevertheless possible that Leigh was questioned about Howard involvement with Pole just as the Marquis of Exeter's wife had been when her husband was executed for his dealings with Pole two years earlier. Leigh does say in his letter that he had previously relayed other information about his links with Pole to the Council, and throughout his sojourn in Italy he had maintained contact with Thomas Cromwell and may even have acted as his agent.[10] According to Edmund Harvel, Leigh was not a malicious man, but was guilty of 'weakness of reason and imprudency in his government'.[11] This assessment is borne out by his later meddling in Queen Mary's marriage negotiations in 1553 and by his future moonlighting as an informant for the French ambassador.[12]

At the beginning of 1542 a Venetian called Pasqual had been ordered to leave England on account of 'unfitting words lewdly spoken to the London Watch touching the King's Highness'.[13] It has been suggested that this man might be the same 'Pasquil, an Italian', who later served in Surrey's household as a jester, but was suspected by the Earl's enemies of being a spy.[14] Surrey was accused four years later of having another servant who 'had been in Italy with Cardinal Pole, and was received again [by Surrey] at his return'.[15] Had Pasqual's deportation prompted Leigh to slander Surrey? Could he have suggested that Surrey had had dealings with the traitor Pole? Or perhaps Leigh had accused the Howards of turning a blind eye to Catherine Howard's wantonness, thereby tarnishing the reputations of all those, including the Leighs, associated with her. Whatever it was that Leigh said or did to provoke Surrey, the Privy Council decreed that the Earl's reaction was in breach of the law and on 13 July 1542, exactly five months after the execution of Catherine Howard, Surrey was languishing in the Fleet.

Once known as the 'Gaol of London', the Fleet was the city's oldest prison. It was situated on the east side of what is now Farringdon Street on the north-eastern corner of Ludgate Circus. In Surrey's time it lay just outside the city walls, on the bank of the Fleet – the river, now bricked in, that dissected Westminster and the City. The river served as the repository for all manner of filth; it received the citizens' rubbish and sewage, the discharge of the tanneries and the breweries, the carcasses from the slaughterhouses and even the odd corpse. Fever-bearing mists rose from its frothy surface and it was said that the miasma was so noxious that some of the prison's inmates had died from it.

On entering this wretched place, Surrey erupted with 'the fury of reckless youth'. Without delay he dispatched his servant, William Pickering, to every member of the Council with a demand for his immediate release. The Council made it clear they had no truck with Pickering and that Surrey's lack of humility would only impair his prospects of liberty. On 25 July Surrey tried again, this time with a formal letter to the Council. Ostensibly it was a humble petition for release. He assured the Council that his will was 'conformable and contented with the quiet learning of the just reward of my folly'. He accepted 'that a Prince offended hast none other redress upon his subject but condign punishment, *without respect of the person*'. Here Surrey betrays his feigned contrition, his inference being that the Earl of Surrey should not in fact be so treated. Evidently he considered it somewhat infra dig to have to submit to the Council and there are strong undertones of mock sincerity and self-justification throughout the letter. 'My Lords,' Surrey continued,

> if it were lawful to persuade by the precedent of other young men reconciled, I would affirm that this might sound to me a happy fault: by so gentle a warning to learn how to bridle my heady will, which in youth is rarely attained without adversity. Where might I, without vaunt, lay before you the quiet conversation of my passed life, which (unstained with any unhonest touch, unseeming in such a man as it hath pleased God and the King to make me*) might perfectly promise new amendment of mine offence.
>
> Whereof, if you doubt in any point, I shall humbly desire you that during my affliction (in which time malice is most ready to slander the innocent) there may be made a whole examination of my life; wishing, for the better trial thereof, rather to have the time of my durance redoubled and so (declared and well tried as unsuspected) by your mediations to be restored to the King's favour than condemned in your grave heads [and] without answer or further examination to be quickly delivered; this heinous offence always unexcused, whereupon I was committed to this so noisome prison whose pestilent airs are not unlike to bring some alteration of health.

Surrey then beseeched the Council to petition the King 'as well for his favour as for my liberty' or, failing that, for a transfer 'into the country, to some place of open air'. He added that separation from the King was 'unto every loving subject, *specially unto me*' no less than 'a living death'.

> Finally, albeit no part of this my trespass in any way to do me good, I should yet judge me happy if it should please the King's Majesty to think that this simple body [that] rashly adventured in the revenge of his own quarrel, shall be without respect always ready to be employed in his service.[16]

---

* This is a reminder to the Council that Surrey had recently been installed as a Knight of the Order of the Garter.

This profession of fidelity and zeal for active service seems to have softened Henry VIII's heart. Four days later the Warden of the Fleet was ordered to deliver Surrey to the Court at Windsor Castle. On 1 August 1542 the Earl was bound by a recognisance of ten thousand marks against committing 'by himself, his servants or any other at his procurement, any bodily displeasure either by word or deed to Jhon a Legh esquire or to any of his'.[17] A few days later Surrey was formally released and, the following month, he found himself on the road to Scotland.[18]

Ever since the Wars of Independence (1296–1328), English kings had squabbled and fought with their northern counterparts. Henry VIII and his nephew, James V of Scotland,* were no different. The English looked down on their neighbours with undisguised contempt. A stanza from Richard Grafton's verse dedication of Harding's *Chronicle* (1543) to the Duke of Norfolk is typical of the English attitude to the Scots:

For the Scots will aye be boasting and crakyng,
Ever seeking causes of rebellion;
Spoils, booties and preades ever taking,
Ever sowing quarrels of dissension;
To burn and steal is all their intention
And yet as people, whom God doth hate and curse,
They always begin, and ever have the worse.[19]

In January 1537 James V had cemented the 'auld alliance' with the French by marrying Francis I's daughter Madeleine; following her early death, he wed Marie, daughter of the duc de Guise. In 1541 Henry VIII attempted reconciliation but was publicly snubbed when James refused to meet him at York. A year later, after a spate of border raids and the capture by the Scots of an English March Warden, Henry announced that the blood between himself and James V had been 'frozen with the cold air of Scotland'. Safe in the knowledge that Francis I was too busy fighting Charles V on the Continent to assist his Scottish allies, Henry declared war on his nephew. He appointed the Duke of Norfolk as his Lieutenant General and ordered him to lead an army across the Border and perform 'some notable exploit'.[20]

* James' mother Margaret was Henry VIII's elder sister. She had married James IV of Scotland in 1503.

'Spite drave me into Boreas' reign', Surrey announced in one of his poems,

Where hoary frosts the fruits do bite,
When hills were spread and every plain
With stormy winter's mantle white.[21]

In spite of the cold and a scarcity of bread and beer, despite the 'poor and feeble' carriages, 'exceedingly foul' roads, the collapse of a bridge, the drowning of five men and the wounding of many more, Surrey, his father and an army of over twenty thousand crossed the Tweed at Berwick on 21 October 1542.[22] Scotland was traditionally the arena in which Howard reputations were made. According to Richard Grafton, the House of Howard was 'appointed by God, to be to the Scots a sharp scourge and rod'.[23] But if Surrey was hoping for his own Flodden, he would be sorely disappointed.

Norfolk had vowed to shock and awe the Scots into submission: 'We shall do as much as is possible for men to do to make the enemies speak according to the King's pleasure, or else to make them such a smoke as never was in Scotland these 100 years.' In the space of eight days his men destroyed over twenty towns and villages, 'utterly devastating all the corn about the same,' Norfolk bragged, 'in such sort as they shall not be able to recover this displeasure many years hereafter.'[24] On 25 October they met with some resistance around Kelso, but it was easily suppressed by Norfolk's gunners.[25] The following day Surrey and his servant Thomas Clere stood together and watched as the town and abbey of Kelso were put to fire and reduced to smouldering embers. But there was no 'notable exploit' and before October was out, a combination of appalling weather, inadequate supplies and infirmity had forced Norfolk to abort the campaign and withdraw to Berwick.

Henry VIII was less than impressed. On 2 November he sent Norfolk and his fellow commissioners a letter full of barbs about 'the loss of this enterprise' which was 'not of such sort as we did trust and desired'.[26] Howard pride received a further blow on 24 November when the Warden of the West Marches, Sir Thomas Wharton, achieved what the Howards could not. On the western edge of the border at Solway Moss, Wharton routed a Scottish retaliatory force and claimed over a thousand prisoners. Within a month James V was dead. The future of his kingdom rested on the tiny shoulders of his one-week-old daughter Mary, Queen of Scots.

Surrey returned to England more restless than ever. His instinctive aggression, always simmering near the surface, had been unleashed by the authorised hooliganism that was the Scottish campaign, but not sated by it. Adrenaline pumped through his veins and so he headed for the one place where it could best be expended.

Tudor London was only a fraction of the size of the city we know today. A thick defensive wall enclosed an area of about one square mile that stretched from the Greyfriars in the west to Aldgate in the east and Moorgate in the north down to the Thames. But it was growing fast. Mansions and tenements soon overtook the open spaces within the city walls and further housing sprawled across the green suburbs. London's population, around fifty thousand at the beginning of the sixteenth century, had quadrupled by the beginning of the next.[27] Each street had its own peculiar character and was named accordingly. Competitors for the tourneys traditionally rode down Knightrider Street before exiting the city. The entrails of butchered animals were cast out of the scalding houses and swept down Pudding Lane towards the dung boats on the Thames. Fenchurch Street once had a river running through it and used to be little more than marshland. Pissing Lane, set between St Paul's and Paternoster Row, needs no explanation, though even that quintessential Londoner, Thomas More, was revolted by the sight of a 'beastly body' shamelessly defecating 'in the open street'.[28]

The throbbing heart of the city was Cheapside, where market traders hawked their wares and cutpurses drifted numinously through crowded stalls. There was nothing that could not be found here: malmsey wine from Crete, oil from Calabria, Turkish carpets, buttons, hats, spices, strawberries, gemstones, medicine, candles, horseshoes, quills, woodcuts, playing cards, hawks' bells, birchrods, the services of porters and water carriers, fish and meat at the Stocks (a covered market in East Cheap) and yet more cuts of meat from the butchers of St Nicholas Shambles in the west. In the wider streets bands of apprentices played football with stuffed pig bladders and down the alleys, darkened by the overhang of the houses, gangs of sturdy beggars lurked with menace. Writing a century later, Henry Peacham observed that London was 'like a vast sea, full of gusts, fearful dangerous shelves and rocks, ready at every storm to sink and cast away the weak and unexperienced.'[29]

At the west end of Cheapside was St Paul's Cathedral, where God
and money were worshipped in unequal measure. According to the
Bishop of Durham in 1561, St Paul's could be divided thus: 'the south
alley for Popery and usury, the north for simony, the horse fair in the
midst for all kinds of bargains, meetings, brawlings, murders, conspiracies, and the font for ordinary payment of money, as well known to
all men as the beggar knows his bush.'[30] As Surrey walked east along
Cheapside, the first great landmark he encountered was the Eleanor
Cross, erected by Edward I in 1290 in honour of his late Queen. Further
along was the Standard, a stone fountain, where punishments were
meted out and, further still, the Great Conduit, which contained fresh
water piped from Paddington. The first street left after the Standard,
set between Milk Street and Ironmonger Lane, was St Lawrence Lane
and it was here, at the guesthouse of one Mistress Milicent Arundel,
that Surrey and his companions raised their temporary quarters.

It was a far cry from the luxury to which Surrey was accustomed –
perhaps that was part of its appeal – but the street contained 'many
fair houses' and Mistress Arundel was an attentive and obliging host.
When a knuckle of veal proved unsatisfactory, she dispatched one of
her maids to the butcher with a sharp message of rebuke and when
Surrey fell into a rage after being conned into buying substandard cloth,
she pandered to his ego. 'I marvel they will thus mock a prince', she
bleated to her maids in the kitchen.[31]

The following episode of Surrey's life contains an element of Shakespearian farce. There is the garrulous hostess, the Cheapside inn, the
heir determined to evade his responsibilities and a crew of Falstaffian
characters more than willing to assist.[32] Thomas Hussey, the Duke of
Norfolk's treasurer, was 'a fat-bellied lump of a man', who could often
be found at the carding and dicing tables; in two years' time, he would
endure a spell in the Fleet when an argument over a game of primero
got out of hand. Surrey's servant, William Pickering, another keen
gambler with a weakness for high jinks and loose women, would stand
accused in six years' time of breaking the London curfew and bearing
a 'light and evil demeanour' towards the city constables. William
Stafford, who had defied the King a decade earlier by marrying Mary
Boleyn, would be committed to the Fleet for affray in 1552.

Surrey had known the Clere brothers from childhood. Thomas, his
faithful squire, had been in trouble two years earlier for brawling on
the King's tennis court at Greenwich, while Sir John, the elder brother,

was well known to the officials of the Star Chamber and had been criticised there for his 'covetous appetite and ungodly disposition'. Davy Seymour seemed content to lurk in the shadow of his famous family. Thomas Wyatt, the son of the poet, had only recently been pardoned for robbery and Thomas Wyndham, whose half-brother had been with Surrey in France, would later become a great explorer. In 1551, he participated in what Hakluyt called 'the first voyage for traffic into the Kingdom of Morocco in Barbary' and the following year he was, according to his page, the first Englishman who 'fairly rounded Cape Verde and sailed into the Southern Sea'. His reputation among the French was less heroic; they knew him as an accomplished pirate. The boisterous troupe was completed by another servant of Surrey's called Shelley, and George Blagge, a squat man whose frame spawned various nicknames; to Ralph Vane he was Tom Trubbe, while Henry VIII referred to him as 'my pig'.

The records are silent for their first few weeks, but there was much in the city and its environs to divert them. They could have honed their archery skills at Finsbury fields, tilted at the quintain on Cornhill, enjoyed the wrestling at Clerkenwell or the horse racing at Smithfield. Had they wandered down to the Thames, they might have witnessed the ducking of prostitutes in the river from the 'cucking-stool' at the Three Cranes.[33] They could have ventured east to see the lions and the rest of Henry VIII's menagerie at the Tower of London or west beyond the walls to Domingo's, a notorious gambling den favoured by the high-rollers of the Court. Had they felt partial to an afternoon of blood sports, they could have taken a wherry across the river to Paris Garden in Southwark, where bulls and bears were baited by fierce mastiffs. Alternatively, they could have crossed London Bridge, where the heads of traitors were impaled on spikes. According to a Greek envoy who toured London around 1545, the skulls of Catherine Howard's executed lovers could still be seen there, though somewhat 'denuded of flesh'.[34]

At eight o'clock on Sunday, 21 January 1543 the bell of St Mary-le-Bow was rung, signalling the evening curfew. Apprentices put down their tools, shopkeepers packed away their wares, taverns were cleared, candles were snuffed out and the city gates were locked. An hour later Surrey, Wyatt, Thomas Clere, Shelley and Pickering put on their cloaks, armed themselves with stonebows and ventured into the darkness. They strode purposefully through the alleys west of their lodging and arrived in a matter of seconds at Milk Street, an affluent neighbourhood lined with the sumptuous houses of the more successful members of London's merchant community.[35] Sir Richard Gresham lived here. He was a Norfolk man by birth, but had made his fortune in the capital through trade and usury and had served a term as Lord Mayor in 1537. A few well-aimed shots from Surrey's stonebow put paid to Gresham's expensive glass windows.

Surrey's gang then ran amok through Cheapside, the Poultry and the Stocks Market, abusing passers-by as they went. Continuing east, they hurtled along Lombard Street and onto Fenchurch Street, where a mercer by the name of William Birch resided. His windows went the way of Gresham's, as did those of other merchant dwellings and even some churches. Their next port of call was the Thames, where they commandeered some boats and rowed along the river, shouting obscenities and shooting missiles at the prostitutes who plied their trade on the South Bank. When they eventually tired of their sport, they headed back to their lodgings, leaving a trail of broken glass in their wake. According to one of the maids, 'it was two of the clock in the morning 'or that they came in again.'[36]

The following night, in response to a reprimand from George Blagge, Surrey admitted to the folly of his deed. 'He had liever [rather] than all the good in the world it were undone,' he said, not because he felt any guilt, but because 'he was sure it should come before the King and his Council'. There was already 'a great clamour' over the vandalism 'and the voice was that those hurts were done by my Lord and his company'.[37]

Within days Surrey was the subject of a municipal enquiry headed by the Lord Mayor, but on 13 February he was granted a royal licence 'to alienate the manor of Larlingforth'.[38] The Earl of Surrey, it seemed, was untouchable and so he might have remained had Henry VIII not then authorised a new heresy commission. One line of attack, co-ordinated by Stephen Gardiner, Bishop of Winchester, was to target all those who had disobeyed the fasting laws. Surrey, who had flagrantly eaten meat not only over Lent but also on other proscribed days, was caught in Gardiner's net. As Easter approached, a full investigation was launched into his misconduct.

On 24 March Alice Flaner, a maid of Mistress Arundel, was examined by the Privy Council. Four days later it was the turn of her mistress, who was recalled on 2 April along with another maid by the name of Joan Whetnall. Their revelations uncovered further transgressions,

including the Earl of Surrey's regal pretensions. Joan claimed that she
thought that the armorial bearings above Surrey's bed 'were very like
the King's arms'. Surrey's rage over his ill-advised cloth purchase was
also brought up and it was remembered that Mistress Arundel had
called him a prince. There was nothing particularly unusual in a
nobleman being referred to thus, but the maids had followed it up with
questions about Surrey's status.

'Is he a prince?'

'Yea,' Mistress Arundel had replied, 'and if ought should come at
the King but good, his father should stand for King.' By this she meant
that if Henry VIII should die before Prince Edward had reached his
majority, then the Duke of Norfolk deserved to be regent. However,
the maids soon confused her words. Joan Whetnall thought that 'if
ought came at the King and my Lord Prince, then [Surrey] would be
King after his father', while Alice Flaner had announced at the butchers
that 'if ought came to the King otherwise than well, [Surrey] is like to
be King'. 'It is not so,' challenged a merchant-tailor. 'It is said so,' Alice
had retorted.[39] Such chatter was dangerous in the extreme. Discussing
the succession, if only hypothetically, was potentially treasonous as it
presupposed – 'imagined' in the language of the day – the King's death.
The three deponents denied 'that ever they heard any other person
speak of this or any like matter', but Mistress Arundel's statement
reflected Surrey's own sentiments as his words, uttered three years later,
would reveal.

Surrey appreciated the seriousness of the situation. He knew that the
authorities had called his allegiance into question and he feared for his
life 'notwithstanding mine innocency'. On 1 April 1543 he was examined at St James's Palace by four privy councillors: Thomas Wriothesley,
John Russell, Stephen Gardiner and Anthony Browne. All were, at this
stage in their careers, on good terms with Surrey's father and they proffered a sympathetic line of questioning, so much so that when Surrey
later became the subject of a more serious enquiry, he asked that the
same four men might conduct it.[40]

Surrey was not charged with any treasonable muttering about the
succession, nor for bearing royal arms above his bed.* Instead he faced

---

* In all likelihood the arms were Surrey's own. The Howards were entitled to bear the arms
of Thomas of Brotherton – three white lions with three silver labels. This bearing was similar
to, but not the same as, the King's, though it is easy to see how a maidservant, unversed in
heraldry, could have confused the two.

the two lesser charges: 'of eating of flesh' and 'of a lewd and unseemly manner of walking in the night about the streets and breaking with stonebows of certain windows'. To the first charge Surrey claimed he had a licence, 'albeit he had not so secretly used the same as appertained'. But he confessed to the second offence: 'He could not deny but he had very evil done therein,' the Privy Council recorded, 'submitting himself therefore to such punishment as should to them be thought good.'[41] Two of Surrey's crew – Wyatt and Pickering – initially denied any involvement in the rampage and when they eventually confessed, they were dispatched to the Tower. Surrey and his other roistering confederates could therefore consider themselves lucky only to be sent to the Fleet.[42]

Back in the river prison, amid the 'pestilent airs' that so offended his aristocratic nose, Surrey raged, brooded, then took up his quill. The result was an extraordinary poem that offered a justification for his nocturnal activities. 'London!' the poem begins in shocked tones emphasised by the heavy stresses of the metre, 'hast *thou* accused *me* / Of breach of laws the root of strife?' London, whose 'wicked walls' embrace the devil and the seven deadly sins, has the temerity to accuse the Earl of Surrey, 'whose breast did boil to see / So fervent hot thy dissolute life.' Indeed, the poet explains, it was the very degeneracy of London, whose citizens had closed their ears to the gentle chastisements of preachers, that had spurred him to express his 'hidden burden'. As words had failed to rouse the citizens from their torpor, Surrey's speaker explains, more extreme methods of persuasion had been necessary:

> In secret silence of the night
> This made me, with a reckless breast,
> To wake thy sluggards with my bow:
> A figure of the Lord's behest,
> Whose scourge for sin the Scriptures show.

With characteristic hubris, Surrey has fashioned himself as God's agent on earth. He is the vigilante-prophet sent out with his stonebow to warn the citizens of the 'fearful thunder clap' and 'dreadful plague' at hand if God's wrath is not assuaged:

> In loathsome vice each drunken wight
> To stir to God, this was my mind.

'Thy windows,' he tells the city, 'had done me no spite',

> But proud people that dread no fall,
> Clothed with falsehood and unright
> Bred in the closures of thy wall.

The poem climaxes with a terrifying vision of London as Babylon, the mystical city of the Apocalypse:

> Oh Shameless whore! Is dread then gone
> By such thy foes as meant thy weal?
> Oh member of false Babylon!
> The shop of craft! The den of ire!
> Thy dreadful doom draws fast upon.
> Thy martrys' blood, by sword and fire,
> In Heaven and earth for justice call.
> The Lord shall hear their just desire;
> The flame of wrath shall on thee fall;
> With famine and pest lamentably
> Stricken shall be thy lechers all;
> Thy proud towers and turrets high,
> Enemies to God, beat stone from stone;
> Thine idols burnt, that wrought iniquity;
> When none thy ruin shall bemoan,
> But render unto the right wise Lord,
> That so hath judged Babylon,
> Immortal praise with one accord.[43]

For this poem, Surrey drew on the Scriptural voices of the prophets Jeremiah and Ezekiel, on Juvenal's invectives against first-century Rome, and on Petrarch's denunciation of the Papacy at Avignon. But Surrey's is a poem very much of its moment, pregnant with contemporary issues and loaded with reformed rhetoric. Opinion is divided over his true intentions. Some critics have taken his iconoclastic defence at face value, arguing that the poem, and the rampage, were heartfelt expressions of faith, a faith that was distinctly evangelical and would be endorsed again by Surrey in his biblical paraphrases. Others doubt the Earl's sincerity, claiming that he appropriated the bombastic language of the pulpits in order to mock his detractors and voice his own personal outrage at being punished. A third possibility is that the poem, written as it was when London had become the battleground for the Reformation, might convey 'a protest against the self-righteousness and inflexibility of both confessional sides, certain of their monopoly of truth.'[44]

It is unlikely, though not impossible, that a religious motive drove Surrey to the streets on the night of 21 January 1543. We do not even know if the church windows that he smashed were under the care of traditional or reforming clerics, and the targeting of Gresham and Birch, who both seemed more reform-minded than otherwise, points to personal antagonism rather than any instance of faith. Gresham and Birch, both 'new men' in Surrey's eyes, had been supporters of Thomas Cromwell and were closely acquainted; Gresham's wife had attended the christening of Birch's son (named Thomas after his godfather Cromwell).[45] Gresham was a very wealthy man, who enjoyed a lucrative sideline in moneylending. He had risen quickly through the ranks of London society, but not without making enemies. An anonymous poem written after his death in 1549 denounced him as a fraudulent merchant who had sold his own honour for profit and called on all those who had owed him money to rejoice in his death and cast excrement upon his corpse.[46]

Both Gresham and Birch traded in cloth and it is tempting to speculate that either one or both of them had had a hand in the swindling of Surrey over his purchase of shoddy linen. Even if they had not, Surrey may have decided that as figureheads of the industry that had conned him, they were fair game. Alternatively, many of Surrey's consorts were, like him, avid gamblers and frequently in debt. Birch the gambler and Gresham the moneylender could easily have made themselves targets.[47]

Surrey instantly regretted the rampage because it was, he readily admitted, juvenile and reckless. 'We will have a madding time in our youth,' he explained to Blagge. One might add that it was probably a far from sober time too. Nor did Surrey present any kind of religious defence during his examination. Instead he once again admitted 'that he had very evil done therein'.[48] Only after the event, languishing in prison, did Surrey devise a justification that attempted to play down his disgrace. But if he was cocking a snook at the authorities in his poem, if he was winking conspiratorially at his friends, if, even, he was partially sending himself up as the lone champion of the Reformation, it does not necessarily follow that his professed zeal was contrived. Indeed, a mass of cumulative evidence strongly suggests that Surrey's early flirtation with reform had by now grown into ardent commitment.

First there are his companions: they were all adherents to the new faith, some with the zeal of a fanatic. In three years' time, George Blagge would be condemned for sacramentarianism and only the personal intervention of the King would save him from the fires of Smithfield. Wyatt would lose his head after his rebellion against Queen Mary in 1554 (for which Pickering was also indicted) and Stafford became a Marian exile in Calvin's Geneva. Surrey was not the only one to flout the fasting laws; at least eight of his crew had done so too. Traditionalists viewed such defiance as damnable heresy; reformers as an admirable rebellion against a superstitious custom.

Then there is the place: Mistress Arundel and her husband had disobeyed the Lenten laws themselves and their contacts with evangelical butchers had ensured a ready supply of black-market meat at Surrey's table.[49] On the west side of St Lawrence Lane, through an open passage called Duke Street, was All Hallows, Honey Lane, a parish notorious for its radical stance. To the conservatives, well aware that it harboured an illegal trade in reformist literature, the church was a bastion for 'the secret sowing and setting forth of Luther's heresies'. One of its rectors, Thomas Garrard, had been burned for heresy in 1540 and at the time of Surrey's sojourn the curate incumbent was William Reed, soon to be examined for abuses of religion.[50] Three other churches within Cheap Ward – St Pancras, St Martin Ironmonger Lane and St Mary Colechurch – employed reforming clerics and St Mary Aldermary, a church in the neighbouring ward, was under the heterodox care of Edward Crome. The sermon given there that Lent landed the reformer, Robert Wisdom, in prison.[51] One of those who stood surety for Wisdom was Henry Brinklow, an evangelical campaigner whose *Lamentacyon of a Christen Agaynst the Cytye of London* exhorted sinful Londoners to repent – 'Awake! Awake! For the Lord sleepeth not.' His rented tenement between St Lawrence Lane and Ironmonger Lane was only a stone's throw from Mistress Arundel's inn.[52]

If all this appears too circumstantial, then there is firmer evidence of Surrey's evangelical commitment. The Imperial ambassador Eustace Chapuys, who was well informed on such matters, reported that Surrey, Wyatt and Pickering were 'suspected of professing Lutheranism, to which heretical sect the above-mentioned Earl is said to belong'.[53] Surrey's faith had recently been encouraged by his friend's father, the poet Sir Thomas Wyatt, whose paraphrases of the seven penitential psalms had endorsed the evangelical message – 'For lo, thou loves the truth of inward heart / Which yet doth live in my fidelity'; 'thou delights not in no such gloze / Of outward deed as men dream and devise'; 'Inward Zion, the Zion of the ghost / Of heart's Jerusalem'. In Surrey's opinion, Wyatt's psalms taught 'the lively faith and pure'.[54] One of them may even have been dedicated to him. Inserted in the Arundel Harington Manuscript, just after Wyatt's paraphrase of psalm 37 and presumably before another psalm, now missing, is a *strambotto* that is commonly thought to be addressed to the Earl:

> Sometime the pride of my assured truth
> Contemned all help of God and eke of man.
> But when I saw man blindly how he go'th
> In deeming hearts, which none but God there can,
> And his dooms hid, whereby man's malice grow'th,
> *Mine Earl*, this doubt my heart did humble then,
> For error so might murder innocents.
> Then sang I thus in God my confidence.[55]

On 11 October 1542, as Surrey was marching towards the Scottish border, Sir Thomas Wyatt died. Surrey was distraught and composed several poems lamenting his death. In the sonnet beginning 'Diverse thy death do diversely bemoan', he pictures himself kissing the ground where Wyatt's body lay and weeping tears of true love 'as Pyramus did on Thisbe's breast bewail'.[56] In another, Surrey defends his excessive grief. 'In the rude age,' he begins, 'when science was not so rife', pagans erected temples in honour of those who 'taught / Arts to revert to profit of our life'. Enlightened Christians eschew purgatory and prayers for the dead, but, Surrey argues, they can hardly be blamed for remembering Wyatt, who gave the greatest lesson of all:

> In days of truth if Wyatt's friends then wail
> (the only debt that dead of quick may claim)
> That rare wit spent employed to our avail
> Where Christ is taught, deserve they monnis blame?[57]

Surrey's longer elegy on Wyatt, wrought in the heroic quatrains that he had invented for the Duke of Richmond, lauds the late poet as an exemplar of virtue and, in the last lines, as a Christian gospeller, selflessly dedicated to the promotion of the godly commonwealth:

But to the heavens that simple soul is fled,
Which left with such as covet Christ to know
Witness of faith that never shall be dead;
Sent for our health, but not received so.

Thus, for our guilt, this jewel have we lost.
The earth his bones, the heavens possess his ghost.[58]

Surrey's implication in these lines is that God took Wyatt from his countrymen as a punishment for their sins. Yet there is hope. Wyatt bequeathed his psalm paraphrases to his evangelical brethren; they are a 'witness of faith', a faith everlasting, a faith that true Christians will continue to uphold.

Within weeks of Wyatt's death, the antiquarian John Leland published his *Naeniae* ('funeral songs') in honour of the late poet. He dedicated them to 'the most learned and most noble young Earl of Surrey'. One, entitled *Unicus Phoenix*, called on Surrey to continue the work of his predecessor:

The world a single Phoenix can contain,
And when one dies, another one is born.
When Wyatt, that rare bird, was taken away
By death, he gave us Howard as his heir.[59]

It was a calling that Surrey chose to interpret in terms of religion as well as poetry. He would strive to emulate Wyatt and produce works that would stand as a 'witness of faith'. Thus, after praising Wyatt's psalms in another poem written around this time, Surrey exhibited his fidelity by warning contemporary rulers of 'God's scourge' and praying that they might 'awake out of their sinful sleep'.[60] Surrey's apocalyptic, threatening language chimes with that of his London satire. There he made a point of bewailing the heedlessness of Londoners; goodly preachers were, like Wyatt, 'sent for our health, but not received so'. Unlike his Wyatt elegy, Surrey's London satire was not published, but nor was it kept secret. It is an epideictic poem modelled along the lines of a judicial oration, which Surrey dedicated to a public figure, Sir Nicholas Poyntz, and it would resurface three years later when he once again faced investigation.[61]

Surrey's Wyatt poems identify the speaker as a member of the evangelical brethren – 'with such as covet Christ'; in his London satire he acts as God's spokesman. In terms of faith, though not of politics, the son of the foremost Catholic peer in England had proudly and defiantly declared his allegiance to the Opposition.

Henry VIII proved remarkably forgiving. It can be assumed that Surrey was free by 11 May 1543, when he was appointed to the Commission of the Peace for Norfolk.[62] The King probably dismissed the rampage as a London matter of little import. He did not even seem unduly concerned by the stories of Surrey's allegedly royal coat of arms or the loose talk about the succession. Not yet, anyway.

We can only guess at the Duke of Norfolk's reaction to Surrey's behaviour. In public he remained tight-lipped. But his son had declared himself a reformer. He had suffered three imprisonments in six years. He had rebelled openly against authority and displayed little contrition thereafter. Surrey seemed to be systematically destroying all the props that defined him as a scion of the Howards. He had come a long way from the dutiful heir praised by the French princes for his 'wisdom and soberness'. On Surrey's shoulders rested the future of the House of Howard. Norfolk had already shown that he was willing to destroy Court rivals and sacrifice two nieces and countless cousins for this cause. It remained to be seen if, or for how much longer, he would continue to tolerate his son's excesses.

PART THREE

WAR

NOBLE HEART

On 11 February 1543 a secret treaty between Henry VIII and the Holy Roman Emperor Charles V was signed. On 27 May Surrey was present at Hampton Court to witness Henry VIII's pledge to honour the treaty and just under a month later, on 22 June 1543, an Anglo-Imperial intimation of war was presented to the French ambassador.[1]

The Emperor Charles V and Francis I of France were natural foes. As respective heads of the houses of Habsburg and Valois, they fought each other for land, especially in Northern Italy, for honour and for the ultimate ascendancy of Europe. Despite Henry VIII's best efforts, England could not compete directly with these two superpowers. When, as had happened during 1538 and 1539, Charles and Francis joined forces, England became, in the words of Thomas Wriothesley, 'but a morsel among these choppers'.[2] But such unions rarely lasted long and Henry's decisions were sometimes pivotal in upsetting the balance of power. By the summer of 1542 Francis and Charles were once again in open conflict and for the rest of the year Henry found himself in the glorious position of being courted by both rulers.

Despite past clashes with Charles, Henry's instinct was always to oppose Francis. Their relationship was characterised by an intense personal rivalry and Henry made no secret of his desire to emulate his ancestors, especially Henry V, and revive the ancient English claim to suzerainty over France. In the first two decades of his reign, Henry had launched two major expeditions into France, neither with much lasting success. Since then Francis had kept him at bay with an annual pension, but he frequently defaulted on the payments and by 1543 he owed arrears of a million crowns. At the beginning of 1543, in retaliation for Henry's seizure of some French pirate ships in the Channel, Francis arrested all English merchant ships in French ports. This act of aggression, along with Francis' 'auld alliance' with Scotland and his new amity with the Turks, meant that Henry had few qualms about allying with Charles. In 1543 Henry was entering his fifty-third year and, on 12 July, he married his sixth wife, Catherine Parr. War with France provided one more chance, maybe his last, to honour the pledge he had made in 1512, 'not merely to equal but indeed to exceed the glorious deeds of his ancestors'.[3]

For the twenty-six-year-old Surrey the war presented a similar prize. 'My kind,' he had announced in his beast fable, 'is to desire the honour of the field' – and there was no better field than that of France. According to Thomas Churchyard, 'he was counted nobody that had not been known to be at some valiant enterprise.'[4] Here was Surrey's chance to be a somebody, or rather, to gain renown rather than notoriety. Finally he had an opportunity to prove himself worthy of the name of Howard and relieve the burden that weighed so heavily on his shoulders.

The Anglo-Imperial treaty pledged an ambitious plan. A two-pronged invasion of France would be mounted the following year. The English would march from Calais in the north and Charles' army from the Low Countries in the east. Both would then drive towards Paris. In the interim, Henry agreed to assist Charles in checking French expansionism in the Low Countries. At the end of July 1543 a force of around six thousand men led by Sir John Wallop crossed the Channel and marched towards Landrecy, a town on the Sambre that had been taken by the French the previous month. Surrey begged the King for permission to join them. Twenty years earlier, when the Scots had been threatening England's borders, Surrey's father had written to Wolsey in exasperation:

God knoweth, if the poorest gentleman in the King's house were here, and I at London and were advertised of these news, I would not fail to kneel upon my knees before the King's Grace to have licence to come hither in post to be at the day of battle. And if young noblemen and gentlemen be not desirous and willing to be at such journeys and to take the pain and give the adventure – and the King's Highness well contented with those that will do so and not regarding others that will be but dancers, dicers and carders – His Grace shall not be well served when he would be. For men without experience shall do small service and experience of war will not be had without it be sought for and the adventure given.[5]

One can assume, therefore, that Norfolk heartily approved of his son's volunteering. So too did Henry VIII, who was avuncular in his support. Not only did he grant Surrey the necessary licence to go over-seas, but he also wrote a personal letter of recommendation to the Emperor: 'Tres hault, tres excellent, et tres puissant Prince, nostre tres chier et tres ame frere et cousin,' Henry addressed his ally from Woodstock on 1 October,

> Our very dear and most beloved cousin the Earl of Surrey, Knight of our Order, has applied to us for permission to visit Your Majesty's camp. This petition we have readily granted [so] that we may, through him, have news of your successes, which we hope will continue to be prosperous, [and] that he may at the same time acquire that experience in military affairs that will make him the true heir and successor of his ancestors.
>
> We beg to recommend him most particularly to Your Imperial Majesty, praying you to order the captains and lieutenants of your army to help and assist in all things in which the said Earl may advance and improve his knowledge of military affairs.[6]

Three days later the Earl of Surrey, flanked by Thomas Clere and George Blagge, joined the camp besieging Landrecy.

The siege was the favoured mode of warfare in this period. Pitched battles were occasionally still fought and lances were still levelled. Sir John Wallop had even attempted to revive the world of Froissart's *Chronicles* on his march through France by challenging the garrison-ners at Théouranne to break a staff 'for their lady's sake'.[7] Increas-ingly, though, the enemy was the faceless foe beyond the trench and behind the gun. The changing nature of warfare was a result of devel-opments in ballistics. Gunpowder had been around for some time but its full potential was only just being realised. Large guns and cannon were superior in range, shock and impact, if not yet in rate of fire, to traditional weaponry. The culverin, for example, weighed four thousand pounds, had a calibre of five-and-a-half inches and a range of four hundred and sixty yards when fired horizontally; at a ten-degree elevation the yardage was well over two thousand. It was cumbersome and slow but could smash through walls previously deemed impregnable. Other forms of artillery such as the falcon were lighter and could discharge up to one hundred and twenty rounds a day. By the end of his reign Henry VIII had over two thousand pieces of artillery in his fortifications and a well-stocked arsenal at the Tower of London.[8]

English munitions were by no means the most impressive in Europe. The Imperial army at Landrecy contained an assortment of Germans, Dutchmen, Burgundians, Spaniards and Italians, who all took advantage of the increasingly sophisticated technology. On 22 October 1543 Sir John Wallop described a German mortar that he had seen at the camp. It was 'the fairest that ever I saw, made of cannon metal, and shooteth the greatest bullet that ever I saw; diverse of them made of stone and the others artificial, full of wild fire and a forty or fifty shot of guns within them, every one of them able to kill a man.' Indeed, Wallop assured the King, 'in all the wars that I have been in, I have not seen such another time for youth to learn.'[9]

Much to Wallop's approbation, Surrey immediately strove to familiarise himself with his new environment. On 26 October Wallop wrote to Paget, 'praying you to make my humble recommendations to my good Lord of Norfolk, showing him that my Lord of Surrey hath lost no time sithen [since] his being here, for he visiteth all things that be meet for a man of war to look upon for his learning.' Surrey liaised with the various camps and toured the trenches, though on one occasion he strayed too close to the enemy lines and was 'somewhat saluted' by their fire. Another time he stayed up through the night to witness the operation of the mortar that had so impressed Wallop and 'it was a strange and a dreadful sight to see the bullet fly into the air, spouting fire on every side.'[10]

On 27 October 'a certain foolish letter' of Surrey's was leaked to Eustace Chapuys, Charles V's ambassador in London. It has not survived, but it seems to have been critical of some of the Imperial officers. Henry VIII was piqued and Surrey was ordered 'to abstain in future from making such reports'.[11] But this was the only blot on an otherwise faultless copybook. A few days earlier Charles V had met Surrey and been so impressed by what he had seen that he mentioned the Earl in his next dispatch to Henry VIII:

> As for your recommendation that the son of our cousin the Duke of Norfolk be initiated into the arts of war, he is such a good example of your race that he cannot fail to profit thereby. All our men will respect him as he deserves, for the valour of his father and for his own noble heart and we thank you for your recommendation.[12]

Henry was delighted by Charles' letter, while the Duke of Norfolk, Chapuys informed Charles V, was 'so grateful at this show of kindness on Your Imperial Majesty's part that he has been heard to say in public that nothing would be so agreeable to him as to find an opportunity of risking his person, his family and his property for Your Majesty's service.'[13] These are more than the sentiments of a proud father. If Norfolk's gratitude is palpable, then so too is his sense of relief.

Wallop's dispatches for the end of October 1543 were confident of victory. On the 22nd he reported that Landrecy would fall in twelve days, on the 26th that parts of the city were on fire and on the 29th that 'a practicable breach' had been made in the city walls.[14] But all the while Francis I had been marching towards them with a great army and on 29 October he was encamped at nearby Cateau-Cambrésis. 'Verily,' the English chronicler, Raphael Holinshed, recorded, 'it was thought that two such powers as were there at that time so near together, should never have departed without battle.'[15] Charles V assumed as much. He immediately raised the siege and began to commit his men to the field. On the morning of 4 November Charles summoned his Imperial generals, along with Sir John Wallop, Sir Francis Bryan and the Earl of Surrey, to a council of war. It was agreed that they would advance the next day and give the French battle.

Francis had no intention of engaging his foes. Having lured them away from Landrecy, he replenished the town with men, munitions and provisions. On the day that Surrey and the others sat in the Emperor's tent discussing battle plans, Francis prepared to withdraw. As night fell, he and his army crept away. 'Trumpet there blew none,' Wallop noted bitterly 'ne yet stroke with drum.' As soon as they received news of the retreat, the Anglo-Imperial army gave chase. They were, Holinshed tells us, 'as eager as tigers', but the French had made too much ground. A few days later, with 'the weather waxing extreme foul and contrary to an army that should lie in the fields', it was agreed that camp should be broken and the armies sent home.[16]

On Sunday, 18 November 1543 Surrey took his formal leave of the Emperor. Charles V 'handled him after a very gentle sort' and entrusted him with some delicate information concerning the latest overtures of the French to treat for peace. Then he placed a sealed letter in Surrey's hands and asked him to deliver it personally to Henry VIII.[17]

Surrey returned to the English Court in good time for the Chapter of the Order of the Garter held at Hampton Court on Christmas Eve.[18]

Although the enterprise at Landrecy had ultimately proved disap-
pointing, Surrey himself had never been in higher favour. The letter
that Charles V had asked him to deliver to Henry VIII feted him as a
rising star of the allied army. The Earl of Surrey, his King read,

> has provided good witness in our army of whose son he is and how he does
> not wish to falter in following his father and his ancestors. With so noble
> a heart and such dexterity there has been no need for him to learn anything.
> In fact, you cannot command him anything he does not know how to do.[19]

The foolish proud boy, it seemed, might finally have grown up.

On 14 January 1544, the same day that Holinshed's *Chronicles* recorded
an eclipse of the sun,[20] the third session of Henry VIII's fourth Parliament
was opened. One of the acts passed confirmed a land indenture between
Henry VIII and the Duke of Norfolk, his heir and daughter-in-law.[21]
Just under two years earlier Surrey had signed a ninety-nine-year lease
for the house, buildings, orchards, grounds and woods appertaining to
the dissolved priory of St Leonard's, within the manor of Thorpe,
Norwich.[22] Now, in exchange for some properties in Suffolk, Henry VIII
granted the Howards the manors of Gaywood, Rising and Thorpe. The
Duke of Norfolk handed St Leonard's Priory over to Surrey and Frances.
Much work needed to be done to make it fit for their habitation, but
finally they could plan a future away from Kenninghall.

The following month Henry VIII broadcast his new-found confidence in Surrey by sending him 'to visit and offer compliments on his
part to the Duke'. Don Juan Estaban Manrique de Lara, third Duke
of Najera, had served at Landrecy and was one of Charles V's most
respected generals. His visit was unofficial but Henry VIII determined
to honour him with a formal reception. Surrey met him in London on
12 February 1544 and was told to divert him for five days until the
King was ready to receive him. During this period the Duke's secretary
kept a diary in which he recorded his impressions of London. The city,
he decided, was 'one of the largest in Christendom', and the Thames
one of the greatest rivers: 'It is not possible, in my opinion, that a more
beautiful river should exist in the world . . . The bridge on this river
is the finest I ever beheld, or have heard of; nor do I believe its equal
is to be found.' Never, he concluded, 'did I see a river so thickly covered
with swans'.

The Duke's party visited the Tower of London, where 'we saw four lions, very large and fierce, and two leopards, confined within wooden railings'. But it was the entertainment at Paris Garden that most amused the Spaniards:

We saw seven bears, some of them of great size. They are led out every day into an enclosure where, being tied with a long rope, large and intrepid dogs are thrown to them in order that they may bite and make them furious. It is not bad sport to see them fight and the assaults they give each other. To each of the large bears are matched three or four dogs, which some-times get the better and sometimes are worsted, for besides the fierceness and great strength of the bears to defend themselves with their teeth, they hug the dogs with their paws so tightly that, unless the masters come to assist them, they would be strangled by such soft embraces.

Into the same place they brought a pony with an ape fastened on its back, and to see the animal kicking amongst the dogs, with the screams of the ape, beholding the curs hanging from the neck of the pony, is very laughable.[23]

On Sunday, 17 February Surrey and the Queen's brother Lord William Parr dined with the Duke of Najera and then escorted him to Court, where he had his audience with Henry VIII. The formalities dispensed with, Surrey and Parr accompanied the Spanish party to the Queen's Chamber where they were entertained for the rest of the evening with music and dancing. At the end of May Surrey performed a similar role when he rode out 'with a gallant and numerous suite' to meet the Duke of Albuquerque, another Spanish luminary, who had come to England to finalise plans for the invasion of France.[24]

By now the soldiers had been mustered and the generals appointed. Henry VIII's army was the largest body of English troops ever sent across the Channel, four times the size of that at Agincourt and twice the number of men sent into France in 1522. Including the German and Burgundian auxiliaries sent by the Emperor and the English militiamen summoned in September, Henry VIII had some forty-eight thousand men at his command.[25] The Duke of Norfolk, now entering his seventy-second year, was appointed Captain of the Vanguard and the Earl of Surrey, at only twenty-seven, was made Marshal of the Field.

Surrey's excitement over his first posting and the imminent invasion was tempered by the fear and uncertainty of the enterprise. He knew that there was a chance that he might not see his wife and children again. His squire Thomas Clere, 'now being ready to pass into the realm of France to serve the King, my sovereign Lord, in his wars there', made his will on 6 June 1544. Lord Mountjoy also made provisions. His will contained orders for his tombstone to be laid 'in the place where I am slain' and engraved with his autobiographical epitaph, which he hoped would serve as 'a monument to my children to continue and keep themselves worthy of so much honour as to be called hereafter to die for their master and country'.[26] Neither Clere nor Mountjoy would survive the war.

Surrey's emotions may be gleaned from two poems that he is thought to have composed around this time. The first (cited in chapter 8) depicts Frances pining after her husband and fondly imagining him in the sanctuary of the nursery, 'playing where I shall find him with T. his little son'.[27] The second poem, 'O happy dames', was inscribed by Surrey's sister into the Devonshire Manuscript and explores similar themes of absence, longing and uncertainty. The speaker of this poem is also a woman – possibly, though not necessarily, Frances – who watches from her window as her lover sails away. 'Good Ladies,' she implores her companions, 'help to fill my mourning voice':

> Alas, how oft in dreams I see
> Those eyes that were my food,
> Which sometime so delighted me,
> That yet they do me good;
> Wherewith I wake with his return
> Whose absent flame doth make me burn.
> But when I find the lack, Lord how I mourn!
>
> When other lovers in arms across
> Rejoice their chief delight,
> Drowned in tears to mourn my loss
> I stand the bitter nights
> In my window, where I may see
> Before the winds how the clouds flee.
> Lo, what a mariner love has made me!
>
> And in green waves when the salt flood
> Doth swell by rages of wind,

A thousand fancies in that mood
Assails my restless mind.
Alas, now drenches my sweet foe,
That with spoil of my heart did go,
And left me; but, alas, why did he so?

And when the seas wax calm again,
To chase from me annoy,
My doubtful hope makes me to plain
So dread cuts off my joy.
Thus is my mirth mingled with woe,
And of each thought a doubt doth grow,
Now he comes, will he come? Alas, no, no![28]

Surrey crossed the Channel in June 1544 and joined the thousands of
soldiers amassing at Calais. The strike on Paris was ostensibly still on,
but, Henry VIII reasoned, supply lines and strongholds had to be secured
before such an assault could be attempted. In fact, Henry had no intention of venturing beyond the Somme. On previous campaigns he had
acted as little more than a stooge for his self-interested allies. This time
he resolved to make his own way in the war, on his terms and with
his own conquests. The plan, therefore, was for the Duke of Suffolk
to lay siege to Boulogne with the 'King's Battle', the largest division of
the army, while the vanguard under Norfolk, the rearguard under Lord
John Russell and a division of Imperial cavalry commanded by the
Count de Buren would besiege Montreuil, a fortress town just over
twenty miles south of Boulogne.

The logistics for the Montreuil campaign were complex and daunting
and a great part of the responsibility for them lay with the Earl of
Surrey as Marshal of the Field. It was a remarkable first posting,
especially for one so young. 'The Lord High Marshal,' Barnabe Rich
wrote in 1587, 'ought to be a man of such perfection and knowledge
that of his own experience he may as well instruct inferior officers in
their duties as correct and chastise them for their misdemeanours.'

To his office appertaineth the administering of justice, the punishing of
abuses, the correcting of all disorders and to give every man his right. The
High Marshal is to appoint the camping place, wherein he must have this
ordinary consideration for wood, water and forage. He is to quarter the

camp, assigning to the Quarter Master where the regiments of footmen shall be lodged and where the horsemen shall likewise have their places. He must appoint the watch and, surveying the places of greatest peril, he must give order to his inferior officers to have them furnish with requisite guard, directing the scout to places of most convenience . . .

When the camp shall remove, he is first to appoint the Scout Master to send out discoverers which way the army must pass, that must warily survey straits, copses and all places fit to hide ambushments and according as they find occasion, so to give intelligence. He must then signify to the Master of the Ordnance, and in like manner to the Carriage Master, that the artillery, munitions and all other carriages may be made ready and set forwards. He must then give order to the Sergeant Major in what form he will have the battle to march, wherein he hath to consider both of straits and otherwise of the nature of his passage, assigning both guides to conduct them and pioneers [sappers] to mend or make ways for the carriages and army the easier to pass.[29]

Co-ordinating the movements of two divisions comprising almost twenty thousand footmen and a thousand horsemen was no mean feat.[30] Carts and wagons were needed to transport the ammunition, gunpowder, axle-grease, spades, shovels, scythes, crowbars, horseshoes, nails, rope, candles, tents (for the officers; the rest had to sleep in the open), harness, horse armour, the forges for the smiths, vessels for brewing ale and all the other baggage and paraphernalia required for the maintenance of an effective fighting force. The larger sections of the siege train were conveyed by gun carriages that sometimes needed as many as twenty-four horses to draw them. Ovens were crucial for baking bread, but those sent over from England were faulty and the horses 'so evil that they be not able to draw one of them under fourteen or fifteen horses'.[31] The marching pace was slow. Wagons and carriages were frequently held up or overturned by the rough terrain and there was the constant threat of ambush.

Planning the route to Montreuil and finding night quarters presented further challenges to Surrey. He had no detailed maps and had to rely on the advice of de Buren, who sought to preserve the border territories in the Low Countries from the ravages of a marching army. 'We might have been at Montreuil three or four days past,' Surrey, Norfolk and the war council complained on 4 July, but we, knowing no part of the country, nor having no guides but such as they gave us, have been brought such ways as we think never army passed, up and down the hills, through hedges, woods and marshes, and all to cause us to lodge upon the French grounds, saving their own friends.

These practices invariably bred resentment and mistrust. Only yesterday, the letter continued, de Buren had recommended a spot within a couple of miles of Montreuil: 'Whereupon, being often deceived, we, the Earl of Surrey, Lord Warden and Poynings went to view the ground, where was neither grass nor forage for horses and such hills and passages that it was impossible for the army to pass that way; and therefore [we] are enforced this day not to go so far, but to take another [site] near hand.' The English had no choice but to liaise with their Imperial allies, who not only provided a division of troops, but also supplied them with food and drink from Flanders. 'Though we speak quickly,' the English acknowledged, 'we must of force handle them with gentle words, or else they may displease us at their pleasure in keeping victuals from us.'[32]

Even when Surrey's scouts did manage to locate suitable camping ground, the 'strange and horrible' weather conspired to disrupt their progress. Writing from Wymminghen, 'this 5th foul night of July', the English command reported that 'by our own search, without help of guides sent unto us by the lords of those parts, we found yesterday (as we thought) a good way to bring us thither, yet this excessive rain hath so moisted the ground that we doubt very much (though the weather break up this day or night following) that we shall not [sic] be able to reach the place of a good time where we determined to have lyen tomorrow.'[33]

Nor were their problems alleviated when they finally arrived at Montreuil, for it was immediately apparent that the plans of the town that Norfolk had been given were wholly misleading. Far from being an easy town to approach, Montreuil rose on a high mound above the River Canche and was surrounded by flat lands that offered very little cover. The French had anticipated the siege well. The Governor of Boulogne, Marshal du Biez, had tracked the progress of the allied host and foreseen that the intended target was Montreuil. Accordingly he had hastened there with four thousand men from the Boulogne garrison and set to work on external defences and bulwarks. When the English finally arrived, the town was well fortified and supplied. On 8 July 1544 Norfolk viewed Montreuil with the Imperial generals. The following morning he reported succinctly that 'none of us ever saw so evil a town to make approach unto.'[34]

His misgivings were brushed aside by Henry VIII. The figure of four thousand Frenchmen defending the town was bound to be an exaggeration, he said. 'My Lord of Norfolk knoweth well enough the counts the French make of their number which vaunt always commonly two for one.' Norfolk, Henry argued, should have been neither surprised nor cowed by his findings. Montreuil was a frontier town and all such towns were well fortified. If 'no man have courage to essay the winning of them', then little good would be achieved in France.[35] In other words, if Norfolk wished to preserve his honour and his favour with the King, he would just have to get on with it.

The following day the siege began, 'but to say truth,' Norfolk wrote, 'not like a siege for they have two of their gates open and in manner one other at their liberty to go in and out all the night through'. Lord John Russell and the rearguard were encamped 'in a little vale within two flight shots of the town, being continually visited with their ordnance very quickly', while Norfolk, Surrey and the vanguard were lodged a little further away, 'half a mile from Abbeville Gate, because,' Norfolk explained, 'I can find no place to lay my company out of danger of the shot of the town, nor scant sure there, for often they shoot into my camp.' In the same letter Norfolk lamented the fact that while the town was well manned and armed, 'we have but 4 cannons, 8 demi-cannons and 4 culverins, which the Burgundians do say is too little to make one battery.' They were also short of victuals, 'specially of drink', and only had enough powder and shot for '8 or 10 days' battery at the most'.[36]

Nevertheless, Norfolk promised to do his best and immediately set his sappers to work on trenches and a mount from which he hoped to batter the defences along Abbeville Gate. By 2 August he could report that work on the mount was progressing well:

We think it hath not been seen more diligence than made in raising our mount. There is neither lord nor gentleman but doth continually (as their time cometh about) labour in their own person to give example how the soldiers should travail. And there is ever both forenoon and afternoon four hundred men working thereupon and 600 other soldiers making of faggots in the forenoon and as many at afternoon. And all day 160 carts carrying of faggots to raise the said mount. The Burgundians do wonder to see the great diligence [that] is made here and the great pain taken of every part as well great personages as small.[37]

According to a Welsh infantryman called Elis Gruffydd, though, it was simply a face-saving operation. The English works were 'as profitless as rowing against the wind and the tide'.[38] The French pounded the English with up to a thousand shot a day, while at night they attacked the trenches in person.[39] Montreuil never looked like falling. Too many gates remained open, making it easy for the French to reinforce the town, and although Norfolk heard that some of the enemy were reduced to eating horse-flesh and were 'glad to eat of a cat well larded and call it dainty meat', it was in fact his own men who were more likely to starve.[40]

The sheer size of the army, its distance from English territory and the length of the campaign meant that the English had to rely on a steady supply of foodstuffs from Flanders. Frequently, however, the promised provisions never arrived and even when they did, they were sold at such inflated prices that few English soldiers could afford them. Even before they had reached Montreuil, Norfolk was complaining that 'we cannot get drink to serve our men by the twentieth part that we do need and yet that little we have, sold at so unreasonable price that no soldier can live off their wages unless they live with water.'*[41]

As the siege progressed, matters grew steadily worse. Demand within the camp rose, but supply dwindled as French troops, led by the Duke of Vendôme, executed a series of devastating attacks on the allied convoys.[42] With provisions so scarce, Norfolk was forced to send raiding parties deep into French country where Vendôme and his men held sway. On the night of Saturday, 30 August Surrey rode out of Montreuil with a band of noblemen. They burned the walled towns of St Riquier and Rue and only had to advance upon Crotoy before its terrified citizens burned it themselves. On the outskirts of Abbeville, they had 'a right hot skirmish' with the French, but fought well and were able to withdraw 'without loss of any man slain'. They returned to the camp before Montreuil at seven o'clock on Tuesday evening with 'a very great booty of all sorts of cattle'. Norfolk, who reported these events to the Council three hours later, praised the 'very honest journey' made by

---

* Water was commonly polluted and only ever drunk when the beer ration dried up.

Surrey and his men. They have, Norfolk wrote, 'made such an excourse that the like hath not been made since these wars began'.[43]

But it was a rare triumph and the spoils of their raid did not stretch far. Many of the soldiers were so hungry that they went foraging without escort. The Welshman Gruffydd kept a chronicle of his experiences at Montreuil. 'I often saw,' he wrote, 'a dozen able-bodied lusty men seven or eight miles from the camp in orchards and fields without three weapons among them to face their enemies with; and sometimes one could see forty men without even six weapons to protect them.' In one orchard not far from the camp, the bodies of some of them were later discovered hanging grotesquely from the trees, 'after the French had crammed their jaws and bosoms with cherries'.[44]

The obstacles facing the English camp might yet have been surmounted had Henry VIII fully committed to the siege. This, however, he refused to do. The King's priority was always Boulogne. Success there would almost double the size of the Calais Pale and effectively cut France off from the Low Countries, thereby reviving some of England's early dominance in Europe. According to ambassador Chapuys, Henry VIII valued Boulogne above Paris itself and, on 14 July 1544, he crossed the Channel in order to prosecute the siege in person.[45] Not only did Norfolk's petitions for reinforcements fall on deaf ears, but he was actually ordered to transfer some of his own men to Boulogne. While the besiegers at Boulogne were given 'enough cannons to conquer hell', Norfolk and his men were left to suffer the purgatory of Montreuil alone. As Gruffydd noted shrewdly and with justifiable bitterness, 'the King did not intend to capture Montreuil but only set them to lie there so that he and his host might take their ease and sleep more easily in their beds in the camp round Boulogne.'[46]

On 11 September Surrey and his half-uncle Lord William Howard set out for Boulogne with their servants in one last attempt to convince the King of the desperate state of their camp. As they travelled through the scarred countryside, peasants rushed towards the road and 'cried piteously in God's name for the help of a piece of bread to keep alive some of the little ones who were dying for want of food'. As Gruffydd, who made the same trip four days later wrote:

Their words and appearance would have made the hardest heart melt into tears from pity at seeing as many as a hundred people, old and young, with not one healthy man among them, but all shivering with ague, and death in their faces from the scarcity and lack of bread to strengthen them.[47]

Surrey arrived in Boulogne just in time to accompany Henry VIII to his viewing platform. Together they stood and watched as an English mine was detonated under the castle.[48] The following day the acting Governor of Boulogne, Seigneur de Vervins, offered to surrender. It was, perhaps, with a tinge of regret that Surrey took his leave of the conquering party and returned post-haste to Montreuil. But he had encouraging news. Henry VIII had finally promised to send men and provisions to the camp. As Norfolk wrote in his dispatch of 14 September, the news was as welcome as it was timely: 'The corn, now growing on the ground, doth begin to shake out of the ear . . . Also, our soldiers fall daily so sick, and in such numbers, that we remaining here shall have need of good reinforce[ments] as well of footmen and of horsemen, for our horses do daily die in great number.'[49]

Norfolk's relief was short-lived. The reinforcements did not leave Boulogne until 25 September, by which time it was too late. On 18 September Charles V had made his peace with Francis I, independently of Henry VIII and in breach of the Anglo-Imperial treaty, which stipulated that neither ally could treat for peace without the consent and inclusion of the other. Francis I, now able to concentrate solely on the North of France, sent his son, the Dauphin Henri,* to raise the siege of Montreuil. Henri had once shared apartments with Surrey in the Louvre. Now he marched against him with a force of some fifty thousand men. On 26 September his advance guard was spotted only ten miles away.

With the Dauphin so close and England's erstwhile allies withdrawn from the war, the only viable option was retreat. On 28 September the camp at Montreuil was broken. Few carriages were operable as so many horses had succumbed to disease and starvation. Mills, ovens and tents were therefore destroyed in order to prevent the incoming French from taking them. As Marshal of the Field, Surrey bore the responsibility for the evacuation and upon him also devolved the dangerous task of bringing up the rear. It is to his immense credit, therefore, that the retreat over the river, 'across hill and dale', through waterlogged fields and 'freezing wind', with the French constantly snapping at their heels,

* Henri was Francis I's second son. He became Dauphin on the death of his elder brother François in 1536.

was executed with precision and efficiency. On 30 September 1544 the English arrived at Boulogne 'safe and sound', if somewhat bedraggled. The same day Henry VIII took ship back to England.[50]

The Dauphin stalked the region until the night of 9 October, when he launched a surprise attack on the garrison at Boulogne. The English managed to repel their assailants and thereafter the Dauphin lost heart and soon retired to Paris. Boulogne had been won and retained, but Henry VIII was under no illusion that the French would seek to avenge it at the next opportunity. For the first time in his reign, thanks to the perfidy of the Emperor, he was going to have to face them alone.

Surrey was back in England in good time for Christmas, but the effects of the war lingered well into the following year. The appalling weather, especially the relentless storms of mid-September, the scarcity of victuals, which had driven men to eat rotting food and drink polluted water, and the inadequate living conditions, made worse by 'the stink of the carrion of the mares and horses that died among the host', had created a breeding ground for disease. Dysentery, plague, typhus, cholera, malaria and fevers 'so fierce that they took away people's memory and senses' had cut swathes through the allied camp.[51] Some had died instantly; others made it out of Montreuil, only to succumb later. As Gruffydd powerfully recalled,

> the soldiers coming from Calais and Boulogne were dying along the road from Dover to London and along the roads from London to every quarter of the Kingdom while trying to go to their homes. After they had come home, those who were well fell sick and those who were sick got worse and from this sickness and feebleness and pest they died in every part of England, mostly the people who had been in the camps by Montreuil among whom both before and after there was the greatest pest that ever was among people.[52]

One of the late casualties was Surrey's squire Thomas Clere, who died the following April. He was the same age as Surrey and had served him for many years. He had fought alongside him in Scotland and at Landrecy and had rampaged with him through London. The two had hunted, hawked, gambled and played tennis together. Clere had fallen in love with Surrey's close friend Mary Shelton, and he had served his master throughout with faith and constancy. Surrey's grief for Clere was comparable only to that which he had felt for his childhood companion the Duke of Richmond, and just as he had honoured Richmond's memory in verse, so now he honoured Clere's.

Surrey's elegy, or more accurately his epitaph, was later engraved on a tablet above Clere's tomb in the Howard chapel at St Mary's, Lambeth. It is one of Surrey's most moving poems and bears witness to a sensitivity and generosity of spirit that was all too frequently hidden from his contemporaries:

Norfolk sprang thee, Lambeth holds thee dead,
Clere of the County of Cleremont though hight;
Within the womb of Ormonde's race thou bred,
And sawest thy cousin crowned in thy sight.
Shelton for love, Surrey for lord thou chase:
Ay me! While life did last that league was tender;
Tracing whose steps thou sawest Kelsall blaze,
Laundersey burnt and battered Bullen render.
At Muttrell gates, hopeless of all recure,
Thine Earl, half dead, gave in thy hand his will;
Which cause did thee this pining death procure,
Ere summers four times seven thou couldest fulfil.
    Ah Clere, if love had booted, care or cost,
    Heaven had not won, nor Earth so timely lost.*[53]

From the first end-stopped line to the last, an elevated strain runs through Surrey's sonnet. Clere is emblazoned with all the virtues of a chivalric knight: gentility (both of manner and birth), loyalty, liberty, self-sacrifice, courage and constancy. The exact cause of his death is unknown, but the suggestion that he might have died from a wound

---

* line 2: *hight*: named. The sense of the first two lines is: *Although your name is Clere, you were born in Norfolk and lie buried in Lambeth*. The rest of the poem justifies Clere's place of honour in the Howard chapel.

line 3: the Cleres claimed descent from the Irish Earls of Ormonde.

line 4: a reference to the coronation of Anne Boleyn, both Surrey's and Clere's cousin (Anne's father, Thomas Boleyn, was Clere's uncle; her mother, Elizabeth née Howard, was Surrey's aunt).

line 5: *chase*: chose.

line 7: *Kelsall*: Kelso: one of the towns burnt during the 1542 campaign in Scotland.

line 8: *Laundersey*: Landrecy; *Bullen*: Boulogne.

line 9: *Muttrell*: Montreuil; *recure*: recovery.

line 13: *booted*: availed.

he had picked up while saving Surrey's life during an assault on Abbeville Gate – an assault that is nowhere mentioned in the records and almost certainly never happened – is unlikely. More convincing is the argument that Clere could have been felled by one of the diseases that ravaged the camp.[54] He may even have contracted something from Surrey himself, who claims that he lay 'half dead' at one point of the siege and with little chance of recovery. Surrey's rendering of Clere's death is ambiguous. What mattered to him was not so much its nature as what it represented. For Surrey it is the ultimate realisation of a 'tender league', a league that tied Surrey to Clere as strongly as it tied Clere to his lady. When Surrey places his 'will' in Clere's hands – literally his last will and testament but also perhaps his instructions or, more broadly, his aspirations – he reveals, in this act of giving, the mutual bond of trust that underlay that league.

Thomas Clere's descendants were rightly proud of him and proud, too, of Surrey's tribute. When Sir Edward Clere found himself slandered in 1606 by the Earl of Salisbury, one of Surrey's own descendants, he referred his accuser to Surrey's poem. That 'your honourable ancestor, the noble Earl of Surrey', he wrote, had been pleased 'to grace my ancestor with an epitaph wherein his great honour and my ancestor's faithful service and ancient lineage' were set forth, was surely, Edward Clere argued, sufficient testimony 'of the worth of our poor house'. Surrey's inscription of honour had proved to be, in the words of his grandson Lord William Howard, 'an argument of special eloquence'.[55]

But Surrey's epitaph, like his Windsor elegies, has another effect. In trumpeting the values of chivalry, Surrey draws attention to the gulf between theory and practice. His nostrils still smarted from the stench of rotting flesh and his ears rung with the pitiful pleas of the roadside peasants. He had seen death dealt out indiscriminately by disease and shot. He had witnessed the iniquities of his Imperial allies and his own King's celebrations at Boulogne as the rest of his men died in their hundreds twenty miles away. Surrey's elegy is a celebration of the pristine virtues of his squire, but it acts too as a kind of reverse foil for the gritty realities of Henry VIII's wars.

IN EVERY MAN'S EYE

War was a costly business, especially for the nobility. Unlike Francis I, Henry VIII had no standing army and, although he made use of mercenaries and militiamen, the vast bulk of his force was recruited on a 'quasi-feudal' basis whereby the nobility were obliged to supply as many able-bodied men as they could muster from their tenantry.[1] For the 1544 campaign, Norfolk and Surrey had provided one hundred and fifty horsemen and five hundred footmen.[2] Each soldier was paid sixpence a day by the King, ninepence if he had a horse, but the cost of equipping him was usually borne by his lord, as was the inevitable shortfall in farming revenue caused by the reduction in labour, livestock, horses and wagons.

According to *A Supplication to . . . Henry the Eyght*, printed in 1544, men who were ordered to perform military service were often 'compelled to sell their lands or else to burden their friends or else to danger themselves in debt to many'. This was not empty rhetoric. Sir George Blount claimed that he had been forced to sell one of his manors in order to gather 'some store of money for his ready furniture and provision of horses and other things necessary' to fulfil his duty.[3] Even someone as parsimonious as Norfolk found it hard to balance the books in wartime. Complaints about his 'decayed purse' were a refrain in every campaign he served.

Surrey, by contrast, was unconcerned by the pecuniary effects of the war and continued to spend, and borrow, with reckless abandon. The folding bedstead adorned with arms and Garter insignia that he commissioned 'for the wars' or the brand-new suit of armour that had cost him £8 might be considered permissible extravagances.[4] The huge sums he poured into rebuilding and furnishing his new house in Norwich were less easy to justify.

The estate of St Leonard's Priory, which Surrey had received the previous year, stood on a hill that rose steeply from the bank of the River Wensum. Surrey House, as it was re-christened (the hill becoming 'Mount Surrey'), became the Earl's pet project between the wars and he made no secret of his vision for the place. When he later made a translation of chapter two of Ecclesiastes, he rendered the lines *Magnificavi opera mea. Edificavi mihi domos et plantavi vineas* ('I made me great works; I builded me houses; I planted me vineyards') so freely that his own aspirations for Surrey House can surely be read into them:

> To build my houses fair then set I all my cure:
> By princely acts thus strave I still to make my fame endure.[5]

Surrey House was intended as a vehicle for magnificence. No one leaving its gates was to be allowed to forget the power of its owner. The grounds commanded spectacular views of the thriving city of Norwich* and contained three pavilions designed to resemble forts, replete with military insignia and ornamental cannon. In Surrey's vision for the house, the Howard lion would be everywhere, stalking the windows and plate that he would commission in 1545 and flying from the flag of the crenellated tower. In the inventory of Surrey House, taken in December 1546, there is an entry for 'the Lord of Surrey's picture'. This would have been hung in a position of prominence, reminding guests that it was Surrey, not his father, who represented the future of the dynasty.[6]

By modern standards the interior of the house might sound gaudy, but in Surrey's time it was the height of style. Reds and yellows and blues all vied for attention amidst a profusion of royal purple. Surrey's curtains and quilts were paned with purple and yellow silk. His chair of state was upholstered in purple velvet and satin, as was the canopy over his bed, which was 'embroidered with white lions of silver and passement lace fringed gold and silver'. Surrey's taste for the exotic was indulged by Turkish carpets, Spanish blankets and bedsteads from Flanders. Tapestries were an indication of status; a set of around ten, woven with silver and gold yarn, could cost 'more than a fully rigged

---

* Throughout the sixteenth and seventeenth centuries, Norwich was the largest and most affluent provincial city in England.

and armed warship'.[7] By the end of 1546 Surrey owned at least one set of hangings, though probably not of the finest quality, and over fifteen other pieces, bordered with garlands of flowers, pomegranates, cucumbers, grapes and birds.*

In the summer of 1545 Surrey decided that he needed a more imposing coat of arms to fit in with the Surrey House aesthetic. He experimented with various quarterings, including those of Edward the Confessor, Geoffrey Plantagenet, Count of Anjou, and even, it seems, those of his mythical hero Lancelot du Lac. According to his sister, Surrey had over seven rolls of heraldic devices.[8] By the beginning of August he had made up his mind and summoned England's chief herald, Christopher Barker, for official approval. Unfortunately Barker was not happy with Surrey's shield. In particular he seems to have objected to the Anjou quarter. He probably also queried Surrey's use of St Edward's arms, though he may not have specifically forbidden them. Surrey returned to the drawing board, took out the Anjou quarter, but retained the arms of Edward the Confessor as he had a legitimate claim to them through his Mowbray ancestors.[9] This seemingly innocuous decision would prove a fatal error of judgement.

On 23 April 1545 Surrey attended the Chapter of the Order of the Garter at St James's Palace.[10] It was an occasion of heightened solemnity, for it was rumoured that Francis I of France was ready to avenge the loss of Boulogne. Not only was he said to be sending forty thousand soldiers to besiege the town, but he was also planning to hamstring Henry VIII's defences by invading England from the North with the help of his Scottish allies and by blockading the Channel with a great fleet that he was amassing at Le Havre.

Henry determined to meet the threat head on. Surrey and the rest of the nobility returned to their counties to muster men and collect taxes. In addition to levies and subsidies, merchants and landowners were expected to contribute to a loan called the Benevolence. It was anything but; an alderman who refused to pay was sent to the borders, where he was subsequently captured by the Scots.[11] Henry VIII's three commanders from the previous year were entrusted with the security of England's shores. The Duke of Norfolk guarded the East Anglian coastline, the Duke of Suffolk the South-East, and Lord Russell the

* Surrey House was sacked during Kett's Rebellion of 1549 and later fell to ruin. There is nothing to visit today, but the view from what is now Gas Hill is worth the climb.

West. The King himself took personal command of the navy in Portsmouth. Surrey had been earmarked for the defence of Boulogne, but before he set sail he rode south to serve as liaison officer to Henry VIII and John Dudley, who as Lord Admiral, occupied Spitsand on the Solent with a fleet of sixty ships.

On 18 July 1545 the French Armada appeared on the horizon. It comprised two hundred and thirty-five ships, far more than the Spanish would put out in 1588, and four times the number of the English fleet. However the English, protected by the shallows and swirling currents of the Solent and covered by the guns of the forts and blockhouses behind them, held the strategic advantage. For the next few days Surrey dashed back and forth exchanging messages between Henry VIII at Southsea Castle and the Lord Admiral aboard the *Great Harry*. 'I would,' Dudley assured his King, 'for my own part little pass to shed the best blood in my body to remove them out of your sight.'[12]

But it was all bluster. Henry VIII ordered Dudley to hold position. The French tried to lure him out by invading the Isle of Wight. If the King was tempted, the vagaries of wind and current forestalled a general engagement. Most of the ships that were lost were victims not of artillery, but of human error and misfortune. Francis' first flagship had caught fire in Le Havre; its replacement sprang a leak and had to be run ashore. The fate of Henry VIII's old warship, the *Mary Rose*, is the saddest of all. Someone forgot to close the gunports so that when the dangerously overloaded ship began to heel as she turned in the wind, water flooded the ports taking down the ship and over four hundred men with her. By mid-August the French Admiral, Claude d'Annebault, admitted defeat. With his fleet riddled with plague, he raised anchor on 16 August and sailed back to France.[13]

Francis I's proposed invasion from the North never amounted to much either, but it was calamitous for the Scots. Henry VIII vowed revenge and in Edward Seymour, Earl of Hertford, he had a willing and ruthless instrument. In the space of two weeks Seymour 'burnt, razed and cast down' towns, abbeys, hospitals and a total of two hundred and forty-three villages.[14] That just left Boulogne. Francis I, it was said, 'hath so much spoken of Boulogne that he will have [it] and it hath been so noised in the world that in Boulogne consisteth now all his reputation, as he taketh it.'[15] By mid-August Thomas Poynings, the Captain of the English garrison at Boulogne, reported that twenty thousand French footmen, one thousand horsemen and twelve thousand sappers were encamped opposite the town with more on their way. By contrast, the whole garrison at Boulogne, including sappers, clerks, bakers, brewers and other labourers numbered well under ten thousand.[16] Hundreds had died of the plague or been sent home and those that remained lacked munitions, armour and provisions.

In response to the crisis, Surrey had left Portsmouth for Kenninghall at the end of July. Within two weeks he was ready to cross the Channel with four thousand men from East Anglia and a further thousand drawn from the London musters. This was the vanguard of the army sent to reinforce Poynings. The Duke of Suffolk, who was due to leave shortly with the rest of the army, would assume overall command and Surrey would captain the vanguard.[17] However, an extraordinary sequence of events soon presented Surrey with an even greater opportunity to shine.

On 18 August Poynings died of 'the bloody flux'. Four days later the Duke of Suffolk also died.[18] The Captaincy of Boulogne then passed to Lord Grey of Wilton, who had hitherto served the King as Captain of all the 'crews' within the marches of Guisnes and Calais. Surrey was ordered to fill Grey's vacancy, but only days later Henry VIII changed his mind. Grey was told to resume his old post and Surrey, whose desire 'to see and serve' had already been noted by the King's Secretary William Paget, was promoted to the Boulogne command.[19] Unlike his predecessors, who had only had the charge of the town, Surrey was also given ultimate responsibility for all English operations across the Channel. There could be no greater indication of Henry VIII's unique estimation of Surrey at this time. Only three years earlier the King had refused to appoint Henry Clifford, Earl of Cumberland, as Lord Warden of the North Marches because 'we think him to be yet of too few years for that office'.[20] Clifford had been twenty-five, only three years younger than Surrey was now, and yet Henry VIII appeared to have no qualms about entrusting Surrey with the greatest position of honour in his army. On the last day of August the Privy Council wrote to Surrey informing him of his appointment and on 3 September 1545 it was confirmed by letters patent. He was now Lieutenant General of the King on Sea and Land for all the English possessions on the Continent.[21]

Boulogne was in poor shape after the battering it had received the previous year. The infrastructure had to be completely overhauled, the

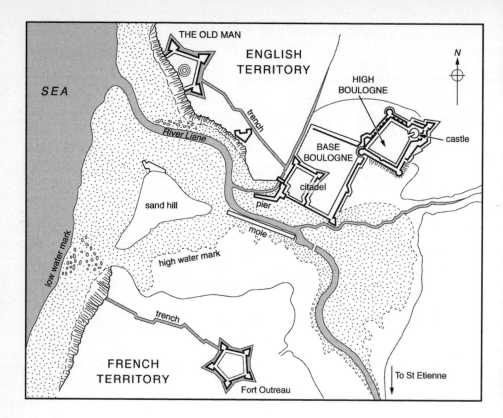

houses needed rebuilding, the sanitation was poor and communications had to be revived. To the dismay of his more reform-minded friends, Surrey even erected an altar in the church. One of the earliest sets of instructions he received from the Privy Council concerned the imposition of order and the reduction of waste. He was told 'to send away all sick and maimed men', to launch an investigation into any malpractices committed by the head officers and 'to rid all harlots and common women out of Boulogne'.*[22]

The town's fortifications were crucial to the retention of Boulogne. There were three main strongholds. First was the bastioned watchtower, which stood on a cliff overlooking the Liane estuary and was known to the English as 'the Old Man'. A little downstream was Base Boulogne, which controlled the harbour, and leading off from its north-east tower

---

* Overseas garrisons were magnets for prostitution, especially the following spring when the King suppressed the Southwark brothels. According to one soldier, 'shameless prostitutes came at every tide from England' and 'descended on Boulogne dressed as gallantly as they knew how in velvet and silk of the finest cloth and the soldiers took them up so that no one could call himself worthy without a whore or two following him from every house like the sheath after the dagger' (Gruffydd II, pp. 13–14).

Map of the Pas de Calais by Nicholas de Nicolay, 1558

was High Boulogne, where the castle stood and the main garrison was quartered. Surrey's predecessors had already begun to re-fortify these sections and re-establish the lines of defence between them. Surrey consolidated and expanded their work, overseeing new ditches, trenches, gun-platforms, bulwarks, bastions and jetties.

By the end of Henry VIII's reign Boulogne could boast an elaborate network of fortifications, characterised by the short, squat structures and angled bastions pioneered by the Italians. These 'modern' defences were a direct response to the recent improvements made in artillery and were far better at absorbing, and directing, cannon fire than the high-walled medieval castle. Surrey was by no means responsible for all the defences erected at Boulogne and, as he readily admitted, there was still much to be done by the end of his tenure, but the progress made under his watch was crucial. Indeed he assumed such an active role in the town's defences that he clashed with John Rogers, the surveyor of the town, whose plans were as precious to him as any artist's work-in-progress. 'Your Lordship knoweth that the man is plain and blunt,' Surrey had to be reminded, but he 'must be borne withal as long as he is well meaning and mindeth the service of the King's Majesty.'[23]

It was not enough just to defend Boulogne from a direct assault; the town also had to be able to receive supplies. As the French controlled the outlying territory and were able to intercept any convoys travelling overland from Calais and Guisnes, the only viable supply line was from the sea. It was vital, therefore, that Surrey guaranteed protection to the ships entering and leaving the haven. The French commander, Marshal du Biez, who had defended Montreuil so effectively the previous year, was equally determined that Surrey should not. He had nearly finished work on Fort Outreau, an impressive pentagonal fortress built on the high ground opposite Base Boulogne across the River Liane. Its guns were not within accurate range of the town but its presence so close to the harbour was alarming, especially as du Biez was also setting up other strongholds along the coast and further inland.[24]

Surrey's options were therefore limited. The great army that was supposed to have been sent over with Suffolk had been stayed on his death.[25] If Surrey were to attempt anything major against the French, he would be outnumbered and outgunned and the town would be left vulnerable. But if he sat back and did nothing but improve his own defences, the French would be free to work on their own fortifications and threaten his supplies. He therefore resolved upon a number of short, sharp sallies against the convoys sent to sustain the French works with materials and provisions from the south. In this, he was remarkably effective.

Among his many successful raids was the burning of Samer 'and all the country thereabout', the ambush of a French force around St Etienne – 'we drove them from place to place to the Sandhills and so from hill to hill to Hardelot' – and the putting to flight of forty French supply ships, seven of which were captured – 'whereby, besides the ruin of their horsemen and footmen by the extremity of the weather, their whole purpose is for this present disappointed.' Each triumph was joyfully narrated by Surrey in the glossy chivalric language that appealed to the King: 'the cavalry offered the charge'; the enemy were 'upon the spur' and 'well dagged with arrows'; 'Francis Aslebye, that hurt Mons. d'Aumale break his staff very honestly'; 'Mr Marshal very honestly and hardily brake his mace upon a Frenchman; Mr Shelley brake his staff upon a tall young gentleman of Monsieur de Botyer's band and took him prisoner; and in effect, all the men at arms of this town brake their staves'.[26]

Swept away by the thrill of it all, Surrey sometimes took unnecessary risks. On 25 September the King's Secretary William Paget wrote to him warning him not to 'admit any light ruffians to be of counsel with you, or be persuaded by any of them to put yourself at any skirmish further in danger than were expedient either for the Earl of Surrey or the King's Lieutenant there to enter into.' Paget knew how to play on Surrey's sense of honour. His letter was supremely tactful:

His Majesty thinketh your Lordship hath right well showed your courage and likewise your dexterity and wisdom and trusteth that, by over too great adventure, you will not commit anything that shall detract [from] that which is passed. You must now, my Lord, think that you are in every man's eye. Men before this time hoped well of you and, by these your happy and wise proceedings, you have given them occasion to look for greater and better every day. . . Wherein fear not but you shall be able to answer to all.[27]

But neither this letter, nor another written two days later by the Duke of Norfolk, could temper Surrey's zeal. On 6 November he was upbraided for venturing too close to the French lines. 'The King's Majesty,' Surrey read, 'took it in very ill part that ye should adventure your presence in standing upon the bridge of the fortress for the better viewing of the same.'[28] But even if the King was genuinely annoyed by Surrey's 'negligence', he was heartened by his passion. Henry VIII and Surrey were at one in their vision for Boulogne. To them it was not a French town under English occupation, but an honourable conquest that had to be conserved. Henry called Boulogne 'his daughter' and Surrey was equally sentimental, referring to it as a 'jewel'.[29] Both were die-hard hawks, committed to further success in arms and desperate for lasting glory. So Surrey continued to send his jingoistic letters. Henry VIII, beguiled, spurred him on and Surrey wrote back, urging his King to share in the honour of the enterprise by coming in person: You should have seen, If only you could see, When you come soon you will see: the courage of your men, the desperation of the French, 'how easy it is to keep the strait'. Each swept the other along upon a tide of hubris.

Practically everyone else touched by the war lamented its prolongation. Morale in the camp was very low. Those who had been in the garrison before Surrey's arrival had not been paid for several months. Of the five thousand men that Surrey had brought over from England many, especially those from London, 'who were delicate and disliked lying on the ground and on planks', found the privations of war intolerable. According to Elis Gruffydd, who served in the Calais garrison and considered himself a hardened professional, the men who arrived from England at this time were a motley crew – 'among them many a flatfooted, crooked ankled, squint-eyed, crooked shouldered, skew headed, unshapely man, unfit to carry arms; in fact many admitted they had never carried any.'[30]

As winter approached and the camp became colder, wetter and increasingly diseased, the mood of the men darkened. There were not even enough fresh supplies. According to Gruffydd, his colleagues in Boulogne had to rely on the mouldy old provisions of the King's storehouses:

> The bread was hard and baked with corn and meal, which had lost its taste and savour, and the salt beef stank when it was lifted out of the brine. The butter was of many colours and the cheese dry and hard, and this was the best they could get from the King's stores, which made most of the soldiers miserable and reckless.[31]

To make matters worse, the foreign mercenaries, who formed an essential part of the Boulogne garrison, were paid more, and more regularly, than the Englishmen. This caused considerable resentment. As Paget explained, an English horseman on a wage of ninepence a day, 'if his horse is killed, is not able to buy another, and seeing a stranger have £3 a month, and he but 20 shillings, his heart is killed.'[32]

The mercenaries were an ongoing headache for Surrey. Whenever their high wage demands were not met, they threatened to up weapons and leave or, worse still, to join the French. If the majority of English complaints are to be credited, the mercenary captains were little more than conmen. They knew how to siphon and pilfer and embezzle. They concocted wild stories about how the King's money had managed to go missing and, on occasion, they even held the King's agents to ransom. 'Happy is he that hath no need of Almains [Germans]', Stephen Vaughn, the King's financier, wrote from Antwerp, 'for of all the nations under the heavens, they be the worst, most rudest and unreasonablest to deal withal.' For Paget, the Italians were just as bad, if not worse, because they set such 'naughty examples' to the rest of the men. The English captains, Paget wrote despairingly, were now following them 'in deceiving of the King's Majesty in their musters and other encroachments of wages and polling and nipping of their poor soldiers' wages'. The Italian proverb, he concluded sadly, 'is now true': *Ung Inglese Italianato e ung diavolo incarnato.*[33]

Surrey took his pastoral responsibilities very seriously and showed genuine concern for his men. His letters to the King and Council were full of enquiries into the wage and food situation. After the King had agreed to waive the customs duties on all the victuals entering Boulogne, Surrey wrote on behalf of his 'poor men' who still 'complain they are much exacted by the customers' and went on to request that 'there may be redress had in that behalf accordingly'. Having noticed that the goods of his dead men were running 'to the common sack and not to the heir', he requested that a commissioner learned in the law be sent to supervise his men's wills.[34] Surrey also made a point of commending individuals for exceptional work, as the following extract from a letter to the King, dated 4 December 1545, illustrates:

I beseech Your Highness to be good and gracious Lord to this bearer, Mr Dudley, who, for his towardness and good will to serve hath few fellows in this town and hath a brother in the Old Man, a gentleman of as good a sort and as serviceable as I have much seen. Mr Arden also, both now and at sundry times for his service, hath deserved to be humble commended by me unto Your Majesty. Mr Adrian Poynings, I assure Your Majesty, is a man for his discretion and hardiness of great service.[35]

On 14 September Surrey wrote on behalf of Thomas Norwick of London and Richard Songar of Dover, whose supply boats had been captured by the French. In Surrey's opinion each 'poor man' deserved 'some reasonable recompense'. So did three 'maimed men' for whom Surrey wrote separate letters in February.[36] He showed similar kindness to 'poor Sir Andrew Flammock, whose service, as I observed in the town and field, hath been always of such sort, as me thinketh he hath well deserved to be defended from poverty now in his old days.' Another case that received Surrey's support was that of Sir Richard Wingfield. He had been held hostage by the French for seventeen months and 'is now returned, ransomed so high, that scarce all that the poor gentleman hath to be sold will suffice to redeem him.' Surrey's concern here was not just for the individual. As he explained when he interceded for Wingfield, if the King would be gracious enough to show the man favour, the rest of the men shall be encouraged 'to adventure their lives in the service of so noble and thankful a Prince as never yet left acceptable service unrewarded.'[37]

But no matter how hard Surrey tried to rally the troops, morale remained low. The tough conditions, the rotten food, even the unpaid wages might have been bearable had the men been stimulated by the cause. But there was little sense of this. Not even the garrisons at Calais and Guisnes were particularly supportive and Surrey had real difficulty gaining reinforcements from the commanders there.[38] Back at home, Henry VIII's financial impositions ensured that patriotic fervour was in short supply. 'Touching the public opinion of the English regarding the war,' the Imperial ambassador reported on 18 June 1545, 'so far as I can learn – and I have heard it from innumerable people – there is not a soul with any wit in England who does not blaspheme at the war.'[39]

Around Henry VIII's Council table the hostility to the retention of Boulogne was even greater. Just after the English had won the town, Paget had estimated that the cost of war for the next six months would be £90,000. In fact the military expenses for the year following Michaelmas 1544 amounted to £560,000 and the majority of this was spent on operations in France.[40] Every source of revenue had been drained. Even the coinage was reminted with a lower precious metal content. On 11 November 1545 Lord Chancellor Wriothesley presented

Paget with a detailed assessment of the King's finances. It made depressing reading. 'If you tarry for more money to be sent to Boulogne at this time,' he wrote, 'you may percase tarry too long before you have the sum desired . . . I assure you, Master Secretary, I am at my wits' end how we shall possibly shift for three months following, and specially for the two next. For I see not any great likelihood that any good sum will come in till after Christmas.'[41]

The Council implored their King to relinquish Boulogne. He would strike a very good peace deal, they argued, if only he agreed to put the town on the table. But Henry was immovable: 'He had honourably won the place at the sword's point and he meant to keep it.'[42] There seemed to be only one possible way by which the King might be persuaded to abandon his dream, and that was through the mediation of his fellow-visionary, the Earl of Surrey. But hitherto Surrey had proved as blinkered and stubborn as his King, perhaps even more so.

Before he had completed even a month in Boulogne, Surrey had received a letter from his father warning him to 'animate not the King too much for the keeping of Boulogne, for who so doth, at length shall get small thanks.'[43] A month later, his letter having had no discernible effect, Norfolk resorted to other measures. Surrey had asked that Frances and the children be allowed to join him in Boulogne. Norfolk now sent a message to his son, informing him that his request had been denied. Norfolk also knew that Surrey was in financial straits and that he owed a lot of people a lot of money, including his own servant, Richard Fulmerston. On 26 October Norfolk's treasurer, Thomas Hussey, sent Surrey a letter in which he detailed a conversation he had just had with the Duke. 'What way,' Norfolk had asked Hussey, 'taketh my son for payment of his debts?'

'I answered & saith "I know not".

"Well," quod he, "he oweth Fulmerston an honest sum, and what oweth he you?"

I answered: "so much as I can be content to forbear in respect of his necessity."'

Norfolk had then enquired into a manor that Surrey had been licensed to sell two months earlier.[44] Hussey warned Surrey that his father was prepared to 'make some stop' in order to sabotage the deal. Norfolk had also made it clear that he was no longer prepared to underwrite any of Surrey's loans and that the provisions the Earl wanted for Surrey House 'will not be attained at my Lord's hand'. Hussey promised to help by borrowing some money 'upon my credit in this town', but 'to be plain with you, I cannot see how ye can both pay your whole debts and finance your necessities at the present.' Just in case Surrey had not already guessed the reason for his father's obstructiveness, Hussey made it perfectly clear: 'by these means and others ye may be made weary of your will of Boulogne.' Then, aware of the sensitive nature of the letter and the potential disaster that might ensue if it fell into the King's hands, Hussey implored Surrey, 'as my trust is in you, burn this letter'.[45] Surrey clearly did not honour Hussey's request.

Just eleven days later Norfolk felt the need to adopt a more direct approach. Once again, Thomas Hussey was the intermediary. On 6 November he wrote to Surrey:

> I see my Lord's Grace somewhat offended in seeing your private letters to the King's Majesty of such vehemency as touching the animating of the King's Majesty for the keeping of Boulogne and in especial considering his diverse letters addressed to your Lordship, to the which, as he thinketh, ye have given simple credence. For what His Grace and the rest of the Council worketh in for the rendry of Boulogne and the concluding of a peace in six days, ye with your letters set back in six hours, such importance be your letters in the King's opinion at this time. Albeit that my Lord concludeth ye may, by your practices, sustain the same Boulogne for 2 or 3 months, yet he thinketh it impossible that it may continue 6 months, forasmuch as he certainly knoweth the realm of England not possible to bear the charges of the same.

Boulogne had to be abandoned. The King was in debt by four hundred thousand marks. 'Every councillor saith "Away with it"; and the King and your Lordship saith "We will keep it".' Surrey would not, Hussey assured him, receive 'any recompense out of the King's coffers' for his own expenses, but 'if Boulogne be rendered', then Norfolk would push hard for Surrey to be granted 'either the Captainship of the Castle of Guisnes or the Deputyship of Calais'. Having proffered the carrot, Hussey then wielded the stick: 'Assuring your Lordship that I heard my Lord say that he had rather bury you and the rest of his children before he should give his consent to the ruin of this realm, not doubting but that ye should be removed in spite of your head [obstinacy] work what ye could.'[46] Here was the Duke of Norfolk unmasked. Surrey and his siblings were not indispensable. They could be sacrificed, as their cousins had been, for the greater good of the House of Howard. Surrey was useful only for as long as he played the part of the dutiful heir. If he stepped out of line, or entertained ideas above his station, then he would be on his own.

But nothing could douse the flames of Surrey's ardour, not separation from his wife and children, not the threat of bankruptcy and political marginalisation, not even the prospect of alienation from his father. Despite all the hardships and sacrifices, Surrey felt Boulogne was worth it. He was, according to the final lines of an oblique poem he composed in Boulogne,

> as restless to remain,
> Against my will, full pleased with my pain.[47]

Such was the extent of Surrey's vainglory and so warm did he feel from the glow of the King's favour that he continued to work on his controversial coat of arms. Quite openly, 'in the presence of the King's Highness's Council there', Surrey had the new quarterings painted into escutcheons and forwarded to his agent at Surrey House.[48] Around the same time he commissioned a new portrait of himself. Hussey's second letter makes reference to it, stating that its progress was being held up because the artist was working on a portrait of the Queen. If, as is probable, the artist was William Scrots, a Dutchman who had recently succeeded Holbein as the official Court painter, then the work mentioned by Hussey may be identified as Surrey's famous last portrait, an early seventeenth-century version of which now hangs in Arundel Castle (plate 26).*[49]

Here Surrey is depicted in full-length, standing under an archway. He seems to have just emerged from a ruined landscape. His fur cloak is still billowing. He leans on a broken column (a symbol of suffering and endurance), his left hand casually resting on his hip, his right clasping a white glove (denoting wealth and power) and pointing towards his codpiece (a sign of virility). On the plinth of the column, Surrey instructed the artist to paint a miniature of the Duke of Richmond. The broken pillar topos had previously been adopted by Surrey's two literary heroes, Francesco Petrarch and Sir Thomas Wyatt. 'Broken is the high column and the green laurel that made shade for my tired thought,' Petrarch wrote as he mourned the loss of his lover, Laura, and his patron, Cardinal Giovanni Colonna. For Wyatt, writing

* Later versions of this portrait also exist at Parham Park, Knole and Castle Howard.

on the occasion of Thomas Cromwell's execution, 'the pillar perished
is whereto I leant / the strongest stay of mine unquiet mind.'[50]

Why would Surrey want to resurrect the painful memory of the Duke
of Richmond almost ten years after his death? Was he drawing attention to the bond of honour that he had shared with Richmond and
now thought he shared with the King? Under pressure from his father
and the rest of the Privy Council to cede Boulogne, he may have drawn
strength from the chivalric vision that Richmond represented for him.
Or could Surrey have been advertising his suitability for a role as the
King's other son's *incitateur*, even, perhaps, his Protector? The portrait
is complex and full of esoteric symbols, but Surrey's charisma is unequiv-
ocal. He stands there as a hero, dressed in sumptuous Italianate clothes,
adorned in the insignia of the Order of the Garter, staring directly out
of the canvas as if promising that through his agency good things will
arise from the ruins behind him.

It never seemed to have occurred to Surrey that his confidence may
have been misplaced or that the King's favour could be anything but
permanent. Like Aeneas, whose story he rendered into English blank
verse, Surrey had a destiny to fulfil. Yet only divinely ordained kings
had the right to indulge grand visions. As long as Surrey continued to
report successes, Henry VIII would be pleased to claim them. But if
anything were to go wrong, it was the King's prerogative to absolve
himself from blame. There would always be scapegoats, as Wolsey,
Cromwell and a long line of other faithful servants had shown.

'God hath given you much of his grace, courage, knowledge of the
war, liberality and good luck,' Paget had written to Surrey in September,
'all which, if you shall join in one and use together, you shall serve
well the King's Majesty and go beyond all your ancestors in honour
and renown and give great cause of joy to all your friends.' 'But,' Paget
continued – and it was an important but – 'among all other things
forget not to give the praise and glory to God of all good that cometh
to you, and so shall you prosper.'[51] God had so far graced Surrey with
the good luck needed by all great military leaders. But as the new year
approached and Henry VIII and his Lieutenant resolved upon a more
offensive approach towards the retention of Boulogne, Surrey, as Paget
had warned, had better pray, and pray hard, for his luck to continue.

LOSS OF REPUTATION

The favours of great princes (which exceed all bonds of moderation) were never durable. The sun arrives no sooner to his height but he declines again. The waters ebb when the flood is past.

Henry Howard, second son of the Earl of Surrey, 1583.[1]

On the night of Wednesday, 6 January 1546 smoke was seen curling up from the valleys before Montreuil. It came from the campfires of du Biez, who was marching towards Boulogne with a great force. His destination was Fort Outreau and he intended to escort over a hundred wagons laden with provisions safely into the fort. Surrey's recent raids had necessitated such a measure. In the past sixteen days over four hundred Frenchmen had reportedly died in the fort, 'partly for want of victuals, partly for want of wood, houses and other necessaries'.[2] Surrey had written to the King only the day before about the 'misery' of the French at Outreau and had forwarded a plan 'to famish the same' into submission by encamping 'so strongly in the strait in diverse places, trenched the one from the other, as no relief of victuals may pass'.[3] There was no time now for Surrey to implement his stratagem. To prevent the convoy from reaching the fort, he would have to meet it head on.

At the break of the following day Surrey sent an advance guard of around six hundred footmen to occupy the hill and trenches of St Etienne, a small village on the other side of the river that the French would have to pass on their way to the fort.[4] Surrey also ordered Ralph

Ellerker, 'with all the horsemen of this town', and George Pollard, 'with two hundred that he brought the night before from Guisnes', to scout the area further south and monitor the progress of the French. As they passed Hardelot, a culverin was fired from the castle. Pollard was struck in the knee and died soon after from his wounds. It was an inauspicious start.

Once Surrey received news that the French had passed Hardelot, he raised his banner and led two thousand footmen out of the garrison. Linking up with the scouts and advance guard at St Etienne, Surrey set his troops in order of battle. The majority of his force consisted of pike and billmen. He also had one wing of archers and two armed with handguns, known as harquebuses. On the right flank, blocking the path to Fort Outreau, Surrey positioned his horsemen. As the evening approached, the enemy came into view: four thousand footmen and around five hundred horsemen, including two troops of German mercenaries and two wings of harquebusiers.

Surrey was outnumbered and, bizarrely, his front line contained many men of rank. According to Surrey, they had volunteered for such a vulnerable position 'because they were well armed in corselets'. Another, equally plausible, reason is given by Elis Gruffydd, who claimed that Surrey's underpaid, undernourished soldiers had balked at the thought of front-line duty and, despite much 'beating and shoving' by Surrey and his officers, had refused to advance, 'so that the Earl ordered the captains to go forward'.[5]

Surrey decided to risk all. He ordered his cavalry to attack. Thundering down the hill, they managed to break through the enemy's harquebusiers and charge directly at the French horse. Then, Surrey tells us, 'their horsemen fled and ours followed the victory and killed and slew till they came to the carriages, where they brake four score and ten.' Surrey scented victory. Over four-fifths of the convoy had been destroyed and the French were in disarray. The English front line now charged 'with a cry of as great courage and in as good order as we could wish'. The enemy countered fiercely, encouraged, if one French commentator is to be credited, by du Biez himself, who 'leapt down from his horse' and 'threw himself all alone' at one of the English battalions.[6] With the handgunners on both sides falling back to re-load, the footmen of the second line found themselves at 'the push of the pike'. Suddenly some of the Englishmen panicked and bolted. Seeing this, the back lines also began to flee leaving the front line dangerously exposed. The French then turned on them 'as cruel as wolves among sheep'.

Surrey tried to rally the troops, riding up and down the lines, crying 'loudly on the people to turn and fight in order to face the attack, but they would not listen and only retreated faster'. Instead of seeking sanctuary in the trenches around St Etienne, the Englishmen were now so terrified of the French army 'which was pursuing and killing without quarter', that they continued their flight towards the river. There was only one crossing here, a small bridge known as Pont de Brique, 'where there was not much room for men to cross together'. Wave upon wave stormed the bridge, desperate man. after desperate man bent only on making it to the other side. 'Many of the footmen were forced off the bridge'; those in armour had mercifully swift deaths; others were left thrashing about in the deep water, clambering over each other, screaming for succour and gasping for air. The men that did survive traipsed back to the garrison, 'which they reached about nine o'clock at night like defeated men, one after the other'.[7]

As soon as Surrey and the surviving members of his council returned to Boulogne, they threw off their armour and hurried to the council house where they drafted letters to Henry VIII and the Privy Council. There was 'loss and victory on both sides,' Surrey informed the King; 'the enemy took more loss than we.' There are no accurate figures for the number of French dead (the Privy Council said three hundred; Gardiner heard six hundred[8]) and accounts vary wildly over the extent of the English casualties. Surrey recorded two hundred and five losses; the Frenchman, Martin du Bellay, said that between seven and eight hundred Englishmen had perished and the Spanish and Venetians heard from their sources that the figure was over a thousand.[9]

Surrey's claim that du Biez sustained heavier losses than he seems dubious, but even if this was the case, it was the quality of men lost rather than the quantity that provided the more accurate barometer of success. The common soldier was expendable, but an experienced officer was a rare commodity. Accordingly, Surrey had suffered a terrible defeat at St Etienne for the majority of the captains and gentlemen fighting in the front line had been slain. Surrey's list of dead officers is a roll call of top-flight military talent: 'Mr Edward Poynings, Captain Story, Captain Jones, Spencer, Roberts, Basford, Wourth, Wynchcombe, Mr Vawse and a man at arms called Harvy. Captain Crayford and Mr John Palmer and Captain Shelley and Captain Cobham, missed but not found. All these were slain in the first rank.' Their loss, Surrey admitted, 'was much to be lamented'.[10]

The rest of Surrey's letter attempts to play down the loss. He points out that less than twenty wagons had entered Fort Outreau and they only contained biscuit:

And thus beseeching Your Highness to accept our poor service, albeit the success in all things was not such as we wished, yet was the enemy's enterprise disappointed, which could not have been otherwise done; and more of their part slain than of ours; and the fortress in as great misery as before; and a sudden flight the let of a full victory. And if any disorder there were, we assure Your Majesty there was no default in the rulers, nor lack of courage to be given them, but a humour that sometime reigneth in Englishmen.

Surrey's next sentence alludes to the cause of this 'humour':

Most humbly thanking Your Majesty that it hath pleased the same to consider their payment, which shall much revive their hearts to adventure most willingly their lives according to their most bounden duty in Your Majesty's service to make recompense for the disorder that now they have made.[11]

The chronicle of Elis Gruffydd confirms Surrey's view of his footmen. 'Lack of food' and 'lack of money' had made them 'miserable and reckless'. Indeed Gruffydd went much further than Surrey in his criticism: 'Among them were many obstinate men who did not want to fight and were very sluggish in advancing to meet the enemy.' But for Gruffydd these 'ignorant, cowardly soldiers' were ultimately not to blame. Their behaviour was merely a symptom of a failure of command. According to Gruffydd, the fault lay squarely with the Earl of Surrey:

When the time came, he called the soldiers suddenly, without warning, and without giving any reason, which could have raised their hearts, which had fallen from sadness and pity at their great poverty.

. . .

[Surrey] wanted nothing better than to turn on them [the French] and fight, but not like a saintly godly soldier, who would put his trust and hope in God and look to victory more from the intervention of God than from the strength of brutish men, as testified by John and Judas Maccabaeus and many other devout soldiers as recorded in the Holy Scriptures. No, the Earl paid no heed either to the hand of God and his favours, nor to the unwilling-ness and lassitude of his soldiers, but in the pride of his folly.

. . .

Most sensible men thought it [the defeat] happened because of the lack of any sense of the virtue in praying to God and trusting in him for the victory, but chiefly because of the Earl, their leader, whose head and heart were swollen with pride, arrogance and empty confidence in his own unreasoning bravery.[12]

Gruffydd's commentary is not wholly convincing. He was at Calais at the time and did not witness the events before, during or after the battle. Nor was he possessed of all the facts. He castigated Surrey for not summoning reinforcements from Calais and Guisnes – 'this his pride would not allow him to do, for he wanted the glory for himself alone' – but Surrey had, in fact, asked for aid and consequently a division of troops from Guisnes did fight at St Etienne. Gruffydd assumed Surrey cared little for his men, but he had not seen the countless letters the Earl had written on their behalf throughout his command. He was a cantankerous old veteran who had regularly and mercilessly vented his spleen on many of the King's former generals. He was an ardent religious reformer who resented the Duke of Norfolk for attempting to launch a heresy investigation into the Calais garrison in 1540, and he seemed to have been unaware that Surrey's beliefs differed from his father's. When Gruffydd attacks Surrey for not paying heed to God, his comments probably tell us more about his own zeal than Surrey's lack of it.[13]

Nevertheless, his account cannot be dismissed. Events described else-where in his chronicle often correspond with the recollections of contem-porary eyewitnesses.[14] Although Gruffydd did not serve in the Boulogne garrison, he did visit it and he certainly maintained contact with some of the men who served there. Many of Gruffydd's details about the Battle of St Etienne and its aftermath are corroborated by those given by Surrey himself. For example, both Surrey and Gruffydd relate how the Earl had tried to rally the troops during the chaos and both reveal too how Surrey immediately drew up a report of the battle for the King despite the Council's later protestations to the contrary. The character sketch that Gruffydd gives of Surrey – the posturing and overweening

pride, the recklessness, the supreme confidence in his own ability –
although exaggerated to the point of caricature, does accord with the
impression that many people gained of Surrey. Elis Gruffydd was
without doubt a harsh critic, especially of his superiors, but he gave
praise where he felt it was due. In his eyes, Surrey's predecessor, Thomas
Poynings, about whom he wrote with admiration, deserved it; the Earl
of Surrey emphatically did not. Against Gruffydd's account, though,
should be read the long Latin poem composed by Thomas Chaloner
on the death of Captain Shelley at St Etienne. For the author, Surrey's
martial *vigor* was one of his greatest assets. He was 'the hero' who
'bent the [French] empire under the power of the English'.[15] Surrey's
approach to war, like his approach to all things, tended to divide
opinion.

Was Gruffydd fair in attributing the defeat to Surrey's 'lack of
patience'?[16] Had Surrey blundered? Perhaps. His horsemen performed
heroically, but in chasing their French counterparts beyond Hardelot,
they withdrew their support from the footmen. Surrey had sensed
disaffection among the common soldiers, but nevertheless ordered the
attack, assuring the King of 'the courage and good will that seemed in
our men'. On the other hand, Surrey knew his King. Had he not
presented the fight, not only would Fort Outreau have been rescued
and Surrey's past successes have been nullified, but Henry VIII's honour
would have been touched. Victory that day 'might have imported no
less success than the winning of the fortress'. Therefore, Surrey
beseeched the King, 'accept the good intent of us all considering that
it seemed to us, in a matter of such importance, a necessary thing to
present the fight.'[17]

Surrey had taken a risk, one that a less enterprising and more experienced commander might not have. But it was a calculated risk and had
been paying off marvellously until the second line suddenly bolted. Had
luck, or God, been with Surrey on 7 January 1546, the victory might
have been his. As it was he was left flailing in the field, powerless to
prevent the flight of his men and eventually, as the seventeenth-century
historian Lord Herbert of Cherbury delicately put it, 'also being
constrained to save himself as he could'.[18]

Flight from battle was utterly reprehensible. It was one of the three
ways (along with heresy and treason) by which a Knight Companion
could be degraded from the Order of the Garter.[19] For a man of Surrey's
sensibility and with his family history, nothing could be worse. Surrey

immediately knew that the shame of St Etienne belonged to him. In an echo of his grandfather's cry at Bosworth, Surrey yelled out 'like a man in a frenzy and he begged Sir John Bridges and some of the gentlemen who were with him to stick their swords through his guts and make him forget the day.'[20]

Surrey sent his letter to the King on 8 January, the day after the battle. He also determined to dispatch Ralph Ellerker to the King in person, but 'the present tempest being such, we have thought it meet to send these before, and stay him for a better passage.'[21] Letters sent from Boulogne usually took about three days to arrive at Hampton Court. In theory, though, an urgent letter could be sent and received on the same day. Surrey's letter did not arrive at Court for over a week. The bad weather to which Surrey refers was probably the cause of the delay, yet some vessels evidently had managed to cross the Channel and by the night of 8 January, rumours of an English defeat had already begun to spread through the streets of London.[22] On 13 January the Imperial ambassador reported that the English had lost twelve hundred footmen at St Etienne. 'The Earl of Surrey has consequently lost greatly in reputation,' he concluded, 'and there is considerable discontent at these heavy losses.'[23]

Around the same time, Surrey received an angry letter from the Privy Council. Henry VIII, having heard about St Etienne, 'cannot but marvel very much that in so many days you have advertised hither no part of that matter.' If Surrey had triumphed, then the King would have 'rejoiced with you' and 'tended to your further success and comfort'. If Surrey had suffered a setback, then the King, 'who of his great clemency considereth the uncertainty and unstable chance of the wars', would have helped Surrey redress the loss. 'And therefore His Majesty hath specially commanded us to require you to advertise, without further delay, the very truth and whole circumstances of this chance; and that, from henceforth, as often as any such matter or worthy advertisement shall grow, that you fail not from time to time to advertise His Majesty of the full truth thereof accordingly.'[24]

By 15 January there was still no sign of Surrey's report. Ralph Ellerker arrived later that day, but only after the Privy Council had written letters to the English ambassadors abroad, ordering them to quell any 'vain and untrue' rumours that might be circulating in the European Courts. The councillors, 'advertised by some that were present', attempted to downplay the 'skirmish' at St Etienne, but ominously for Surrey, they seemed to imply that 'overmuch courage' was the real cause of the defeat and that had Surrey's horsemen not chased the French so far from the field of battle, the disorder might have been prevented.[25] Stephen Gardiner demonstrated his diplomatic nous in his response from Utrecht: although 'somewhat troubled' by the boldness of the horsemen, 'we kept the ground of the truth of that was done and fashioned it with circumstances meet for the same.'[26]

That Surrey's letter did eventually surface at Court is proven by the fact that it now sits in the National Archives. However, it is not clear if it had arrived by the morning of 17 January when William Paget wrote to Surrey from Hampton Court. 'My good Lord,' he began,

> with most hearty commendations, these shall be to signify unto you that your skirmish with the Frenchmen being done the 7th of this present, in the evening upon Friday [8 Jan.] at night in the street, letters written of the same from some of that town were read & say in Lombard Street so lewdly written to your disadvantage and discouraging that all we here which saw the same were much dismayed therewith and much the more for that there was nothing written from your Lordship nor any others of the council there.
>
> The bruit [rumour] brought it so terribly to our ears here that we rather lamented your chances there than were angry hoping yet still to receive better news from thence because I know the iniquity of our English nature to be such as commonly will report the worst of our own things. And so I wrote to the King's Majesty from London where as at that time, with His Highness' licence, I passed days two or three for the buying of my own things. But when 5 or 6 days together no word came, then we began to note some negligence for your silence still longing to hear the truth.

Following this rebuke, Paget proceeded to reassure Surrey that he was not to blame:

> Albeit we had heard before the worst and as ill as might be, yet I promise you there was no displeasure in the world conceived, nor not one jot of fault arrected to any person, and so shall appear unto your Lordship by the report of Sir Ralph Ellerker and also by His Majesty's letters of content-ation and thanks to you and his council there for the honest meaning of the enterprise, which, I assure you, is not written for the manner sake but ever for that you be so thought worthy, His Majesty knowing like a Prince

of wisdom and experience that whosoever playeth at any game of chance must sometime look to lose.

So as my Lord neither want of knowledge, neither in you, nor in no man there, nor lack of consideration for the enterprise, nor of foresight for the execution of it, is thought here but altogether laid upon the fondness of the footmen flying of whom, as I would wish, some few to be made an example to all the rest, so I would have wished that jointly you and all the rest of the council there had informed the truth where the great fault was to His Majesty.

Although Paget claimed to be ignorant of military matters – 'By God, my Lord, I am no man of war' – he was keen to provide counsel: 'For God's sake be ever plain with the King. Praise no further than your men be praiseworthy and praise no further than you may honestly, upon good cause, dispraise again.' Surrey, Paget continued, should not be swayed by his more jingoistic colleagues in Boulogne (probably the 'light ruffians' to whom Paget had referred the previous September), for they will cause you 'to hinder all the rest, to hinder yourself and to hinder also the King's Majesty's affairs.'

There are enough innuendoes in Paget's letter to suggest that he believed that Surrey had not, in fact, executed his command satisfactorily:

'I am sure, my Lord, that in the rearguard of the battle, you had placed some men of wit and experience, which, when against all order of flight and against the appointment of the chieftain, seeing the horsemen fly (as they took it), if they so thought and fled, so were not greatly to be blamed.'

'If your horsemen had just executed their part and duty (which had been done if they either had experience or wit), the victory and the fort had been yours.'

Never mind, Paget concluded, 'let it go. All is well.'

And learn the lesson, my Lord, that as long as you work . . . with the advice of his council (as I know you did this and agreed upon it together upon good ground and consideration) and that you have always a clear conscience, void of iniquity or fond affects, be never afraid nor discouraged. There can no more be had of a man than he can do. The King and all the Council think well of you . . . and I am your poor friend that will honestly stick to you. Give God thanks that hath beaten you with so soft a rod.[27]

A month later Surrey was demoted.

In response to Francis I's redoubled efforts to seize the initiative in Northern France, Henry VIII made preparations for a new army and fleet to be sent there. Edward Seymour, Earl of Hertford, fresh from his successes in Scotland, was appointed Lieutenant General of the army and the Lord Admiral, John Dudley, was given control of all matters naval. Surrey retained the Captaincy of Boulogne, but he was no longer Henry VIII's main man in France. There were fears that he would take the news badly and it was left once again to Paget to assuage his hurt pride.

It was no accident that William Paget had risen from humble beginnings to become Henry VIII's Principal Secretary. He was an astute observer, an excellent judge of character and an extremely subtle manipulator. In an age of suspicion, Paget was trusted. Both conservatives and reformers claimed him as one of their own. As one contemporary put it, he 'will have one part in every pageant if he may by praying or paying put in his foot'.[28] Paget knew exactly how to handle people, empathising with their problems one moment, playing on their insecurities the next. Even when he had to get tough – and as Henry VIII's mouthpiece this was fairly often – he did so with such reluctance and proceeded to offer such sound advice that his recipients were usually persuaded that he had their best interests at heart. All these techniques are evident in the above-cited letter and they were deployed again on 20 February 1546, when Paget wrote to inform Surrey of Seymour's appointment as Lieutenant General. The two extant drafts of Paget's letter are full of crossings-out and insertions, revealing that considerable care was taken in its composition. Initially, he empathises with Surrey: 'I fear your authority of Lieutenant shall be touched for I believe that the later ordering of a Lieutenant taketh away the commission of him that was there before.' Then he works on the Earl's sense of honour:

> Now, my Lord, because you have been pleased I should write mine advice to your Lordship in things concerning your honour or benefit, I could no less do than put you in remembrance how much in mine opinion this shall touch your honour if you should pass the thing over in silence until the very time of my Lord of Hertford's [Seymour's] coming over thither, for so should both your authority be taken away, as I fear is Boulonnais,* and

* *Boulonnais*: the county to which the town of Boulogne belonged.

also it should fortune ye to come abroad without any place of estimation
in the field, which the world would much muse at and, though there be no
such matter, think you were rejected upon occasion of some either negligence or inexperience or such other like fault – for so many heads so many
judgements.

Instead, Paget advises, Surrey should apply to the King for a post in
the new army – 'the Captainship of the foreward, or rearward, or to
such other place of honour as should be meet for you, for so should
you be where knowledge and experience will be gotten.' Indeed, Paget
continues – and here we see him at the height of his skills – with a
position of command in the army, 'you should the better be able hereafter to serve and also have peradventure occasion to do some notable
service in revenge of your men at the last encounter with the enemies,
which should be to your reputation in the world'.* Hitherto, Paget
states, Surrey has been regarded as 'a man of a noble courage and of
a desire to show the same to the face of your enemies'. But, he warns,
'if you should now tarry at home within a wall, having I doubt [not]
a show of your authority touched, it would be thought abroad, I fear,
that either you were desirous to tarry in a sure place of rest or else
that the credit of your courage and forwardness to serve were diminished and that you were taken here for a man of none activity or
service.' Of course Surrey will ever remain Paget's 'special good Lord'.
The King's Secretary will fight Surrey's corner and 'if it shall please you
to use me as a mean to His Majesty, I trust so to set forth the matter
to His Majesty as he shall take the same in gracious part and be
contented to appoint you to such a place as may best stand with your
honour.'[29]

Surrey took the bait, as Paget knew he would, and five days later
he was named Captain of the Rearward.[30] The theatre of conflict would
soon move north to the port of Ambleteuse, where the English were
preparing a camp, and to Marquise, where the French planned to erect
a new fort. Seymour was expected towards the end of March and Surrey
kept up a stream of correspondence informing the King and Council

---

* Paget reworked this passage considerably. Originally it read: 'you should the better be able
hereafter to serve and also have peradventure occasion to do some notable service in revenge
OF THE LOSS of your men at the last encounter YOU HAD with the enemies, which should be
BOTH GREATLY TO THE SATISFACTION OF HIS HIGHNESS AND THE REST HERE AND ALSO
TO THE RECOVERY OF REPUTATION in the world.'

of enemy movements. Otherwise it was business as usual in Boulogne. Surrey continued to petition the King for the payment and provisioning of his men; he persevered with the fortification of the Old Man, Base Boulogne and High Boulogne and he persisted in his efforts to prevent supplies from entering the French fort. But it was a wretched time for him and St Etienne never strayed far from his mind. On 13 February he wrote to the King, 'assuring Your Highness that the service here is more accident to losses than in any other place where Your Majesty is served'. The following month, having reported a successful skirmish against the French, Surrey concluded wryly: 'now I see that the Frenchmen can run as fast away up the hill as the Englishmen not long ago ran down.'[31]

There were sure signs now that he had lost favour with the King. His renewed petition for Frances to be allowed to join him in Boulogne was denied on the grounds that the King thought the new campaign 'will bring some trouble and disquietness unmeet for women's imbecilities'.[32] Increasingly Surrey was isolated from the decision-making process. On 10 February he recommended one Crofts as Lieutenant of the Old Man, 'assuring Your Highness that his service hath been such, both for his diligence and hardiness, that he meriteth' such a post. It went to Thomas Audley.[33] On 8 March Surrey was informed that because of the 'uncertainty' of his opinions, he would henceforth have to relinquish control of all the fortifications in Boulogne to the surveyor John Rogers.[34] In a letter to the Council of Calais on 2 March, Surrey admitted that 'I have received from His Majesty no letters of like effect as you have done', and a week later he wrote to the Privy Council, informing them that one thousand sappers had arrived in Boulogne 'and we, having none advertisement from your good Lordships thereof, know not how to use the same'.[35]

To his credit, Surrey continued to serve the King with zeal, but it was increasingly apparent that he was deemed a liability, especially now that Henry VIII was considering the prospect of peace. When once Paget had ended his letters to Surrey with a hearty flourish – on 25 September 1545, for example, he prayed to God for Surrey 'to be as good a captain as ever was and as good a man withal' – now he signed off with weary dispassion: 'And now, having answered to all your things, I take my leave of you and pray God to send you to do no worse than I do wish you.'[36]

On 22 March 1546 Seymour landed in Calais. A day or two later

Surrey received a letter from the Privy Council recalling him to England. He had previously expressed some concern about the state of the fortifications in Boulogne and this was used as the pretext for the summons – 'considering that you cannot be so well able in writing to express your mind in these matters to the understanding of His Majesty as if you were here present to say, and hear again, what can be said in that behalf.'[37]

The news of Surrey's imminent return was greeted with joy at Kenninghall, still his main residence despite his attempts to get Surrey House up and running. Hadrianus Junius, the children's tutor, set one of them the task of composing a welcoming epistle in Latin. The result is highly stylised and reveals the strong influence of Junius, whose own letters are cloyed with floridity and hyperbole. But there is also a child-like sweetness to the letter and a touching reverence undiminished by recent events. As it is the only surviving letter addressed to Surrey from his children, it is worth quoting in full:

I do not know what words or what expressions to use in describing the enormous joy experienced by us, your children and dearest objects of your affections, by your most illustrious and heroic father, by your sister, the renowned Duchess, by that most glorious woman our mother, your wife, and finally by all your dependants and your whole household, at your unexpected but so greatly desired return, my most honoured father. Certainly our joy is so great that the strength of this little body of mine is inadequate to express it. In order to bear witness to it even these walls of our house would break into speech, unless this were forbidden by nature, and so it is that they reluctantly remain silent.

We try, without succeeding as much as we would wish, but at least to the limits of our abilities, to express the sure signs of our undoubted joy with words, gesture and facial expression and so to reveal the hidden seeds of our feelings. There are very proper reasons for us to do this: the demands of duty require it and our love towards our most deserving father calls for it in its own right. And so we all congratulate you on your return, you, my most loving father and the bravest of commanders, who have so many times killed and routed the French and emerged as victor over the most bitter enemies of the English race. In the words of all it is said that you have preserved the King's interests with the greatest good faith that you could have applied.

You have battled hitherto against the stormy waves of war with amazing success to your own great glory, with great spirit, unbelievable bravery, equal prudence, the utmost toil and an outcome worthy of so great a hero, by opposing yourself to our enemies and driving them back by, as it were, thrusting your body against them like an invincible rampart guarding altars and hearths. We also congratulate the King, the father of our country, who, by his very act of choosing you as his Lieutenant in preference to all others, readily revealed how much he values your qualities; and now he rejoices that his judgement has been vindicated and that he has not been disappointed in his expectations. We also congratulate the whole Kingdom, because, resting as it does on the shoulders of Henry, our invincible and greatest King, and defended by his arms, it appears to have won a most illustrious name among foreign nations thanks to the efforts of you, a second Henry, whilst leaving nothing for the French except envy, lamentation, and a dread of yourself. I have spoken.*[38]

At Court, the reaction to Surrey's return was less fulsome. On 28 March 1546 the special Imperial emissary recorded that 'the Earl of Surrey, formerly Captain of Boulogne, arrived at Court yesterday, but was coldly received and did not have access to the King.' Although Surrey had been demoted from his Lieutenancy, he was officially still Captain of Boulogne. But the reference to Surrey as 'formerly Captain of Boulogne' suggests otherwise. Sure enough, Surrey was 'revoked' two days later 'from his late charge at Boulogne'.[39]

He was still confident of returning to the town after his audience with the King. He had left it in a hurry and needed to clear his 'raw and uncertain' accounts before the arrival of his successor as Captain, Lord Grey of Wilton. On 30 March Paget wrote to Seymour in France, informing him that 'my Lord of Surrey shall within a day or two repair thither for five or six days for the ordering of his things there.' Surrey

---

* This letter was probably written by Jane who was nine years old. She was Surrey's eldest child and the one who most clearly inherited his linguistic skills. When John Foxe took over from Junius as the children's tutor the following year, he was so impressed by Jane's knowledge of Greek and Latin that he thought 'she might well stand in competition with the most learned men of that time, for the praise of elegancy in both' (Foxe, I, p. 24).

The congratulatory tone of the epistle has led some to suspect it was written before the Battle of St Etienne. However, Surrey is not known to have returned home before then. Some passages in the letter are perhaps suggestive of recent events – 'your unexpected but so greatly desired return'; 'you have battled hitherto [hactenus] against the stormy waves of war with amazing success'; 'in the words of all it is said that you have preserved the King's interests with the greatest good faith that you could have applied'. It is hardly surprising that there is no direct reference to St Etienne – even Paget was wary of mentioning it (see his letter of 20 Feb. 1546) – and it probably would have been downplayed to the children at the time.

was also the nominal Captain of the Rearguard of the new army and the Council, after announcing Surrey's revocation from Boulogne, confirmed that the Earl was 'appointed otherwise to serve His Highness there'.[40] But it was a charade. Surrey was not allowed to return to France and his position in the new army was conveniently forgotten.

On 7 April 1546 Surrey was granted, 'for his services', the manor of Wymondham, which he had previously only held for the duration of his father's life.[41] Yet he was far from placated. His restless lyrics, reckless behaviour and constant protestations of 'the zeal that I bear to His Majesty's service'[42] all testify to an energy that could not be bridled. Now he was going to have to 'tarry at home within a wall' and, as Paget had insinuated in February, the Earl of Surrey deprived of command in France might no longer be seen as 'a man of a noble courage', but as 'a man of none activity or service'.[43]

'It may be here,' Lord Herbert of Cherbury suspected, that 'began his discontent which after undid him.'[44]

15

MY FOOLISH SON'S DEMEANOUR

Henry VIII's nature was such that some of his subjects were able to extricate themselves from positions of disfavour with a certain amount of politic handling. The old master of the game was the Duke of Norfolk, who had suffered temporary disgraces throughout his long life of service. The secret to clawing one's way back was to absorb the King's abuse, profess one's innocence, make grand, and in Norfolk's case oleaginous, protestations of loyalty and liaise with those in high favour.

Such tactics were especially requisite in 1546. The health of the King, who turned fifty-five in June, had deteriorated dramatically. The ulcers on his legs kept flaring up and throughout the year he was struck by a series of debilitating fevers. After each attack he would assure the foreign ambassadors that he was fully recovered, but his appearance revealed the lie.[1] He was unable to climb stairs without the aid of a winching device and was frequently carried through his palaces on a velvet chair like some kind of living effigy. The lack of exercise led to further weight gain for a man already so fat in 1543 that it was said that 'three of the biggest men that could be found could get inside his doublet'.[2] Ambassadors gave regular updates on the King's physical decline. They also noted his 'continued melancholy'.[3]

It was apparent to all but perhaps Henry himself that he was coming to the end of his days. Nothing terrified him more than the prospect of his own mortality and he 'was loath to hear any mention of death'.[4] In 1540 he had been confident that 'with God's help' he would leave his Kingdom 'in as good case to his son as his father before left it unto him, and better'.[5] Six years on and his coffers were empty, his Church was schismatic and his counsellors divided. Prince Edward, aged eight at the beginning of 1546, was a long way off his majority. It was hardly a secure legacy and Henry grew increasingly fearful of threats to the succession, and correspondingly vulnerable to intrigue. Like the medlar fruit that he gorged upon at state banquets, Henry seemed only to ripen with his own corruption. As his physical health deteriorated, he evolved into the worst kind of tyrant: paranoid, vindictive, unpredictable and desperate to prove his 'absolute power and independence of everyone'.[6]

Although he had put in an impressive performance at the prorogation of Parliament on Christmas Eve 1545, moving people to tears with his calls for 'charity', 'Christian fraternity' and 'perfect love and concord',[7] the fissures that ran through his Court were largely of his own making. Sometimes he appeared to be toying with his factions, teasing them into thinking they had their victim, only to offer a last-minute reprieve. At other times it seemed that 'the impressions privately given him by any court-whisperer were hardly or never to be effaced.'[8]

For the first half of 1546 the conservatives were on the offensive, searching out heretics 'as well of the Court as of the City'.[9] Some, including John Lascelles, the man who had uncovered Catherine Howard's adultery in 1541, were burnt at the stake. Many more fled abroad to escape the same fate.[10] But Henry did not allow the conservatives to have it all their own way. He foiled their plan to destroy Queen Catherine Parr* – 'Arrant knave! Beast and fool!' he bellowed at Lord Chancellor Wriothesley when he arrived with an armed guard to arrest her[11] – and he also extended his protection to his Privy Chamber companion, George Blagge.

Blagge, it will be remembered, was Surrey's portly friend who had rebuked him for rampaging through London in 1543 and then accompanied him to the trenches of Landrecy. Blagge had been an ardent reformer then, and in the three years since, his commitment had crystallised. On 9 May 1546 he uttered some derisory comments about the Mass. Two months later he was arrested, arraigned for the heresy of denying the Real Presence in the Sacrament of the Altar and sentenced to death by burning. However, the King, 'sore offended' by the probing into his Privy Chamber, intervened to save Blagge, who received a full pardon on 17 July. 'Ah! my pig,' Henry exclaimed on Blagge's return to Court; 'Yea,' Blagge replied, 'if Your Majesty had not been better to me than your bishops were, your pig had been roasted ere this time.'[12]

---

* An ardent supporter of reform, Catherine Parr was an influential patroness – and indeed an author herself – of evangelical literature.

Anne Askew was not so fortunate. In June she was arrested, arraigned and condemned without trial for the same sacramentarian heresy that had been levelled at Blagge. Still only in her twenties, Askew was a Lincolnshire gentlewoman who had been deliberately targeted because of her links with reformers at the heart of the Court. For the next two weeks she was interrogated and put to the rack – 'a strange thing', it was said, to be inflicted upon a woman of her status.[13] Who shared her beliefs, Askew's interrogators enquired; who supported her? The wives of some very powerful men were implicated. She admitted that a man in a blue coat had given her maid ten shillings and another, wearing a violet coat, had passed on a further eight. The former claimed to have been sent by the Countess of Hertford, the latter by Lady Denny, but 'whether it were true or no, I cannot tell'. She refused to say any more, even when Richard Rich and Thomas Wriothesley rolled up their sleeves and turned the rack themselves.

Such was the climate at Court in 1546. The times, Paget later remembered, were 'too straight', for 'then was it dangerous to do or speak though the meaning were not evil'.[14] Surrey would have been advised, therefore, to be unobtrusive, circumspect and calm. But his father's tactics were not his. Surrey returned to England with a point to prove. He was sensitive to any perceived slight and, after the King's refusal to grant him an audience, he grew increasingly bitter. As ever, when he was feeling defensive he lashed out. Soon after his return from France he had a furious row with his old friend Blagge.

It began with a discussion about 'the rule and government of the Prince' in the event of the King's death. Blagge envisaged a corporate regency government formed by men that Henry VIII 'should specially thereunto appoint'. Surrey refused to accept this. His father, he announced, 'was the meetest personage to be deputed to that room as well in respect of the good service that he had done as also for his estate'. The thought of a Catholic aristocrat dominating the kingdom was too much for the rotund reformer. 'I trust never to see that day!' Blagge squealed before launching into a savage attack on the Duke's beliefs and the 'evil' influence he would have upon young Edward. 'Rather than it should come to pass that the Prince should be under the government of your father or you,' Blagge said as he reached for his scabbard, 'I would bide the adventure to thrust this dagger in you.' Surrey had no weapon at hand so he resorted to a proverb that his father sometimes used to belittle the authority of his critics: 'God sent a shrewd cow short horns.'[15] Quick as a flash Blagge snorted 'yea, my Lord, and I trust your horns also shall be kept so short as you shall not be able to do any hurt with them.'

Few men had the temerity to stand up to Surrey and fewer, if any, were able to better him in an argument. Surrey flounced off 'in choler', but there was no way he was going to let Blagge have the last word. According to the evangelical courtier Edward Rogers, who heard about it from Blagge himself, Surrey 'put on his sword and dagger and came incontinent to seek Blagge at his own house'. He accused Blagge of being 'very hasty with him'. 'But as for the rest of that their second talk,' Rogers added unhelpfully, 'I do not call to remembrance.'[16]

Soon after, Surrey returned to Norfolk, where he was commissioned to collect taxes or, as it was euphemistically termed, 'to assess a loving contribution to be given by the King's subjects'.[17] During this period, while her husband was tarrying at home 'within a wall', Frances became pregnant. But she could do little to mend Surrey's hurt pride. His resentment festered throughout the spring and into the summer, when he ventured once again to Court.

Twice in July 1546 he looked back in anger at Boulogne. Hostilities between England and France had officially ceased in June on the signature of a treaty that stipulated the return of Boulogne to the French in eight years' time upon the payment of a hefty indemnity. The peace owed much to Lord Admiral Dudley, Surrey's old rival from the May tournament of 1540, who had replaced him as Lieutenant General upon the Sea in France. Not only had Dudley handled the peace negotiations alongside Seymour and Paget, but he had also been instrumental in setting the whole process in motion.[18] Dudley planned to ratify the treaty at the French Court, but on 12 July, the day before his departure, he received a letter from Surrey that troubled him. The same day he wrote to William Paget:

I do send you herewith a letter which my Lord of Surrey sent unto my lodging this morning, wherein is contained so many parables that I do not perfectly understand it; which letter (if you think it meet), I require you to show unto the King's Majesty . . . also to send me your advice touching an answer, which I have briefly made unto the same letter, the copy whereof I do send you.[19]

According to a servant of Surrey called Hugh Ellis, his master's letter concerned 'a discord between him and my Lord Admiral', but as neither Surrey's letter nor Dudley's response to it has survived, the circumstances of that discord remain hidden.[20] Fortunately another letter, written by Surrey two days later, has survived. It concerned an allegation made by his successor in Boulogne, Lord Grey of Wilton. There were no parables here. On the contrary, Surrey begged his recipient, Paget, to 'pardon my frankness'. What had caused Surrey to lose his composure again?

The problems between Surrey and Grey had begun the moment the whippersnapper Earl displaced the older, more experienced man in Boulogne. Grey had first been appointed to the Captaincy of the town at the end of August 1545, but had only been allowed to serve there for a week before Henry VIII changed his mind and appointed Surrey in his stead. Grey's fractious personality was well known in France, as his clashes with Sir John Wallop, Richard Blount and John Rogers revealed.[21] The tension between him and Surrey had simmered beneath a veneer of cordiality throughout much of Surrey's command, but had eventually surfaced in the spring of 1546 over a dispute about foreign mercenaries. Paget had warned Surrey then that the 'variance' between him and Grey not only caused the 'continual torment' of them both, but also 'the dangerous hindrance of His Majesty's affairs'.[22] Yet it continued unabated and when Grey eventually took over from Surrey in Boulogne at the beginning of April, he seized for himself the keepership of the tolls, a post held by one of Surrey's servants.

Surrey was furious when he found out about it in July. The servant in question, he wrote in his 'frank' letter to Paget, 'was placed there for his merits by Mr Southwell and me' and deserved recompense for what, Surrey implied, was a vindictive and petty action of Grey's, taken only 'for some displeasure borne to me'. Worse still, Grey then claimed he was only following the lead of Surrey and his predecessors, who had always pocketed the income from the post. This, Surrey swore, 'upon mine honour, is untrue'.[23]

Grey knew that Henry VIII was open to accusations of corruption for they provided a useful diversion from his own reckless expenditure. One of the first orders Surrey had been given when he had arrived in Boulogne was 'to enquire whether any of the head officers had used to receive any sums of money above their ordinary entertainment and whether the same had used to appoint their household servants to certain charges, whereby the King's Highness had ill service.'[24] Even Lord Admiral Dudley felt compelled to write in April that 'I never meddled with His Majesty's money' and Grey himself would later stand accused not only of putting the King's appointees out of office, but also of 'neglecting' the King's accounts in favour of his 'private commodities'.[25]

Money was never a priority for Surrey. He seemed to think that it only really mattered to merchants and mercenaries. That is why he was unmoved by his father's attempts to make him 'weary' of Boulogne, why he sacrificed 'an hundred ducats of mine own purse and some-what else' in order to relieve some soldiers that the King had refused to pay and why he emerged from France so indebted that he had to mortgage all the interior furnishings at Surrey House.[26] His innocence is also borne out by later events. The Council had all the account books relating to Surrey's command in Boulogne and, as 'raw and uncertain' as they were, they contained no grounds for corruption.[27] Had they done so, they would surely have been cited in December when every kind of calumny was hurled at the Earl.

Surrey's reaction to Grey's allegation was predictable. In suggesting that he could have risked his reputation for the sake of a few pounds, Surrey wrote to Paget, Grey 'can have none honour, for there be in Boulogne too many witnesses that Henry of Surrey was never for singular profit corrupted, nor never yet bribe closed his hand.' Surrey claimed to be, in contrast to his accuser, a true nobleman who under-stood the values of his class. The 'lesson' of integrity, he wrote, 'I learned of my father and wish to succeed him therein as in the rest'.[28]

Surrey was rebuked by the Privy Council either for this 'frank' attack upon Grey's honour or, more likely, for his earlier letter of 'parables' to Dudley. On 15 July the Duke of Norfolk wrote to the Lords of the Council asking them 'to give the King thanks that it hath pleased His Majesty to will you to advertise me of my foolish son's demeanour'. The admonition of the Council, Norfolk wrote, 'may do him much good . . . and much more if His Majesty be pleaded to cause the same to be spoke on his behalf'. Norfolk was 'glad', he said, that on this occasion Surrey had 'used himself humbly and repentantly, which I pray God he may often remember and not trust too much to his own wit'. But the old Duke knew that he could no longer control his heir: 'I desire you that my son may be so earnestly handled that he may have regard hereafter so to use himself that he give His Majesty no cause of discontent.'[29]

Had Henry VIII read the paraphrases of the first five chapters of Ecclesiastes that Surrey probably composed around this time, he would have had far greater cause for concern. On lines 44–6 of chapter three, Surrey paints a terrifying picture of a tyrant:

> I saw a royal throne whereas that Justice should have sit;
>> Instead of whom I saw, with fierce and cruel mode,
> Where Wrong was set, that bloody beast, that drunk the guiltless
>> blood.[30]

The similarities here with a ballad attributed to Anne Askew are striking.

> I saw a royal throne,
> Where justice should have sit,
> But in her stead was one
> Of moody, cruel wit.
>
> Absorbed was righteousness,
> As of the raging flood:
> Satan, in his excess,
> Sucked up the guiltless blood.[31]

It is impossible to say for sure who originated this image, as Surrey's Ecclesiastes poems cannot be dated with precision.[32] The lines from the Vulgate* – 'I saw under the sun impiety in the seat of judgement and evil in the place of justice' – suggest that although Surrey was translating very freely, he was 'following the thought and the sequence' of the original.[33] Surrey had previously shown, in his poem about the tyrant Sardanapalus, who 'had lost his honour and his right' to rule, that he did not shy away from accusatory imagery and he had written about 'guiltless blood' before, in a poem about Wyatt.[34] Askew admitted she was a literary novice – 'not oft use I to write / in prose nor yet in rhyme'[35] – and her poem is not particularly accomplished. Surrey frequently polished and improved upon the work of others and had strong empathy for the voice of female complaint. Nor was he averse to reworking phrases and images that appealed to him, as his borrowings from Gavin Douglas (for the *Aeneid*) and Johannes Campensis (for

---

* Surrey's main source for his biblical paraphrases, the Vulgate was the Latin version of the Bible established by St Jerome in the late fourth century.

his biblical paraphrases) show. When, in his version of chapter three of Ecclesiastes, Surrey writes about 'the slipper top of worldly wealth', he is echoing Wyatt's 'slipper top of Court's estates'.[36] Therefore the possibility, however remote, exists that Surrey could have appropriated Askew's poem, rather than the other way around.[37]

Either scenario begs the question: how did the one get hold of the other's work? Anne's ballad was written in Newgate prison and then smuggled to Germany, where it was published by John Bale. Could Surrey's poem have been slipped into Anne's cell in order to provide comfort and support in her hour of need? Or had Surrey's contacts (perhaps his sister Mary, who sheltered John Bale on his return to England) helped him get hold of a copy of Anne's ballad before it was shipped abroad? Whatever the exact provenance of the image of the satanic beast feeding on 'guiltless blood', both Anne and Surrey claimed it as their own. But only the one had nothing to lose. On 16 July 1546 Anne Askew, 'so racked that she could not stand', was burned alive as a heretic.[38]

The story of what would be the last full year of Henry VIII's reign cannot be told without reference to the religious differences at the Council board and in the Privy Chamber. Foreign ambassadors often reported events in terms of religious factionalism, and so did many domestic commentators. Staunch conservatives like Bishops Gardiner of Winchester and Bonner of London ('puffed up porklings of the Pope' according to John Bale[39]) were determined to destroy reform and, in targeting their enemies, they utilised the heresy card again and again. Ardent reformers like Blagge were equally determined to spread the Word of God and work towards a reforming protectorate for Prince Edward following his father's death. But little was black and white at Henry's Court. Most politicians rated power above religion, or at least appreciated that their beliefs were best protected and advanced from a position of authority. Other factors such as kinship, clientage, local issues, financial considerations, foreign policy and personality shaped allegiances at Court. Nor should the instinct for self-preservation be underestimated. Bets were hedged and unholy alliances forged for the sake of survival.

Thomas Wriothesley was the archetypal Court chameleon. He emerged on the scene in the 1520s as one of Stephen Gardiner's protégés, but very quickly entered the Cromwell camp. During the chief minister's fall, Wriothesley aligned himself with leading conservatives and throughout the summer of 1546 he was the principal persecutor of evangelicals. It was Wriothesley who tried to destroy both Catherine Parr and George Blagge and it was Wriothesley who turned the rack on Anne Askew till 'the strings of her arms and eyes were perished'.[40] By the end of the year, though, having noted in a list of memoranda 'things in common: Paget, Hertford, Admiral, Denny', he had drifted towards that camp.[41] Wriothesley was accused of being a ruthless opportunist, but he was the King's loyal servant and the path he chose was well trodden.

Of the four men noted by Wriothesley to be in the ascendant, Paget was Henry VIII's trusted Secretary, Edward Seymour, Earl of Hertford, was Prince Edward's uncle and, like Lord Admiral Dudley, the King's military darling, while Anthony Denny of the Privy Chamber was Henry VIII's chief confidant. All four seemed to embrace reform, but each was careful, outwardly, to cut his beliefs according to Henry VIII's protean cloth. Whether each man's end game was the dissemination of the Word of God throughout the country or the mastery of government was a question of priority and a matter of conscience. If all went to plan, no differentiation would be necessary. The two goals were inextricably linked.

Like Wriothesley, the Duke of Norfolk was prepared to compromise when necessary. In 1538 he had proposed a marriage between his daughter Mary and Edward Seymour's younger brother Thomas.[42] Nothing came of it then but in June 1546 Norfolk tried again. The Seymours were amenable to the idea and so was the King. In order to consolidate the alliance Norfolk also proposed a 'cross-marriage' between several of Surrey and Edward's children.[43] The Seymours were linked by blood to the future King; the Howards were the figureheads of the old nobility. A dynastic alliance would fare well for both families in the reign to come.

Surrey saw things differently. His relationship with the Seymours had always been ambivalent. In the 1530s he had enjoyed Seymour hospitality numerous times and, over the past three years, he had nominated Thomas Seymour to the Order of the Garter.[44] On the other hand, his scathing beast fable had attacked Edward Seymour's wife and left no doubt as to his opinion of the craven ways of her 'kind' in general. More recently, Surrey had suffered the ignominy of being replaced by Edward as Lieutenant General on Land in France. According to his sister Mary, Surrey took Seymour to be 'his enemy' and was 'so much incensed' against him that the Duke of Norfolk feared 'his son would lose as much as he had gathered together'.[45]

Mary was also hostile to the union because 'her fantasy' – or, as we would today term it, fancy – did not incline her to Thomas. According to Gawain Carew's later testimony, Mary told him that summer that she had consulted Surrey about the marriage and that he had proffered the following advice: she should feign indecision about the Seymour match so that the King would send for her. At the ensuing interview, 'she should in nowise utterly make refusal' of Thomas, but 'should leave the matter so diffusedly that the King's Majesty should take occasion to speak with her again'. And again and again until, 'by length of time', Henry VIII might 'take such a fantasy' to her that she might rise to the status and attain the power that Francis I's mistress enjoyed in France. Mary told Carew that she had been horrified by her brother's suggestion and had screamed at him that 'all they should perish and she would cut her own throat rather than she would consent to such a villainy'.[46]

At his trial half a year later Surrey 'emphatically denied the truth of the allegation', and when he was presented with Mary's written statement confirming the story, he exclaimed: 'must I, then, be condemned on the word of a wretched woman?'[47] Surrey's apologists have long maintained that he should not have been. He was, they argue, incapable of such ignoble advice; his words were not intended literally, but sarcastically; they were uttered in a fit of pique at the thought of the Howard–Seymour union and were subsequently distorted by his malicious sister and her evangelical friends. Without any evidence, Edmond Bapst, Edwin Casady and their followers argue that Mary had probably been keen on the marriage and that her enthusiasm had provoked Surrey's outburst. These writers even went so far as to submit their own versions of the episode. 'Go to!' Casady's Surrey shrieks at Mary, 'such would be a grand farce of a marriage.' Apparently 'in tones of bitter scorn', the Earl continued: 'You had best conclude your marriage quickly, while your husband-to-be is in such high favour. Then you can profit from your position to insinuate yourself into the good graces of the King. If you can submit yourself to such a husband, why not make the most of your chance?'[48]

Such an interpretation gets Surrey off the hook. His virtue is preserved and Mary becomes the villain of the piece. It is convenient, but is it plausible? If Mary deliberately distorted Surrey's words, then she did not do so after his arrest in December, when it would have been expedient for her to distance herself from him, but in August, when she told Sir Gawain Carew all about it. That month Surrey was ostensibly still in favour, or at least not conspicuously out of favour. He participated in the reception of the Admiral of France, who had come to Hampton Court to ratify the Anglo-French peace treaty, and he was ranked above Hertford and the rest of the earls in the order of precedence drawn up for the accompanying celebrations.[49] Mary and Surrey had a volatile relationship and just recently they had quarrelled about religion, but it seems highly unlikely that she would deliberately seek to undo her brother (as any kind of fabrication of the story would necessarily imply), not least because her own status would be affected by the fall-out.

Another argument put forward is that Mary genuinely and guilelessly mistook her brother's sarcasm for literalism.[50] Yet she was a bright lady – 'too wise for a woman' according to her father – and if Surrey had adopted a sarcastic tone, it is hard to imagine her not picking up on it. Might Sir Gawain Carew, then, be the one who wilfully misconstrued Surrey's 'ironic' outburst when he retold the story to his friend Edward Rogers in August? This cannot entirely be discounted. Carew was a reformer and was related by marriage to Sir Anthony Denny. But surely if he had conspired to discredit Surrey in August, he would have informed Denny and others about the conversation then rather than passed it on to Rogers as a piece of juicy gossip.

It is neither necessary nor helpful to bend over backwards to exonerate Surrey in this affair. Carew's detailed testimony has a ring of authenticity to it, as does the corroborative deposition provided by Rogers and, though Mary's testimony is at times confusing, it too appears genuine. Besides, if Mary had actually wanted to marry Thomas Seymour, as Surrey's apologists suggest, then it would have been in her interests to say so in December as the Seymours had by then emerged as the likeliest contenders for the regency government. It seems more reasonable to conclude that it was neither Mary nor Carew, but Surrey's apologists, who later twisted his words, that Surrey was as ambitious as the next man, that he was desperate, as he had already shown to Blagge, to gain a footing in the next reign and that he was not above proposing the use of female bait to catch the King as his own father and the Seymours had so successfully done before. Surrey had probably not thought his proposal through – Mary was, after all, Henry VIII's son's widow – and it is unlikely that he pursued it further. His servant Hugh Ellis later testified that he knew nothing about it.[51] It was probably as rash and unthinking as Surrey's riotous behaviour in London had been in 1543, but it was no less real, nor any less shameful, for that.

The Duke of Norfolk had always been adept at sensing changes in the political climate. As the year progressed and the days shortened, he must have rued the failure of the Howard–Seymour alliance. War with France had put the reformers on the back foot. Its prosecution relied, at the very least, on Imperial neutrality and, in his vigorous courtship of Charles V, Henry VIII had been at pains to display his religious orthodoxy. The June peace lifted these restrictions and it was no coincidence that the heresy hunts began to peter out once Seymour and Dudley had wrapped the negotiations and resumed their residence at Court.[52] On the last day of August 1546 Anthony Denny was granted access to the King's dry stamp. This was a device that created an impression of Henry VIII's signature, which could then be filled in with ink. Denny had, in effect, a licence to forge the King's signature on all public documents with the only proviso being that the King would sign a monthly schedule listing the documents stamped.[53]

The following month Henry had another health scare. He was reportedly 'in great danger' and his doctors gave 'very little hope of his recovery'. He rallied, but his condition worsened at the end of October when he was at Windsor.[54] Access to him was restricted and the reformers, including the royal doctors and a nexus of Privy Chamber companions, further tightened their grip. Denny was now appointed first Chief Gentleman of the Privy Chamber, while his vacancy in the secondary post was filled by another reformer, the Queen's brother-in-law Sir William Herbert. The Imperial ambassador filed unhappy reports on 'the evils and dangers threatened by these sects'. Only those 'specially sent for' were now allowed at Court. Howard affiliates like Sir Francis Bryan and Sir Nicholas Hare found themselves excluded and Norfolk himself complained that he was no longer part of the King's 'privy Privy Council'.[55]

At a Council meeting at the end of September, John Dudley astounded his colleagues by striking Stephen Gardiner, the conservative Bishop of Winchester, across the face. He was absented from Court for a month but retained the King's favour. Gardiner, Henry VIII protested, had a 'troublesome' nature and the Bishop's reluctance at the end of November to exchange some land with the Crown was enough to secure his exile from Court. Gardiner wrote desperate letters begging to be allowed to return, but was tersely told by the King not to 'molest us any further'.[56] Affairs 'change almost daily', ambassador Van der Delft noted late in December 1546, but though they still centred on the King, increasingly they revolved around the reformed axis.[57]

It is possible that the Duke of Norfolk might have been tolerated by these men. He had taken a back seat in the summer persecutions and his overtures to the Seymours had shown a willingness to adapt. He was an old man now, in his eighth decade, and the autumn and winter months saw him attend the Council board only twice.[58] His daughter Mary was a zealous reformer and his younger son Thomas had been censured by the Privy Council in May for his 'indiscreet proceedings touching talking of Scripture matters'.[59] Surrey's children's Dutch tutor, Hadrianus Junius, complained incessantly about his distasteful lifestyle at Kenninghall. He despaired of the 'wanton and precipitate behaviour' of Surrey's 'insolent' sons and claimed to be engulfed by 'an unpleasant and almost depressing loneliness'. Above all, he was 'disgusted' by the anti-Imperial taunts directed at him by those who sympathised with Charles V's Lutheran enemies.[60] If the Duke of Norfolk was unable to control the beliefs within his own household, the reformers might have mused, then he might not pose a threat to their plans for a godly commonwealth.

The Earl of Surrey was a different matter entirely. There had been a time back in 1543 when he was seen as a champion of the reformed faith. His translations of Ecclesiastes, with their emphasis on 'simple faith' and disavowal of 'outward works', suggest that privately he still valued the Word of God and the principle of *Sola Fide*.[61] They also revealed some kind of association with the evangelical heroine, Anne Askew. Further, in October 1546 Surrey justified his request for the belfry and dormitory of a former monastery in Norwich on the grounds that they were 'unserviceable' remnants of 'the old superstition'. But he had also erected an altar at Boulogne; he had counselled Mary against 'going too far in reading the Scripture' and, as he later admitted to Blagge, his faith had faltered.[62]

Politically and personally, Surrey was an even greater liability. As Henry's Lieutenant in France, he had valued honour (his own and the

King's) above the financial security of the realm. 'Who so doth, at length shall get small thanks,' Norfolk had warned, and so it now seemed. In his belligerence, Surrey had alienated the Privy Council. Had he only acquiesced to the dynastic union with the Seymours, things could have been very different. But Surrey's 'defiant aristocratic singularity' disqualified him from any kind of alliance.[63] He envisaged no other way after the King's death than a noble protectorate headed by the Howards. As far as Surrey was concerned, the 'new erected men' had no right to govern. They 'loved no nobility,' he said, 'and if God called away the King, they should smart for it'.[64] Snobbish jibes were one thing but overt threats, in this environment, were quite another.

It is impossible to determine exactly when the decision was first taken to target Surrey, and by whom, if such a decision was ever so baldly stated. The deposition of Sir Edward Warner, made in December 1546, suggests that Surrey's argument with Blagge had been the catalyst:

> In summer last past Master Devereux did tell me upon certain communications of the pride & vain glory of the said Earl that it was possible it might be abated one day & I asked what he meant thereby & he said:
>
> 'What if he be accused to the King that he should say if God should call the King to his mercy, who were so meet to govern the Prince as my Lord his father?'
>
> I asked then if there were any such thing & he said, 'It may be so'. Whereupon I gathered that it was so.[65]

Warner and Devereux had both been in trouble in the spring for their reformist views, as had Sir Gawain Carew and Edward Rogers.[66] All four men had escaped with a warning and all four now seemed very interested in the Earl of Surrey. At the August reception of the French Admiral, Carew had told Rogers about Surrey's recent contretemps with Mary, and Rogers had reciprocated with details of the Earl's quarrel with Blagge. It was not long before Surrey's every move was being watched. His aggressive behaviour, impolitic utterances, boasts about his pedigree, flamboyant manner, flashy house and even his 'gown of gold' and his habit of 'riding with many men in the streets' were noted.[67] Each instance of Surrey's 'pride and vainglory' fed the ailing King's paranoia about the succession. A few whispers in Henry VIII's ear easily poisoned his mind against the Earl who had let him down in France. 'It was notorious,' Lord Herbert of Cherbury noted a century later, 'how the King had not only withdrawn much of his wonted favour, but promised impunity to such as could discover anything concerning him.'[68]

Although Surrey's arguments with Mary and Blagge reveal astounding political naivety, he was sensitive enough thereafter to appreciate the need for a little caution. The grandiose, avant-garde portrait that he had commissioned in France was still a work in progress. Its depiction of the Earl emerging from a ruined landscape (the classic symbol of degeneration) and leaning on a broken pillar (a sign of endurance) could be seen as a defiant, perhaps even treasonous, gesture.[69] But the inclusion on the plinth of the pillar of the image of the Duke of Richmond, with all that could be read into it in terms of Surrey's ambition for Henry VIII's other son, was deemed too risky now even by Surrey. He therefore sent a note from Kenninghall to his servant Hugh Ellis at Lambeth, with instructions for the artist 'to leave out the tablet where my Lord of Richmond's picture should stand'.[70] Instead, the place was filled by a Latin motto, *Sat Superest* – Enough Survives. Exactly what Surrey meant by this pithy epithet has been the subject of endless debate. Its most likely derivation is from Seneca's *Epistulae Morales* (I:5): 'Non puto pauperem, cui quantulumcumque superest sat est' – 'I do not regard a man as poor, if the little which remains is enough for him.'[71]

Hugh Ellis claimed that he had heard Surrey say that 'if he survived his father he should have enough and that he would never covet more', and in Wriothesley's list of memoranda is the phrase: 'they will let me alone as long as my father lives and after I shall do well enough.'[72] Surrey's younger son Henry later appropriated the phrase in the context of his own loss of royal favour. In the dedicatory epistle of a translation to Queen Elizabeth, Henry assured his monarch of his loyalty:

Angels bathe themselves, as St Basile writes, in streams of sinners' tears and happy is that subject's face, which you vouchsafe to look upon with pity when it is most richly garnished with pearls of this water. Wherefore, if the dew of my devotion may be drawn up by the beams of your remorse, *Sat Superest* as once my father wrote upon the breach of a distressed hope; if not yet such is my belief in your administration of right as with the daughter of Darius, while I live, I will deem me *captum esse quamdui* [sic] *Regina vixerit*. [I will consider myself a prisoner as long as the Queen shall still live][73]

There is an ambivalence in Surrey's adoption of the phrase. If 'enough survives' in the body of Surrey himself, then it could be seen as a defiant, challenging statement: enough survives in the Earl of Surrey to rescue something from the ruins of Tudor England. But if 'enough survives' despite Surrey's poverty, despite the defeat at St Etienne, despite the King's disfavour, then it may be read as a statement of Senecan stoicism. Considering the context and the fact that Surrey substituted *Sat Superest* for the image of Richmond 'upon the breach of a distressed hope', it seems that the latter interpretation is more likely. Surrey, far from vaunting his ambition, may actually have been attempting to play it down: if the King could find it in himself to forgive Surrey, accept his allegiance and allow him to survive his father, then it would be enough for the Earl, and 'he would never covet more'.

Surrey evidently thought he was protected by his father and that by replacing the miniature with the motto, he would be safe. But he was unaware that the religious conservative Sir Richard Southwell, Surrey's old East Anglian friend and colleague from Boulogne, had defected.*

Along with the note Surrey had sent Ellis was a letter for Mary Shelton, the lady whom Thomas Clere had chosen 'for love' and who formed the third member of the 'tender league' in Surrey's epitaph for his late squire. Some time after Clere's death, probably in late 1545 or early 1546, Mary had married Anthony Heveningham. Surrey's letter for her, Ellis was told, must be delivered 'with all speed' and 'to none but her own hands'. Ellis seems to have handed it over safely, but his own letter from Surrey was seized and at the bottom, in Richard Southwell's hand, is the message: 'It may please your good Lordships to examine Mrs Heveningham, late Mary Shelton, of the effect of the Earl of Surrey his letter sent unto her; for it is thought that many secrets hath passed between them before her marriage and sithens.'[74]

In October Surrey retired once more to Kenninghall and attempted to extricate himself from 'the misery of debt'. On 19 October he wrote to William Paget asking him to intercede with the King for the belfry and dormitory of Christ Church in Norwich. 'If it were His Most

---

* It is sometimes assumed that Southwell was brought up alongside Surrey in the Howard household. This is unlikely as he was over ten years older than the Earl. They did, however, know each other very well. The Southwells were clients of the Howards and had been regular visitors at Tendring Hall in the 1520s. In 1536, Surrey regarded 'my friend Mr Southwell' as one of his chief confidants (California MS, fos. 29, 29v, 82, 96, 96v; Pembroke MS, dinner, 22 September 1527; Bindoff: Richard Southwell; Bapst, p. 220).

Excellent Majesty's pleasure to give it me,' Surrey pleaded in what might be seen as another version of *Sat Superest*, 'I will faithfully promise never to trouble His Majesty with any suit of profit to myself hereafter and [to] spend that and the rest in His Majesty's service with the old zeal that I have served with always.' Wishing Paget 'health and me relief in this necessity', he signed off 'your assured loving friend, H. Surrey'.[75]

Nine months earlier Paget had promised Surrey that 'I am your poor friend that will honestly stick to you.'[76] Surrey clearly believed his word was true. But Paget, like Southwell, Blagge, Wriothesley and so many others, as Surrey would soon find out, had turned. This rather pathetic letter is the last surviving piece of correspondence written by Surrey as a free man.

16

UNBRIDLED TONGUES

'Welcome, my Lord', said the Captain of the Guard as he approached the Earl of Surrey at the palace of Whitehall. 'I wish to ask you to intercede for me with the Duke your father in a matter in which I need his favour, if you will deign to listen to me.' Surrey was happy to grace such a deferential request and followed the Captain to a quiet corridor. Suddenly, twelve haldberdiers jumped out of the shadows, seized the Earl and bundled him into a waiting boat. Thus, the *Spanish Chronicle* tells us, was the Earl of Surrey arrested 'without attracting notice' on Thursday, 2 December 1546.[1]

Accounts differ over the exact reason for Surrey's arrest. Indeed the controversy surrounding his fall from grace, the rumours and innuendoes, the accusations, denials and counter-accusations, the disparities between foreign reports, Court circulars and recorded depositions and the subsequent disappearance of key documents might challenge the accuracy of any interpretation of the following events. According to the Imperial ambassador, Surrey's arrest was triggered by 'a letter of his, full of threats, written to a gentleman'. This could be the letter of 'parables' sent to Dudley in July, or it may have been a letter sent to Richard Southwell, for he now stepped forward saying 'he knew certain things of the Earl that touched his fidelity to the King'.[2] According to the French ambassador in London, Southwell accused Surrey of 'two principal charges: one, that he had the means of attempting the castle of Hardelot when he was at Boulogne and neglected it; the other, that he said there were some who made no great account of him but he trusted one day to make them very small.'[3]

Surrey reacted to his arrest with characteristic bravado. From Lord

Chancellor Wriothesley's house in Holborn, where he spent the first ten days of his confinement, he 'vehemently affirmed himself a true man' and demanded a judicial trial or, better still, a trial by combat with Southwell. So confident was Surrey that his truth would bear him out that he offered to fight 'in his shirt' against his armed accuser.[4] The Council was unmoved by his histrionics. They had arrested Southwell at the same time, but soon released him. Surrey, on the other hand, was transferred to the Tower of London on Sunday, 12 December. He was transported not by water, as would befit a titled peer, but overland and on foot, as would befit a commoner. Technically, this was the correct procedure. The Earldom of Surrey had been granted to Thomas Howard for life in 1514. When he inherited the Dukedom of Norfolk in 1524, he transferred the junior title to his heir, but it was by courtesy only. Legally, Surrey had no right to it. Thus Henry Howard, stripped of all courtesies, angry, humiliated and 'making great lamentation' was forcibly marched through London's busy streets.[5]

That same Sunday the Duke of Norfolk was arrested and taken by barge to the Tower. Neither he nor the public was given a reason and it was 'still unknown' two days later when the Imperial ambassador, Van der Delft, dispatched his reports. The ambassador was sceptical about the stories he had heard from 'some people who assume to know' that Norfolk and Surrey had 'held secretly some ambiguous discourse against the King, whilst the latter was ill at Windsor six weeks ago, the object being to obtain the government of the Prince.' But he immediately grasped the significance of the arrests. 'The chance of their liberation is very small,' he wrote, 'for the Garter and his staff of office were taken from the father before he was sent to the Tower, and the son was led thither publicly through the streets.' The French ambassador offered an even bleaker forecast: 'many hold that Surrey will suffer death.'[6]

Having heard about his father's arrest, Surrey sent a letter to the Privy Council. 'Since the beginning of my durance,' he wrote, 'the displeasure of my master, much loss of blood with other distemperance of nature, with my sorrow to see the long approved truth of mine old father brought in question by any stir between Southwell & me hath sore feebled me as is to be seen.' Surrey had not yet been formally examined and 'lest sickness might follow by mean whereof my wit should not be so fresh to unburden my conscience', he 'most humbly' requested a sympathetic hearing. Nearly four years earlier he had been questioned by Thomas Wriothesley, John Russell, Stephen Gardiner and Anthony Browne about his riotous behaviour in London and the dangerous gossip of Mistress Arundel's maids. Ever since, Surrey wrote, he had held these men in high estimation. Thus, 'my desire is [that] you four and only you may be sent to me' for the formal examination, 'trusting in your honourable Lordships that, with respect of my particular deserts towards you, ye will make report of my tale to His Majesty according as ye shall hear.'

Surrey acknowledged that his request might seem impudent, but if the King thinks 'that I overshoot myself', he will be 'contented therewith when I am heard'. He stressed once again that 'my matter is prejudicial to no creature unless to myself' and then signed off, either out of habit or in defiance of his recent degradation, 'Henry Surrey'.[7] He had no idea what he was up against.

On 14 December Richard Fulmerston was questioned about his dealings with the Howards. His response, written in a letter the following day, suggests that Southwell's opposition to Surrey may have been motivated as much by local as central issues. Fulmerston had been 'a most earnest drudge and servant' to the Howards for almost a decade, first as a yeoman servant to the Duke of Norfolk, then as Mary's under steward and finally as steward to the Earl of Surrey. He admitted that Surrey was heavily in debt, not least to Fulmerston himself, but he denied that he had ever blackmailed, bribed or intimidated anyone in his capacity as Surrey's steward: 'I never shifted any farmer or tenant of his from their farms, demesne lands or other their holds. I never from the beginning exacted any of them by payment of any fine, amercement or by any other kind of exaction by any mean.'[8]

Fulmerston's letter dwells heavily on one specific issue that the Council had raised the previous day. It concerned a dispute between Surrey and one John Corbet over the dissolved chapel and lands of St Mary Magdalen in Sprowston, near Norwich. Corbet owned the manor of Sprowston and other properties in the outlying region.[9] His cousin and business associate was none other than Richard Southwell, who owned a slew of properties just north of Sprowston.[10] To the south was the manor of Thorpe, where Surrey House lay. According to Corbet's allegation, Surrey and Fulmerston had bullied him into surrendering the chapel in 1544. 'It was not so,' Fulmerston protested; 'It was quite contrary of the other side.' Because the chapel had originally formed part of the manor of Thorpe, Fulmerston explained, Corbet, 'fearing my Lord my master's displeasure for so purchasing the same, came first to Kenninghall to declare himself therein'. Indeed, so desperate was Corbet to curry favour with the Earl that he eventually gave him the chapel 'frankly and freely'. Fulmerston claimed to have letters that would confirm this as well as witnesses, three of whom were lawyers, who would testify to the same.[11] Surrey's arrest was thus a boon to Corbet and Southwell. Following the confiscation of Surrey's lands, the chapel of St Mary Magdalen, Sprowston was awarded jointly to Corbet and Richard Southwell's younger brother Robert.[12]

Fulmerston was also questioned more generally about anything that he 'heard or knew' about Norfolk and Surrey 'in any such thing as by treason might any ways touch His Highness or my Lord Prince or my Lords and others of His Majesty's most honourable Council or the commonwealth of this His Highness' realm.' Fulmerston swore 'by the faith I owe to God and by mine allegiance I owe to the King' that he knew nothing, nor 'ever mistrusted' the allegiance of either father or son. Moreover, he insisted that 'their talk, since their coming to the city, in my poor fantasy, weigheth so much to their declaration of their truth as I dare not meddle in writing or otherwise setting forth the same, unless I shall be thereunto commanded.'[13]

The Council now changed tack. Seymour and Paget went to the Tower to interrogate Norfolk about events which had allegedly happened years before. Had he ever communicated with anyone in code, they wanted to know, and had he ever contrived to reunite the King with the Pope? In his letter of response, Norfolk presented a robust defence. 'There was never cipher between me and any man, save only such as I have had for the King's Majesty when I was in his service.' As for his alleged support of the Pope, 'if I had twenty lives,' he protested, 'I would rather have spent them all against him than ever he should have any power in this realm.' Indeed, 'no living man' has 'spoken more sore' against the Pope 'than I have done, as I can prove by good witness'. Norfolk was all too aware of the importance of the King's ear at this time and he begged to be brought 'face to face' with his accusers in the presence of Henry VIII: 'I am in no doubt so to declare myself that it shall appear I am falsely accused.' Still unaware of the grounds for his arrest, Norfolk pleaded with the Council to 'be made privy what the causes are; and if I do not answer truly to every point, let me not live one hour after for surely I would hide nothing of any question that I shall know that doth concern myself, nor any other creature.'

The rest of Norfolk's long letter is a manifesto for his loyalty to the Crown: 'There was never gold tried better by fire and water than I have been, nor hath had greater enemies about my Sovereign Lord than I have had, and yet, God be thanked, my truth hath ever tried me as I doubt not it shall do in these causes.' In his faithful service to the King, Norfolk had set himself against Wolsey, Cromwell, his royal nieces and many others besides: 'Who tried out the falsehood' of the Pilgrims of Grace 'but only I!'

> Who showed His Majesty of the words of my mother-in-law, for which she was attainted of misprision but only I!* In all times past unto this time I have showed myself a most true man to my Sovereign Lord . . . Alas! who can think that I, having been so long a true man, should now be false to His Majesty? . . . Alas! Alas! my Lords, that ever it should be thought any untruth to be in me.

In conclusion, Norfolk beseeched the Council 'to show this scribble letter to His Majesty' and to exhort him 'to remit out of his most noble, gentle heart such displeasure as he hath conceived against me'.[14] The Duke's letter succeeded in quashing the specific points raised in his interrogation. No mention would be made again of a cipher or of Rome. But now that the King and Council had Norfolk and Surrey in custody, they had no intention of releasing them. The lack of evidence was something that could be remedied later. Now it was important to tell the world of their disgrace.

On 16 December Wriothesley fed Van der Delft the official line and the following day the Imperial ambassador dispatched his report:

> It was, he [Wriothesley] said, pitiable that persons of such high and noble lineage should have undertaken so shameful a business as to plan the seizure of the government of the King by sinister means. The King, he said, was too old to allow himself to be governed and in order absolutely to usurp the government, they intended to kill all the Council, whilst they alone obtained complete control over the Prince.[15]

* Norfolk is referring here to Agnes, the Dowager Duchess of Norfolk, who was arrested for her alleged concealment of Catherine Howard's adultery. Agnes was in fact Norfolk's stepmother, not his mother-in-law.

Falsified reports were soon spread abroad that two 'gentlemen of faith and honour' had accused Norfolk and Surrey of the conspiracy and that Surrey had subsequently confessed.[16]

Meanwhile Richard Southwell and Anthony Denny's brothers-in-law, Wymond Carew and John Gates, were rummaging through various Howard properties in search of evidence to substantiate the lie. They had arrived at Kenninghall before daybreak on Tuesday, 14 December and had found Mary and Norfolk's mistress Bess Holland 'newly risen and not ready'. They announced the arrests and ordered the gates and back doors to be bolted. Then they trawled through every room in the house, seizing money, jewels and papers. Having inventoried every item right down to the last candlestick, they proceeded to break up the household. They were unsure, though, what to do with Surrey's children or his pregnant wife, noting with some embarrassment that she was 'looking her time to lie in at this next Candlemas'. Eventually it was decided to send Frances away. An old nightgown, 'much worn and furred with cony and lamb', was plucked from the Duke's wardrobe and placed on her lap.[17] Then her chariot rattled out of the drive. Little T. was placed in the custody of Sir John Williams, the Treasurer of the Court of Augmentations, while the other four children were entrusted to the care of the East Anglian landowner Sir Thomas Wentworth.[18]

On the evening of the dawn raid, the commissioners reported to the King that Mary's 'coffers and chambers [were] so bare as Your Majesty would hardly think, her jewels, such as she had, sold or lent to gage to pay her debts'. But if the Duke had neglected his daughter, the same could not be said for his mistress. The commissioners uncovered a horde of treasure in Bess Holland's chamber: rings set with pointed diamonds, square emeralds, rubies and white sapphires; gold brooches bearing images of 'our Lady of Pity', the Trinity, and Cupid; strings of pearls, diamond-encrusted crosses and 'a valentine of gold with three diamonds, three rubies and eight pearls'. There were also ivory tables, silver spoons and girdles studded with pearl. Bess' reluctance to lose her sparkle proved useful to the Council and her collection was only returned after she had travelled to London and testified against her generous lover and his son.[19]

After nearly fainting from the shock of the news, Mary also agreed to co-operate. 'She was not,' the commissioners assured the King,

forgetful of her duty, and did most humbly and reverently, upon her knees, humble herself in all unto Your Highness, saying that although nature constrained her sore to love her father, whom she hath ever thought to be a true and faithful subject, and also to desire the well doing of his son, her natural brother, whom she noteth to be a rash man, yet, for her part, she would, nor will, hide or conceal anything from Your Majesty's knowledge, specially if it be of weight or otherwise as it shall fall in her remembrance . . . And, perceiving her humble conformity, we did comfort her in your great mercy, whereof, using a truth and frankness in all things, we advised her not to despair.[20]

A few days later Mary and Bess arrived in London for their interviews. Their depositions have not survived, but they were seen in the seventeenth century by Lord Herbert of Cherbury, who abstracted them into his *Life and Raigne of King Henry the Eighth*:

Mrs Elizabeth Holland, being deposed, confessed that the Duke had told her that none of the King's Council loved him because they were no noblemen born themselves as also because he believed too truly in the Sacrament of the Altar.

Moreover, that the King loved him not because he was too much loved in his country, but that he would follow his father's lesson, which was that the less others set by him, the more he would set by himself.

As also that the Duke complained that he was not of the most secret (or, as it is there termed, the privy Privy) Council and that the King was much grown of his body and that he could not go up and down the stairs, but was let up and down by a device. And that His Majesty was sickly and could not long endure, and the realm like to be in an ill case through diversity of opinions.[21]

This was little more than pillow talk, hardly evidence of a *coup d'état*. The Council seems to have suspected Norfolk of bearing an illegal coat of arms. Questioned about this, Bess denied that she had heard the Duke speak of his own arms, but admitted he had 'found fault' with his son's heraldic experiments. 'He liked them not,' Bess said, and 'knew not from whence' they came. He had said that Surrey had 'placed the Norfolk arms wrong' and had told Bess to refuse to 'work them with her needle'. In conclusion, 'she confessed that the Earl of Surrey loved her not' and that his sister Mary loved him not and that Bess 'addicted herself much' to Mary.

The Council then turned to Mary. She admitted that she had argued with her brother over her proposed marriage to Thomas Seymour and that he had advised her 'to endear herself so into the King's favour as she might the better rule here as others had done'. She also confessed that Surrey had been 'much incensed' against Edward Seymour and that he had once said: 'these new men loved no nobility and, if God called away the King, they should smart for it.' Ever since his confinement at Windsor Castle in 1537, Mary continued, Surrey had 'hated' all new men. Norfolk, on the other hand, 'seemed not to care for their ill will, saying his truth should bear him out'.

Like Bess, Mary was ordered to declare anything strange or untoward in her father or her brother's armorial bearings. According to Herbert's abstract, Mary 'said that she thought that her brother had more than seven rolls'. She claimed that he had added the arms of Anjou and Lancelot du Lac to some of his escutcheons and had also assumed his attainted grandfather's Woodstock arms. Furthermore, he had 'put to his arms a cap of maintenance, purple with powdered fur, and with a crown, to her judgement, much like to a close crown and underneath the arms was a cipher, which she took to be the King's cipher, *HR*'. Mary added that 'her father never said that the King hated him, but his councillors', though Surrey had said that 'the King was displeased with him (as he thought) for the loss of the great journey [at St Etienne], which displeasure he conceived was set forward by them who hated him for setting up an altar in the church at Boulogne.' She also claimed that Surrey had 'dissuaded her from going too far in reading the Scripture', that he had said 'God long save my father's life for, if he were dead, they would shortly have my head' and that 'he reviled some of the present Council'. According to Herbert, Mary repeated other 'passionate words of her brother' and also 'some circumstantial speeches little for his advantage; yet so, as they seemed, much to clear her father'.[22]

More depositions soon followed.[23] Sir Edmund Knyvet, whose late mother Muriel was the Duke of Norfolk's younger sister, claimed to know 'no untruth directly by the Earl of Surrey, but suspected him of dissimulation and vanity'. He recalled that he had recently left Kenninghall after his 'unnatural' uncle had refused to support him in a private quarrel. Surrey had subsequently enquired into his absence and, when told by Knyvet that 'the burden of their malice' was too hard to bear, Surrey had replied, 'No, no, cousin Knyvet, I malice not so low; my malice is higher; my malice climbs higher.' Knyvet added that Surrey felt threatened by the 'new erected men' of the Court, that he kept Italians in his household and 'loved to converse with strangers and to conform his behaviour to them'. In this, Knyvet suspected, 'he had therein some ill device'.[24]

Sir Edward Warner was next. Like Knyvet and Southwell, he hailed from Norfolk. Unlike them, he was the dedicatee of one of Surrey's poems, one of his best in fact: a beautiful translation of Martial's epigram advocating the 'happy life', the 'quiet mind' and the 'equal friend'.[25] Warner was ordered by Secretary Paget to reveal all he knew about Surrey's armorial bearings and 'to put in writing all such words and communications as hath heretofore been betwixt me and the Earl of Surrey that might in any wise touch the King's Highness and his posterity, or of any other person, what I have heard of the said Earl that might in any wise tend to the same effect.' Warner recalled that Richard Devereux had told him the previous summer that Surrey's championing of his father's right to the protectorate might be reported to the King – 'whereupon, I looked every day to see him in the case that he is now in which, me thought, with those words, he well deserved.' But Warner stressed that he had never heard anything from Surrey himself 'that was any prejudice to the King's Majesty or his posterity'.[26]

Edward Rogers also lacked first-hand evidence against Surrey. He did, however, reveal the substance of the Earl's arguments with Blagge and Mary. The former he claimed to have heard from Blagge himself, the latter from Sir Gawain Carew, who confirmed the story in his own deposition. Carew added that Surrey had once said to him: 'Note those men which are made by the King's Majesty of vile birth hath been the distraction of all the nobility of this realm' – a statement that the Earl reinforced by claiming that both Cardinal Wolsey and Thomas Cromwell had 'by diverse means sought the death of his father'.[27]

Next a spy called John Torre, who had defected to Francis I in the 1530s and had been attempting to prove his allegiance to Henry VIII ever since, testified that the Duke of Norfolk used to pay secret nocturnal visits to the French ambassador.[28] There was nothing sinister here. Norfolk had gone to the French ambassador's house in the past, but with the full knowledge, indeed on the orders, of Henry VIII.[29] That this testimony was taken down and placed in the records suggests a certain amount of straw-clutching on the part of the Council. According to Lord Herbert of Cherbury, Thomas Pope's allegation against the

Duke of Norfolk from the time of the Pilgrimage of Grace was also dredged up and even Surrey's mother, who offered up all her old grievances against her estranged husband, 'was not unwillingly heard'.[30]

'When a man is imprisoned in the Tower,' the French ambassador once observed, 'there is no one living that dare meddle with his affairs or open his mouth, unless to speak ill of him, for fear of being suspected of the same crime.'[31] Despite this, and the fact that he had a young family to protect, Surrey's servant Hugh Ellis refused to buckle under the pressure of Wriothesley's interrogations.[32] To the charge that Surrey had counselled his sister to become the King's concubine, Ellis quipped: 'I never knew them so great together [for Surrey] to wish her so good a turn', adding 'by my faith and truth to God and the King's Majesty, that in my remembrance I did never see with him the countenance of any such purpose.' Nor, Ellis insisted, had he ever heard Surrey mention the King's death or the future protectorate, nor had Surrey spoken against any of the Lords of the Council, except for John Dudley, to whom 'he did write his mind in a letter', and Richard Rich, who had earned Surrey's scorn by turning up at Hardilot Castle in France 'in his best apparel'. Asked 'whether you have heard him say that the King's Majesty loved him not or such like words and what purpose he held of the same', Ellis replied candidly that 'after the overthrow of the great skirmish at St Etienne, if ever I heard him say he had the King's Majesty's displeasure or disfavour, it was then; for the which, ever since, he hath taken great thought.'[33]

Although the Public Record Office only contains the original depositions of Knyvet, Rogers, Torre and Ellis (the two given by Warner are unsigned and Carew's is in a modern hand), we can be sure that more were taken down at the time. Apart from Torre's, all the original depositions are numbered. Knyvet's was 7, Ellis' 19 and Rogers' 22. Others have clearly been lost or removed. Mary Howard, Bess Holland and Richard Southwell definitely gave statements. One would assume that George Blagge would have been questioned over his quarrel with Surrey. Mary Shelton, too, was surely worth investigating after Southwell's tip that she knew 'many secrets' of Surrey's. A page also seems to have been expurgated from Richard Fulmerston's statement and there is no longer any sign of the 'two chests full of evidence and other writings of the Duke' that were discovered in a closet at Kenninghall.[34] There was also once a 'bag of books . . . wherein were contained writings concerning the attainder of the Duke of Norfolk and the Earl of Surrey'. An entry in the Privy Council register for 5 July 1547 reveals that the bag had been given to the Master of the Rolls 'to peruse'. He had then delivered it, 'sealed with his seal', to the members of the Privy Council, who ordered that it 'be bestowed in the Study at Westminster Palace, where other records do lie'.[35] It was never seen again. It is interesting, and perhaps instructive, to note that the Master of the Rolls at this time was Sir Robert Southwell, brother of Richard.

Surrey was convinced that he was the victim of a conspiracy. 'Rein those unbridled tongues!' he wrote from the Tower in his paraphrase of psalm 55, 'break that conjured league!'[36] But he too had secrets at which we can now only grasp blindly. Who, for example, is 'Friowr', who appears at the end of the same paraphrase, but is nowhere in the Vulgate?

> Friowr, whose harm and tongue presents the wicked sort
> Of those false wolves, with coats which do their ravin hide,
> That swear to me by heaven, the footstool of the Lord,
> Who though force had hurt my fame, they did not touch my life:
> Such patching* care I loathe as feeds the wealth with lies.[37]

It is usually supposed that Surrey was referring either to a friar from one of the dissolved orders or to someone whose surname was Friowr, or Fryer, as it would more commonly be spelt. Yet no conclusive identification has been made.[38] Surrey's reference could be to any one of the turncoats who had abetted his fall. It was commonplace in medieval and early modern literature for friars to be represented as hypocrites, wolves in sheep's clothing, and 'the image of disguised wolves who "raven" the innocent sheep has its source in Christ's warning against "false prophets" in Matthew 7.15'.[39] Surrey may have had the same person in mind when he wrote twenty lines earlier:

> It was a friendly foe, by shadow of good will,
> Mine old fere† and dear friend, my guide, that trapped me;
> Where I was wont to fetch the cure of all my care,
> And in his bosom hide my secret zeal to God.[40]

---

* *patching*: deceitful.
† *fere*: companion.

Other mysteries are contained in Surrey's verse letter to Sir Thomas Radcliffe – a friend and cousin of his, but also the son-in-law of Chancellor Wriothesley – who remained at Court over Christmas.[41] Surrey begins his six-line poem with some advice drawn from his own bitter experience:

> My Ratclif, when thy reckless youth offends,
> Receive thy scourge by others' chastisement;
> For such calling, when it works none amends,
> Then plagues are sent without advertisement.

But the final couplet harbours a warning:

> Yet Solomon said, the wronged shall recure*;
> But Wyatt said true, the scar doth aye† endure.[42]

This precept alerts Radcliffe to a *strambotto* written by Sir Thomas Wyatt in 1541 to his fellow ambassador and friend, Sir Francis Bryan. It was penned in the Tower following Wyatt's sudden, and probably unjust, arrest for treason ('Innocency is all the hope I have'). Wyatt and Bryan had liaised closely on their respective embassies to Spain and France and shared many secrets. 'Sure I am, Bryan,' Wyatt wrote, 'this wound shall heal again / But yet, alas, the scar shall still remain.'[43] Bryan was a poet himself and, like Wyatt, he knew his proverbs and his Bible. Wyatt's message, drawn from the Book of Ecclesiasticus, was therefore clear:

> As for wounds, they may be bound up again and an evil word may be reconciled: but who so bewrayeth the secrets of a friend, there is no more hope to be had unto him.[44]

By referring to Wyatt's use of the proverb, Surrey alerts Radcliffe to the urgency of his plight. Like Wyatt, he seems to be saying, he is innocent, but also has secrets. These must not be betrayed, for though a wound may heal, its scar is indelible. It is the threat of a desperate man. And it may well have worked. There is no record of Radcliffe in any of the surviving documents relating to Surrey's fall. Whatever secrets

* *recure*: regain health.
† *aye*: ever.

the two men shared, they were probably taken to the grave.

Another sidelight on Surrey's clandestine activities is provided by a treatise that his younger son Henry wrote in 1583. *A defensative against the poyson of supposed Prophesies* is, as the title suggests, a tirade against the sixteenth-century vogue for prophecy, astrology and divination. The previous year Henry had been forced to deny all knowledge of 'a certain painted treatise', containing prophecies about Queen Elizabeth.[45] The *defensative*, dedicated to his examiner, the Queen's spymaster and principal secretary Sir Francis Walsingham, was thus a politic and timely exercise. Yet the venom Henry directs at his subject – 'the froth of folly, the scum of pride, the shipwreck of honour, and the poison of nobility' – is considerable and gives credibility to his claim that his treatise was engendered by 'a mortal malice against prophecies in respect of some progenitors and ancestors of mine, which smarted for presuming overmuch upon their hopes'.[46]

Henry's beheaded great-grandfather, the Duke of Buckingham, had listened to prophecies that he would be King, and a prognostication on the overthrow of Queen Elizabeth was introduced at the trial of Henry's elder brother Thomas, who was found guilty of conspiring with Mary, Queen of Scots.[47] Yet Henry claimed to have conceived his 'mortal malice' in his teenage years, long before his brother's execution. Twice in the 1580s, Henry wrote about his father's demise, and he leaves broad hints in the *defensative* that he was referring to him again. Not only does his reference to family members 'presuming overmuch upon their hopes' echo his statement that Surrey composed *Sat Superest* 'upon the breach of a distressed hope', but he also recalls circumstances that sound very similar to Surrey's own:

> The last but notwithstanding the most pestilent and bitter root from whence the prophecies have drawn their head and received, as it were, their life and soul is curiosity: to search and hunt for deeper knowledge of the future causes and affairs of the commonwealth than it pleaseth God to discover and reveal by ordinary means. As how long the Prince shall reign? Who shall succeed and by what mean? What houses shall recover or decay? Of what quality the Prince shall be? with such like mysteries. And the reason why this fountain is more pestilent than any of the rest is chiefly because it pierceth and approacheth nearer to the quick of man's delight insomuch as I myself have been acquainted with some godly persons and such as neither doubted of God's sure defence, nor lent their ears to winds of light

report, which were notwithstanding wonderfully ravished and bewitched with this enticing humour.[48]

Elsewhere in the *defensative* Henry writes:

It hath been an ancient practice of discoursing sycophants, sometime by figures, sometime by pedigrees, sometime by popular reports and rumours, to bring that person whom they most detest and fear into so deep mistrust and jealousy of those that bear rule as none but he must be regarded, watched, and observed by the spies of the State, while they bring things to pass according to the compass of their own intent, and cover drifts of treason with a mask of hypocrisy.[49]

In June 1546 a servant of Surrey called Robert Barker was examined for discussing 'prophecies and other things stirring to commotion against the King's Majesty'. The Duke of Norfolk's secretary, John Clerke, who dedicated several books to Surrey, was known to dabble in necromancy. Surrey's friend, Thomas Wyatt junior, was another dilettante of the dark arts as, later, would be Surrey's daughter Katherine. Surrey himself, and Henry VIII too, it must be said, were fascinated by astronomy.[50] It is possible, therefore, as his son strongly implies, that Surrey had indulged a soothsayer and presumed 'overmuch' on his hopes. His final portrait could have been the context for some kind of prophecy, especially if one credits the unsupported statement in the *Spanish Chronicle* that the motto 'till then thus' was also inscribed upon it.[51] Several of his comments might also be interpreted prophetically. Apparently there were friends 'to whom in figure he had promised the coming of a fair day', while his enemies 'he trusted one day to make . . . very small'.[52] The ravenous 'Friowr', who 'feeds the wealth with lies', may even have been a false prophet in the literal sense as opposed to one of Surrey's back-stabbing friends. An anonymous seventeenth-century manuscript also suggests that 'diabolical divination' played a part in Surrey's fall.[53] But there is nothing in the surviving skeleton of official evidence to suggest this. It is a ghost of a possibility, one that dissolves as soon as it is investigated too closely.

By Christmas 1546 the Court was seething with rumour: that Surrey had established an illegal power base in Norwich; that the cannon that adorned the pavilions at Surrey House were not ornamental; that he had given weapons to strangers; that he had had traitorous talks with the Emperor at Landrecy; that his portrait had been 'inspired by evil thoughts'; that he and Norfolk had planned to assassinate Henry VIII and Prince Edward; that he had secretly sought to surrender Boulogne to the French. To the last, patently absurd, charge, Hugh Ellis had retorted: 'as God shall be my judge, I did never see in him a spot of any likelihood thereof.'[54]

Surrey's reputation was submerged in gossip and innuendo, but it must be said that he himself had opened the gates to the flood. Henry VIII might not have read his recent paraphrases of Ecclesiastes, with their references to bloody beasts and 'aged kings wedded to will that work without advice',[55] but he was well aware of the Earl's inflammatory behaviour. In his argument with Blagge, Surrey had exposed his ambition for the protectorate and, to Mary, he had implied that the King was little more than a manipulable roué. This was particularly offensive in light of the Howards' previous successes with Anne Boleyn and Catherine Howard.

In spite of 'a sharp attack of fever' in December, which 'lasted in its burning stage for thirty hours' and left him 'greatly fallen away', Henry VIII was 'deeply engaged and much perplexed in the consideration of this affair'.[56] Just how engaged is revealed by a set of charges against Surrey and Norfolk drawn up by Wriothesley. In a tremulous hand, Henry carefully edited the text. His annotations can be seen in the following extract:

> If a man compassing ~~to govern the King~~ with himself to govern the realm, do actually go about to rule the King and should, for that purpose, advise his daughter, or sister, to become his harlot, ~~what it importeth?~~ thinking thereby to bring it to pass, and so would rule both father and son, as by this next article doth more appear, what this importeth?

> If a man ~~should~~ say these words: 'If the King die, who should have the rule of the Prince but my father or I', what it importeth?[57]

If proven, these charges might import treason according to a law that stipulated that 'imagining' the King's death and seeking to deprive the King, the Queen or the heir of the 'dignity' of the royal estate were capital offences. A case against Surrey based on these charges would rest solely on words rather than deeds, but the statute of 1534 had made words treason, and even before then words had been 'constructed' as treasonable by the courts. Surrey's maternal grandfather had been executed on the basis of a servant's testimony, while his cousin Anne Boleyn had been convicted of treason according to hearsay and innuendo. Subjects could also be condemned by *ex post facto* rulings, as the act of attainder hurried through Parliament to deal with Surrey's half-uncle, Lord Thomas Howard, had shown. Given the elasticity of the treason legislation, the current climate and the King's paranoia about the succession, Surrey's reported comments might be construed as treason by those determined to make him a traitor.

'I hear,' ambassador Van der Delft wrote on 27 December, 'that the councillors have been several times, and indeed go daily, to the Tower to examine the two prisoners.'[58] But no confessions had yet been extracted. Perhaps the evidence was deemed too circumstantial. Perhaps Surrey and Norfolk's denials, backed up by the testimonies of Fulmerston and Ellis, were thought too convincing. Perhaps Henry VIII balked at the thought of his sexual appetite being debated as a key issue in open court. Whatever the reason, neither of these charges, nor others drawn up by Wriothesley – vilifying members of the King's Council, exceeding manorial rights, giving arms to strangers – were to feature in the indictment against Surrey.

In fact it contained just a single charge and it applied, not to the Act of Treason, but to the Second Succession Act of 1536. Surrey was accused of the *lèse-majesté* of bearing the arms of Edward the Confessor. This is not as extraordinary as it may sound. In sixteenth-century England, where the majority of the population was illiterate, the power of image was tremendous. The Flodden Duke's funeral, Holbein's portrait of Henry VIII at Whitehall, the tournament of May 1540 and the ceremonies and insignia of the Order of the Garter are just a few instances of the potency of symbolism and spectacle in this age. Coats of arms were not just adornments, but vivid expressions of lineage, identity and power. The image of Edward the Confessor symbolised sanctity, legitimacy and majesty. Most English kings were crowned (using his regalia) and buried at Westminster Abbey, where his shrine lay. Five English kings had been named after him and Henry VIII maintained the tradition with his heir. An unlawful display of the Confessor's arms could therefore be interpreted, especially in these perilous times, as a sign of ambition, perhaps even as a threat to the succession.

The armorial charge against Surrey had not originally been considered. Neither the Duke of Norfolk nor Richard Fulmerston was questioned about it, but when Southwell, Gates and Carew had searched for evidence against the Howards in Norfolk, they had also looked into the possibility of heraldic violation. Their initial target was the Duke of Norfolk, whom they suspected, wrongly, of bearing an illegal version of his ancestor, Thomas of Brotherton's arms. However, at Thetford Priory, the burial place of the Howard Dukes of Norfolk and their Mowbray ancestors, the inspectors stumbled across an instance of the display of Edward the Confessor's coat of arms.[59]

When Bess and Mary gave their depositions in mid-December, both confirmed that there was nothing untoward in the Duke of Norfolk's coat of arms, but both spoke out against Surrey's. Bess had been vague, only specifying that Surrey had placed the Norfolk arms in the wrong quarter and, though Mary's statement was more detailed, she had been careful to add caveats – 'to her judgement'; 'which she took to be'. Surrey's 'seven rolls' that Mary claimed to have seen were never found or, if they were, they were subsequently destroyed. In any case, they hardly amounted to a case for public heraldic display. But it was a start and Wriothesley soon focused the investigation.

Surrey, it will be remembered, had experimented with a new coat of arms in the summer of 1545 and a few months later, when he was at Boulogne, 'he devised the same to be painted amongst other his coats in scutcheons, which were sent from thence to Norwich'. According to Hugh Ellis, Surrey did not do this sneakily, but openly 'in the presence of the King's Highness' Council there'.[60] On his return to England Surrey sent the glaziers and silversmiths of Norwich patterns of his arms and on 7 October, he displayed them 'in full public view' at Kenninghall. This last instance was the only one cited in the indictment.[61]

Surrey's new coat of arms was certainly controversial. Originally, he had wanted to bear the arms of Edward the Confessor and Geoffrey Plantagenet, Count of Anjou, but it seems that Christopher Barker, the Garter King of Arms, had successfully dissuaded him from the latter.[62] Surrey had, however, persisted with St Edward's arms with the difference, on the upper portion of the shield, of a silver label of

three points.* This is confirmed by a heraldic drawing of a shield in
the British Library entitled 'Howard Earle of Surry, for which he was
attainted' (plate 35). There is no sign here of the arms of Anjou (which
were not mentioned in the indictment or at the trial), but in the fifth
quarter are the arms of Edward the Confessor with a label of three
points.[63]

Surrey was incredibly foolish to tinker with royal quarterings at a
time when the King was increasingly suspicious of threats to the succession. He was even more foolish to cross over into the realm of myth,
as he did when he told Hugh Ellis that his predecessors had been granted
the arms by King Edward himself.[64] Surrey was probably drawing on
the spurious tradition within the Howard family that their ancestor
was Hereward the Wake, the Saxon hero who had rebelled against
William the Conqueror. But even if Surrey could have traced his Howard
roots back to Hereward – which he could not – it was still absurd to
claim that Edward the Confessor had given Hereward his arms because
Edward had never actually borne them himself. The Confessor lived in
an age before the science of heraldry had been established. The arms
attributed to him were modelled on a stamp used on his coins and were
awarded posthumously in the thirteenth century.[65] Nevertheless, some
of the early Howards had asserted this mythical claim as their display
of St Edward's arms at the church of East Winch in Norfolk showed.[66]

Surrey did, however, have a valid claim to the arms attributed to
Edward the Confessor. In 1397 Richard II had granted Surrey's ancestor,
Thomas Mowbray, first Duke of Norfolk, the right to display those
arms in his shield. In subsequent years the Mowbray and Howard
Dukes of Norfolk had exercised that right as the noted instances of
display at Thetford Priory, Framlingham Castle and Kegworth Church
in Leicestershire revealed.[67] Had Surrey's ancestry been less impressive,
his actions might have been overlooked. But the fact that he could, and
did, boast of his descent from kings (and not only from Edward I by
virtue of his Mowbray and Brotherton ancestors, but also from Edward
III through his mother's line) made his heraldic pretensions appear more

---

* This was one of the marks of difference used to distinguish the arms of the father from
those of his sons. The eldest son used a label of three points, the second son a crescent, the
third a mullet, the fourth a martlet, the fifth an annulet and so on. The colour of the mark
of difference was a matter of preference and, although it is commonly assumed that from
1340 the silver label was reserved for royalty, this was never officially delineated (A. C. Fox-
Davies, *A Complete Guide to Heraldry*, rev. and annot., J. P. Brooke-Little (1969), p. 373,
n. 222).

threatening. 'For what intent and purpose you put the arms of St Edward in your coat armour or escutcheon?' Surrey was asked, and why 'at this time more than . . . at any other time before?'[68]

Lord Chancellor Wriothesley, whose father, uncle and grandfather had all been heralds, knew of Surrey's rightful claim to the arms of Edward the Confessor through his Mowbray ancestry. This presented a huge obstacle in any attempt to charge Surrey with heraldic treason. Wriothesley sought to overcome it by concentrating, in his interrogation of Surrey, on the mythological claim. We do not know how Surrey responded, as all his answers have been lost, but Wriothesley's approach was clearly adopted in order to undermine Surrey's credibility and divert attention from the valid claim. It also served to highlight Surrey's regal pretensions, especially if he could be entrapped into claiming legitimate descent from the last Saxon King.[69]

Wriothesly faced another obstacle in the actions – or rather, the lack thereof – of Christopher Barker, Garter King of Arms. He was England's chief herald and it was his job to investigate and, if necessary, report any abuses. He had challenged the validity of Surrey's arms at a meeting with the Earl in August 1545 and also claimed to have sought the aid of Surrey's friend, Sir Edward Warner. But thereafter he had not deemed it necessary to report Surrey either to the Duke of Norfolk, who as Earl Marshal presided over the College of Arms for the King, or to Lord Chancellor Wriothesley. Why not? The logical answer is that Surrey, as he maintained at his trial, 'had the opinion of the heralds therein'.[70] In other words, Barker had been satisfied with Surrey's armorial display once he had removed the offending Anjou quarter.

Much, therefore, hinged on Barker's deposition:

Also concerning the Earl of Surrey, a little before he went to Boulogne, Richmond Herald wrote a letter to me to come with all speed to speak with the said Earl in a morning and thither I came and tarried the same morning the space of an hour 'or I spake with him. And at the last, he sent for me into a gallery in his house at Lambeth and there showed me a scutcheon of the arms of Brotherton and St Edward and Anjou and Mowbray quartered and said he would bear it. And I asked him by what title and he said that Brotherton bare it so. And I showed him it was not in his pedigree and he said he found it in a house in Norfolk in stone graven so and he would bear it. And I told him it was not his honour so to do. And so, at the last, he said he would bear it and that he might lawfully do it. And after that I saw him so wilful, I spake to Mr Warner in Paul's to tell him that he might not do it.[71]

As a recent study of the heraldic charge against Surrey has shown, 'three features of Barker's deposition should have raised red flags in the mind of any well-informed reader'.[72] First is the 'also' at the beginning – a telltale sign that the record we now have is incomplete. One plausible suggestion is that the missing text probably gave details about the quartering that Barker had forbidden.[73] This raises the second flag: Barker does not actually specify which quarter or quarters he objected to. Instead he fudges the issue by referring to the whole coat, including the arms of Mowbray and Brotherton which the Howard Dukes of Norfolk and their heirs had always borne. Finally, the statement that Surrey had a right to the coat because 'Brotherton bare it so' is ludicrous. Thomas of Brotherton had no Mowbray ancestors, only Mowbray descendants (Thomas Mowbray was his great-grandson). Therefore, he could never have borne the Mowbray quarter. Surrey had either said Brotherton by mistake or Barker had written it down in error. Either way, the intention was 'Mowbray bare it so', not Brotherton, and Surrey backed up his defence by citing solid visual evidence.

The error was realised before Barker's deposition was shown to Henry VIII.[74] But Surrey's imputed words were not corrected. Instead Barker's reference to the Mowbray and Brotherton quarters was cut. The only specific references left were to Anjou and St Edward, thus covering up the error and limiting the appearance of Barker's equivocation over what he had specifically forbidden Surrey to bear. It also wilfully misled the King over Surrey's right to the arms of Edward the Confessor. Henry VIII read in the doctored version of Barker's deposition that 'the Earl said that Brotherton bare them', but this was impossible as St Edward's arms were granted to Thomas Mowbray by Richard II in 1397, fifty-nine years after Brotherton's death in 1338. Thus Wriothesley, who had already diverted Henry VIII from Surrey's legitimate Mowbray right by concentrating on the mythological claim, further clouded the issue by allowing another invalid claim to be introduced.

There is, however, one aspect of the King's version of Barker's deposition that works in Surrey's favour. Whereas the original statement is unclear as to why Richmond Herald wrote his letter summoning Barker to Lambeth, the King's copy states that he had done so at Surrey's behest. This means that Surrey had actively sought heraldic approval. That his coat afterwards bore no trace of the Anjou quarter also suggests a willingness to follow any directive that Barker may have expressly given.

It was said that Barker was 'a much honester man' than his predecessor as Garter King of Arms, but his attempt before his appointment to the office to bribe one of his rivals into dropping out of the running suggests otherwise. The knighthood he received a month after Surrey's trial also raises suspicion.*[75] Yet he was, at least, honest enough never to claim that he had specifically forbidden Surrey from bearing the arms of Edward the Confessor. His discomfort is apparent at the end of his deposition where he attempts to shift the responsibility towards Surrey's friend, Sir Edward Warner.

In his own deposition, Warner admitted that he had 'at diverse times' spoken to Surrey about his pedigree. He claimed that he had questioned the propriety of Surrey's adoption of the Confessor's arms, but had not, he admitted, advised against it 'with precise words'. He had also spoken to Barker 'diverse times' about Surrey's bearing of the arms of Anjou and Edward the Confessor and both had agreed 'that he might not bear these said arms lawfully'. Barker had claimed that Surrey's obstinacy had driven him to seek Warner's aid. Warner, though, was under the impression that Barker had already dealt with the matter:

> whereof I was glad thinking it was more seemly for him who, by his office had authority so to do, than for me to whom the matter did no whit appertain, nor at that time, for lack of skill, so well weighed the matter and his abuse therein as I have done since by better understanding. This is all I can say in this matter to my remembrance.[76]

At the last resort, then, neither Barker nor Warner had expressly forbidden Surrey from bearing the arms of Edward the Confessor. Nor should they have done, for although Surrey's appropriation of the arms was ill considered, it was not illegal. Nevertheless, Wriothesley's gentle massaging of the complex evidence made it seem, at least to the King, as though Surrey had committed the double crime of thwarting the rules of heraldry and of defying the arbiter of those rules, in this case the Garter King of Arms.

*

* 'A special exemption had to be procured to enable him to accept the honour as the officials of the College of Arms were legally ineligible for such distinctions, and on no other member of the college before or since has a like dignity been conferred' (*DNB*).

Wriothesley was still not satisfied. Section twelve of the Second Succession Act of 1536 stated that any kind of malicious threat to the King or the succession, or any attempt to disturb or deprive the King and his heirs of their royal titles and dignities 'by words, writing, imprinting or by any exterior act or deed' was high treason.[77] The usurpation of royal arms, though not explicitly mentioned, was arguably covered by this section. But Surrey was a master of language, perfectly capable of justifying his bearing of the Confessor's arms and arguing against any treasonable intent in so doing. The case against him had to be watertight. He simply could not be allowed to conjure an acquittal through linguistic wizardry. So the bill of indictment against Surrey was drawn up in such a way that he would have to be found guilty, no matter what.

It begins by citing the pertinent clauses of the Second Succession Act and then blazons the arms of Edward the Confessor – '*azure, a cross fleury, between five martlets gold.*' These arms, the indictment states, 'are the unique and singular property of our present Lord the King alone and of his aforementioned most noble ancestors, the kings of this realm of England, and not of any other persons whatsoever in the shape and form in which the aforesaid present Lord King and his aforesaid ancestors used, bore and possessed them as a privilege of the said Crown of England.' Moreover, 'the aforesaid arms and insignia with three labels called *three labels silver*' belong 'uniquely' to Prince Edward as heir to the throne 'and not to any other subjects'.

Yet Henry Howard, a Knight of the Most Noble Order of the Garter, lately of Kenninghall in the county of Norfolk, otherwise called Henry, Earl of Surrey, who has not kept God before his eyes, but has been seduced at the devil's instigation and who, by taking no account of the allegiance he owes and his aforesaid rank, but like a false and malicious traitor and a public enemy of the aforesaid most mighty and most serene Lord our present King . . . in order to accomplish and fulfil his false, malicious and treasonable intentions and aim and encompass the peril, scandal and disinheritance of the said Lord King and the overthrow of this his realm of England as far as lies within his powers, contrary to the allegiance which he owes his monarch, did, on the 7th day of October in the 38th year of the reign of the aforesaid Lord the King, at Kenninghall in the aforesaid county of Norfolk, in the house of his father Thomas the Duke of Norfolk, falsely, maliciously and treasonously, in full public view in that same place, have, raise and bear and in addition treasonably in that same place and time did cause to be made and painted right next to his own coat of arms, that is, those of Henry Howard, the aforesaid arms and insignia of our Lord the present King, along with the three labels called 'three labels silver', in order to crush, destroy, bring to nought and scandalise the true and indubitable title of the aforesaid Lord the present King to the Crown of this his realm of England.

In addition his purpose was treasonously to disinherit and block the advancement of the said most excellent Lord Prince Edward from his true and indubitable title in the case of, and towards, the Crown of this realm of England . . .[78]

Surrey, the indictment concludes, not only went against the 'form and effect' of the Second Succession Act as well as 'diverse other statutes recently published' in his attempt 'to cause scandal, peril, derogation and contempt' towards Henry VIII and his title, but he also threatened rebellion in his 'opposition to the peace of the said Lord King and his rank'. The indictment is long and full of convoluted clauses, but at its heart is a basic syllogism: it was treason to threaten the succession; in usurping royal arms and insignia, Surrey had threatened the succession; ergo Surrey was a traitor.

Of course the indictment was specious. The arms of Edward the Confessor were not the exclusive preserve of royalty. Surrey had a legitimate right to bear them, although Wriothesley, as we have seen, had done his level best to obscure that right. On this particular issue, therefore, no treason had been committed. Yet the indictment ruled out any arguments of justification. Surrey's jury would have no cause to debate the niceties of the case. If the indictment's interpretation of the statute, and its practical application of Surrey's 'crime' to it, was ruled valid, then the jury would have to determine Surrey's guilt or innocence according to its flawed logic.

On 31 December 1546 a special commission was appointed to enquire into treasons in Norfolk and on New Year's Day it issued a precept to the sheriff of the county to summon a grand jury to determine the validity of the indictment. On 7 January that jury met at Norwich Castle and found the indictment a 'true bill', grounded upon the Second Act of Succession. A commission of 'oyer and terminer' was then appointed to hold sessions in London to try, with a jury from Norfolk, the Earl of Surrey upon the indictment returned against him. The date was set for 13 January 1547.[79]

CONDEMNED FOR SUCH TRIFLES

Surrey was oblivious to the goings on beyond his cell. His interrogations would have given him an inkling of the charges against him, and the people who had traduced him, but only on the day of his trial would he discover the precise nature of the indictment. Until then, he had to wait and wonder, his mind swirling with hypothetical conspiracies and poisoned by thoughts of revenge.

A record of the Lieutenant of the Tower's expenses for this period reveals that Surrey was made as comfortable as possible in the circumstances. He was allowed two attendants, who served him meals on plate borrowed from the King's Jewel House. He slept on a feather bed with two pillows, sheets, a pair of fustian blankets and a quilt. The winter chill and the lacerating Thames draughts were minimised by five tapestries which were hung around his cell. He also had a fire that consumed two loads of coal during the thirty-nine days of his confinement. In addition to five dozen candles, Surrey must also have had access to writing materials, for it was during this period that he undertook his last literary enterprise.[1]

Within the Tower, Surrey made paraphrase translations of psalms 88, 73 and 55.[2] The psalms appealed to sixteenth-century men and women for many reasons. They offered models for introspective contemplation, springboards to spiritual edification and, in the case of the seven penitential psalms, which Wyatt had versified, they gave direction to those wishing to go on the difficult journey through repentance to absolution. The psalms mined the depths of human emotion and offered a mirror to men's souls. People identified with the lyrical voice in the Book of Psalms more readily and more completely than with any other form of biblical expression. 'Whosoever take this book in his hand,' St Athanasius declared, 'he reputeth and thinketh all the words he readeth . . . to be as his very own words spoken in his own person.'[3]

By the mid-sixteenth century, translation of the psalms was seen predominantly, though not exclusively, as an evangelical act of faith. When Surrey translates 'sapientia' as 'grace' and 'filiorum tuorum' as 'thy chosen', his psalms, like Wyatt's, 'breathe the language of the reformers'.[4] But Surrey did not work on the psalms purely for his own edification. They were meant for public consumption and he had a specific audience in mind. Two verse prologues accompanied his versions of psalms 73 and 88. They were addressed to George Blagge and Sir Anthony Denny, two men at the vanguard of English reform. In the first, Surrey tries to reach out to his former friend Blagge. He admits to, and attempts to justify, his once faltering faith, but assures Blagge that the psalms of David have shown him the light:

> The sudden storms that heave me to and fro
> Had well-near pierced faith, my guiding sail,
> For I, that on the noble voyage go
> To succour truth and falsehood to assail,
> Constrained am to bear my sails full low
> And never could attain some pleasant gale,
> For unto such the prosperous winds do blow
> As run from port to port to seek avail.
> This bred despair, whereof such doubts did grow
> That I gan faint, and all my courage fail.
>   But now, my Blagge, mine error well I see:
>   Such goodly light King David giveth me.[5]

Whether the sentiments are genuine or not, Surrey's *apologia* is a cry for help. But once again, he underestimates the gravity of his plight. A vigorous protestation of faith and a show of repentance could not save him now. In his second psalm prologue, Surrey attempts to win over Sir Anthony Denny, the Chief Gentleman of the Privy Chamber and purveyor of the King's dry stamp:

> When reckless youth in an unquiet breast,
> Set on by wrath, revenge and cruelty,
> After long war patience had oppressed,

And justice wrought by princely equity;
My Denny, then mine error, deep impressed,
Began to work despair of liberty,
    Had not David, the perfect warrior, taught
    That of my fault thus pardon should be sought.[6]

There is a scrappy desperation to these two prologues, but even now, Surrey is not quite able to shake off his aristocratic hauteur. He writes of 'mine error' and 'my fault', but his contrition lacks depth. Indeed, he seems to have learnt nothing from his previous incarcerations. His prologues share the same grudging remorse evident in the letter that Surrey had sent from the Fleet in 1542. Now (at the age of twenty-nine), as then (at twenty-five), 'reckless youth' is presented as justification. Surrey has undertaken a 'noble voyage'. He is determined 'to succour truth' and attack falseness. The psalms of David have made him realise that he should seek a pardon, but the inference is that Surrey, like 'David, the perfect warrior' with whom he identifies, fully deserves that pardon.

Surrey's sense of injustice is even more pronounced in his ensuing psalms. Here any sense of humility or regret is overridden by far more powerful feelings of terror, anger, alienation and despair. The psalms, it was said, could be the 'particular prayers of particular persons, in particular griefs'.[7] Languishing in his cell, Surrey eschewed the traditional penitential psalms in favour of psalms 88, 73 and 55. Here the psalmist, like Surrey, is more sinned against than sinning. He is the victim of persecution and betrayal, the righteous witness to vice and sin. He suffers a profound trial of faith. In his paraphrases, Surrey identifies with the psalmist's voice so completely that he elides it with his own. The psalms thus become vehicles for Surrey's 'particular griefs'.

Sometimes he stayed close to the original Vulgate Latin; sometimes he strayed from its strict sense, and at other times, especially in psalm 55, he departed from it entirely. He drew on other sources, including Wyatt's psalms, Coverdale's 'Great Bible' of 1539 and the Latin paraphrases produced by the Dutch Lutheran, Johannes Campensis. But Surrey made the psalms his own. His choice of metre – unrhymed hexameters for psalm 55, poulter's measure for 73 and 88 – allowed for long, discursive lines that gave room for amplification. His adoption of blank hexameters, an innovation in English poetry, may be seen as an attempt to inject an epic quality into his version of psalm 55, while his resort to the 'infernal jog-trot'[8] of poulter's measure for psalms 88 and 73 set up a dramatic contrast between the lilting, lulling rhythm and the raw immediacy of Surrey's words. Frequently his images are more vivid than the original, his sentiments more intense, his fury more violent.

In psalm 73, Surrey picks up from where he left off in his prologue to Blagge:

> Though, Lord, to Israel thy graces plenteous be:
> I mean to such with pure intent as fix their trust in thee;
> Yet whiles the faith did faint that should have been my guide,
> Like them that walk in slipper paths my feet began to slide,
> Whiles I did grudge at those that glory in their gold,
> Whose loathsome pride rejoiceth wealth, in quiet as they would.

The speaker attributes his spiritual backsliding to the prosperity of the wicked, those,

> Whose glutton cheeks sloth feeds so fat as scant their eyes be seen.
> Unto whose cruel power most men for dread are fain
> To bend and bow with lofty looks, whiles they vaunt in their reign.
> And in their bloody hands, whose cruelty doth frame
> The wailful works that scourge the poor without regard of blame.

The Vulgate condemns the ungodly for their villainy, but makes no distinction between those who wield power and those who fawn before it. Surrey's interpretation was influenced by the work of Campensis,* but his lines are even more stinging than the Dutch reformer's. Was Surrey thinking of Henry VIII, whose piggy little eyes, so vividly depicted in Cornelis Matsys' portrait (plate 27), were sunken deep within his bloated face? Surrey does seem to be evoking the circumstances of a tyrannical Court: the subordination of public good to private pleasure,

---

* 'Their eyes can scarce be seen for fatness, all things prosper with them more than they can desire.

Every man that meeteth them is afraid of them by reason of their power, which is waxen so great, that they give no force whether their wickedness and violence (whereby they oppress the poor) be known or no, but speak openly and boast themselves of such.'

(*A Paraphrasis upon all the Psalmes of David, made by Johannes Campensis . . . and translated out of Latin into Englysshe*, 1539, sig. K.2v)

the shedding of innocent blood, the 'cruelty' of one who vaunts in his 'reign' and the obsequiousness of fearful courtiers.⁹

'In terror of the just,' Surrey's speaker continues, 'thus reigns iniquity, / Armed with power, laden with gold, and dread for cruelty. / Then vain,' he admits, 'the war might seem that I by faith maintain / Against the flesh, whose false effects my pure heart would distain.' Eventually, though, the speaker overcomes his crisis of faith in the knowledge that he is not alone:

> Alas, how oft my foes have framed my decay;
> But when I stood in dread to drench,* thy hands still did me stay.
> And in each voyage that I took to conquer sin,
> Thou wert my guide, and gave me grace to comfort me therein.

The godless men will fall, their glory will fade and the 'sword of vengeance shall / Unto their drunken eyes, in blood disclose their errors all.' By contrast, the speaker, God's fearless witness, can look forward to the time of reckoning for he has put his trust in God and, in another departure from the Vulgate, he has assumed grace:

> Where I, that in thy word have set my trust and joy,
> The high reward that longs thereto shall quietly enjoy.
> And my unworthy lips, inspired with thy grace,
> Shall thus forspeak thy secret works in sight of Adam's race.¹⁰

This final resolution recalls Surrey's earlier Petrarchan lyrics, where the speaker laments his restless state and attempts to draw strength from an internal sense of worth: his morality, his fidelity, his ability to triumph through language. But just as doubt and desperation crept into those lyrics, so the speaker's resolution lacks conviction in the biblical paraphrases. In psalm 88, ostensibly the hymn of repentance promised to Denny, there is a sense of betrayal, not only by friends, but also by God. Time is running out:

> My soul is fraughted full with grief of follies past;
> My restless body doth consume and death approacheth fast.

---

* *in dread to drench*: in dread of being drowned.

Yet God forsakes the speaker:

Oh Lord, thou hast cast me headlong to please my foe,
Into a pit all bottomless, where as I plain my woe.
The burden of thy wrath it doth me sore oppress,
And sundry storms thou hast me sent of terror and distress.
The faithful friends are fled and banished from my sight,
And such as I have held full dear have set my friendship light.

Why, the speaker asks, has God abandoned him? He has never stopped asking for 'thine aid' and he sings forever of mercy and faith. 'The flesh,' he warns 'that feedeth worms cannot thy love declare.' Surrey's speaker is more doubtful of salvation than the biblical psalmist. He tries desperately hard to convince himself that God's mercy is still obtainable:

The lively voice of them that in thy word delight
Must be the trump that must resound the glory of thy might.
Wherefore I shall not cease, in chief of my distress,
To call on thee till that the sleep my wearied limbs oppress.

But an anguished apostrophe draws him back to his lament: 'Within this careful mind, burdened with care and grief, / Why dost thou not appear, Oh Lord, that shouldst be his relief?'

It is not hard to see why Surrey chose this psalm, with its themes of treachery, persecution, alienation and tested faith. He identifies with the psalmist's despair and joins him in concluding bitterly:

The dread, lo, of thine ire hath trod me under feet;
The scourges of thine angry hand hath made death seem full sweet.
Like to the roaring waves the sunken ship surround,
Great heaps of care did swallow me and I no succour found.
For they whom no mischance could from my love divide
Are forced, for my greater grief, from me their face to hide.[11]

In psalm 55, probably the last that he worked on, Surrey's anguish is even more palpable. It wells and surges with a fury that the metre cannot sustain and, ultimately, his innovative hexameters collapse under the strain. He cannot even bring himself to finish his paraphrase. Instead, he pulls himself up with an abrupt couplet and resorts to the original Latin where he claims to find 'ease' in God's love. Yet the vitriol that scorches the body of Surrey's verse might seem to challenge that conclusion. Here he lambasts the 'unbridled tongues', the 'conjured league' and 'the bloody compacts of those / That prelooked on with ire to slaughter me and mine.' Here, too, he rages against the devastating betrayal of the 'friendly foe' and calls once again for divine vengeance. Perhaps with a thought to his seemingly inescapable appointment with the headsman, Surrey reminds his enemies that God's wrath is 'more sharp than any tool can file'.

At the beginning of the poem, in abrasive alliterative diction, Surrey heightens the sense of urgency by depicting the persecuted psalmist as hunted prey:

> My foes they bray so loud, and eke threpe on* so fast,
> Buckled to do me scathe,† so is their malice bent.
> Care pierceth my entrails and travaileth my sprite;
> The grisly fear of death environeth my breast;
> A trembling cold of dread clean overwhelmeth my heart.
> 'O', think I, 'had I wings like to the simple dove,
> This peril might I fly, and seek some place of rest
> In wilder woods, where I might dwell far from these cares.'
> What speedy way of wing my plaints should they lay on,
> To scape the stormy blast that threatened is to me![12]

The image of flight from care and peril is not Surrey's invention. It occurs in the Vulgate. But if the *Spanish Chronicle* is to be credited, Surrey strongly identified with this impulse. Before his trial, the chronicler narrates, the Earl of Surrey attempted an audacious escape from the Tower. The story goes that Surrey ordered his servant, a man named Martin, to smuggle a dagger into his cell. Martin duly delivered the weapon, which he had concealed in his breeches. Surrey then said to him: 'Go to St Katherine's and take a boat, no matter what it costs, and wait for me there. I hope to be with thee at midnight.' According to the *Chronicle*, 'the Earl was confined in a chamber overlooking the river and he saw that he could escape through a retiring room if he killed the two men who slept in it. The tide came up under it, but at low

---

* *eke threpe on*: also press on.
† *buckled to do me scathe*: armed to hurt me.

water it was dry, and that night at midnight the tide was out.'[13]

There was once a room at the Tower of London that fitted the chronicler's description. It was on the first floor of the western half of St Thomas' Tower. Built in 1275 to form the new royal lodgings, St Thomas' was positioned on the outer curtain wall and straddled the moat. Between 1532 and 1533 it was refurbished and partitioned in order to accommodate the Lord Great Chamberlain and Lord Chamberlain of the Household for the coronation of Anne Boleyn. One of the well-appointed suites would have been fitting for a man of Surrey's status, though it must be said that only one record has ever been found of a prisoner having been kept at St Thomas'.[14] Within the west wall was a large shaft that ran vertically through the building and emptied into the moat. This serviced the garderobe (lavatory) and the currents of the Thames would have acted as a natural flush. Part of the shaft is clearly visible today and, in its current form, is just large enough for a man of Surrey's slight build to fit into.

The *Chronicle* continues:

When the night came, the Earl said that he was unwell and wished to go to bed and the guards that slept in his chamber at night said, 'Your Lordship can go to bed; we have to go on the rounds and cannot come until past midnight.' It may well be imagined whether the Earl was sorry when he heard this, for he thought that when they were gone, he could the more easily escape, and every moment seemed a year.

He arose from his bed and went to see whether the tide was low and found that it would be quite midnight before it was low water. So, when midnight came, he went and took off the lid of the closet and saw that there was only about two feet of water. So, as he would not wait any longer, he began to let himself down. But, at that instant, the guards came in and, seeing that he was not in the bed, ran to the closet and one of them just reached his arm. The Earl could not help himself and the guards cried out and other guards came.

It is to be believed that if they had taken him in the chamber instead of in the closet, he was so courageous that he would have killed them both before anyone knew of it; and, if he had waited for another night, he would certainly have killed the guards. The other guards came and put some shackles of his feet and the next day the news was all over London. The servant who had taken the boat went away with the money and nothing more was heard of him.[15]

Surrey would not have been the first, or the last, to attempt escape from the Tower. In the fortress' history there have been at least thirty successful breakouts. Warders have been bribed and drugged, walls have been scaled with knotted sheets, male inmates have disguised themselves as women or servants and, most famously, the Jesuit priest John Gerard escaped in 1597 by means of a rope suspended between the wharf and his cell in the Cradle Tower. This, like St Thomas', was located opposite the Thames on the outer curtain wall where the moat was at its narrowest. Thirteen years before Surrey's imprisonment, a thief called Alice Tankerville effected an escape from the roof of St Thomas' Tower (but was seized by the nightwatchmen at St Katherine's Wharf) and only three months before Surrey joined him at the Tower, Edward Courtenay informed on a fellow inmate, a Spaniard, 'who has often tried to persuade me to break prison'.[16]

But is the story of Surrey's attempted escape credible? No other contemporary source describes it and, although the *Spanish Chronicle* states that the issue was raised at Surrey's trial, no other trial witness mentions it. The *Chronicle* was written by an anonymous Spaniard around 1550. The author was probably a merchant or mercenary captain and he seems to have had a good knowledge of the goings on at St Katherine's Wharf, but he is notoriously unreliable. Time and again he gets his facts wrong. To cite just one glaring error, he placed the King's marriage to Anne of Cleves (his fourth wife) after his marriage to Catherine Howard (his fifth wife). The credibility of the *Chronicle* is also undermined by its frequent resort to detailed dialogue, citing conversations to which the author could never have been privy. At times, though, the *Chronicle* is demonstrably accurate and sometimes, as in the case of Thomas Wyatt's witnessing of the execution of Anne Boleyn's alleged lovers, recollections previously dismissed have been verified by the emergence of new evidence.[17]

Although no contemporary chronicle corroborates the Spaniard's story of Surrey's escape, there are two pieces of evidence to suggest that he might just have been telling the truth. Admittedly, neither is wholly satisfactory. When Surrey's servant, Hugh Ellis, was interrogated about his master's alleged treasons, he was asked 'whether you have heard him devise at any time upon his flying out of the realm and what his purpose was that he held touching that matter?' Ellis' testimony is undated, so it is impossible to tell whether the question referred to a plan concocted before Surrey's incarceration in the Tower, or after. Ellis' reply is also

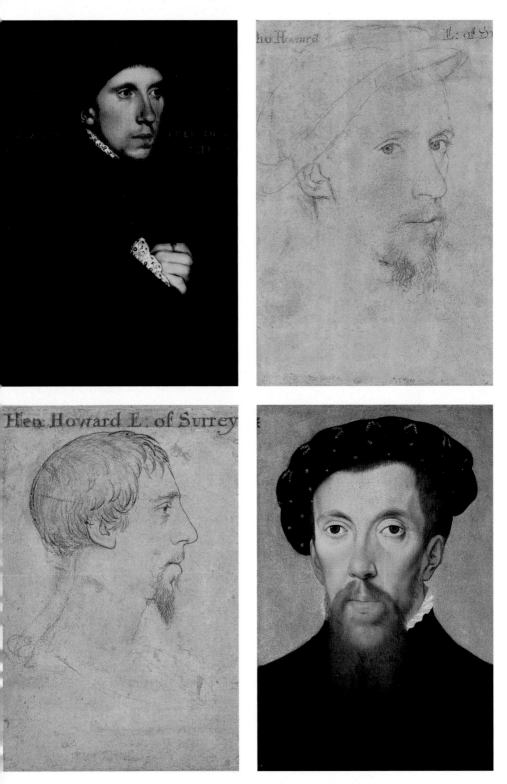

20, 21, 22, 23. The many faces of the Poet Earl. Surrey sat for his portrait more times
than any other Tudor courtier.

24. The sport of kings. Henry VIII jousting before Catherine of Aragon in 1511.

25. (*Left*) The Siege of Boulogne of 1544.

'My foes they bray so loud, and eke threpe on so fast,
Buckled to do me scathe, so is their malice bent.

...

Rein those unbridled tongues! Break that conjured league!'

26-33. Surrey, in the controversial last portrait of him (*above*), stands alone against the combined might of Henry VIII (*facing page centre*) and the 'conjured league' (*opposite clockwise from top left*) Sirs William Paget (detail), Thomas Wriothesley, Edward Seymour, John Dudley, Anthony Denny and Richard Southwell.

34. Extract from the charges drawn up by Lord Chancellor Wriothesley against the Earl of Surrey and Duke of Norfolk. The annotations are in Henry VIII's own hand.

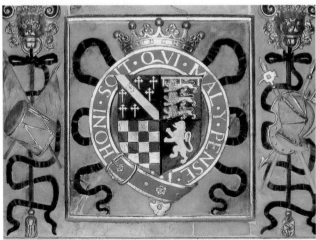

35, 36, 37. (*Above left*) Drawing of a coat of arms in the British Library entitled 'Howard Earle of Surry, for which he was attainted'. The arms of Edward the Confessor with a silver label of three points are in the fifth quarter. Surrey had a right to bear the Confessor's arms as the shield (*above right*) of his ancestor Thomas Mowbray shows. (*Left*) Detail of Surrey's tomb showing the arms more commonly borne by the Howards after 1513.

38. A contemporary drawing of the Tower of London by Anthonis van den Wyngaerde. St Thomas' Tower (or 'Traitors' Gate'), on the outer curtain wall straddling the moat, was the entrance to the Tower from the Thames.

39. The west wall of St Thomas' Tower, photographed during re-presentation work in 1992. Despite much reconstruction, the remnants of part of the garderobe shaft are still visible. If the *Spanish Chronicle* is to be credited, this may have been Surrey's intended escape route from the Tower.

40, 41. *Sat Superest* – Enough Survives. Surrey's tomb at St Michael's Church, Framlingham. His wife Frances reclines in effigy alongside him, while their two sons and three daughters kneel in prayer on the plinth. (*Below*) Surrey's great-grandson, Thomas Howard, Earl of Arundel, celebrates his appointment as Captain General of Charles I's army against the Scots. Holbein's portraits of Surrey and Norfolk are prominent in this picture of Howard pride and regeneration.

ambivalent: 'For his flying out of the realm, I take God to record, I never knew him go about it, but have heard him say if he survived his father he should have enough and that he would never covet more.'[18]

In the Public Record Office there is a manuscript entitled *Account of the Lieutenant of the Tower of money due to him for the expenses of certain prisoners*. The entry for the Duke of Norfolk includes the cost of his lodgings, food, fuel and other necessaries. That for Surrey is similar though the final item is curious: 'To have allowance for the said Earl's irons – 13*li. 6s. 8d.*'[19] Could this be a reference to the 'shackles' that the Spanish chronicler claimed were secured to Surrey's feet after his attempted escape? There are other references in the Lieutenant's accounts to 'irons' and other recorded instances elsewhere of prisoners in the Tower being chained. Anne Boleyn's alleged lover, Mark Smeaton, for example, was kept in irons during his time in the Tower, as were the Carthusian monks following their refusal to acknowledge the Royal Supremacy. Such treatment, though, was practically unheard of for prisoners of Surrey's status.

It is possible that Surrey was being treated as the commoner that he really was and that the irons were part of the deliberate campaign of humiliation that had begun with his forced march through London and would continue with his trial by twelve commoners at the Guildhall rather than by his peers at Westminster. As we have seen, though, the courtesies due to a nobleman – gilt plate, tapestries, soft bedding, writing materials – were extended to Surrey during his tenure in the Tower. Thus it seems likely that if he was physically chained, something had warranted such a stringent measure. An escape attempt would certainly provide a suitable reason, especially if Surrey was armed with a dagger, as the *Spanish Chronicle* claims.

A note of caution must be added, though, as it seems that not all prisoners who were registered for 'irons' were actually chained. The Lieutenant of the Tower could claim a number of perquisites from his office. In addition to fees for bed, board, heating and lighting, he would also, on occasion, charge prisoners for an exemption from being chained, thereby making entries to 'irons' ambiguous in all records that lack external corroboration.* In the Lieutenant's Accounts, Surrey's

* I am grateful to Brett Dolman, Curator of Collections, Historic Royal Palaces, for pointing this out. According to him, the story of Surrey's escape from St Thomas' garderobe 'doesn't sound completely unfeasible' (Letter to the author, 7 May 2004). See too Bellamy, *The Tudor Law of Treason*, p. 100.

irons cost £13 6s. 8d., while 'irons due' for Mr William Conningham cost less than £4 and those for a servant called George Scot were only forty shillings.[20] These sums seem to reflect a variable scale of fees dependent on the status of the prisoner rather than the actual cost of irons; over £13 does seem astronomical for a simple pair of leg irons. Another document, containing accounts for the Tower in the reign of Edward VI, shows that this charge was sometimes levied on members of the nobility. The Countess of Sussex, arrested for dabbling in treasonous prophecies and imprisoned in the Tower for five-and-a-half months in 1552, was charged 'for fees of irons' and the sum was exactly the same as Surrey's: '13*li*. 6s. 8d.'[21]

The Earl of Surrey had the motive and the opportunity to escape from the Tower. Noble inmates were allowed their own servants – though nowhere is there any record of Surrey having had a servant called Martin[22] – and Tower security was sufficiently lax for a dagger to have been smuggled without much difficulty.[23] The shaft at St Thomas' Tower also provided a viable escape route, though Surrey would then have had to have found a way to hoist himself out of the moat and onto the wharf. The story is plausible, then, but without firmer corroborative evidence, it cannot be verified. But even if the Spanish chronicler fabricated the tale or based it on unfounded rumour, he did so in the knowledge that many would believe it. The Earl of Surrey's reputation as a courageous, risk-taking, swashbuckler was widespread. If anyone could have attempted such a daring escape, it was he.

On 12 January 1547, the day before Surrey's trial, Wriothesley, Seymour, Dudley, Paget, four other members of the Privy Council and the two Chief Justices rode through the gates of the Tower of London and headed for the Duke of Norfolk's cell. They left it with a signed confession. Norfolk admitted to having passed on state secrets 'to the great peril of His Highness'. He also confessed that in bearing, in the first quarter of his shield, the arms of Thomas of Brotherton – the three lions of England with three labels silver – he had not only acted 'against all right, unjustly and without authority', but also treasonably, as the arms 'are the proper arms of my said Prince [Edward] to be borne for this realm of England only'.

The arms of Brotherton had been legitimately borne by the Lords of Norfolk since the early fourteenth century. The Duke of Norfolk, as he knew perfectly well, had a lawful right to them. He would also have known that, since 1340, the royal arms of England were not, in fact, the three lions, but the lions and lilies quartered. Norfolk realised the absurdity of the charge, but he confessed to it anyway 'without compulsion, without force, without advice or counsel'. He was willing to admit to anything that might placate Henry VIII, anything that might elicit his 'most gracious pity and mercy', even, as another of his statements revealed, if it meant sacrificing his own son:

> Also, I likewise confess that I have concealed high treason in keeping secret the false and traitorous act most presumptuously committed by my son, Henry Howard, Earl of Surrey, against the King's Majesty and his laws in the putting and using the arms of St Edward the Confessor, King of the realm of England before the Conquest, in his scutcheon or arms; which said arms of St Edward appertain only to the King of this realm and to none other person or persons; whereunto the said Earl by no means or way could make any claim or title, by me, or any of mine, or his, ancestors.[24]

It is likely that the councillors then hastened to Surrey's cell and waved his father's signed statement before him in an attempt to extract his own confession. Surrey refused to buckle. The following day, a Thursday, he rose early and put on the black satin coat furred with cony that the Lieutenant of the Tower had bought him for his trial.[25] His jailers led him out of his cell, across the bridge over the moat, past the King's menagerie at the Lion's Tower and through the gate, where an armed guard was waiting to take him to the Guildhall.

The location of the trial was another sign of Surrey's degradation. Peers of the realm were commonly tried at Westminster, but Surrey's Earldom was no longer recognised and there was no mount for him to ride through the city. 'It was fearful,' the Spanish chronicler observed, 'to see the enormous number of people in the streets.'[26] Surrey was marched past them, through his old stamping ground at Cheapside, and into the eerie silence of Guildhall Yard. Looking down on him from the elaborate porch façade of the civic building were statues of Christ in Majesty, two bearded men symbolising Law and Learning and four female figures representing Discipline, Justice, Fortitude and Temperance.* He would need them all in the hours ahead.[27]

---

* The façade was demolished at the end of the eighteenth century, but the four female statues were preserved and can now be viewed at the Museum of London.

The public gallery was packed with an assortment of well-wishers, ill-willers and voyeurs. A collective murmur of excitement flooded the court as an official, bearing the axe, appeared in the doorway. Surrey was behind him with the Constable of the Tower. Slowly he was conducted through the court to the bar. They were all there, sitting proud on the King's Bench: Wriothesley in the Lord Chancellor's robes, William Paget, who had sworn to 'honestly stick' by Surrey, John Dudley, who had recently received Surrey's letter of 'parables', Edward Seymour, once Surrey's dining companion but now, like the rest, his bitter foe. The only absentee was Henry VIII, who in his majesty did not attend state trials.

The Clerk of the Council spoke: 'Henry Howard, Knight of the Noble Garter of England, otherwise called Henry Howard, Lord of Surrey, hold up thy hand.' Surrey held up his hand. The indictment was read out. Surrey heard how he had 'falsely, maliciously and treasonously' borne the arms of Edward the Confessor; how there could be no justification because the arms pertained only to the King and his heir; how he had therefore encompassed 'the peril, scandal and disinheritance of the said Lord King and the overthrow of this his realm of England'. Surrey was told that he was 'a public enemy', that he had been seduced by the devil, that he deserved death.

This was probably the first time that Surrey had heard the precise nature of the charge against him, for the law did not require the prosecution to present the accused with a copy of the indictment before the trial. Nor would there be any presumption of innocence. Nor was Surrey allowed legal counsel or sworn witnesses on his behalf. And there would be no chance of appeal. As Surrey's elder son put it when he later faced his own treason trial, 'I am brought to fight without a weapon.'[28]

'Henry Howard, how do you plead?'
'Not Guilty.'
'How will you be tried?'
'By God and the country.'

The jury was then sworn in. Surrey saw twelve familiar faces, some friendly, some less so. They were all knights and squires of Norfolk, the county where his crime had allegedly taken place. They were Sir William Paston, Sir James Boleyn, Sir Francis Lovell, Sir Richard

Gresham, Sir John Gresham, Sir John Clere, Sir Thomas Clere, Sir William Woodhouse, Christopher Heydon, Nicholas Lestrange, Miles Hubbert and Henry Bedingfeld. Of the twelve, seven had served with Surrey on county commissions on three or more occasions.[29] One can state with reasonable confidence that each juror, or an immediate member of his family, would have enjoyed Howard hospitality at some stage in his life.[30] Some, like Sir James Boleyn, were related to the Howards by marriage, while others, like Sir John Clere (elder brother to Thomas Clere, whose epitaph Surrey composed), were personal friends. But there were tensions too, be they longstanding rivalries, as with the Pastons, or more recent areas of friction, like the matter of Sir Richard Gresham's windows, smashed by Surrey on his riotous spree through London in 1543.

Several jurors would have faced conflicts of loyalty. Christopher Heydon, for example, was on good terms with the Howards: a 'Mr Heydon' had stayed for several days at Tendring Hall in 1527, a 'Lady Heydon' received an annuity out of one of the Howard manors, Christopher's grandfather had named the Duke of Norfolk supervisor to his will and Christopher's election as a Member of Parliament for Norfolk in 1545 probably owed something to the Duke's influence. But Heydon also had a sister who married the son and heir of John Corbet of Sprowston, the man with whom Surrey had quarrelled over the chapel of St Mary Magdalen. Corbet considered Heydon his 'right worshipful friend' and would later appoint him supervisor to his will.[31] Another juror, Nicholas Lestrange, enjoyed Howard patronage, but was related by marriage to Surrey's original accuser Sir Richard Southwell. Henry Bedingfeld of Oxburgh Hall, whose family had presented the Howards with a gift of poultry in September 1525, was also intimate with Southwell, who referred to him as his 'cousin and assured friend' and would bequeath him his personal armour and his 'best battleaxe'.[32]

If Surrey had objections to any of the jurors, he had to keep quiet; an act passed in 1542 had prohibited the accused in treason trials from challenging the enpanelment of juries.[33] Surrey was probably still assessing his chances when the prosecution introduced their case. The armorial charge was presented and then all the other allegations that had been collated against him in the preceding weeks were read out. These formed no part of the indictment, but were offered up as substantive proof of Surrey's malicious intent. Many of the testimonies, including all of Rogers' and nearly all of Carew's, were based on hearsay, but the rules of evidence in Tudor England were not strict.[34]

There is no transcript of Surrey's trial, but enough has survived in the accounts of eyewitnesses and chroniclers to reveal that he countered the charges with all the strengths and deficiencies of his character. Recalling happier days in the classrooms at Tendring Hall and Kenninghall, Surrey drew on his classical education and the precepts of Quintilian: 'where we cannot deny the truth of facts that are urged against us, we must try to show that the purpose of the act was not what is alleged.'[35] Yes, Surrey admitted, he had assumed the Confessor's arms, but he had meant no harm, and certainly no treason, for 'all his ancestors, Dukes of Norfolk' had borne them 'without challenge or impeachment' and he had 'the opinion of the heralds therein'.

According to Lord Herbert of Cherbury, 'the Earl (as he was of a deep understanding, sharp wit, and deep courage) defended himself many ways: sometimes denying their accusations as false, and together weakening the credit of his adversaries; sometimes interpreting the words he said in a far other sense than in that in which they were represented.' He denied that his portrait had been 'inspired by evil thoughts' and 'excused himself by saying that he had done nothing to the prejudice of anyone, nor had he acted maliciously'. He admitted to having said that his father was the most qualified man to govern the country after the King's death and proceeded to argue his case, presenting the Duke's 'merits and services in comparison with those of those who had been preferred to him'. When questioned about his plan to make his sister the King's concubine, Surrey 'emphatically denied the truth of the allegation', and upon the presentation of Mary's written testimony, exclaimed: 'Must I, then, be condemned on the word of a wretched woman?'

'If he had tempered his answers with such modesty as he showed token of a right perfect and ready wit,' thought the chronicler Raphael Holinshed, 'his praise had been the greater.' According to the Imperial ambassador, watching from the public gallery, Surrey 'did not spare any of the Lords of the King's Council, who were all present, and he addressed words to them that could not have been pleasant for them to hear'. Paget was branded a 'catchpole' – a derogatory reference to his father's employment as a bailiff.[36] 'Thou hadst better hold thy tongue,' Surrey sneered, 'for the Kingdom has never been well since the King put mean creatures like thee into the government.' Surrey also abused one of the King's Justices – 'You are false and to earn a piece of gold would condemn your own father!' – and when one witness, recalling an argument that he had had with Surrey, bragged that he had returned a 'braving answer', Surrey gave the man a withering glare, then turned to the jury and asked them to judge, 'whether it were probable that this man should speak thus to the Earl of Surrey and he not strike him'.

The trial had begun at nine o'clock. Surrey defended himself all morning, through lunch, and long into the afternoon. As the light receded from the courtroom, the lonely figure of the erstwhile Earl, illuminated by the uncertain flicker of candles, stood firm. Commentators marvelled at this feat of endurance, but the King's commissioners were not impressed. The longer Surrey was allowed to talk, the greater his chances of swaying the jury. Finally, court was adjourned and the jurors retired to consider their verdict. According to the *Spanish Chronicle*, they only came to a decision once William Paget, who had slipped away during the proceedings, returned with a direct order from the King. One might dismiss this story as apocryphal were it not for a revealing letter written by Surrey's grandson to Elizabeth I, thirty-eight years after the trial:

> My grandfather was brought to his trial and condemned for such trifles as amazed the standers by at that time and is ridiculous at this day to all that hear the same. Nay, he was so faultless in all respects, as the Earl of Southampton that then was [Wriothesley], being one of his chiefest enemies, fearing lest his innocency would be a mean to save his life, told Sir Christopher Heydon, one of his jury, beforehand, that though they saw no other matter weighty enough to condemn him, yet it were sufficient cause to make him say guilty for that he was an unmeet man to live in a commonwealth.[37]

Heydon had evidently expressed some doubts about Surrey's guilt. Had others done the same? It is impossible to tell, but if they had, it is likely that they too would have received a visit from the Chancellor.

Jurors were not expected to keep the court waiting for long. They were held in virtual imprisonment by a bailiff who ensured that they had no food, drink or fire. Only once they had reached a unanimous verdict were they allowed to leave their chamber and receive sustenance.[38] In this way, many cold, tired, hungry jurors must have been worn down. There was also the threat of reprisals. Those who reached 'unjust' verdicts might find themselves hauled up before the Council in Star Chamber to be rebuked, and sometimes punished, for their decision. Seven years after Surrey's trial, the men who acquitted Sir Nicholas Throckmorton of treason even found themselves behind bars.[39] The tantalising prospect of a share in the confiscated Howard patrimony probably also helped to remind others of their duty. Finally, there was the bill of indictment. Surrey's jury was not allowed to consider arguments of justification, no matter how convincing. The indictment, already adjudged a 'true bill', declared that anyone other than the King or Prince who bore the arms of Edward the Confessor was a traitor. Surrey himself had admitted that he had borne the arms. It was enough.

At five in the afternoon, the jury filed back into the courtroom. The foreman, Sir William Paston, stood up and announced the verdict: 'Guilty and he should die.' The blade of the axe that had preceded Surrey's entry into the courtroom was now turned towards him. 'Of what have you found me guilty?' he is said to have bellowed from the dock, 'surely you will find no law that justifies you, but I know the King wants to get rid of the noble blood around him and to employ none but low people.' After the prisoner had been silenced, Lord Chancellor Wriothesley pronounced the sentence:

> Henry Howard, you are to be taken to the place from whence you came; from there to be dragged through the City of London to the place of execution called Tyburn. There to be hanged, cut down while still alive, your privy parts to be cut off and your bowels to be taken out of your body and burnt before you, your head to be cut off and your body divided into four parts, the head and quarters to be set at such places as the King shall assign.

'The Earl had too great a blood to have so foul a thought. He was known to be thankful to God and too pitiful a man to embrace so wild an act.' Such was the view of one seventeenth-century commentator. It was shared by Gilbert Burnet, who stated in the first part of his *History of the Reformation of the Church of England* (1679) that Surrey's fall 'was generally condemned as an act of high injustice and severity . . . He was much pitied, being a man of great parts and high courage, with many other noble qualities.'[40]

By then a legend had grown up around the Earl of Surrey. One should hardly be surprised. Modern times furnish us with enough examples of the romanticisation of young lives, full of promise, cut short before their time. There seems to be a basic human need to embalm tortured souls, preserve their innocence and hold them up as *exempla* for future generations. Following the publication of Tottel's *Miscellany* in 1557, Surrey was celebrated as the pioneer of polite verse – 'his was love exalted high / By all the glow of chivalry.'[41] It was not an image that sat well with treason. Later writers either ignored the circumstances of Surrey's death or fashioned them into an epic tragedy.

For Thomas Chaloner, writing in the first decade of Queen Elizabeth's reign, the 'wound' of Surrey's execution was still painfully fresh. Had the young 'hero' not fallen victim to 'Envy' and 'Slander' then, thought Chaloner, 'our generation would have seen nothing greater, or more distinguished with illustrious deeds, than this man, so great was the courage in his blazing heart, so great the spirit in his noble visage.'[42] In 1580 Thomas Churchyard, who had spent part of his youth in Surrey's service, painted his master as an almost Christ-like figure:

His virtues could not keep him here, but rather wrought his harms,
And made his enemies murmur oft, & brought them in by swarms.
Whose practice put him to his plunge, and lost his life thereby,
Oh! cancered breasts that have such hearts, wherein such hate doth lie.[43]

At the time, though, few had the temerity, or the inclination, to lament Surrey's fate. A notable exception was the humanist scholar and tutor to Prince Edward, John Cheke, who was a great admirer of Surrey's lyrics. In an elegy, written in Surrey's blank hexameters, Cheke focused on Surrey the poet for 'uncertain is the rest which shame will not descry / nor rage with stroke of tongue that bittrest egg to bite.'[44] Others may have also found the episode unappetising, but most were more concerned with their own futures. The Bishop of Westminster was astonished when he first heard about the treason charges, but sensibly condemned 'those two ungracious, ingrate and inhuman *non homines*, the Duke of Norfolk and his son'.[45]

On 18 January 1547 a bill of attainder against Norfolk and Surrey was introduced in the House of Lords. It adjudged them 'high traitors' and forfeit of all lands, chattels, titles and offices.[46] But long before it was passed, before Surrey's trial even, the vultures had begun to circle. From Boulogne, Lord Grey of Wilton petitioned the King for one of Norfolk or Surrey's offices, while the Earl of Rutland, whose wedding Surrey had attended, busied himself with enquiries into potential acquisitions of Howard land.[47] In Reformed Strasbourg, where the rumour was that the Howards had sought to restore papal authority in England, it was hoped that the 'agreeable' news of their fall would be a fillip for the cause of reform: 'God grant,' Richard Hilles wrote, 'that all these things may be subservient to the glory of His name and the propagation of evangelical doctrine, as many of our friends think it will be!'[48]

The response was more measured among the Imperialists. When, in mid-December 1546, the Emperor's man in London, Francis Van der Delft, was fed the official line about a Howard *coup d'état*, he repeated the details in his dispatch but was careful to add the qualifier 'though I know not with what truth'. In another report, written ten days later, Van der Delft readily admitted that Surrey had invited the suspicion of all his countrymen, but refused to believe that his arrest had come about organically. After reporting the ascendancy of Seymour and Dudley – 'nothing is now done at Court without their intervention' – he concluded that 'the misfortunes that have befallen the house of Norfolk may well have come from the same quarter.'[49]

King Francis I of France was also sceptical when told the news by the English ambassador at his Court, Nicholas Wotton. 'If the Duke of Norfolk and his son, the Earl of Surrey, have gone about or have enterprised those things that [Wotton] had declared to him,' Francis replied, then 'they worthily deserved punishment for it'. He was, he carefully added, 'well assured that no private affection or passion' would cause so 'wise, just and virtuous' a king as Henry VIII to proceed against the Howards 'otherwise than right and justice requireth'. Was the matter, Francis had then asked, 'already sufficiently proved?' Told the lie that Surrey had confessed, 'and yet . . . the matter was in examination still', the Gallic brow had raised and 'he wondered much'.[50]

Wotton may have found it so hard to convince Francis I of the Howards' 'most execrable and most abominable' crimes because he doubted the veracity of the charges himself. The following March he gave a more honest appraisal to Jean St Mauris, his Imperial counterpart in Paris. If Surrey had been permitted to survive Henry VIII, Wotton told St Mauris, 'he would have given the government trouble'. According to St Mauris, Wotton 'greatly censured' Surrey for his 'insolence' and 'hinted that he had been put out of the way because it had been feared he might stir up some commotion'.[51] This, surely, was the real reason for Surrey's fall: not envy or hate or because he was somehow too virtuous for his age, nor because of any popish plot or conspiracy to seize the reins of government. He was 'put out of the way' because of his 'insolence', his regal pretensions, his volatility and his intolerance of the 'new men'. He was simply, Wriothesley told the juror Heydon, 'an unmeet man to live in a commonwealth'.

On Wednesday, 19 January 1547 the Lieutenant and Constable of the Tower led the Earl of Surrey out of his cell for the last time. Mercifully, Henry VIII had commuted the dreadful sentence pronounced at Surrey's trial to death by the axe. At the drawbridge, the prisoner was transferred to the custody of two London sheriffs. They marched him up to Tower Hill and made him climb the steep wooden steps of the scaffold. The executioner begged for forgiveness. A priest administered the last rites. Surrey's gown and doublet were removed. He was given the option of wearing a blindfold – an offer that he, like his son after him, probably declined.[52] Then Surrey lay down, stretched out his arms and placed his neck upon the block. The axe rose and fell.

Two contradictory accounts survive of Surrey's last words on the scaffold. According to the Chronicle of Anthony Anthony, an Officer of the Ordnance of the Tower, Surrey subscribed to the formulaic ending taken by so many of the King's victims:

> The said Henry Howard, submitting himself to the law, saying that he was justly condemned by the law & was come to die under the law & humbly desired God to forgive him his offences & also requiring of the King's Majesty to forgive him his trespasses & so made his petition to God & so he was beheaded.[53]

The *Spanish Chronicle*, on the other hand, recorded that Surrey 'spoke a great deal' in his own defence, until 'they would not let him talk anymore'.[54]

Both calm and panic rise from a poem that Surrey's younger son Henry claimed was 'the last thing that he wrote before his end'.[55] It begins, as some of his other poems had ended, with a stoical acceptance of his fate. Pondering the evil of the outside world, he finds serenity in the sanctuary of his mind. But angry, vengeful thoughts soon force their way in and Surrey's lines eventually splinter in anguish as he finds no respite from the rage that wells within him against the enemies – and one craven 'wretch' in particular – that had ruined him. The poem expresses the anguish of a man on the brink of violent death. But it also testifies to a lifelong struggle to find the right pose, to hide insecurity and mask weakness, to fulfil expectations and to survive in a turbulent world. The poem gives us Surrey's true last words and forms a tragic, though fitting, epitaph:

Bonum est mihi quod humiliasti me
[It is good for me that you have humiliated me]

The storms are past, these clouds are overblown,
And humble cheer great rigour hath repressed;
For the default is set a pain foreknown,
And patience graft in a determed breast.
And in the heart where heaps of griefs were grown
The sweet revenge hath planted mirth and rest;
No company so pleasant as mine own.
                    [missing line]
Thraldom at large hath made this prison free;
Danger well past remembered works delight.
Of lingring doubts such hope is sprung *pardie*,
That nought I find displeasant in my sight
But when my glass presented unto me
The cureless wound that bleedeth day and night.
To think, alas, such hap should granted be
Unto a wretch that hath no heart to fight,
      To spill that blood that hath so oft been shed
      For Britain's sake, alas, and now is dead.[56]

EPILOGUE

Henry VIII survived Surrey by nine days. He breathed his last at two
o'clock in the morning on Friday, 28 January 1547. Had he not died
that day, the Duke of Norfolk may well have done, for only the day
before, his death warrant had effectively been signed by the ratifica-
tion of the act of attainder against him. Royal assent had been granted
by a special commission authorised by the dry stamp, the King being
too ill to attend Parliament or even to sign his own name.[1] As it was,
Norfolk was saved by Henry VIII's death. It was not deemed propi-
tious to begin a new reign with the shedding of blood.

Practically everyone involved in Surrey's fall was rewarded in the
next reign. Barker, Devereux, Rogers and Wymond Carew received
knighthoods.[2] Richard Southwell was appointed to a number of offices,
including the Keepership of Kenninghall and the Stewardship of the
Duke of Norfolk's lands in Norfolk. Knyvet was presented with the
lease of Surrey's manor of Wymondham. Warner received a £50 annuity,
a warship, an export licence and over five hundred sheep from the
Howard flock. Sweeteners also went to several members of Surrey's
jury. And Bess Holland got her jewels back.[3]

A bizarre and controversial clause in Henry VIII's will allowed for
the posthumous bestowal of unspecified gifts that Henry had allegedly
promised, but not yet delivered. Paget, Denny and Herbert swore that
they had been made privy to the King's intentions and at the beginning of February they drew up a book detailing his 'unfulfilled gifts'.
Edward Seymour was accordingly elevated to the Dukedom of Somerset,
his brother Thomas was made Baron Seymour of Sudeley; Dudley and
Wriothesley were made Earls. All four also received generous cash

legacies, as did many others, some of whom were also raised to the peerage.[4]

Henry VIII's will had provided for a Regency Council of sixteen men to govern the country during Edward's minority. There was to be no dominant voice in Council, no *primus inter pares*. The will stated that individual councillors could only act if 'the most part of the whole number of their coexecutors do consent and by writing agree to the same'. Three days after the King's death, the spirit, if not the letter, of the will was jettisoned when the Council, 'by one whole assent, concord and agreement', elected Edward Seymour Governor of the King's Person and Lord Protector of the Realm. Within two months Seymour had assumed sole control over the membership of the Privy Council.[5]

Protector Somerset, as he was henceforth known, ruled autocratically for the next two-and-a-half years. He committed the country to a ruinous war with Scotland and introduced a prayer book so ambiguous that it satisfied no one. He continued the Great Debasement (the reminting of the coinage with a lower precious metal content, begun by Henry VIII to alleviate the costs of the French wars), so that by 1549 it was said that the silver coins were so discoloured by the copper in them that they 'blushed for shame'.[6] Inflation, already at dangerous levels throughout Europe, soared in England. Subjects complained of escalating prices, swingeing taxes and exploitative landlords. Somerset, playing up to his image as 'The Good Duke', authorised a series of enclosure commissions to investigate the abuse of commoners' rights. This aroused hope and, when it was frustrated, deep resentment.

The Protector grew increasingly imperious and aloof. He brooked no opposition and refused all advice. When Wriothesley showed early signs of recalcitrance, he was forced out of Chancery and dumped from the Council.* In March 1549 Somerset committed fratricide when Thomas Seymour revealed himself to possess an ambition that rivalled his own. By the summer of 1549 even Somerset's closest ally, William Paget, was lamenting the state of affairs and, in particular, his own role as a Cassandra. On 7 July he reminded Somerset of broken pledges:

> Remember what you promised me in the gallery at Westminster before the breath was out of the body of the King that dead is. Remember what you promised immediately after, devising with me concerning the place which

---

* Few tears were shed when Wriothesley eventually died amid rumours of suicide. 'This dog is dead,' George Blagge wrote with savage glee, 'the soul is down to hell' (*AH*, I, no. 295).

you now occupy, I trust, in the end to good purpose, howsoever things thwart now. And that was to follow mine advice in all your proceedings more than any other man's. Which promise I wish Your Grace had kept, for then I am sure things had not gone altogether as they go now.[7]

Three months later, following two rebellions (one centred in Norfolk where the rebels quartered at Surrey House), Somerset was toppled in a *coup d'état*. He was executed two years later. John Dudley assumed the reins of power, created the Dukedom of Northumberland for himself and dominated for the rest of the reign.

On 6 July 1553 Edward VI died of tuberculosis at the age of fifteen. During his illness he and Northumberland had conspired to alienate Mary Tudor from the succession in favour of Henry VIII's great-niece (and Northumberland's daughter-in-law) Lady Jane Grey. On 10 July Jane was proclaimed Queen. Her reign lasted just nine days. The English people rallied round their rightful heir at Kenninghall, where Mary initially based herself, and then at the Howard castle of Framlingham. On 19 July Northumberland's cause collapsed. He was arrested two days later and executed the following month.

After Mary had entered the City of London in triumph, she visited the Tower, where the Duke of Norfolk had been lingering since his arrest. The new Queen received the eighty-year-old on his knees, bade him rise and kissed him. An act passed by her first Parliament proclaimed the innocence of the Howards and reversed the 'pretended' attainder against them.[8] Norfolk retired to Kenninghall, where the following August, 'weak with age and sickness', he died. On his deathbed he gave his blessing for his granddaughter (Surrey's daughter Katherine) to marry Henry, Lord Berkeley. They duly married a month later at Kenninghall.[9] Surrey's two other daughters also married well: Jane to the Earl of Westmorland and Margaret to Henry, Lord Scrope of Bolton.

The children had been reunited after their father's execution and placed in the care of their aunt, Mary Howard. They were tutored by the reformer John Foxe, who was later made famous by his *Acts and Monuments* (popularly known as the *Book of Martyrs*). Despite his and Mary's best efforts, not all the children turned out to be perfect Reformed Christians. Mary herself remained committed to her faith and gained renown as a patroness of evangelical writers and churchmen. She never remarried and was to die childless in her late thirties.

Frances, meanwhile, returned to the quiet life she had always seemed to favour. By 1553 she had remarried. Her new husband was an unremarkable country squire called Thomas Steyning, and she seems to have lived comfortably with him in East Anglia, only venturing to Court for the requisite christenings and funerals. We do not know what happened to the child she was carrying when Surrey was arrested. The commissioners had mentioned that it was due in February 1547, but there is no record of the birth. Perhaps the shock of Surrey's execution had made her miscarry.[10] By her second husband she had two children. One was a son. They named him Henry. After her death in June 1577, Frances was reclaimed by her Howard family and buried in the church of St Michael's, Framlingham.[11]

Thomas (Little T.) became the fourth Duke of Norfolk on the death of his grandfather and was, for a time, a favourite of Queen Elizabeth. He married three times, first to the Earl of Arundel's daughter and heiress, Mary Fitzalan. It is from the only son of that marriage that Edward Fitzalan-Howard, the eighteenth and present Duke of Norfolk, descends. Thomas, like his father, ultimately flew too close to the sun. He was beheaded in 1572 for his support of, and secret betrothal to, Mary, Queen of Scots. 'Beware of high degree,' he advised his son in a poignant letter from the Tower. 'To a vainglorious, proud stomach, it seemeth as the first sweet. Look into all chronicles and you shall find that, in the end, it brings heaps of cares, toils in the state and, most commonly, in the end, utter overthrow.'[12] One of his last requests was that his mother be kept away from London, for 'he greatly feareth that if she should happen to be in town at the time of his execution, the sudden news thereof might happen to be the death of her, whose life he chiefly desireth.'[13]

Surrey's younger son Henry lived under a cloud of suspicion for the rest of Elizabeth's reign, but his fortunes changed on the accession of James I. He was made a member of the Privy Council, created Earl of Northampton and, in 1608, appointed Lord Privy Seal. In 1614 he transferred his father's body from the church of All Hallows, Barking, near the Tower, where it had been buried after the execution, to the Howard mausoleum at St Michael's Church, Framlingham. There Surrey was reunited with his wife and laid to rest in a splendid alabaster tomb.*

* By 1974 the tomb was suffering from 'considerable settlement' and was beginning to crack. It was fully restored and, on 9 July 1977, an ecumenical rededication service was held at the church. In what Philip Howard of The Times called 'a roll-call of feudal grandeur', the seventeenth Duke of Norfolk invited the Earls of Carlisle, Effingham, Suffolk and Berkshire, and

The Jacobean monument is instantly recognisable on the left of the chancel. Not only does it differ radically in form and style from the Renaissance tombs, but it is also the only one with any colour. Surrey and Frances recline together in effigy, their hands clasped tightly in prayer. Their three daughters kneel at their heads and their two sons at their feet. Surrey's figure, with darker, thicker hair than he ever possessed in life, is decked out in armour, the collar of St George and a red robe of estate trimmed with ermine. Escutcheons and military insignia adorn the plinth and a Latin inscription bears witness to Surrey's illustrious life and premature death. Modern visitors will also notice a framed print of Surrey's elegy on Thomas Clere carefully propped up against the base of the tomb. The monument thus commemorates Surrey's literary, military and dynastic roles. But there is another symbol there too: a golden coronet that lies, not on Surrey's head, but next to his right thigh. It reminds us that for all his honours, Surrey died in disgrace, a condemned traitor and the last person to be executed by Henry VIII.

Like many extraordinary people, Surrey was riven by contradiction. He could be witty, urbane, innovative, generous, gracious and gentle. He was also petulant, brutish, reactionary, vain, haughty and uncompromising. He was born into immense privilege, but found it hard to sustain the accompanying pressures. He was defensive of his status and sensitive to criticism. Many of his servants revered him; few at the Court could suffer him. His more personable qualities were only apparent to the few who knew him well – if anyone could ever really be said to have known him. People thought him outspoken and predictable, yet he kept his innermost thoughts and fears hidden behind a many-layered mask.

We will probably never know exactly what Surrey meant when he ordered the artist of his final portrait to add the motto 'Enough Survives'. In his lyrics and letters, in external representations like his portraits, his coat of arms and Surrey House, in his imprisonments and

---

Wicklow, and Barons Howard of Penrith and Strathcona, along with other members of the various cadet branches of the family. Around five hundred turned up to hear the Earl of Arundel and Surrey (now the eighteenth Duke of Norfolk) read his ancestor's verse translation of Martial on 'the happy life' and 'the household of continuance'. In his sermon, the Rt. Rev. Alan Clark, Bishop of East Anglia, stressed the importance of 'forgetfulness, forgiveness and thankfulness: forgetfulness of religious differences, forgiveness of Tudor injustice and thankfulness for the sheer brilliance of Henry Howard, Earl of Surrey' (Arundel Castle MS MD 2586–8; *The Times*, 14 March and 11 July 1977).

appointments and in the reactions that he elicited from his peers, there survives something of his personality. That it is not enough is a testament to the allure of the man whom his contemporaries judged a 'hero', 'a worthy and ingenious gentleman', a 'poet without peer', a 'God of spirit', and 'the most foolish proud boy that is in England'.[14]

NOTES

Details of works given in abbreviated form will be found in the Select Bibliography or in the following list:

AH   *The Arundel Harington Manuscript of Tudor Poetry*,
              ed. R. Hughey (2 vols., Columbus, Ohio, 1960)
APC   *Acts of the Privy Council of England*, ed. J. R. Dasent,
              vols. 1–4: *1542–1554* (1890–2)
Bapst   E. Bapst, *Deux Gentilshommes-poètes de la Cour de
              Henry VIII* (Paris, 1891)
Bindoff   *The History of Parliament: The House of Commons
              1509–1558*, ed. S. T. Bindoff (1982)
BL   British Library
California MS Bancroft Library, Univ. of California, Berkeley, MS
              UCB 49
Constantyne   'Transcript of an original Manuscript, containing a
              Memorial from George Constantyne to Thomas Lord
              Cromwell', ed. T. Amyot, *Archaeologia*, 23 (1831)
CS   Camden Society
CSP   *Calendar of State Papers*
CSP Sp.   *Calendar of Letters, Despatches, and State Papers
              relating to the Negotiations between England and Spain*,
              ed. G. A. Bergenroth et al. (15 vols., 1862–1954)
              Reference to document number unless otherwise stated
CSP Ven.   *Calendar of State Papers and Manuscripts relating to
              English Affairs, existing in the Archives and Collections
              of Venice*, ed. R. Brown, vols. 1–6 (1864–84)
              Reference to document number
DNB   *Dictionary of National Biography*

EETS	Early English Text Society
EHR	*The English Historical Review*
Gruffydd I	Extracts from the Welsh chronicle of Elis Gruffydd, transcribed and translated, with commentary, by M. B. Davies, in 'The "Enterprises" of Paris and Boulogne', *Bulletin of the Faculty of Arts*, 11/1 (Fouad I University Press, Cairo, 1949)
Gruffydd II	The same, in 'Boulogne and Calais from 1545 to 1550', ibid., 12/1 (1950)
Gruffydd III	The same, in 'Surrey at Boulogne', *The Huntington Library Quarterly*, 23/4 (1960)
Hall	E. Hall, *The Union of the Two Noble and Illustre Famelies of Lancastre & Yorke*, ed. H. Ellis (1809)
Hartman	*Surrey's Fourth Boke of Virgill*, ed. H. Hartman (1933)
Heale	E. Heale, *Wyatt, Surrey & Early Tudor Poetry* (1988)
Herbert	E. Herbert (Lord Herbert of Cherbury), *The Life and Raigne of King Henry the Eighth* (1649)
HJ	*The Historical Journal*
HMC	Historical Manuscripts Commission
Holinshed	R. Holinshed, *Chronicles of England, Scotland and Ireland*, ed. J. Johnson et al. (6 vols., 1807–8)
LP	*Letters and Papers, Foreign and Domestic, of the Reign of Henry VIII*, ed. J. S. Brewer, J. Gairdner and R. H. Brodie (21 vols. and addenda, 1862–1932) Reference to document number unless otherwise stated
Memoir	'Inventories of the Wardrobes, Plate, Chapel Stuff. etc. of Henry Fitzroy, Duke of Richmond . . . with a Memoir and Letters of the Duke of Richmond', ed. J. G. Nichols, *Camden Miscellany* 3, CS, old series, 61 (1855)
Nott	Vol. 1 of *The Works of Henry Howard Earl of Surrey and of Sir Thomas Wyatt the Elder*, ed. G. F. Nott (2 vols., 1815–16)
NRO	Norfolk Record Office
Pembroke MS	Pembroke College, Cambridge, MS 300
Poems	*Henry Howard Earl of Surrey: Poems*, ed. E. Jones (Oxford, 1973) Reference to poem number unless otherwise stated
PPC	*Proceedings and Ordinances of the Privy Council of England*, ed. N. H. Nicolas, vol. 7: *1540–1542* (1837)
PRO	Public Record Office
Sessions (1999)	W. A. Sessions, *Henry Howard, The Poet Earl of Surrey: A Life* (Oxford, 1999)

Spanish Chronicle	*Chronicle of King Henry VIII of England: Being a Contemporary Record of Some of the Principal Events of the Reigns of Henry VIII and Edward VI, written in Spanish by an unknown hand*, tr. and ed. M. A. S. Hume (1889)
St. P.	*State Papers Published under the Authority of His Majesty's Commission, King Henry VIII* (11 vols., 1830-52)
Wriothesley	C. Wriothesley, *A Chronicle of England During the Reigns of the Tudors, 1485–1559*, ed. W. D. Hamilton, CS, new series, 11, 20 (1875, 1877)

Prologue

1   The above account draws on the material gathered during the enquiry into Surrey's misconduct (PRO SP 1/175, fo. 87; 1/176, fos. 152, 156). For the Bankside brothels, see E. J. Burford, *Bawds and Lodgings: A History of the London Bankside Brothels, c. 100–1675* (1976), and R. M. Karras, 'The Regulation of Brothels in Later Medieval England', *Signs*, 14/2 (1989).

Introduction

1   Thomas, *The Pilgrim*, p. 13; PRO SP 1/227, fo. 97; *Spanish Chronicle*, p. 147; *Poems*, 46, 31.
2   Constantyne, p. 62.
3   Churchyard, *Churchyardes Charge*, p. 2.
4   Brenan and Statham, *The House of Howard* I, p. 188; Chapman, *Two Tudor Portraits*, p. 142; Jordan, *Edward VI* I, p. 49; Sessions (1999), p. x.
5   I. D'Israeli, *Amenities of Literature* (3 vols., 1841), II, p. 116.

1 Only Virtue Unconquered

1   PRO SP 1/227, fo. 97.
2   *The Household Books of John Howard, Duke of Norfolk, 1462–1471, 1481–1483*, intro. A. Crawford (Stroud, 1992), p. ix; Robinson, *The Dukes of Norfolk*, p. 5.
3   *Poems*, 27, line 39.
4   *The Tragedy of King Richard the Third*, Act 1, scene 3, line 244. The Shakespeare edition used here and elsewhere is *The Complete Works*, ed. S. Wells, G. Taylor et al. (Oxford, 1986).
5   Hall, p. 419.

6   Ibid.

7   Beaumont's 'Bosworth Field', cited by Weever, *Ancient Funerall Monuments*, p. 832.

8   Ibid., p. 833.

9   *Letters of Richard Fox*, ed. P. S., and H. M. Allen (Oxford, 1929), p. 58.

10 *The Anglica Historia of Polydore Vergil*, p. 203.

11 *The Eclogues of Alexander Barclay*, ed. B. White, EETS, original series, 175 (1928), p. 179.

12 Hall, p. 555.

13 The epitaph adorned his funerary monument at Thetford Priory. It was destroyed during the Civil War, but not before the antiquarian John Weever had made a careful transcription (Weever, *Ancient Funerall Monuments*, pp. 834–40).

14 R. B. Merriman, *Life and Letters of Thomas Cromwell* (2 vols., Oxford, 1902), I, p. 39.

15 *The Letters of King Henry VIII*, p. 20.

16 Wilson, *In the Lion's Court*, p. 111.

17 J. Skelton, *The Complete English Poems*, ed. J. Scattergood (1983), no. XII, lines 91–2.

18 *LP* I ii, 2684 (1, 2).

2 Henry Howard

1   'The Framlingham Park Game Roll', in J. Cummins, *The Hound and the Hawk: The Art of Medieval Hunting* (2001), p. 264; Stow, *The Annales or Generall Chronicle of England* (1615), p. 506.

2   Giustinian, *Four Years* II, p. 113; *The Travel Journal of Antonio de Beatis*, p. 104.

3   Arundel Castle MS 1638, pp. 35, 123. See too *LP* XX ii, 496; Nott, p. vii.

4   Elyot, *The Governor*, p. 15.

5   Edwardes, *De indiciis et praecognitionibus*, dedication, sig. A.2.

6   T. Phaer, *The Boke of Chyldren*, ed. R. Bowers (Tempe, AZ, 1999), pp. 34–5, 44, 49.

7   Arundel Castle MS 1638, p. 123.

8   C. M. Torlesse, *Some Account of Stoke By Nayland, Suffolk* (1877), p. 1.

9   NRO MS NRS 2378 (11D4), fos. 10Av, 36v–38; Sessions (1999), p. 47.

10 Colvin, *The History of the King's Works* IV, p. 154.

11 *The Regulations and Establishment of the Household of Henry Algernon Percy, the Fifth Earl of Northumberland*, ed. T. Percy (1827), pp. xv, 386–91 (quotation on p. 386).

12 R. Reyce, *The Breviary of Suffolk*, ed. F. Hervey (1902), p. 53.

13 California MS, fos. 116v–17.

14 Boorde, *Introduction of Knowledge*, p. 132.

15 *The Second Book of the Travels of Nicander Nucius*, pp. 23–5.

16 Boorde, *Introduction of Knowledge*, p. 132.

17 Vokes, 'Early Career', p. 194.

18 *St. P.* II, pp. 38–9.

19 PRO SP 1/29, fo. 292.

20 *St. P.* II, p. 43.

21 Ibid., p. 52.

22 Ibid., p. 84.

23 Brewer, 'The Book of Howth', p. 192.

24 Vokes, 'Early Career', p. 212.

25 *CSP Sp.* V i, 87.

26 Brenan and Statham, *The House of Howard* I, pp. 125–6.

27 *The Anglica Historia of Polydore Vergil*, p. 263; *The Papers of George Wyatt Esquire*, ed. D. M. Loades, CS, 4th series, 5 (1968), p. 158.

28 Giustinian, *Four Years* II, p. 315.

29 Hall, p. 624; *CSP Ven.* III, 213.

30 Ellis, *Original Letters*, 3rd series I, p. 221; Hall, p. 624.

31 BL Cottonian MS Titus B I, fo. 101.

32 Miller, *Henry VIII and the English Nobility*, pp. 214–15.

33 *St. P.* IV, p. 149; Wood, *Letters* I, pp. 337–8. See too Sessions (1999), pp. 49–50.

34 BL Cottonian MS Titus B I, fo. 390.

35 Ibid., fo. 388.

36 From January 1520 to December 1524, Thomas spent at least 40 out of 60 months in the field (Head, *Ebbs and Flows*, p. 279).

37 California MS.

38 Ibid., fos. 71, 73. The Pembroke MS of 1526–7 gives further details of Elizabeth's pilgrimages, revealing visits to Walsingham (28 April–1 May 1527), Ipswich (4 May) and the Rood of Grace at Kersey (6 June).

39 Wood, *Letters* III, p. 190.

40 BL Cottonian MS Titus B I, fo. 391.

41 Furnivall, *The Babees Book*, pp. 64–5; Brigden, *New Worlds, Lost Worlds*, p. 56.

42 Furnivall, *The Babees Book*, pp. 69–70.

43 Ibid., pp. 179–80; Starkey, 'The Age of the Household', p. 250.

44 The household account for 1525 records the purchase of soap (Howlett, 'Household Accounts', p. 57).

45 Thurley, *Royal Palaces*, p. 171; Furnivall, *The Babees Book*, pp. 182–5.

46 R. Hughey, *John Harington of Stepney: Tudor Gentleman His Life and Works* (Columbus, OH, 1971), pp. 198–200.

47 Furnivall, *The Babees Book*, pp. 77–9, 135.

48 California MS, fo. 93.

49 'Tudor Kitchens at Hampton Court', *History Today*, 41 (1991), p. 59.

50 Thomas, *The Pilgrim*, p. 6.

51 Boorde, *A Dyetary of Helth*, pp. 263, 279, 281.

52 California and Pembroke MSS, *passim*.

53 California MS, fos. 147v–60.

54 *CSP Ven.* IV, 694; *CSP Sp.* IV ii, 1030.

55 *LP* XVI ii, 1332.

56 PRO SP 1/210, fo. 30v.

57 California MS, fos. 69–70.

58 T. Martin, *The History of the Town of Thetford* (1779), app. VIII, pp. 38–43; 'The Register or Chronicle of Butley Priory', pp. 43–4; Howard, *defensative*, sig. I.i.4r.

3 Earl of Surrey

1 Head, *Ebbs and Flows*, pp. 272–3; H. Miller, 'Subsidy Assessments of the Peerage in the Sixteenth Century', *Bulletin of the Institute of Historical Research*, 28/77 (1955), p. 18.

2 Pembroke MS, 1526: 1–2 Oct., 8 Oct., 20 Nov., 29 Nov., 27 Dec. and 13 Jan. 1527.

3 Brewer, 'The Book of Howth', p. 191. Hermits are mentioned throughout the Pembroke MS, e.g. 31 Dec. 1526, 2–3 Jan. 1527.

4 D. MacCulloch, 'Kett's Rebellion in Context', *Past and Present*, 84 (1979), pp. 55–6.

5 Pembroke MS. On 6 Jan. over 200 guests and 399 servants were given dinner.

6 Thurley, *Royal Palaces*, pp. 41–3.

7 Details drawn from the inventory of Kenninghall, taken after the fall of the Howards: PRO LR 2/115, fos. 36 (Great Chamber), 47v (Long Gallery), 51 (Surrey's lodgings. I have not mentioned the furnishings as they probably changed over time), 54 (Armoury), 47 (Garret), 58–67v (Shelfhanger Farm).

8 *CSP Sp.* IV i, 270; ii, 1030; *St. P.* V, p. 220; PRO SP 1/118, fo. 146. For further references to Norfolk's health, see below and: *St. P.* I, p. 72; II, p. 84; V, pp. 104, 216, 221; PRO SP 1/105, fo. 246; 1/115, fo. 80; 1/116, fo. 1; 1/122, fo. 212; *Hamilton Papers* I, no. 227.

9 PRO SP 60/1, fo. 114.

10 PRO SP 1/48, fo. 94.

11 *LP* IV, intro., pp. ccclxxii *f.*

12 Wood, *Letters* II, pp. 28–30.

13 *Poems*, 35, line 6.

14 Peacham, *The Complete Gentleman*, p. 2.

15 The ideals of the humanist educators are well described by L. V. Ryan in the introduction to his edition of Ascham's *The Schoolmaster*, esp. pp. xxiii–xxvi. Despite protestations to the contrary, most English noblemen were reasonably learned. By 1521 Erasmus could write triumphantly to a fellow humanist that 'there is scarce a nobleman in the land who considers his children fit for their rank except they have been well educated' (*LP* III ii, 1527). It is doubtful that Henry VIII would have allowed his own son to be mentored by Surrey, as he later was, if Surrey had not benefited from a humanist education.

16 Elyot, *The Governor*, p. 70.

17 Pembroke MS, dinner, Fri., 5 October 1526.

18 Elyot, *The Governor*, pp. 19, 57–8.

19 Clerke, *A certayn treatye*. The suggestion that Clerke may have tutored Surrey was first made by G. F. Nott in 1815 (p. xviii). It was accepted as fact by Bapst (pp. 159–62), Padelford (*Poems*, p. 7), Casady (*Henry Howard*, pp. 27–8) and Chapman (*Two Tudor Portraits*, p. 24). The earliest reference to Clerke in the Howard household was previously thought to be in 1541, when he is described as the Duke's secretary (*LP* XVI ii, 1489, fo. 170b). He is later mentioned as the Duke's comptroller (*LP* XXI ii, 557). I have found an earlier reference in the Seymour Papers at Longleat (XVI, fo. 4): 'May 1538, Beauchamplace, Receipts: Item, received of my Lord by the hands of John Clerc, servant to the Duke of Norfolk the same day [28 May] – 100*li*.' For further reading, see S. Baldi, 'The Secretary of the Duke of Norfolk and the First Italian Grammar in England', in *Studies in English Language and Literature presented to Professor Dr. Karl Brunner*, ed. S. Korninger (Vienna and Stuggart, 1957), pp. 1–16.

20 P. Ackroyd, *The Life of Thomas More* (1998), p. 21; Pinchbeck and Hewitt, *Children in English Society*, p. 39.

21 *LP* IV, iii, 6788, p. 3065; D. Galloway and J. Wasson, 'Records of Plays and Players in Norfolk and Suffolk, 1330–1642', *The Malone Society Collections*, 11 (1980–1), pp. 21, 221; *The Register of Thetford Priory* I, pp. 48–52.

22 3 Hen. VIII, c. 3 (*Statutes of the Realm*, pp. 25–6).

23 N. Orme, 'Child's Play in Medieval England', *History Today*, 51/10 (2001), pp. 54–5; Furnivall, *The Babees Book*, p. lv.

24 PRO LR 2/115, fo. 36v.

25 *Poems*, 2. For Petrarch's sonnet, see p. 103 of this edition.

26 Elyot, *The Governor*, pp. 66–7.

27 'The Register or Chronicle of Butley Priory', pp. 50, 57.

28 *Poems*, 25.

29 *CSP Sp*. IV i, 228.

4 With a King's Son

1 Skelton, *The Complete English Poems*, ed. J. Scattergood (1983), no. XIX, lines 644–5.

2 *Two Early Tudor Lives*, p. 12.

3 Wilson, *In the Lion's Court*, p. 53; *Collected Works of Erasmus*, vol. 2: *The Correspondence of Erasmus, 1501–1514*, tr. R. A. B. Mynors and D. F. S. Thomson; ann. W. K. Ferguson (Toronto and Buffalo, 1975), pp. 147–8.

4 Whether Henry VIII decided to marry Anne Boleyn before he had resolved upon an annulment with Catherine or vice versa is the subject of much debate. Most recently David Starkey has argued for the former (*Six Wives*, 2003, pp. xxiv *f.*, 203, 273–88) and Eric Ives for the latter (*The Life and Death of Anne Boleyn*, Oxford, 2004, chapter 6).

5 Quotations from Ives, *Anne Boleyn* (1986), pp. 51–2.

6 *The Letters of King Henry VIII*, p. 82.

7 See MacCulloch, *Thomas Cranmer*, p. 41.

8 *The Letters of King Henry VIII*, p. 86.

9 *CSP Ven.* IV, 701.

10 Holinshed III, p. 719.

11 Ives, *Anne Boleyn*, p. 154.

12 *CSP Sp.* IV i, 194, 211, 232.

13 It is not known exactly when Surrey travelled to Windsor. Chapuys' letter detailing Norfolk's plans for his son is dated 9 December 1529. By the end of April 1530 Henry Fitzroy had taken up residence at Windsor Castle and it is likely that Surrey joined him soon after.

14 Hall, p. 703.

15 *Privy Purse Expences*, pp. 40, 131; Murphy, *Bastard Prince*, p. 127.

16 Dowling, *Humanism in the Age of Henry VIII*, p. 210; *CSP Ven.* III, 1037.

17 *Memoir*, pp. xxi–xxiii, xxvii.

18 BL MS Cottonian Titus B I, fo. 390v.

19 *St. P.* IV, p. 386.

20 *Memoir*, p. xlviii.

21 *St. P.* IV, p. 408.

22 *Memoir*, pp. xxxvii–xliii.

23 Bapst, p. 165.

24 *CSP Sp.* IV i, 228.

25 *Poems*, 27.

26 *Memoir*, pp. 15–17.

27 See Nott, pp. 346–8.

28 *Poems*, 27.

29 *CSP Sp.* IV i, 270: Chapuys to Charles V, 16 March 1530, '[Norfolk's]

eldest daughter . . . died yesterday of the plague at a house near here . . . it will be one of the greatest blows the Duke has ever received.'

30 *CSP Sp.* IV ii, 778.

31 Bapst, p. 169.

32 Guy-Bray, 'We Two Boys', pp. 138–50.

33 The dating is suggested by J. Roberts, *Drawings by Holbein from the Court of Henry VIII* (Orlando, FL, 1987), p. 76.

34 *CSP Sp.* IV i, 182.

35 Ibid., 232.

36 Ibid., 249.

37 Ibid. ii, 934. Anne may also have been prompted by rumours that she might marry Surrey herself. Miguel Mai, the Imperial ambassador to Rome, reported on 14 June 1530, 'they say . . . that Boleyn [Anne's father] desires to marry [Norfolk's] son to Mistress Anne, which may be believed as being good for all parties; first for her, as she cannot marry the King, that she should marry the greatest Lord in the realm; and secondly, to the King, as he cannot marry her' (*LP* IV iii, 6452). This may, however, have been no more than Imperial wishful thinking.

38 *CSP Sp.* IV ii, 934.

39 *CSP Ven.* IV, 694.

40 Harris, *English Aristocratic Women*, pp. 46–7.

41 Nott, pp. xxiii *f.*; 23 Hen. VIII, c. 29 (*Statutes of the Realm*, p. 410).

42 *CSP Sp.* IV i, 481.

43 Vokes, 'Early Career', p. 305.

44 Wood, *Letters* II, p. 12.

45 See J. W. Harris, 'John Bale: A Study in the Minor Literature of the Reformation', *Illinois Studies in Language and Literature*, 25/4 (1940), pp. 68, 75, 100.

46 Pinchbeck and Hewitt, *Children in English Society*, p. 49.

47 No guest list has survived, but we know from his household accounts that the Earl of Rutland attended. HMC, *Report on the Manuscripts of His Grace The Duke of Rutland* IV (1905), p. 272. It is doubtful that Henry VIII was present at the ceremony, but a record of plate delivered from the Jewel House to the Earl and the Countess of Surrey probably refers to the King's wedding present (*LP* V ii, 1711).

48 *The Sarum Missal in English*, tr. F. E. Warren (2 vols., 1913), II, pp. 146–8.

49 Ibid., p. 158.

50 *Privy Purse Expences*, pp. 252–3.

51 *CSP Sp.* IV ii, 980.

52 *LP* V ii, 1239.

53 *CSP Ven.* IV, 802.

5 A Frenchman at Heart

1 HMC, *Report on the Manuscripts of The Most Honourable The Marquess of Bath* IV (1968), pp. 1–3.

2 Hall, p. 790.

3 Sessions (1999), pp. 87–8; Starkey, *Rivals in Power*, p. 31; Scarisbrick, *Henry VIII*, plate 16.

4 'The Manner of the Triumph at Calais and Boulogne', in *Tudor Tracts, 1532–1588*, intro. A. F. Pollard (1903), p. 6.

5 Ibid., p. 7.

6 Giustinian, *Four Years* I, pp. 90–1.

7 Ibid. II, p. 312.

8 *LP* V ii, 1373.

9 Hall, p. 793.

10 Ibid.

11 'The Manner of the Triumph at Calais and Boulogne', op. cit., p. 7.

12 *CSP Ven.* IV, 822.

13 *Entrevue De François Premier Avec Henry VIII à Boulogne-sur-Mer, en 1532*, ed. P. A. Hamy (Paris, 1898), p. xxx; *LP* V ii, 1538. See too *CSP Sp.* IV ii, 1023, 1028; *CSP Ven.* IV, 822.

14 *CSP Ven.* IV, 795, 823; *St. P.* VII, p. 610. But for Francis' denial that there had ever been such a suggestion, see *LP* VIII, 846.

15 *LP* V ii, 1529; Murphy, *Bastard Prince*, p. 132.

16 Hall, p. 794.

17 BL Cottonian MS Caligula E II, fo. 192.

18 Ibid.

19 *CSP Ven.* V, 1036. For the dreadful weather, see Starkey, *Six Wives*, p. 471.

20 BL Cottonian MS Caligula E II, fo. 192; Bapst, p. 184.

21 Pierre de Brantôme quoted by Bapst, p. 185.

22 L. Frieda, *Catherine de Medici* (2003), pp. 37–9.

23 Ibid., p. 40.

24 Smith, *Henry VIII*, p. 70.

25 *St. P.* VIII, p. 500.

26 *The Travel Journal of Antonio de Beatis*, pp. 164–8.

27 N. M. Sutherland, 'Parisian Life in the Sixteenth Century', in *French Humanism, 1470–1600*, ed. W. L. Gundersheimer (1969), p. 59; *St. P.* XI, p. 230.

28 N. M. Sutherland, op. cit., pp. 61–2.

29 *LP* VI i, 692.

30 *The Travel Journal of Antonio de Beatis*, p. 107.

31 *LP* IV i, 606; Knecht, *Francis I*, note on p. 428.

32 Smith, *Henry VIII*, p. 70.

33 Wilson, *In the Lion's Court*, pp. 239–40.

34 Hall, p. 597.

35 *CSP Sp.* VI ii, 127.

36 *The Legend of Sir Nicholas Throckmorton*, ed. J. G. Nichols (1874), p. 3, stanza 10.

37 See C. H. Clough, 'Francis I and the Courtiers of Castiglione's *Courtier*', *European Studies Review*, 8/1 (1978).

38 *The Papers of George Wyatt Esquire*, ed. D. M. Loades, CS, 4th series, 5 (1968), p. 143.

39 R. J. Knecht, *The Lily and the Rose: French Influences on Tudor England* (Birmingham, 1987), unpaginated.

40 Knecht, *Francis I*, p. 268; *St. P.* XI, p. 230.

41 For the best account of Fontainebleau's development under Francis I, see R. J. Knecht, 'Francis I and Fontainebleau', *The Court Historian*, 4/2 (1999).

42 For Francis' itinerary, see *Catalogue des Actes de François Ier*, vol. 8 (Paris, 1905), pp. 480–3. He was at Fontainebleau from 19 to 24 April 1533. Bapst (p. 186) claimed that Surrey and Richmond were at Fontainebleau for 'a fairly long time' and Padelford (*Poems*, p. 11) wrote that they enjoyed 'a prolonged stay' there. Sessions (1999, p. 99) stated that they were there for 'probably a month or so before the King' and that they, 'with the Dauphin and his brothers', greeted Francis on his arrival at Fontainebleau on 19 April. But none of these authors provides evidence to support their chronology. In fact, Marin Giustinian, the Venetian ambassador, reported on 12 March 1533 that 'the King and the whole Court left Paris for Picardy' (*CSP Ven.* IV, 862), and on 19 March he wrote from Soissons, north of Paris: 'The most Christian King, with the Queen and the Dauphin and his other children, came to this city' (*CSP Ven.* IV, 865). On their arrival in Paris Surrey and Richmond were treated as members of the royal household and shared the Dauphin's private apartments. There is no reason to suggest that they would suddenly split from Francis and his children and go on ahead to Fontainebleau.

43 *CSP Ven.* IV, 876.

44 Ibid., 895.

45 L. Romier, 'Lyons and Cosmopolitanism at the Beginning of the French Renaissance', in *French Humanism, 1470–1600*, ed. W. L. Gundersheimer (1969), pp. 108–9. For Lyonnaise women, see *The Travel Journal of Antonio de Beatis*, p. 139.

46 *CSP Ven.* IV, 902.

47 Ibid., 868, 893.

48 24 Hen. VIII, c. 12 (*Statutes of the Realm*, pp. 427–9).

49   Ellis, *Original Letters*, 3rd Series II, p. 276.

50   *St. P.* VII, pp. 473–9.

51   Ibid., pp. 479–80.

52   *CSP Sp.* IV ii, 1072.

53   *LP* VI i, 688.

54   BL Cottonian MS Caligula E II, fo. 196.

55   *St. P.* VII, p. 481; *CSP Sp.* IV ii, 1101.

56   *St. P.* VII, p. 493.

57   *LP* VI ii, 1572.

58   *CSP Sp.* IV ii, 1123.

59   *CSP Ven.* IV, 973.

60   Sessions (1999), p. 105.

61   *The Chronicle of Calais*, p. 44.

62   PRO SP 1/85, fo. 6.

63   PRO SP 1/213, fo. 49.

64   Herbert, p. 564.

65   Hall, p. 597.

66   *King Henry the Eighth (All is True)*, Act 1, scene 3, lines 1–37.

67   Peacham, *The Truth of Our Times*, pp. 201–2.

68   For Anne's French education, see Starkey, *The Reign of Henry VIII*, pp. 92, 94.

69   *St. P.* II, p. 276; VIII, p. 500; *LP* VII i, 9.

70   Edwardes, *De indiciis et praecognitionibus . . . Eiusdem in Anatomicen introductio luculenta et brevis*. See too the edition by O'Malley and Russell, esp. the introduction and pp. 53–4.

6 Bloody Days

1   BL MS Cottonian Titus B I, fos. 388, 392; Harris, 'Marriage Sixteenth-Century Style', p. 373.

2   For Bess' jewels and apparel, see PRO LR 2/115, fos. 6v–7v, 21–22v.

3   Harris, *English Aristocratic Women*, pp. 82–6.

4   She was particularly obstructive over Mary's marriage to the Duke of Richmond and clashed with Anne Boleyn so forcefully that she 'narrowly escaped being dismissed from Court' (*CSP Sp.* IV i, 460).

5   *CSP Sp.* IV i, 509; ii, 619, 720.

6   PRO SP 1/76, fo.46.

7   *CSP Sp.* V i, 26.

8   BL MS Cottonian Titus B I, fo. 390.

9   Ibid., fo. 391.

10 Ibid., fo. 388; Wood, *Letters* III, p. 164.

11 BL MS Cottonian Titus B I, fos. 388, 391, 392.

12 H. Latimer, *Sermons*, ed. G. E. Corrie, Parker Society (Cambridge, 1844), p. 253.

13 BL MS Cottonian Titus B I, fos. 388v, 390 (*bis*), 391.

14 PRO SP 1/115, fo. 80v.

15 BL MS Cottonian Titus B I, fo. 394.

16 Ibid.; Head, *Ebbs and Flows*, p. 282; *Two Early Tudor Lives*, p. 130; *The Anglica Historia of Polydore Vergil*, p. 264.

17 BL MS Cottonian Titus B I, fo. 388v.

18 See Harris, 'Marriage Sixteenth-Century Style', p. 376.

19 BL MS Cottonian Titus B I, fo. 389.

20 *LP* VI i, 923.

21 *CSP Sp.* V i, 87.

22 BL MS Cottonian Titus B I, fo. 101.

23 Herbert, p. 563; PRO SP 1/210, fo. 31v.

24 BL MS Additional 24493, fo. 234.

25 BL MS Cottonian Titus B I, fos. 391, 392v, 388v, 389.

26 *LP* X, 284.

27 *LP* VIII, 196.

28 'Two London Chronicles from the Collections of John Stow', ed. C. L. Kingsford, *Camden Miscellany* 12, CS, 3rd series, 18 (1910), p. 8.

29 Ives, *Anne Boleyn*, p. 167.

30 *Statutes of the Realm*, pp. 471–4, 492, 508–9.

31 Wriothesley I, p. 27; *CSP Sp.* V i, 156.

32 P. Ackroyd, *The Life of Thomas More* (1998), p. 381.

33 Notes from the archives at Paris and Brussels, in Thomas, *The Pilgrim*, p. 105.

34 *Two Early Tudor Lives*, p. 237.

35 Lucien Febvre quoted by Knecht, *Francis I*, p. 141.

36 *Narratives of the Days of the Reformation*, p. 56. For further reading, see M. Dowling, 'Anne Boleyn and Reform', *Journal of Ecclesiastical History*, 35/1 (1984).

37 Notes from the archives at Paris and Brussels, in Thomas, *The Pilgrim*, p. 99.

38 MacCulloch, *Thomas Cranmer*, p. 88.

39 Giustinian, *Four Years* I, p. 85.

40 Herbert, sig. A.5.

41 *CSP Ven.* IV, 386; Giustinian, *Four Years* I, pp. 85–6; II, p. 312.

42 Starkey, *The Reign of Henry VIII*, p. 125.

43 For further reading, see A. S. MacNalty, *Henry VIII: A Difficult Patient* (1952), pp. 159–65, 198–9; Scarisbrick, *Henry VIII*, pp. 484–7.

44 See D. Cressy, 'Spectacle and Power: Apollo & Solomon at the Court of Henry VIII', *History Today*, 32 (1982). Quotation on p. 21.

45 N. Williams, *Henry VIII and his Court* (1971), p. 222.

46 *Two Early Tudor Lives*, p. 208.

47 Wyatt, *Poems*, no. CXLIX.

48 Miller, *Henry VIII and the English Nobility*, p. 79.

49 Wilson, *In the Lion's Court*, p. 216.

50 *Lisle Letters* II, p. 92.

51 Bryan, *A Dispraise of the life of a Courtier*, chapter 15, sig. K.viii.

52 Wyatt, *Poems*, no. CLI.

53 *Poems*, 18.

54 *CSP Sp.* V ii, 37.

55 There is a long and complex historiography concerning the fall of Anne Boleyn, especially regarding her alleged guilt, Henry's belief in it and the role of faction. The account below mainly draws on the interpretations of Eric Ives and David Starkey.

56 *CSP Sp.* V ii, 29, 13.

57 Ives, *Anne Boleyn*, p. 337.

58 *CSP Sp.* V ii, 43.

59 Abstracted report of Jean de Dinteville, November 1533, in Thomas, *The Pilgrim*, p. 98.

60 *CSP Sp.* V i, 170.

61 Ibid. ii, 61.

62 Ibid. i, 170; Starkey, *Rivals in Power*, p. 76.

63 Ellis, *Original Letters*, 1st series II, pp. 59–60; Strype, *Ecclesiastical Memorials* I i, p. 434.

64 Ibid., p. 55 (Ellis); p. 433 (Strype).

65 *CSP Sp.* V ii, 55.

66 LP X, 876. Also *Third Report of the Deputy Keeper*, app. II, pp. 243–5. The full Latin text is printed in the appendix to the first volume of Wriothesley's *Chronicle*.

67 *The Reports of Sir John Spelman*, ed. J. H. Baker, Selden Society, 93–4 (1976–7), I, p. 71.

68 Wriothesley I, pp. 37–8.

69 *CSP Sp.* V ii, 55.

70 *Third Report of the Deputy Keeper*, app. II, p. 245; Constantyne, p. 66.

71 *CSP Sp.* V ii, 55; Starkey, *Six Wives*, p. 580.

72 *Lisle Letters* III, p. 365.

73 *CSP Sp.* V ii, 55.

74 Notes from the archives at Paris and Brussels, in Thomas, *The Pilgrim*, p. 117.

75 Wyatt, *Poems*, no. CXXIII.

7 So Cruel Prison

1 *CSP Sp.* V ii, 55; *Lisle Letters* III, p. 396.

2 Wriothesley I, pp. 50–1. HMC, *Report on the Manuscripts of His Grace The Duke of Rutland* IV (1905), pp. 278–83.

3 *CSP Sp.* V ii, 61.

4 *The Letters of King Henry VIII*, p. 67.

5 Muir, 'Unpublished Poems in the Devonshire MS', no. 7.

6 See Head, 'Attainder of Lord Thomas Howard'.

7 28 Hen. VIII, c. 24 (*Statutes of the Realm*, p. 680). My italics.

8 *LP* XI, 376.

9 Muir, 'Unpublished Poems in the Devonshire MS', no. 9.

10 Ellis, *Original Letters*, 3rd series III, p. 136.

11 *AH* I, no. 78, lines 35–40. Surrey's phrase 'In towre both strong and high' echoes, or is echoed by, the line 'this tower ye see is strong and high', which was part of a poem – possibly a verse letter written by Lady Margaret Douglas to her father in explanation of her actions – that was inscribed by Margaret into the Devonshire Manuscript. See E. Heale, 'Women and the Courtly Love Lyric: The Devonshire MS (BL Additional 17492)', *The Modern Language Review*, 90/2 (1995), p. 309.

12 *Lisle Letters* III, p. 458; Wriothesley I, p. 53. The chronicler states that Richmond died on 22 July, but 23 July is more likely, for on that day Chapuys wrote: 'I have just this moment heard that the Duke of Richmond died this morning' (*LP* XI, 148).

13 *CSP Sp.* V ii, 71.

14 *Memoir*, p. 20.

15 PRO SP 1/105, fos. 245v–246.

16 BL MS Cottonian Titus B I, fo. 389. See too *CSP Sp.* V ii, 104.

17 *LP* XI, 434, 458.

18 Notes from the archives at Paris and Brussels, in Thomas, *The Pilgrim*, p. 113; *LP* XI, 567.

19 Hoyle, *The Pilgrimage of Grace*, p. 48.

20 Wilson, *In the Lion's Court*, p. 396.

21 *The Letters of King Henry VIII*, p. 144.

22 PRO SP 1/116, fo. 20.

23 *CSP Sp.* V ii, 104.

24 Bapst, p. 220.

25 *LP* XI, 601.

26 Dodds, *Pilgrimage of Grace* I, pp. 259–60; *LP* XI, 864; *The Letters of King Henry VIII*, pp. 147–9.

27 PRO SP 1/110, fo. 6v.

28 Norfolk does not explicitly state that Surrey attended the meeting, but he

was definitely at Doncaster at the time. A few months later Lord Darcy accused Norfolk of favouring the rebels at this meeting. He also slandered Surrey and, though there are no extant details as to what the Earl is supposed to have done, or when he did it, it is probable that it also concerned this meeting.

29 *The Letters of King Henry VIII*, p. 145.

30 Ibid., pp. 158–64.

31 R. W. Hoyle, 'Thomas Master's Narrative of the Pilgrimage of Grace', *Northern History*, 21 (1985), pp. 74–5.

32 *LP* XII i, 439.

33 Surrey had arrived by 31 March as Norfolk's letter to Cromwell of that day reveals (PRO SP 1/117, fo. 181).

34 PRO SP 1/118, fo. 216. For part of Norfolk's schedule, see *LP* XII i, 804.

35 *The Letters of King Henry VIII*, pp. 168–9; *Lisle Letters* IV, p. 233.

36 PRO SP 1/110, fo. 6v; 1/116, fo. 30; *LP* XI, 1195; Dodds, *Pilgrimage of Grace* II, p. 64; Brenan and Statham, *The House of Howard* I, pp. 110–11; *CSP Sp.* V ii, 104.

37 Bindoff: Thomas Pope.

38 PRO SP 1/120, fos. 6, 14–15.

39 Ibid., fo. 14v.

40 *LP* XII i, 594, 667; Brigden, *New Worlds, Lost Worlds*, p. 148.

41 PRO SP 1/120, fos. 14v–15.

42 Ibid., fos. 66–9.

43 Herbert, p. 428; Bodleian MS Jesus 74, fo. 327v; PRO SP 1/110, fo. 7; *LP* XII i, 1064; Miller, *Henry VIII and the English Nobility*, pp. 61–2.

44 PRO SP 1/105, fo. 8; 1/122, fo. 212.

45 PRO SP 1/122, fo. 235v.

46 Strype, *Ecclesiastical Memorials* II ii, pp. 339–40.

47 This is suggested by Pigman in *Grief and English Renaissance Elegy*, note 2, p. 149.

48 PRO SP 1/122, fo. 235v.

49 PRO SP 1/120, fo. 14v.

50 Herbert, p. 564. Although Mary's comment follows a discussion of Surrey's relationship with Edward Seymour, she makes it clear that since 1537 he hated 'all' the new men of the Court. Seymour was the man who benefited most from Surrey's execution and it would be neat indeed if he had been the victim of Surrey's assault in 1537, but there is no evidence to suggest this. Indeed, far from being the implacable enemies of popular legend, the Seymours and the Howards, at least in the 1530s, had a good relationship. Norfolk proposed his 'great friend' Seymour for the stewardship of Abingdon in 1537 and invited him to share his apartments at Hampton Court at the end of October. Surrey and Frances

named their first daughter Jane, probably after the Queen, and Norfolk would stand as godfather to Edward Seymour's son in May 1539. The two families regularly exchanged gifts and entertained each other; Surrey himself dined or supped at Seymour's house in the Strand no less than seventeen times in the last three months of 1539, including once on Christmas Eve (Longleat MSS Seymour Papers XVIII, fos. 11v–55v). Nor would it have been wise for Seymour to draw attention to the Pilgrimage of Grace when it was known that Jane had some sympathy for the rebels. Some people point to a poem of Surrey's which reveals his enmity for Seymour's wife Anne, but this was probably written in the early 1540s when relations between Surrey and the Seymours had cooled. Indeed the poem is probably so vitriolic precisely because a prior friendship had existed, one which Surrey later believed the Seymours had betrayed. For an excellent debunking of the early Seymour–Howard rivalry myth, see M. L. Bush, 'The Rise to Power of Edward Seymour, Protector Somerset, 1500–1547' (Cambridge University Ph.D., 1965), pp. 113–14, 191–3, 424–7.

51 Herbert, p. 564.
52 Holinshed III, p. 820.
53 PRO SP 1/124, fo. 1v.
54 *Poems*, 27.
55 Anstis, *Register* II, pp. 408–9.
56 By Sessions, in "Enough Survives", p. 53. Also see Sessions (1999), pp. 135–9; Berdan, *Early Tudor Poetry*, pp. 544–5; Foley, 'Honorable Style', pp. 119–211; Davis, 'Contexts', pp. 51–3.
57 *Poems*, 26. For further reading, see Sessions (1999), pp. 132–5 and Foley, 'Honorable Style', pp. 101–5.

8 En Famille

1 PRO SP 1/125, fo. 140.
2 *LP* XII ii, 911.
3 *The Manuscript of William Dunche*, ed. A. G. W. Murray and E. F. Bosanquet (Exeter, 1914), pp. 17, 20.
4 Head, *Ebbs and Flows*, pp. 149–50.
5 Longleat MSS Misc. XVIII, fo. 23v (supper, 11 Nov.), fo. 27 (supper, 17 Nov.), fo. 29 (dinner, 21 Nov.), fo. 31 (supper, 24 Nov.); *LP* XIII i, 646 (48); XIII ii, 399.
6 PRO LR 2/115, fos. 23–4.
7 PRO SP 1/227, f. 129.
8 BL Cottonian MS Titus B I, fo. 390. See too Norfolk's letter to Henry VIII of May 1537, where he argues that he had summoned Surrey to the North

so that he could accompany him 'hunting, hawking, *playing at cards*, shooting & other pastimes'.

9 PRO PROB 11/30, fo. 193; BL Harleian MS 283, fo. 329; BL Cottonian MS Titus B II, fo. 39.

10 Among others, Surrey borrowed from the Prior of Bury St Edmunds (see chapter 6), his servant Richard Fulmerston (PRO SP 1/209, fo. 128), his father's treasurer Thomas Hussey (ibid.), and John Spencer of Norwich (PRO LR 2/115, fo. 76). On the death of Sir Richard Cromwell in 1544, a list of his debtors included 'my Lord of Surrey', who owed him money 'for a jennet' (BL Additional MS 34393, fo. 45).

11 PRO SP 1/120, fo. 6.

12 PRO SP 1/131, fo. 36. Also see Mary's letter to her father in BL Cottonian MS Vespasian F XIII, fo. 75.

13 *LP* XIV i, 651 (29), 1355; XVI i, 400.

14 Wood, *Letters* II, p. 375.

15 *Spanish Chronicle*, p. 142; Herbert, p. 564. The Duke of Norfolk was also concerned about Mary's conduct. In November 1536 he feared that if Mary was 'out of my company, she might bestow herself otherwise than I would she should' (Wood, *Letters* II, p. 374).

16 *Poems*, 9.

17 *Tottel's Miscellany* I, nos. 8 and 13; II, p. 141.

18 Nashe, *The Unfortunate Traveller*, p. 315.

19 Ibid., p. 323.

20 *The Works of Michael Drayton* (5 vols., Oxford, 1931–41), II, ed. J. W. Hebel, pp. 277–94; V, ed. K. Tillotson and B. H. Newdigate, pp. 130–3.

21 Pope, *Windsor Forest* (1713), p. 13.

22 Scott, *Lay of the Last Minstrel*, ed. S. G. Dunn (Bombay and Oxford, 1912), canto VI, stanzas XVIII, XIX.

23 Ibid., p. 147.

24 Nott, pp. 8, 5, 29, 15.

25 Foley, 'Honorable Style', pp. 87–97; Sessions (1999), pp. 192–5.

26 PRO SP 1/122, fo. 235v.

27 Bodleian MS Ashmole 394, fos. 93–8. Some of Surrey's past biographers have argued that Thomas was born in 1536 and that it is Henry, Surrey's second son, to whom Norfolk's letter of 14 March 1538 refers. However, Norfolk wrote that the son would only have been called Henry had Frances undergone her full reckoning. His letter, written from Kenninghall, strongly suggests that Frances gave birth there ('the women here would not suffer me to let the child be so long unchristened'), not at Shotisham where Henry, the second son, is known to have been born. Further, in a second letter of 6 April 1538, Norfolk writes again from Kenninghall (not

Shotisham) about the plague that was spreading so quickly that 'I am enforced to send both my sons children out of this house to another house five miles hence' (PRO SP 1/131, fo. 36). For further arguments in favour of Thomas being born in 1538, see Nott, app. XXXV, p. lxxxiii and Williams, *Thomas Howard Fourth Duke of Norfolk*, p. 1.

28 Queen Jane, after whom the baby was probably named, sent Frances 'a girdle of goldsmith's work enamelled' as a christening present (BL Royal MS 7 C XVI, fo. 24).

29 PRO SP 1/130, fo. 43.

30 The evidence is not watertight and alternative dates have been proffered. My sources are: Williams, *Thomas Howard*, p. 4; G. E. Cokayne, *The Complete Peerage*, ed. V. Gibbs et al. (13 vols., 1910–59), IX, p. 674; XI, p. 549, and Smyth, *Lives of the Berkeleys* II, pp. 381, 387. Smyth's comments suggest that Katherine was born in 1538, but as Thomas was born in March of that year, 1539 seems more likely.

31 *Poems*, 24.

32 Junius, *Epistolae*, p. 13; Williams, *Thomas Howard*, p. 6.

33 W. Bercher, *The Nobility of Women*, ed. R. W. Bond (2 vols., 1904–5), I, p. 154.

34 Smyth, *Lives of the Berkeleys* II, pp. 284–5, 337, 382–7.

35 Ibid., p. 386.

36 Junius, *Epistolae*, p. 32; PRO SP 1/143, fo. 186.

37 *Churchyardes Charge*, p. 2.

38 PRO SP 1/120, fo. 15.

39 Junius, *Epistolae*, p. 178.

40 R. Morison, *A Remedy for Sedition* (1536), sig. B.i.

41 *Spanish Chronicle*, p. 147; Herbert, p. 564; PRO SP 1/227, fo. 105.

42 Nashe, *The Unfortunate Traveller*, p. 312.

43 In September 1540 a 'lewd fellow' from Norfolk called John Kynton was punished for 'certain naughty and ungracious words' spoken 'to my l. of Surrey'. It is not clear whether these words were directed at Surrey or simply reported by him. That the Duke of Norfolk consulted legal experts, took depositions from witnesses and reported the incident to the Council suggests that the matter involved more than a few slanderous remarks about his son. Replying to Norfolk, 'upon his information of one, who had spoken *dangerous* words', the Council advised him to 'proceed against the said Kynton as to his desert shall appertain'. It seems likely, therefore, that Kynton had criticised the King or his policies and that Surrey had simply reported him. See *PPC*, pp. 40–2; PRO PC 2/1, fo. 34; BL Harleian MS 6989, fo. 97.

9 Chevalier sans Reproche

1 *St. P.* VIII, p. 165.
2 BL Cottonian MS Titus B I, fo. 473; *LP* XIV i, 398, 529.
3 Holinshed III, pp. 809–10.
4 See Starkey, *The Reign of Henry VIII*, pp. 130–2.
5 Ashdown Forest: PRO SP 1/153, fo. 17 (*LP* XIV ii, 29); J. E. Doyle, *The Official Baronage of England* (3 vols., 1886), III, p. 679. Wymondham Abbey: PRO E 329/484 (*LP* XV, 1032). Duchy of Lancaster: PRO DL 29/313/5047; PRO SP 1/227, fo. 131; R. Somerville, *History of the Duchy of Lancaster*, vol. 1: *1265–1603* (1953), p. 595.
6 Longleat MSS Seymour Papers XVIII, fos. 11v–17v: 18 Oct. (supper), 19 Oct. (supper), 20 Oct. (supper), 21 Oct. (supper), 22 Oct. (dinner), 24 Oct. (dinner and supper), 25 Oct. (dinner), 28 Oct. (dinner and supper).
7 Wriothesley I, p. 99.
8 Constantyne, p. 61.
9 Notes from the archives at Paris and Brussels, in Thomas, *The Pilgrim*, pp. 118–19.
10 W. H. Frere and W. M. Kennedy, *Visitation Articles and Injunctions* II (1910), p. 38.
11 *Lisle Letters* V, p. 478.
12 See MacCulloch, *Thomas Cranmer*, pp. 252–3.
13 See MacCulloch, *Tudor Church Militant: Edward VI and the Protestant Reformation* (1999), pp. 5–6.
14 *Visitation Articles and Injunctions* II, pp. 35–6; MacCulloch, *Thomas Cranmer*, pp. 241–2.
15 Constantyne, p. 60.
16 Ibid., p. 62 (my italics). For Barlow's character, see *CSP Sp.* IV ii, 967; Starkey, *Six Wives*, p. 305.
17 *LP* XIV ii, 572; XV, 14; *CSP Sp.* VI i, p. xi.
18 Strype, *Ecclesiastical Memorials* I ii, app. CXIV, p. 455.
19 Ibid., p. 462.
20 Scarisbrick, *Henry VIII*, p. 371.
21 Strype, *Ecclesiastical Memorials* I ii, app. CXIV, p. 461.
22 *LP* XV, 616.
23 *Poems*, 27, lines 17–18.
24 Ellis, *Original Letters*, 2nd series I, p. 182.
25 Bindoff: Sir John Dudley; *CSP Sp.* IX, p. 19.
26 Wriothesley I, pp. 116–19; Hall, p. 838; Holinshed III, pp. 815–16; BL Harleian MS 69, fo. 18.
27 Wriothesley I, p. 118.

28 Ibid., p. 117.

29 *LP* XVI ii, 1409 (1).

30 Robinson, *Original Letters* I, p. 202; Smith, *A Tudor Tragedy*, p. 118; *LP* XV, 613 (12).

31 BL Cottonian MS Titus B I, fo. 101.

32 PRO SP 1/92, fo. 147; *Lisle Letters* I, p. 56.

33 Constantyne, p. 77.

34 Starkey, *The Reign of Henry VIII*, p. 129.

35 Starkey, *Rivals in Power*, p. 100.

36 PRO SP 1/227, fo. 97.

37 *LP* XVI i, 12; Notes from the archives at Paris and Brussels, in Thomas, *The Pilgrim*, p. 157.

38 *Spanish Chronicle*, p. 77. Catherine gave one of her new jewels, a diamond- and ruby-encrusted brooch, to Frances Surrey (BL Stowe MS 559, fo. 59).

39 PRO SP 1/161, fo. 147; Nott, app. IX; *LP* XVI i, 305 (68); BL Cottonian MS Claudius C III, fo.124v.

40 Miller, *Henry VIII and the English Nobility*, p. 88.

41 Anstis, *Register* II, pp. 421–3.

42 Ibid., pp. 332–3.

43 PRO SP 1/165, fo. 184v.

44 Holinshed III, pp. 819–20; *CSP Sp.* VI i, 158.

45 *LP* XVI i, 797, 808–9, 811, 813, 820.

46 Anstis, *Register* II, pp. 329–30, 339–40; Begent and Chesshyre, *The Most Noble Order of the Garter*, p. 221; PRO LR 2/115, fo. 3v; *The Inventory of King Henry VIII*, no. 2529.

47 Longleat MSS Misc. XIX, fo. 121v.

48 Begent and Chesshyre, pp. 220–4; Anstis, *Register* II, p. 423.

49 Surrey's previous biographers assumed he was only made cupbearer after Henry VIII's marriage to Catherine Parr. However the Dunche MS reveals that he held the office when Catherine Howard was Queen. See *The Manuscript of William Dunche*, ed. A. G. W. Murray and E. F. Bosanquet (Exeter, 1914), p. 34; Miller, *Henry VIII and the English Nobility*, pp. 83–4. For Surrey's annual wage of £50, see PRO SP 1/227, fo. 131.

50 See D. Starkey, 'Representation Through Intimacy: A Study in the Symbolism of Monarchy and Court Office in Early-modern England', in *Symbols and Sentiments*, ed. I. Lewis (1977), pp. 212–13.

51 *CSP Sp.* VI i, p. vi.

52 Ibid., pp. xvi *f.*

53 *LP* XV, 953; XVI i, 590.

54 PRO SP 1/163, fo. 46.

55 Starkey, *Six Wives*, p. 679. This is the most recent and best account of the rise and fall of Catherine Howard. I am particularly indebted to the author

for the transcriptions within his book of the depositions taken during the investigation into Catherine's misconduct.

56 *PPC*, p. 353.

57 Starkey, *Six Wives*, p. 669.

58 Ibid., p. 667.

59 *PPC*, p. 355.

60 *LP* XVI ii, 1339.

61 Smith, *A Tudor Tragedy*, pp. 168–9.

62 Wriothesley I, p. 132.

63 Kaulek, *Correspondance Politique*, p. 371 (*LP* XVI ii, 1426).

64 *LP* XVI ii, 1457.

65 *St. P.* I, p. 721.

66 *CSP Sp*. VI i, 232; *LP* XVII i, 106.

67 Longleat MSS Seymour Papers XVIII, fo. 55.

68 *AH* I, no. 78.

69 After her husband became Edward VI's Protector in 1547, Anne grew 'more presumptuous than Lucifer', according to one contemporary, while another labelled her 'imperious and insolent'. In his history of the Berkeley family, John Smyth noted that Anne was reputed as 'a woman for many imperfections intolerable, for pride monstrous, exceedingly both subtle and violent in accomplishing her ends, for which she spurned over all respects both of conscience and shame' (*Spanish Chronicle*, p. 156; Jordan, *Edward VI* II, p. 86; Smyth, *Lives of the Berkeleys* II, p. 430).

70 See Heale, pp. 23–4.

71 BL Lansdowne MS 2, fo. 34; *LP* XVII i, 362 (66); XVI ii, 1488 (18).

10 Poet without Peer

1 Stevens, *Music & Poetry*, app. A, pp. 344–5.

2 Quoted by Heale, p. 61. See too Junius, *Epistolae*, pp. 30–1.

3 B. J. Harris, 'Women and Politics in Early Tudor England', *HJ*, 33/2 (1990), p. 279; Thomas, *The Pilgrim*, p. 13.

4 This is Starkey's phrase ('The Age of the Household', p. 253).

5 Heale, p. 53. For the poem, see Wyatt, *Poems*, no. LXXX. In his epistolary satires, Wyatt addressed the courtier's dilemma – whether to retire from the Court to a life of ease in the country (but with the nagging guilt of having renounced one's civic duty to provide the King with good counsel), or to remain at Court in the King's service, where innocence, honour and even life are under threat. For an incisive reading of Wyatt's *Third Satire* and its debunking of Castiglione's theory that the perfect courtier, by means of his accomplishments, can speak candidly to his King and lead him towards virtue, see D. Starkey, 'The Court: Castiglione's Ideal

and Tudor Reality; being a discussion of Sir Thomas Wyatt's "Satire addressed to Sir Francis Bryan"', *Journal of the Warburg and Courtauld Institutes*, 45 (1982).

6 *Poems*, 28.

7 See Heale, p. 93.

8 *Poems*, 13.

9 Wyatt, *Poems*, no. XLIX.

10 *Poems*, 28.

11 Wyatt, *Poems*, no. CLII. For his imprisonment, see Brigden, '"The Shadow that you Know"'.

12 In Henry VIII's Psalter, presented to him by Jean Mallard and now in the British Library (BL Royal MS 2 A XVI), there are miniature portraits of David clearly fashioned from Henry VIII's own likeness. Francis I's Book of Hours had included an illustration of Francis as David kneeling in prayer with a bathing Bathsheba in the background, but in the miniature portrait accompanying psalm 69 (associated with 'David in Penance') in Henry VIII's Psalter, Bathsheba is conspicuous by her absence. See P. Tudor-Craig, 'Henry VIII and King David', in *Early Tudor England: Proceedings of the 1987 Harlaxton Symposium*, ed. D. Williams (Woodbridge, 1989), pp. 195–8; J. N. King, 'Henry VIII as David', in *Rethinking the Henrician Era*, ed. Herman, pp. 83–6.

13 *Poems*, 29, line 9.

14 Ibid., 31.

15 Sidney, *An Apology for Poetry*, p. 98. Also, p. 115.

16 See Worden, *LRB*, p. 14.

17 *Poems*, 32.

18 See Davis, 'Contexts', pp. 45–6.

19 P. B. Shelley, 'A Defence of Poetry', in *Political Tracts of Wordsworth, Coleridge and Shelley*, ed. R. J. White (Cambridge, 1953), p. 201.

20 *Poems*, 17.

21 Ibid., 3.

22 For an excellent analysis of Surrey's poetry within the context of his public image, see Foley, 'Honorable Style'.

23 Edwardes, *Introduction to Anatomy*, p. 54.

24 Castiglione, *The Book of the Courtier*, p. 54.

25 *Poems*, 11. For an insightful reading of this poem, see Sessions, *Henry Howard, Earl of Surrey* (1986), pp. 81–3.

26 Strong, *Tudor & Jacobean Portraits* I, p. 307.

27 *Poems*, 49.

28 Ibid., 44.

29 Ibid., 40.

30 *LP* XVIII ii, 190.

31 Peacham, *The Complete Gentleman*, p. 95.

32 Burrow, *LRB*, p. 14.

33 *The Aeneid*, tr. C. Day Lewis (Oxford, 1986), p. 179 (lines 662–3).

34 Clerke, *A certayn treatye*.

35 Surrey's studied economy is illustrated by the brevity of his text. Book IV of Virgil's *Aeneid* is 705 lines long. Gavin Douglas, who rendered his *Eneados* in heroic couplets and was not interested in literal precision, required 1,374 lines. Surrey completed his translation in 943 lines. See Ridley (ed.), *The Aeneid of Henry Howard*, p. 36.

36 Warton, *The History of English Poetry*, vol. 3 (1781), p. 27.

37 It has been suggested that Nicholas Grimald's blank verse poems, 'The Death of Zoroas' and 'Marcus Tullius Ciceroes Death', might predate Surrey's translations. There is no way of knowing with absolute certainty whose came first, but Grimald's reliance for his second poem on the work of Beza, first published in 1548 (one year after Surrey's death), points to Surrey as the founder of English blank verse. Furthermore, Surrey's translation of Book IV of the *Aeneid* was almost certainly published in 1554, three years before Grimald's poems were published, and was therefore the first instance of English blank verse in print. See Hartman, pp. xii–xv; H. H. Hudson, 'Grimald's Translations from Beza', *Modern Language Notes*, 39/7 (1924), pp. 388–94; Lathrop, 'Translations from the Classics', pp. 103–4.

38 A facsimile of the title-page is printed in Hartman.

39 For commentary, see the bibliography, in particular Oras, Jones (under *Poems* in abbreviations), Richardson and Sessions. For less complimentary readings, see Ridley, Mason and Lewis.

40 Hartman, pp. 50–1 (lines 844–72).

41 J. A. Symonds, *Blank Verse* (1895), pp. 16–17.

42 Cf. *Poems*, 39 and 40.

43 Mason, *Humanism and Poetry*, pp. 236, 240.

44 Lewis, *English Literature in the Sixteenth Century*, p. 234.

45 See Evans, *English Poetry in the Sixteenth Century*, pp. 33–4.

46 Ibid., pp. 37–8, 78; Nott, p. cxciv.

47 Turberville, *Epitaphes, Epigrams, Songs and Sonets*, p. 49. See too Sessions, *Henry Howard, Earl of Surrey* (1986), pp. 24–7; Davis, 'Contexts', pp. 40–55.

48 Turberville, *Epitaphes, Epigrams, Songs and Sonnets*, pp. 48–9.

49 Puttenham, *The Arte of English Poesie*, p. 60; *AH* I, no. 282; *Churchyardes Charge*, p. 2.

50 Camden, *Remains*, p. 183.

51 *Tottel's Miscellany* I, p. 2.

52 Ibid. II, pp. 4–5, 107–9, 121, 285 (quotation from Rollins on p. 4).

53 No autograph manuscript of Surrey's poetry has survived, so it is impossible

to determine just how much revision took place. When Tottel later published Surrey's translations of the *Aeneid*, it is evident from a comparison with the earlier Day-Owen text of Surrey's translation of Book IV that the metres had been regularised by Tottel, or whoever edited the work for him. The same might be said for Tottel's handling of Surrey's poem 'O happy dames', previously inscribed by his sister Mary into the Devonshire Manuscript. That the editor of the *Songes and Sonettes* had no qualms about tampering with original texts is evident from a study of Wyatt's poems, which have survived in autograph. See Hartman, pp. xvi–xxii; R. Southall, 'Mary Fitzroy and "O happy dames" in the Devonshire Manuscript', *The Review of English Studies*, new series, 45/179 (1994), p. 317; *Tottel's Miscellany* II, *passim*; Padelford, 'Manuscript Poems', pp. 284–6. For the best assessments of the Tottel effect on Surrey's literary reputation, see Heale, pp. 191–5; Duncan-Jones, *TLS*, pp. 26–7; Burrow, *LRB*, pp. 13–14.

54 Puttenham, *The Arte of English Poesie*, p. 60.
55 Scott, *Lay of the Last Minstrel*, canto VI, stanza XIII.

11 The Fury of Reckless Youth

1 *APC* I, p. 17.
2 Furthermore, John's uncle Sir John Legh of Stockwell (d. 1523), whose estate he inherited, was the second husband of Catherine Howard's maternal grandmother Isabel née Worsley (Brenan and Statham, *The House of Howard* I, pp. 242–3). However, there is some debate over the nature of John Leigh's kinship with Catherine Howard. See 'Genealogical Notices of Sir John Legh and his Family', in J. W. Burgon, *The Life and Times of Sir Thomas Gresham* (2 vols., 1839), app. IX; PRO PROB 11/21, fos. 112–16; 11/22, fos. 143–4; 11/48, fos. 281–284v.
3 BL Cottonian MS Cleopatra E VI, fo. 395; PRO SP 1/158, fo. 68. For Leigh's epitaph in St Margaret's, Lothbury, see Stow, *Survey* I, p. 283. This definitely refers to John Leigh of Stockwell, as his will made it clear that he wanted to be buried either in St Mary's Lambeth 'or else in the parish church of St Margaret in Lothbury in the city of London where I do presently inhabit' (PRO PROB 11/48, fo. 281v).
4 *APC* II, pp. 111, 142.
5 *APC* II, p. 384; III, pp. 54, 97, 108, 127, 301; *CSP Sp.* X, p. 9; M. Fléchier, *La Vie du Cardinal Jean François Commendon* (Paris, 1694), pp. 45–6.
6 *Ambassades de Messieurs de Noailles en Angleterre*, ed. R. A. de Vertot and C. Villaret, vol. 2 (Leyden, 1763), pp. 244–5, 247. At the beginning of Mary's reign Leigh helped the Pope's secret emissary Cardinal Commendone, whom he had met at Rome, gain access to the Queen. See Fléchier, op. cit., pp. 45–6, and Burgon, *Gresham*, op. cit., I, pp. 122–6.

7 Strype, *Ecclesiastical Memorials* III ii, p. 181; Catholic Record Society, *Miscellanea* I (1905), p. 45.

8 That the John Leigh who had been in Italy with Pole was the same John Leigh who hailed from Stockwell is strongly inferred not only from the reference to Leigh of Stockwell's travels in his epitaph, but also by a grant in May 1541, which pardoned 'John Legh of Lambeth *alias* Stockwell . . . of all offences committed before 20 March, 32 Hen. VIII', which is surely a reference to his illegal flight from England and his dealings with the traitor Pole (*LP* XVI i, 878 [28]).

9 BL Cottonian MS Cleopatra E VI, fos. 394–395v. See too Strype, *Ecclesiastical Memorials* I i, pp. 481–4; *St. P.* I, pp. 624–7; *LP* XV, 615, 697, 721; T. F. Mayer, *Reginald Pole: Prince & Prophet* (Cambridge, 2000), p. 80.

10 In the Public Record Office (SP 1/141, fo. 159), there is a curious letter from Leigh to Cromwell, in which he refers to the 'ancient love' he bears for Cromwell 'and of duty likewise', and signs off, 'ever yours to command'. Leigh's letter also makes it clear that Cromwell expected to receive regular newsletters from him. Anthony Budgegood, another exile in Italy, suspected Leigh of being there 'for the King of England' (*LP* XIV i, 1). See too *LP* XV, 615, Cromwell's Remembrances, 1540: 'For John a Lee and what the King's pleasure shall be therein.'

11 PRO SP 1/158, fo. 74v.

12 E. H. Harbison, *Rival Ambassadors at the Court of Queen Mary* (Princeton, 1940), pp. 76–7, 93, 109–10. Also Harbison's article, 'French Intrigue at the Court of Queen Mary', *The American Historical Review*, 45/3 (1940), pp. 542–5.

13 *PPC*, pp. 288, 291, 303, 319.

14 Brigden, 'Conjured League', p. 532.

15 Herbert, p. 564.

16 BL Harleian MS 78, fo. 24.

17 *APC* I, p. 19.

18 He set out with his father from Kenninghall on 11 September. *LP* XVII i, 729, 770; *Hamilton Papers* I, no. 153.

19 *The Chronicle of Jhon Hardyng* (1543), dedication by the printer Richard Grafton to the Duke of Norfolk, stanza 8.

20 *The Letters of King Henry VIII*, pp. 296–302; *Hamilton Papers* I, no. 204.

21 *Poems*, 20, lines 7–10.

22 *Hamilton Papers* I, no. 221.

23 *The Chronicle of Jhon Hardyng*, op. cit., penultimate stanza, lines 6–7.

24 *Hamilton Papers* I, nos. 218, 226.

25 BL Additional MS 10110, fo. 237.

26 *Hamilton Papers* I, no. 231.

27 C. M. Barron, *London in the Later Middle Ages: Government and People 1200–1500* (Oxford, 2004), pp. 4, 242.

28 Stow, *Survey* I, pp. 200, 211, 245; T. More, *The Answer to a Poisoned Book*, ed. S. M. Foley and C. H. Miller, vol. 11 of Yale *Complete Works* (1985), p. 12.

29 Peacham, *The Art of Living in London*, p. 243.

30 Stow, *Survey* II, p. 316.

31 Ibid. I, p. 270; PRO SP 1/176, fo. 178.

32 The resemblance to 'the merry escapades of Prince Hal' was first noted by Padelford (*Poems*, p. 22). For the following character sketches, see Bindoff and *DNB*. Also:

Hussey: Gruffydd I, p. 60; *APC* I, p. 289; *CSP Domestic, Elizabeth 1601–1603 with addenda 1547–1565*, ed. M. A. Green (1870), p. 528.

Pickering: Corp. of London Record Office Repertory 12, fo. 92; *LP* VII ii, 1672 (2); *Privy Purse Expences*, p. 220.

Thomas Clere: *PPC*, p. 181.

Stafford: *APC* IV, pp. 178, 185.

Blagge: *LP* XVIII ii, 190; Foxe, *Acts and Monuments* V, p. 564.

33 Wriothesley I, pp. 145–6.

34 *The Second Book of the Travels of Nicander Nucius*, pp. 48–9.

35 Stow, *Survey* I, p. 295; II, p. 338.

36 PRO SP 1/175, fo. 87; 1/176, fo. 156. Surrey and his fellows may have taken to the streets on other occasions. The Imperial ambassador reported to the Queen of Hungary that they had terrorised London for 'two or three nights' (*CSP Sp*. VI ii, 127).

37 PRO SP 1/176, fo. 156. Blagge was right to be concerned; his association with Surrey may have impaired his chances at gaining the mastership of the Weigh House, an office in the gift of the City. Despite a personal recommendation from the King on 6 March, Blagge was turned down. See Brigden, 'Conjured League', p. 519; Corp. of London Record Office Journal 15, fo. 20.

38 PRO SP 1/175, fos. 85–89v; *LP* XVIII i, 226 (50).

39 PRO SP 1/176, fos. 151–2, 155–6, 178.

40 PRO SP 1/227, fo. 76, Surrey to the Council, Dec. 1546. It is sometimes assumed that Surrey's reference in 1546 to his previous examination relates to the John Leigh affair, but the names subscribed on the depositions of Mistress Arundel and Joan Whetnal (PRO SP 1/176, fo. 178) show that the four men who conducted the questioning over his misbehaviour in London were the same four that he requested nearly four years later.

41 *APC* I, p. 104.

42 Ibid., pp. 104–6. It has been suggested that Edward Seymour intervened in Surrey's case, arguing in favour of his committal to the Fleet. This is

based on a manuscript in the Sloane collection of the British Library, which contains a book of 'maxims, sayings and short accounts of several eminent men who lived mostly in the reign of Henry VIII'. Under the heading *The Seymours* is the entry: 'The Earl of Surrey & other nobility were imprisoned for eating flesh in Lent.' The next two entries are as follows: 'A secret & unobserved contempt of the law is a close undermining of authority; which must be either itself in indulging nothing or be nothing in allowing all'; 'Liberty knows no restraint, no limit, when winked at' (BL Sloane MS 1523, fo. 37). The provenance and reliability of the manuscript are difficult to ascertain. The handwriting does not accord with the Henrician period. Samuel Ayscough, the eighteenth-century compiler of British Museum manuscripts, ascribed it, without explanation, to one John Wright and to c.1607. However, folio 36v of the manuscript contains a passage entitled *Lord Herbert's Character of Cardinal Wolsey*. This is extracted from Lord Herbert of Cherbury's *Life and Raigne of King Henry the Eighth* (pp. 314–15), which was begun in 1632 and first published in 1649. The impression of the whole manuscript book, which also includes extracted notes on trees, is that each part has been transcribed from another source. There is a remarkable correlation between the Henrician maxim section of the manuscript and David Lloyd's *The Statesmen and Favourites of England Since the Reformation* (1665). Not only are all the statements in the manuscript, including the Seymour maxims, present in Lloyd's book, but also in exactly the same order (see esp. p. 148, where Lloyd explicitly states that Seymour had a hand in Surrey's sentencing). Either Lloyd, who is described in the *DNB* as 'a most impudent plagiary . . . a false writer and mere scribbler', appropriated the manuscript and elaborated upon it for his own book or, more likely, the manuscript contains Lloyd's own notes for his book, or someone else's notes extracted from his book. The style of the manuscript does seem remarkably similar to Lloyd's own, and we know that Lloyd made extensive use of Herbert's *Life and Raigne* (cf. pp. 99–100 of Lloyd with Herbert, pp. 563–5, and fo. 32v of the manuscript). Whatever the provenance of the manuscript, its reliability cannot be confirmed, and unless further evidence comes to light about Seymour's involvement in Surrey's imprisonment, it would be advisable to treat the story with scepticism.

43 *Poems*, 33. See too Jones' comments, pp. 127–8.

44 See Brigden, 'Conjured League', pp. 517–19 (quotation on p. 519). For the first reading, see Nott, pp. liii *f.*, 365–6; Mason, *Humanism and Poetry*, pp. 243–5. For variations on the second, Bapst, p. 272; Brenan and Statham, *The House of Howard* II, pp. 377–9; Padelford, *Poems*, p. 24; Casady, *Henry Howard*, pp. 100–1; Chapman, *Two Tudor Portraits*, p. 81; *AH* II, pp. 90–1. For the third, Foley, 'Honorable Style', pp. 176, 189–200. For

further reading, see Heale, pp. 142–6; Sessions (1999), pp. 234–8; Burrow, *LRB*, p. 13.

45 *LP* XIII ii, 125.

46 For Gresham, see Bindoff and *DNB*. Also: 'Two Poems on the Death of Sir Richard Gresham', ed. A. G. Rigg, *The Guildhall Miscellany*, 2/9 (1967), pp. 389–91; Brigden, *London and the Reformation*, pp. 239, 293–4; Wriothesley I, p. 67; *LP* XIV ii, 782; Longleat MSS Seymour Papers XVI, fos. 5, 87v; XVII, fos. 2, 6v.
   For Birch, see PRO PROB 11/34, fo. 107; *LP* VII ii, 1672 (2); XII ii, 1136, 1151, 1191; XVII ii, 1154 (92); XVIII i, 226 (60); Longleat MSS Seymour Papers XIV, fo. 63.

47 Brigden, 'Conjured League', p. 517.

48 PRO SP 1/176, fo. 156; *APC* I, p. 104.

49 PRO SP 1/176, fo. 156; *APC* I, p. 106. The wife of Andrew Castle, the Arundels' butcher, had been indicted in 1540 for her reforming activities (Brigden, *London and the Reformation*, pp. 343–4, 412, 444).

50 Brigden, *London and the Reformation*, pp. 113, 402; *APC* I, pp. 126, 128.

51 Brigden, *London and the Reformation*, pp. 349, 399–400, 402, 424.

52 H. Brinklow, *The Lamentacyon of a Christen Agaynst the Cytye of London*, ed. J. M. Cowper, EETS, extra series, 22 (1874), p. 92; D. Keene and V. Harding, *Historical Gazetteer of London Before the Great Fire*, vol. 1: *Cheapside* (Cambridge, 1987), app. 1, p. 537.

53 *CSP Sp.* VI ii, 127.

54 Wyatt, *Poems*, no. CLII, lines 461–2, 498–9, 504–5; *Poems*, 31.

55 Wyatt, *Poems*, no. CCLXVII. Also see Heale, p. 177, and note 59 on p. 189.

56 *Poems*, 29.

57 Ibid., 30. See too, Brigden, 'Conjured League', p. 514.

58 *Poems*, 28.

59 Printed by K. Muir, *Life and Letters of Sir Thomas Wyatt* (Liverpool, 1963), app. A, pp. 262, 265.

60 *Poems*, 31.

61 PRO SP 1/227, fo. 129; Jentoft, 'Orations', pp. 257–62. Brigden ('Conjured League', p. 519) suggests that Poyntz 'was probably avant garde in religion as in his taste'.

62 *LP* XX i, 622 (vii). The exact date of Surrey's release is unknown, but Stafford, Hussey and Sir John Clere were free by 1 May and Wyatt and Pickering were released from the Tower two days later (*APC* I, pp. 125–6). It is unlikely that Surrey's confinement would have lasted longer than theirs.

12 Noble Heart

1   *LP* XVIII i, 603; *CSP Sp*. VI ii, 163.

2   *St. P*. VIII, p. 166.

3   *The Anglica Historia of Polydore Vergil*, p. 197.

4   T. Churchyard, *A generall rehearsall of warres* (1579), sig. A.i.

5   Starkey, *Rivals in Power*, p. 60.

6   *CSP Sp*. VI ii, 235.

7   *St. P*. IX, p. 459.

8   Hale, 'Armies, Navies, and the Art of War', p. 554; *The Inventory of King Henry VIII*, p. x.

9   *St. P*. IX, pp. 528, 551–2.

10 PRO SP 1/182, fos. 41–2.

11 *CSP Sp*. VI ii, 250.

12 Charles V to Henry VIII, 21 October 1543. The original French is cited by Bapst, p. 282.

13 *CSP Sp*. VI ii, 254.

14 Nott, app. X.

15 Holinshed III, p. 833.

16 Ibid.; *LP* XVIII ii, 346; *St. P*. IX, pp. 538–42, 544–5.

17 *St. P*. IX, pp. 556–7; *CSP Sp*. VI ii, 260.

18 Anstis, *Register* II, pp. 427–8.

19 Charles V to Henry VIII, 18 November 1543. The original French is cited by Bapst, p. 287. I have used Sessions' translation (Sessions, 1999, p. 295).

20 Holinshed III, p. 834.

21 House of Lords Record Office PO/PB/1/1543/38H8 n22 (copy at Arundel Castle in bundle G1/5); *LP* XIX i, 25.

22 NRO MS NRS DCN 47/1, fos. 18–20v.

23 'Narrative of the Visit of the Duke de Najera to England, in the year 1543–4; written by his Secretary, Pedro de Gante', ed. F. Madden, *Archaeologia*, 23 (1831).

24 *CSP Sp*. VII, 111.

25 Davies, 'The English People and War', p. 2.

26 PRO PROB 11/30, fos. 192v, 343.

27 *Poems*, 24.

28 Baron, 'Mary Fitzroy's Transcript'. See too ibid., 'Mary (Howard) Fitzroy's Hand'; *AH* II, pp. 286–9; Heale, pp. 61–2; Sessions (1999), pp. 213–14. The anguished final line was partially inscribed by Lady Margaret Douglas.

29 B. Rich, *A Path-Way To Military Practise, 1587* (Amsterdam and New York, 1969), sigs., E.2v–3.

30 The vanguard comprised 372 horse and 9,606 foot; the rearguard, 547 horse and 9,017 foot (*LP* XIX i, 274, 276).

31 PRO SP 1/189, fo. 52. See too 1/188, fos. 89–90v.
32 *St. P.* IX, pp. 727–8.
33 PRO SP 1/189, fos. 207–8v.
34 Ibid., fo. 235.
35 PRO SP 1/190, fo. 24.
36 Ibid., fos. 27–8.
37 PRO SP 1/191, fo. 8.
38 Gruffydd I, p. 59.
39 PRO SP 1/191, fos. 8v–9.
40 *St. P.* X, p. 70.
41 PRO SP 1/189, fo. 207v. But see too *CSP Sp.* VII, *passim*.
42 For example, see PRO SP 1/191, fos. 30–1.
43 Nott, app. XVI. But see too Holinshed (III, p. 843), who claims that Surrey, finding only women and children at Rue, spared the town from fire.
44 Gruffydd I, p. 59.
45 *CSP Sp.* VII, 193.
46 Smith, *Henry VIII*, p. 239; Gruffydd I, p. 69. See too Norfolk's postscript to his letter of 2 August (PRO SP 1/191, fo. 9).
47 Gruffydd I, p. 72.
48 Rymer, *Foedera*, p. 56.
49 *St. P.* X, p. 70.
50 *CSP Sp.* VII, 215, 218; Gruffydd I, pp. 82–7; Holinshed III, p. 844.
51 Gruffydd I, pp. 59, 87.
52 Ibid., p. 94.
53 *Poems*, 35.
54 See Zitner, 'Truth and Mourning in a Sonnet by Surrey'.
55 PRO SP 14/19, fo. 107; Sessions (1999), p. 304.

13 In Every Man's Eye

1 By the mid-sixteenth century the 'quasi-feudal' system of recruitment had begun to be replaced by a 'national' system based on shire levies. See J. Goring, 'Social Change and Military Decline in Mid-Tudor England', *History*, 60/199 (1975).
2 *LP* XIX i, 274. See too Norfolk's 'instructions for the setting out of the men which shall go in the vanguard' (College of Arms MS M 16 *bis*, fo. 97v).
3 Goring, op. cit., p. 191.
4 *LP* XX i, 558 (Receipts Anno 36 Hen. VIII and see Anno 28 Hen. VIII too); PRO LR 2/115, fo. 51.
5 *Poems*, 44, lines 11–12; Fox, *Politics and Literature*, p. 292.
6 PRO LR 2/115, fo. 75; see fos. 73–6 for the rest of the inventory. Also Sessions (1999), pp. 143–9, 168–72.

7 S. Thurley, 'Palaces for a Nouveau Riche King', *History Today*, 41 (1991), p. 14.

8 Herbert, p. 564.

9 I owe this interpretation to the scholarship of Peter R. Moore ('Heraldic Charge', pp. 565, 575).

10 Anstis, *Register* II, p. 432.

11 *LP* XX i, 623 (viii); Holinshed III, pp. 846–7.

12 *A Collection of State Papers . . . left by William Cecil, Lord Burghley*, ed. S. Haynes (1740), p. 52.

13 See A. McKee, 'Henry VIII as Military Commander', *History Today*, 41 (1991); Smith, *Henry VIII*, pp. 247–8.

14 *A Collection of State Papers*, ed. Haynes, op. cit., pp. 52–4.

15 *The Letters of Stephen Gardiner*, ed. J. A. Muller (Cambridge, 1933), pp. 183–4.

16 *St. P.* X, p. 569; *LP* XX ii, 200.

17 *APC* I, pp. 223, 229–31; Nott, app. XXIV, XXVI.

18 *St. P.* X, p. 569; Nott, app. XXVI.

19 *APC* I, pp. 235–6, 238; Nott, app. XXV, XXVI.

20 *Hamilton Papers* I, no. 232.

21 *APC* I, p. 238; Rymer, *Foedera*, p. 80.

22 *APC* I, p. 249.

23 PRO SP 1/215, fo. 35v; Nott, letters XX, XXVI; *LP* XXI i, 481. For Rogers' prickly character and the English works at Boulogne, see Shelby, *John Rogers*.

24 *LP* XX i, 1210, 1264. For the best survey of the French defences, see Shelby. Fort Chatillon, which is sometimes thought to have been under construction during Surrey's Lieutenancy, was not in fact begun until July 1546. Two months later it was destroyed by the English and it was only in May 1548 that work on the fort recommenced.

25 Nott, app. XXV.

26 Nott, letters XI, XII. Surrey was not the only one to use the language of the joust in his military reportage. In his account of the taking of Bray-sur-Somme in 1523, the chronicler Edward Hall wrote that, 'Sir Robert Jerningham brake a spear on the Lord Pountdormy; the Lord Leonard Grey did valiantly that day', and in a letter to Henry VIII of May 1546, Edward Seymour, Earl of Hertford, praised a number of men who 'brake their staves and did very honestly' (Hall, p. 668; *LP* XXI i, 908).

27 Oxburgh Hall Bedingfeld MS: Paget to Surrey, 25 Sept. 1545.

28 PRO SP 1/210, fo. 31.

29 *CSP Sp.* VIII, 126; Nott, letters XXVI.

30 Gruffydd II, pp. 23, 25.

31 Gruffydd III, p. 343.

32 *St. P.* XI, p. 118.

33 *LP* XX ii, 671; PRO SP 1/212, fos. 49v–50.

34 Nott, letters XIX.

35 Ibid. XI.

36 Ibid. IV, V; *APC* I, p. 337.

37 Nott, letters XXVI, XXII.

38 *LP* XX ii, 780.

39 *CSP Sp.* VIII, 70.

40 R. Hoyle, 'War and Public Finance', in *The Reign of Henry VIII*, ed. MacCulloch, p. 92.

41 *St. P.* I, pp. 839–40.

42 *CSP Sp.* VIII, 140.

43 Nott, letters VIII.

44 *LP* XX ii, 266 (36).

45 PRO SP 1/209, fos. 128–9.

46 PRO SP 1/210, fos. 30–2.

47 *Poems*, 10.

48 PRO SP 1/227, fo. 109.

49 Sessions, 'Surrey and Catherine Parr', pp. 128–30; Sessions (1999), pp. 341–2; R. Strong, 'Some Early Portraits at Arundel Castle: Lord Lumley, the Earl of Arundel and Inigo Jones', *The Connoisseur*, 197/793 (1978), pp. 198–200; BL Royal MS 18 C XXIV, fo. 69v. There is some debate over the provenance of the Arundel portrait. For the suggestion that it may be the original painting by Scrots and an unknown collaborator, see C. MacLeod, 'Guillim Scrots in England' (Courtauld Institute, University of London MA, 1990), chapter 3, and *Dynasties: Painting in Tudor and Jacobean England 1530–1630*, ed. K. Hearn (1995), pp. 50–2. I am inclined to agree with Strong that the Arundel portrait is a Jacobean copy.

50 See Sessions (1999), p. 348.

51 Oxburgh Hall Bedingfeld MS: Paget to Surrey, 25 Sept. 1545.

14 Loss of Reputation

1 Howard, *defensative*, sig. H.h.iiiv.

2 *St. P.* XI, pp. 16–17.

3 Nott, letters XIV.

4 The following narrative is mainly drawn from the letter sent by Surrey and his council to the King on 8 January (PRO SP 1/213, fos. 47–50v), and the chronicle of Elis Gruffydd (Gruffydd III, pp. 343–6). See too the *Mémoire* of Martin du Bellay (cited by Nott, p. 202), which differs in many particulars from all other accounts.

5 PRO SP 1/213, fo. 47v; Gruffydd III, p. 344.

6 Montluc cited by Bapst, p. 329. *St. P.* XI, p. 18; *LP* XXI i, 128. According to the English, though, du Biez fled with his horsemen.

7 Gruffydd III, p. 345.

8 *St. P.* XI, p. 17; *LP* XXI i, 128.

9 PRO SP 1/213, fo. 48v; Nott, p. 202; *CSP Sp.* VIII, 184; *CSP Ven.* V, 373.

10 PRO SP 1/213, fo. 48v.

11 Ibid., fo. 49.

12 Gruffydd III, pp. 343–5.

13 For Gruffydd, see all Davies' articles cited in the abbreviations. Also, T. Jones, 'A Welsh Chronicler in Tudor England', *The Welsh History Review*, 1/1 (1960); P. Morgan, 'Elis Gruffudd of Gronant: Tudor Chronicler Extraordinary', *Flintshire Historical Society Publications*, 25 (1971–2); *Lisle Letters* VI, p. 43.

14 For example, his account of the Dauphin's camisado of 1544 is consistent with the *Commentaires* of Montluc (Gruffydd III, note 5 on p. 342).

15 Cited and translated by Sessions (1999), pp. 291–2.

16 Gruffydd III, p. 345.

17 PRO SP 1/213, fo. 47v, 49.

18 Herbert, p. 538.

19 Anstis, *Register* II, p. 298.

20 Gruffydd III, p. 345.

21 PRO SP 1/213, fo. 50. On 10 January Surrey sent Thomas Wyatt to report to Lord Cobham in Calais and Lord Grey in Guisnes (BL Harleian MS 283, fo. 341).

22 See Paget's letter to Surrey below.

23 *CSP Sp.* VIII, 184.

24 PRO SP 1/213, fo. 57x. There is some doubt over the date of this letter. It is endorsed '11 December 1545', but this is manifestly wrong, as St Etienne was fought the following month. It is often assumed that the correct date must be 11 January, but this may be a little early for the Council to be complaining of 'so many days' having passed. See the editor's comments on p. xx of *LP* XXI i.

25 *St. P.* XI, pp. 16–18. See too Gardiner and Paget's letters below, which also imply some fault in the ordering of the horsemen.

26 PRO SP 1/213, fo. 170. This manuscript is partially mutilated.

27 Oxburgh Hall Bedingfeld MS: Paget to Surrey, 17 Jan. 1546.

28 J. Ponet, *A Shorte Treatise of Politike Power, 1556* (Amsterdam and New York, 1972), sig. I.iiiv.

29 PRO SP 1/214, fos. 115–16v.

30 *St. P.* IX, p. 60.

31 Nott, letters XVIII, XXVI.

32 PRO SP 1/215, fo. 34.

33 Nott, letters XVII; PRO SP 1/214, fo. 115v–16. Crofts' disappointment did not last long. The following month he was appointed Under Marshal (PRO SP 1/215, fo. 145v).

34 PRO SP 1/215, fo. 35.

35 Nott, letters XXI, XXIV.

36 Oxburgh Hall Bedingfeld MS: Paget to Surrey, 25 Sept. 1545; PRO SP 1/215, fo. 35v.

37 PRO SP 1/215, fo. 145.

38 Junius, *Epistolae*, pp. 89–91.

39 *CSP Sp.* VIII, 226; *APC* I, p. 364.

40 *APC* I, p. 366; *LP* XXI i, 488.

41 *LP* XXI i, 716 (9).

42 Nott, letters XXVI.

43 PRO SP 1/214, fo. 115v.

44 Bodleian MS Jesus 74, fo. 280v.

15 My Foolish Son's Demeanour

1 See, for example, *CSP Sp.* VIII, 216.

2 *Spanish Chronicle*, p. 108.

3 *CSP Sp.* VIII, 291.

4 Foxe, *Acts and Monuments* V, p. 689.

5 *The Letters of King Henry VIII*, p. 418.

6 Smith, *Henry VIII*, p. 303.

7 *The Letters of King Henry VIII*, pp. 418–22.

8 Herbert, p. 572.

9 Wriothesley I, p. 167.

10 *LP* XXI i, 1491.

11 Foxe, *Acts and Monuments* V, p. 560.

12 Ibid., p. 564; *LP* XXI i, 1383 (72).

13 *LP* XXI i, 1180. For her interrogation and torture, see 'Examinations of Anne Askew', in *Select Works of John Bale*, pp. 135–248.

14 'A Critique of the Protectorate: An Unpublished Letter of Sir William Paget to the Duke of Somerset', ed. B. L. Beer, *The Huntington Library Quarterly*, 34/3 (1971), p. 280.

15 PRO SP 1/11, fo. 80v. See too M. P. Tilley, *A Dictionary of the Proverbs in England in the Sixteenth and Seventeenth Centuries* (University of Michigan Press, 1966), pp. 125, 262; Foxe, *Acts and Monuments* V, p. 492.

16 PRO SP 1/227, fos. 103–4, 105v. See too Starkey, *The Reign of Henry VIII*, pp. 149–50.

17 *LP* XXI i, 970 (31 & 32).

18 Ibid., 515. Also the preface to vol. XXI, p. xxvi.

19 PRO SP 1/221, fo. 181.

20 PRO SP 1/227, fo. 109.

21 *St. P.* X, p. 251; *LP* XX ii, 787; Shelby, *John Rogers*, pp. 89–90.

22 PRO SP 1/215, fo. 34v.

23 BL Cottonian MS Titus B II, fos. 39–40. See too Foley, 'Honorable Style', pp. 14–16.

24 *APC* I, p. 249.

25 *LP* XXI i, 527, 553; ii, 102, 601; *APC* I, pp. 559–60.

26 BL Cottonian MS Titus B II, fo. 39; PRO LR 2/115, fos. 75v–76; PRO DL 41/504.

27 *APC* I, p. 366.

28 BL Cottonian MS Titus B II, fos. 39v–40.

29 Norfolk's original letter has not survived, but it was seen by Lord Herbert of Cherbury's amanuensis Thomas Master, whose abstracted version of it can be found in the the Bodleian Library (Jesus MS 74, fo. 282). It is dated 15 July, but Master was unsure whether to attribute it to 1545 or 1546. As Surrey was in high favour in July 1545 and had done nothing to warrant a rebuke from the Council, it seems likely that the letter was written in 1546. It has been suggested that Norfolk's letter may refer to his other son, Lord Thomas Howard, who had been admonished by the Council in May 1546 for 'his undiscreet meddling in Scripture things'. The Privy Council register reveals that Norfolk was indeed advertised of the matter by the Council (though not at the King's specific request), and that the Council dismissed the matter on 8 May upon Thomas' 'submission and promise of reformation'. Whether Thomas could be described as having 'used himself humbly and repentantly' is debatable, as the Council was initially vexed that he 'did not yet confess the particulars which [they] would have had him confess of himself' (*APC* I, pp. 400, 408, 411). Norfolk was an efficient correspondent and it is extremely unlikely that he would have waited two whole months before thanking the Council for their advertisements. The chronology therefore suggests that Norfolk, who was in London at this time, was referring to Surrey. Thomas Master, who had seen the whole letter, was convinced of this. Above his abstracted version, he wrote the words: 'Duke of Norfolk & Earl of Surrey'.

30 *Poems*, 45.

31 *Select Works of John Bale*, p. 240.

32 *AH* II, p. 101; Zim, *English Metrical Psalms*, p. 90, and note 40 on p. 282; Heale, p. 173.

33 Heale, p. 174.

34 *Poems*, 32, 29.

35 *Select Works of John Bale*, p. 240.

36 *Poems*, 45; Wyatt, *Poems*, no. XLIX.

37 Mason (*Humanism and Poetry*, p. 244), Brigden ('"Conjured League"', p. 525), Heale (p. 174), and Sessions (1999, pp. 353–7) argue that Askew borrowed from Surrey. For the suggestion that the influence might have flowed in the other direction, see Burrow, *LRB*, p. 14.

38 *Narratives of the Days of the Reformation*, p. 43.

39 *Select Works of John Bale*, p. 242.

40 Ibid., p. 142.

41 PRO SP 1/227, fo. 129.

42 *St. P.* I, pp. 576–8.

43 BL Cottonian MS Titus B I, fo. 100v.

44 Anstis, *Register* II, pp. 428, 431, 434.

45 Herbert, p. 563.

46 PRO SP 1/227, fo. 105. See too fo. 104v, and Herbert, p. 563 for Edward Rogers' and Mary's corroborations of Carew's testimony.

47 *CSP Sp.* IX, p. 4.

48 Casady, *Henry Howard*, pp. 179–80, 197–9. See too Bapst, pp. 338–9, 354; Brenan and Statham, *The House of Howard* II, pp. 423–4; Padelford, *Poems*, pp. 34, 38; Chapman, *Two Tudor Portraits*, pp. 112–13.

49 BL Royal MS app. 89, fo. 103. For the lavish reception given to the French ambassadors, see BL Cottonian MS Vespasian C XIV, fos. 80–8; Wriothesley I, pp. 171–3.

50 Murphy, *Bastard Prince*, pp. 230–2.

51 PRO SP 1/227, fo. 109.

52 *CSP Sp.* VIII, 370.

53 *LP* XXI i, 1537 (34).

54 *CSP Sp.* VIII, 325; Tucker, 'The Commons in the Parliament of 1545', p. 306.

55 *CSP Sp.* VIII, 370; *St. P.* I, p. 884; Tucker, 'The Commons in the Parliament of 1545', p. 395; Herbert, p. 563.

56 *LP* XXI ii, 347; Foxe, *Acts and Monuments* V, p. 691; VI, p. 139; *St. P.* I, pp. 883–5.

57 *CSP Sp.* VIII, 370.

58 Tucker, 'The Commons in the Parliament of 1545', pp. 325, 361.

59 *APC* I, pp. 400, 408, 411.

60 Junius, *Epistolae*, pp. 84–9, 459–60. Also Sessions (1999), note on p. 81.

61 *Poems*, 43–6; *AH* I, no. 90. See too Brigden, 'Conjured League', pp. 514–15; Mason, *Humanism and Poetry*, pp. 241–3.

62 PRO SP 1/225, fo. 210; Herbert, p. 564; *Poems*, 37.

63 The phrase is Burrow's (*LRB*, p. 13).

64 Herbert, p. 564.

65 PRO SP 1/227, fo. 101.

66 *APC* I, pp. 114–15, 401, 411.

67 PRO SP 1/227, fo. 129.

68 Herbert, p. 562.

69 For a detailed analysis of this portrait, see Sessions (1999), pp. 3–4, 333–51. For contemporary rumours surrounding Surrey's symbolic intent, see *Spanish Chronicle*, pp. 143–7; *CSP Sp.* IX, p. 3; Thomas, *The Pilgrim*, p. 73. Also BL Stowe MS 396, fo. 8.

70 PRO SP 1/223, fo. 36.

71 L. A. Seneca, *Ad Lucilium Epistulae Morales*, tr. R. M. Gummere (3 vols., 1917–25), I, pp. 4–5.

72 PRO SP 1/227, fos. 109v, 129.

73 BL Lansdowne MS 792, fo. 7v.

74 PRO SP 1/223, fo. 36.

75 PRO SP 1/225, fo. 210.

76 Oxburgh Hall Bedingfeld MS: Paget to Surrey, 17 Jan. 1546.

16 Unbridled Tongues

 1 *Spanish Chronicle*, p. 144. For the reliability of this source, see the discussion of Surrey's alleged escape from the Tower in the following chapter.

 2 *CSP Sp.* VIII, 370; Herbert, p. 562.

 3 *LP* XXI ii, 533.

 4 Herbert, p. 562.

 5 *Chronicle of the Grey Friars of London*, p. 52.

 6 *CSP Sp.* VIII, 364–5; *LP* XXI ii, 533.

 7 PRO SP 1/227, fo. 76.

 8 Ibid., fos. 92–3.

 9 Bindoff: John Corbet; *LP* XV, 942 (84); XVIII ii, 449 (18); XX ii, 707 (8); NRO MS NRS DCN 47/1, fo. 315; NRO Norwich Consistory Court, 163 Ingold.

10 PRO PROB 11/47, fo. 151v; *LP* XX ii, 496 (68); XXI i, 1519.

11 PRO SP 1/227, fos. 93v–5.

12 *Calendar of the Patent Rolls, Edward VI 1548–9*, pp. 18–19. On 22 December 1546 Surrey's servant John Spencer was ordered by John Gates to produce a bill that 'mentioned and remembered such deeds, indentures, *evidences* and stuff of the Earl of Surrey's'. One item recorded a 'deed of grant of the advowson' of the chapel of Mary Magdalen, 'made by John Corbet esquire to the said Earl and his heir' on 27 May 1544 (PRO DL 41/504).

13 PRO SP 1/227, fos. 90–1.

14 BL Cottonian MS Titus B I, fos. 99–101v. See too Herbert, pp. 565–6.

15 *CSP Sp.* VIII, 367.

16 Ibid., 370, 372; *St. P.* XI, p. 388. See too, P. R. Moore, 'Hamlet and the Two Witness Rule', *Notes and Queries*, new series, 44/4 (1997).

17 PRO LR 2/115, fo. 18.

18 A local official called Thomas Gawdy seems to have looked after the younger children on Wentworth's behalf. See *APC* II, p. 28; Bindoff: Sir Thomas Wentworth I; Williams, *Thomas Howard*, p. 24.

19 PRO LR 2/115, fos. 6v–7v.

20 PRO SP 1/227, fos. 82–3 (*St. P.* II, pp. 888–90).

21 Herbert, p. 563.

22 Ibid., pp. 563–4.

23 These are undated, so it is impossible to determine exactly when they were taken. Written at the end of Knyvet's deposition, now in the Public Record Office, is 'Sir Edmund Knyvet the iide.'. This could be read as 2 December, although it could just be a reference to Knyvet's second deposition, as it seems from Herbert that Knyvet testified more than once. See too Moore, 'Heraldic Charge', p. 559.

24 PRO SP 1/227, fo. 97; Herbert, p. 564.

25 *Poems*, 40; E. Hood, 'A translation of the Earl of Surrey's out of Martial, directed by him to one Master Warner', *The Gentleman's Magazine*, 97/2 (1827), p. 392.

26 PRO SP 1/227, fo. 101.

27 Ibid., fos. 103–105v.

28 Ibid., fo. 106.

29 Moore, 'Heraldic Charge', pp. 568–9.

30 Herbert, pp, 562, 564.

31 Kaulek, *Correspondance Politique*, p. 261.

32 PRO PROB 11/48, fo. 25v; PRO SP 1/227, fos. 109v–110.

33 PRO SP 1/227, fos. 107–110v.

34 PRO LR 2/115, fo. 39v. Letters E and F are missing from Richard Fulmerston's deposition after fo. 91v in PRO SP 1/227.

35 PRO PC 2/2, fo. 36v (*APC* II, p. 106).

36 *Poems*, 50, line 13.

37 Ibid., lines 42–6.

38 See Brigden, '"Conjured League"', pp. 534–6. Brigden's case for the candidacy of Dr John Fryer is impressive, but raises too many red flags to be accepted out of hand. There is no evidence to indicate that Surrey would have secretly revealed his religious beliefs to the doctor. Fryer had been part of Cardinal Pole's circle in Italy and, if Sir Edmund Knyvet's deposition is to be credited, Surrey had a servant who 'had been in Italy with Cardinal Pole and was received again at his return'. But nothing in any surviving record links the two men. Moreoever, the suggestion that Fryer was the servant of Edward Foxe that had burnt a letter written by the

Duke of Norfolk to his master, concerning 'lewd speaking of the northern men after the time of the commotion', rests on the assumption that Fryer was in the service of Anthony Denny in December 1546. There is no evidence to confirm this. Indeed it is more likely that Fryer was still working for Wriothesley whose service he had joined in 1545 and was known to belong to in 1549.

39 Heale, p. 182, and note 71 on p. 190.

40 *Poems*, 50, lines 22–5; Brigden, '"Conjured League"', pp. 534–5.

41 Brigden, '"Conjured League"', p. 533; *LP* XXI ii, 523.

42 *Poems*, 34.

43 Wyatt, *Poems*, no. LXII. See also no. XXXIV.

44 Ecclus. xxvii. I owe this reading to the scholarship of Susan Brigden. See her articles, 'The Shadow that you Know', pp. 1–2, 26, 30, and '"Conjured League"', pp. 533–4.

45 *CSP Domestic, Elizabeth 1581–90*, ed. R. Lemon (1865), p. 70. Also, pp. 1, 32, 38–40; Howard, *defensative*, sig. K.k.ir.

46 Howard, *defensative*, sig. K.k.ir.

47 Scarisbrick, *Henry VIII*, p. 121; Henry Howard's speech against Father Garnet in *A True and Perfect Relation*; Thomas, *Religion and the Decline of Magic*, p. 480.

48 Howard, *defensative*, sig. E.3r.

49 Ibid., sig. H.h.iiiv.

50 *LP* XXI i, 1027; *APC* I, p. 449; IV, p. 13; Howard, *defensative*, sig. L.l.ir; Smyth, *Lives of the Berkeleys* II, p. 379; Lloyd, *Statesmen and Favourites*, p. 556.

51 *Spanish Chronicle*, pp. 143–7.

52 Thomas, *The Pilgrim*, p. 73; *LP* XXI ii, 533.

53 BL Harleian MS 1579, fo. 6.

54 PRO SP 1/227, fos. 107, 109v, 125v; Camden, *Remains*, p. 183; Thomas, *The Pilgrim*, pp. 73–4; *CSP Sp.* IX, p. 3; Robinson, *Original Letters* I, p. 42.

55 *Poems*, 45–6.

56 *CSP Sp.* VIII, 370.

57 PRO SP 1/227, fo. 123 (*St. P.* II, pp. 891–2). Wriothesley's original draft is on fo. 125.

58 *CSP Sp.* VIII, 373.

59 PRO SP 1/227, fo. 128. See also, Moore, 'Heraldic Charge', p. 560.

60 PRO SP 1/227, fo. 109.

61 PRO KB 8/14, m. 9 (printed in Nott, app. XXXIII).

62 Moore, 'Heraldic Charge', pp. 565, 575.

63 BL Harleian MS 1453, fo. 69. The illustration contains a few errors. Moore ('Heraldic Charge', p. 575) urges the plausible thesis that it was drawn up

for Surrey's trial according to 'a hurried or careless description'. The other arms in the shield are: Howard, Brotherton, Warenne, Mowbray, Hamlin Plantagenet, Marshal, Braose, Arundel, Ranulf Gernon, Earl of Chester, Ranulf Meschines, Earl of Chester, Segrave.

64 PRO SP 1/227, fo. 109.

65 Keen, *Chivalry*, chapter 7; Moore, 'Heraldic Charge', note 1 on p. 561.

66 Moore, 'Heraldic Charge', p. 573; Weever, *Ancient Funerall Monuments*, p. 843.

67 BL Cottonian MS Julius C VII, fo. 238; Howard of Corby, *Indications*, apps. IV, VII; PRO SP 1/227, fo. 128.

68 PRO SP 1/227, fo. 111v.

69 Moore, 'Heraldic Charge', p. 564.

70 Holinshed III, p. 861; Herbert, p. 565.

71 College of Arms MS L14, pt. II, fo. 227. See too, BL Harleian MS 297, fo. 256v; PRO SP 1/223, fo. 34.

72 Moore, 'Heraldic Charge', p. 565. I am indebted to Peter R. Moore for his shrewd and incisive article and have relied upon his findings for the following account.

73 Ibid.

74 Although signed by Barker, the King's copy was reported indirectly: 'Garter saith that the Earl of Surrey . . . etc'. The original has not survived, but a modern copy exists in the Public Record Office (SP 1/223, fo. 34).

75 *Lisle Letters* IV, p. 286; Strype, *Ecclesiastical Memorials* II ii, p. 328.

76 PRO SP 1/227, fo. 99.

77 28 Hen. VIII, c. 7, section XII (*Statutes of the Realm*, pp. 660–1).

78 PRO KB 8/14, m. 9 (printed in Nott, app. XXXIII).

79 PRO KB 8/14; *LP* XXI ii, 697; *Third Report of the Deputy Keeper*, app. II, pp. 267–8. See too Baker, *An Introduction to English Legal History*, pp. 276–7. For an analysis of the grand jury and their connections with the Howards, see Tucker, 'The Commons in the Parliament of 1545', pp. 391–9.

17 Condemned for Such Trifles

1 PRO E 101/60/22, fo. 1. See too BL Additional MS 5751 A, fo. 281.

2 He also paraphrased psalm 8 (though its equanimity points to a date prior to his Tower imprisonment), and he may also have paraphrased psalms 31 and 51. See C. A. Huttar, 'Poems by Surrey and Others in a Printed Miscellany circa 1550', *English Miscellany*, 16 (1965); M. Rudick, 'Two Notes on Surrey's Psalms', *Notes and Queries*, new series, 22/7 (1975); Heale, note 50 on pp. 188–9. For psalms 8, 55, 73 and 88, see *Poems*, 47–50. Psalms 31 and 51 can be found in *Certayne Chapters of the*

prouerbes of Salomon drawen into metre by Thomas sterneholde, late grome of the kynges Magesties robes, printed by John Case for William Seres (*c.* 1550). The most incisive readings of Surrey's psalms are *AH* II, pp. 99–110; Zim, *English Metrical Psalms, passim*, but esp. pp. 88–98; Brigden, '"Conjured League"', *passim*; Sessions, 'Surrey's Psalms in the Tower', pp. 17–31; Heale, pp. 154–9, 173–84.

3 Quoted by J. N. King, in *English Reformation Literature: The Tudor Origins of the Protestant Tradition* (Princeton, 1982), p. 233.

4 Brigden, '"Conjured League"', pp. 514–15; Sessions, 'Surrey's Psalms in the Tower', p. 25.

5 *Poems*, 37.

6 Ibid., 36.

7 Thomas Wilcox quoted by Zim, *English Metrical Psalms*, p. 27.

8 Mason, *Humanism and Poetry*, p. 240.

9 See *AH* II, p. 106; Sessions, 'Surrey's Psalms in the Tower', p. 24.

10 *Poems*, 49.

11 Ibid., 48.

12 Ibid., 50.

13 *Spanish Chronicle*, p. 145.

14 A. Keay, *The Elizabethan Tower of London* (2001), pp. 31–2; S. Thurley, 'Royal Lodgings at the Tower of London 1216–1327', *Architectural History*, 38 (1995), pp. 47–51. For the Tudor alterations, see PRO SP 1/70, fos. 113–19; PRO E 101/474/12, fos. 3–5; /13, fos. 1, 3v, 8–9; Bodleian MS Rawlinson D 775, fos. 202–3, 206, 211v.

15 *Spanish Chronicle*, pp. 145–6.

16 *LP* XXI ii, 141.

17 See Ives, *Anne Boleyn*, p. 65, and Hume's introduction in *Spanish Chronicle*.

18 PRO SP 1/227, fos. 107, 109v.

19 PRO E 101/60/22, fo. 1 (fo. 2 for Norfolk).

20 Ibid., fos. 2v–3.

21 PRO E 351/2960.

22 Surrey's grandfather once had a servant called Richard Martyn (PRO C 1/101, fo. 11), so there may have been a tradition of members of the Martin family serving the Howards. One 'Marten', a carpenter, served alongside Surrey at Montreuil, but there is no evidence to suggest that he was then or thereafter Surrey's servant (*LP* XIX i, 763, 876; XIX ii, 306).

23 Problems with Tower security persisted well into the reign of Elizabeth. See Bodleian MS Engl. Hist. E. 195, app. B, fos. 60–1.

24 Herbert, pp. 567–9. An early draft of Norfolk's confession can be found in the British Library (Harleian MS 297, fo. 257). Also see Moore, 'Heraldic Charge', pp. 568–70, 575–7.

25 PRO E 101/60/22, fo. 1.

26 *Spanish Chronicle*, p. 146.

27 The following account of Surrey's trial has been collated from these sources: PRO KB 8/14 (*LP* XXI ii, 697); *Third Report of the Deputy Keeper*, app. II, pp. 267–8; *CSP Sp.* IX, pp. 3–4; Herbert, p. 565, and the marginal notes transcribed by Thomas Tourneur from the Chronicle of Anthony Anthony into the Bodleian Library's copy of Herbert: Fol. Δ 624, interleaf between pp. 564–5; *Spanish Chronicle*, pp. 146–8; Thomas, *The Pilgrim*, pp. 72–3; *Chronicle of the Grey Friars of London*, p. 53; *The Accession of Queen Mary: Being the Contemporary Narrative of Antonio de Guaras, a Spanish Merchant Resident in London*, ed. and tr. R. Garnett (1892), pp. 34, 80 (for this, also see Moore, 'Heraldic Charge', p. 573); Wriothesley I, pp. 176–7; Holinshed III, p. 861; R. Grafton, *Chronicle or History of England* (1569, repr. in 2 vols., 1809), II, p. 498; Camden, *Remains*, p. 183. Baker (*An Introduction to English Legal History*, pp. 276–9) and Bellamy (*The Tudor Law of Treason*) give very good accounts of Tudor trial procedure in general.

28 Starkey, *Rivals in Power*, p. 255.

29 *LP* XIII i, 646 (48); XIV i, 398; XVI i, 305 (68); XVII i, 362 (66); XX i, 622 (VII), 623 (VIII).

30 Household accounts provide the best record of a family's day-to-day activities, but they were irregularly maintained and rarely preserved. One series that has survived, that of the Lestranges of Hunstanton, reveals regular contact with the Howards and frequent visits to Kenninghall ('Extracts from the Household and Privy Purse Accounts of the Lestranges of Hunstanton, 1519–1578', ed. D. Gurney, *Archaeologia*, 25 (1834), pp. 419, 420, 451, 473, 496, 497, 501, 522, 523, 542, 549).

31 Bindoff: Christopher Heydon; Pembroke MS, 8–10 Sept.; NRO Norwich Consistory Court, 163 Ingold.

32 Bindoff: Nicholas Lestrange; 'Extracts from the Household and Privy Purse Accounts of the Lestranges', op. cit.; Howlett, 'Household Accounts', p. 57; PRO PROB 11/47, fo. 149v. Southwell also left bequests to 'Henry Paston, my son-in-law', and 'my very good neighbour and assured friend, Sir Thomas Lovell' (fos. 145, 150).

33 33 Hen. VIII, c. 23 (*Statutes of the Realm*, p. 864).

34 See Bellamy, *The Tudor Law of Treason*, pp. 157–8; J. H. Wigmore, 'The History of the Hearsay Rule', *Harvard Law Review*, 17/7 (1904).

35 Quoted by Jentoft, 'Orations', p. 259.

36 Surrey was not the only one to deride Paget's background. In 1556 a London bricklayer called William Crowe dismissed Paget as 'but a catchpole's son'. *CSP Domestic, Mary 1553–1558*, ed. C. S. Knighton (1998), no. 445.

37 BL Sloane MS 2172, fo. 42.

38 *The Reports of Sir John Spelman*, ed. J. H. Baker, Selden Society, 93–4 (1976–7), II, pp. 112–13.

39 Foxe, *Acts and Monuments* VI, p. 549. Also Bellamy, *The Tudor Law of Treason*, p. 172.

40 BL Harleian MS 1579, fo. 6; G. Burnet, *The History of the Reformation of the Church of England*, ed. N. Pocock (7 vols., Oxford, 1865), I, p. 544.

41 W. Scott, *Lay of the Last Minstrel*, canto VI, stanza XIII.

42 Chaloner, *De Rep. Anglorum Instauranda Libri Decem*, 'Liber Secundus', pp. 45–6. The book was written in the early 1560s and published posthumously in 1579.

43 *Churchyardes Charge*, p. 2.

44 *AH* I, no. 282; II, pp. 428–30.

45 *St. P.* XI, p. 391.

46 House of Lords Record Office PO/PB/1/1546/37H8 n32; *Journals of the House of Lords* I, p. 285.

47 *LP* XXI ii, 665; HMC, *Report on the Manuscripts of His Grace The Duke of Rutland* I (1888), p. 32.

48 Robinson, *Original Letters* II, p. 639; I, p. 256.

49 *CSP Sp.* VIII, 365, 370.

50 *St. P.* XI, pp. 387–8.

51 *CSP Sp.* IX, p. 496. See also, Moore, 'Heraldic Charge', p. 581.

52 J. Strype, *Annals of the Reformation* (4 vols., Oxford, 1824), II ii, p. 465; Bellamy, *The Tudor Law of Treason*, p. 206.

53 Bodleian Fol. Δ 624, interleaf between pp. 564–5.

54 *Spanish Chronicle*, p. 148.

55 Bodleian MS Bodley 903, fo. 6.

56 *Poems*, 38. The title, originating in psalm 118 of the Vulgate, occurs in *Tottel's Miscellany* I, no. 34. Heale, pp. 183–4: 'So different is the title from those normally invented by Tottel that in this case he may have authority for its use from the manuscript copy he is using. Surrey may here be composing his own psalm, as Blagge had done, or as Sir Thomas Smith later composed "Other Psalms" alongside his paraphrsases during his own imprisonment in the Tower in 1549.'

Epilogue

1 Both the attainder and the Latin document authorising the commission are in the House of Lords Record Office (PO/PB/1/1546/37H8 n32) and have been printed by Nott (app. L). See too *Journals of the House of Lords* I, pp. 289–90; *St. P.* I, p. 898; Lehmberg, *The Later Parliaments of Henry VIII*, pp. 234–5.

2 Strype, *Ecclesiastical Memorials* II ii, pp. 327–8.

3 Southwell: *APC* II, p. 19; Knyvet: *APC* II, p. 17; Warner: Bindoff; *St. P.* I, p. 893; PRO LR 2/115, fo. 86; Bess: PRO LR 2/115, fo. 6v. For the jury, see Bindoff: Nicholas Lestrange, John Clere, Thomas Paston (son of William); *LP* XXI ii, 771 (35); *APC* II, p. 447; *Calendar of the Patent Rolls, Edward VI 1547–8*, pp. 56, 113.

4 The will is printed in Rymer, *Foedera*, pp. 110–17 (pp. 114–15 for the unfulfilled gifts clause); *APC* II, pp. 15–22.

5 Rymer, *Foedera*, p. 114; *APC* II, pp. 5–6, 67–74. Henry VIII's will is the most controversial document of his reign and a lively debate surrounds the circumstances by which it was drafted, amended and stamped. See Jordan, *Edward VI* I, pp. 51–60; G. R. Elton, *Reform and Reformation* (1977), pp. 331–2; H. Miller, 'Henry VIII's Unwritten Will: Grants of Lands and Honours in 1547', in *Wealth and Power in Tudor England*; Starkey, *The Reign of Henry VIII*, pp. 159–66; E. W. Ives, 'Henry VIII's Will: A Forensic Conundrum', *HJ*, 35/4 (1992); Ives, 'Henry VIII's Will: The Protectorate Provisions of 1546–7', and R. Houlbrooke, 'Henry VIII's Wills: A Comment', both in *HJ*, 37/4 (1994).

6 Latimer quoted by Brigden, *New Worlds, Lost Worlds*, p. 183.

7 Strype, *Ecclesiastical Memorials* II ii, p. 430.

8 Nott, app. L.

9 Smyth, *Lives of the Berkeleys* II, pp. 381–2.

10 This is suggested by Williams, *Thomas Howard*, p. 22.

11 *The History of Parliament: The House of Commons 1558–1603*, ed. P. W. Hasler (1981): Thomas Steyning; Sessions (1999), pp. 210–11.

12 Nott, app. XXXV.

13 PRO SP 12/84, fo. 36.

14 Chaloner, *De Rep. Anglorum Instauranda Libri Decem*, 'Liber Secundus', p. 45; Foxe, *Acts and Monuments* VI, p. 412; Nashe, *The Unfortunate Traveller*, p. 287; Churchyard, *Churchyardes Charge*, p. 2; Constantyne, p. 62.

MANUSCRIPT SOURCES

ARUNDEL CASTLE, SUSSEX

MSS G 1/4–6: documents relating to the second and third Howard Dukes of Norfolk and to Henry Howard, Earl of Surrey

MSS MD 2586–8: documents relating to the restoration of Surrey's tomb, 1974–1977

MS 1638: Henry Lilly, *The Genealogie of the Princelie familie of the Howards*, 1638

The Arundel Harington MS of Tudor Poetry

BANCROFT LIBRARY, UNIVERSITY OF CALIFORNIA, BERKELEY

MS UCB 49 (formerly MS HF 5616.E5N6): Howard household book, 1523–4

BODLEIAN LIBRARY, OXFORD

MS Ashmole 394: horoscope made for Thomas Howard (later fourth Duke of Norfolk)

MS Ashmole 861: Elias Ashmole's transcripts from the Chronicle of Anthony Anthony

MS Bodley 903: Henry Howard (later Earl of Northampton), 'A dutifull defence of the lawfull Regiment of Weomen', with an address to Elizabeth I

MS Engl. Hist. E 195, Appendix B: Sir John Peyton, 'A declaration of the state of the Tower of London', 1598

MS Jesus 74: notes by Thomas Master, amanuensis to Lord Herbert of Cherbury

MS Rawlinson B 146: treatise on the office of Earl Marshal

MS Rawlinson D 775: accounts of the Royal Surveyor of the Works: The Tower of London, 1533

Bod. Folio Δ 624: Lord Herbert of Cherbury, *The Life and Raigne of King*

Henry the Eighth interleaved with extracts from the Chronicle of Anthony Anthony

BRITISH LIBRARY, LONDON
Additional MSS
  5751 A: warrants and accounts of the Royal Household
  10110: acts done in Scotland under the Duke of Norfolk, 1542
  17492: the Devonshire Manuscript of Tudor poetry
  19193: account of the opening of the tombs of the Dukes of Richmond and
    Norfolk, 1841
  24493: Surrey's request for a loan from the Prior of Bury St Edmunds
  34393: debts owing to Sir Richard Cromwell on his death
  36529: Tudor poetry miscellany formed by the Haringtons of Stepney and
    Kelston
Cottonian MSS
  Caligula E II: correspondence relating to Surrey's sojourn in France
  Claudius C III: a chronological list of the dubbing of knights
  Cleopatra E VI: letter from John Leigh to the Privy Council, 1540
  Julius C VII: patents
  Titus B I: letters of the Duke and Duchess of Norfolk; Cromwell's Remem-
    brances
  Titus B II: letter from Surrey to Sir William Paget, 14 July 1546
  Vespasian C XIV: preparations for the reception of the Admiral of France,
    1546
  Vespasian F III: letter from the Duke of Richmond to Cardinal Wolsey
  Vespasian F XIII: letters of the Duchess of Norfolk, the Duchess of Rich-
    mond and Lady Margaret Douglas
Egerton MS 985: the disgrading of the Duke of Norfolk and the Earl of Surrey
  from the Order of the Garter
Hargrave MS 205: Surrey's translation of Book IV of Virgil's *Aeneid*
Harleian MSS
  69: details of the tournament held at Westminster, May 1540
  78: letter from Surrey to the Council, Fleet Prison, July 1542; poems
  283: correspondence between Surrey and the Council of Calais, 1545–6
  297: deposition of Christopher Barker against Surrey; an early draft of the
    Duke of Norfolk's confession
  1453: drawing of a coat of arms entitled 'Howard Earle of Surry, for which
    he was attainted'
  1579: seventeenth-century commentary on the fall of Surrey
  6989: miscellaneous letters from the Council
Lansdowne MS 2: list of those entitled to 'bouche of court', *c.* 1544–5
Lansdowne MS 792: translation of Emperor Charles V's political instructions

to his son made by Henry Howard (later Earl of Northampton) and dedicated to Elizabeth I

Royal MSS

    2 A XVI: Henry VIII's Psalter

    7 C XVI: book of Jane Seymour's jewels

    18 C XXIV: record of payment made to the Court painter William Scrots

    Appendix 89: preparations for the reception of the Admiral of France, 1546

Sloane MS 1523: maxims, sayings and short accounts of several eminent men

Sloane MS 2172: letter of Philip Howard, Earl of Arundel, to Elizabeth I, 1585

Stowe MS 396: seventeenth-century account of Surrey's trial

Stowe MS 559: book of Catherine Howard's jewels

COLLEGE OF ARMS, LONDON

MS L 14: heralds' copy of Christopher Barker's deposition against Surrey

MS M 16 *bis*: preparations for Henry VIII's war against France, 1544

CORPORATION OF LONDON RECORD OFFICE

Journal 15: the Common Council of London's rejection of Henry VIII's recommendation of George Blagge for the mastership of the Weigh House, 1543

Repertory 12: complaint of the Court of Aldermen against Sir William Pickering, 1549

LONGLEAT HOUSE, WILTSHIRE

Miscellaneous MSS from the archives of the Marquess of Bath, vols. 18–19: household accounts of Edward Seymour, Earl of Hertford, 1538–9, 1540–1 (microfilm at the Institute of Historical Research: XR 52/3)

Seymour Papers, vols. 14–20: the same, 1536–43 (IHR: XR 57/8–9)

HOUSE OF LORDS RECORD OFFICE

PO/PB/1/1543/35H8 n22: act concerning an exchange of lands between the King and the Duke of Norfolk, the Earl and Countess of Surrey

PO/PB/1/1546/37H8 n32: act of attainder against the Duke of Norfolk and the Earl of Surrey with the royal commission of assent

NORFOLK RECORD OFFICE, NORWICH

MS DCN 47/1: indenture between the Dean and Chapter of Norwich and the Earl of Surrey for the lease of St Leonard's Priory, Norwich, 10 May 1542 (abstracted in DCN 47/27)

MS NRS 2378 (11 D4): Howard household book, 1519–20

Norwich Consistory Court wills

OXBURGH HALL, NORFOLK

Bedingfeld MSS: letters from Sir William Paget to the Earl of Surrey, 25 September 1545 and 17 January 1546

PEMBROKE COLLEGE, CAMBRIDGE

MS 300: Howard household book, 1526–7

PUBLIC RECORD OFFICE (now incorporated into the National Archives)

C 1/101: reference to Richard Martyn, servant of Thomas, Earl of Surrey

DL 29/313/5047: appointment of the Earl of Surrey as Steward for the Duchy of Lancaster in Norfolk, Suffolk and Cambridgeshire

DL 41/504: 'deeds, indentures, evidences and stuff' of the Earl of Surrey delivered to John Gates by John Spencer of Norwich, 22 December 1546

E 101/60/22: accounts of the Lieutenant of the Tower, 1546–7

E 101/474/12–13: abstract of certain reparations done within the Tower of London

E 329/484: grant by Henry VIII to the Earl of Surrey of the reversion and rent reserved on a lease of the site of the monastery and manor of Wymondham, December 1539

E 351/2960: accounts of the Lieutenant of the Tower, 1551–2

KB 8/14: documents relating to the trial for high treason of the Earl of Surrey

LR 2/113: receiver's accounts of the property of the attainted Duke of Norfolk

LR 2/115: inventory of Kenninghall, Castle Rising and Surrey House with a declaration of the delivery of all goods and chattels found there

PC 2/1–2: Privy Council Registers

PROB 11: Prerogative Court of Canterbury wills

SP 1: State Papers, general, Henry VIII

SP 12: State Papers, domestic, Elizabeth I

SP 14: State Papers, domestic, James I

SP 60: State Papers, Ireland, Henry VIII

WORK 31/78: plans of St Thomas' Tower by C. Lempriere, 1735

SELECT BIBLIOGRAPHY

A full bibliography is impracticable for reasons of space. Listed below are works frequently cited in the notes (excluding those already given in the list of abbreviations) and suggestions for further reading. If a work is otherwise mentioned in the notes, it is cited in full. Unless otherwise stated, both here and in the notes, the place of publication is, or includes, London. The date refers to the edition used.

Early Works and Primary Sources in Print

Anstis, J. (ed.), *The Register of the Most Noble Order of the Garter* (2 vols., 1724)

Ascham, R., *The Schoolmaster (1570)*, ed. L. V. Ryan (Ithaca, NY, 1967)

Select Works of John Bale, ed. H. Christmas, Parker Society (Cambridge, 1849)

The Travel Journal of Antonio de Beatis, ed. J. R. Hale (1979)

Boorde, A., *Introduction of Knowledge* and *A Dyetary of Helth*, ed. F. J. Furnivall, EETS, extra series, 10 (1870)

Brewer, J. S. (ed. and intro.), 'The Book of Howth', in *Calendar of the Carew Manuscripts, preserved in the Archiepiscopal Library at Lambeth* (1871)

Bryan, F., *A Dispraise of the life of a Courtier, and a commendacion of the life of the labouryng man* (1548)

'The Register or Chronicle of Butley Priory, Suffolk, 1510–1535', in A. G. Dickens, *Late Monasticism and the Reformation* (1994)

Camden, W., *Remains Concerning Britain*, ed. R. D. Dunn (Toronto, 1984)

Castiglione, B., *The Book of the Courtier*, tr. and intro. G. Bull (Harmondsworth, 1967)

Cavendish, G., *Metrical Visions*, ed. A. S. G. Edwards (Columbia, SC, 1980)

Chaloner, T., *De Rep. Anglorum Instauranda Libri Decem* (1579)

The Chronicle of Calais in the Reigns of Henry VII and Henry VIII to the year 1540, ed. J. G. Nichols, CS, old series, 35 (1846)

Chronicle of the Grey Friars of London, ed. J. G. Nichols, CS, old series, 53 (1852)

Churchyard, T., *A light Bondell of livly discourses called Churchyardes Charge* (1580)

Clerke, J., *A certayn treatye moste wyttely devysed orygynally wrytten in the Spaynysshe, lately Traducted in to Frenche entytled, Lamant mal traicte de samye. And nowe out of Frenche in to Englysshe, dedicat to the ryght honorable Lorde Henry Erle of Surrey* (1543)

Edwardes, D., *De indiciis et praecognitionibus, opus apprime utile medicis, . . . Eiusdem in Anatomicen introductio luculenta et brevis* (1532/3)

—*Introduction to Anatomy*, ed. C. D. O'Malley and K. F. Russell (1961)

Ellis, H. (ed.), *Original Letters illustrative of English History* (3 series in 11 vols., 1824, 1827, 1846)

Elyot, T., *The Book named The Governor*, ed. S. E. Lehmberg (1962)

The Acts and Monuments of John Foxe, ed. G. Townsend (8 vols., New York, 1965)

Furnivall, F. J. (ed.), *The Babees Book . . . The Bokes of Nurture*, EETS, original series, 32 (1868)

Four Years at the Court of Henry VIII: Selection of Despatches written by the Venetian Ambassador, Sebastian Giustinian, 1515–1519, tr. R. Brown (2 vols., 1854)

The Hamilton Papers, ed. J. Bain (2 vols., Edinburgh, 1890–2)

The Inventory of King Henry VIII, vol. 1: *The Transcript*, ed. D. Starkey (1998)

The Letters of King Henry VIII: A Selection, with a few other Documents, ed. M. St. Clare Byrne (New York, 1968)

Howard, H. (cr. Earl of Northampton, 1604), *A defensative against the poyson of supposed Prophesies* (1583)

—*A True and Perfect Relation of the whole proceedings against the late most barbarous Traitors, Garnet a Jesuite, and his Confederats, contayning sundry speeches . . . The Earl of Northampton's Speech having been enlarged* (1606)

Howlett, R., 'The Household Accounts of Kenninghall Palace in the Year 1525', *Norfolk Archaeology*, 15 (1904)

Junius, H., *Epistolae, Quibus accedit Eiusdem Vita & Oratio de Artium liberalium dignitate*, ed. P. Junius (Dordrecht, 1652)

Kaulek, J. (ed.), *Correspondance Politique de MM. de Castillon et de Marillac, 1537–1542* (Paris 1885)

Leland, J., *De Rebus Britannicis Collectanea*, ed. T. Hearn (6 vols., 1774)

The Lisle Letters, ed. M. St. Clare Byrne (6 vols., 1981)

Narratives of the Days of the Reformation, ed. J. G. Nichols, CS, old series, 77 (1859)

Nashe, T., *The Unfortunate Traveller and Other Works*, ed. J. B. Steane (Harmondsworth, 1972)

The Second Book of the Travels of Nicander Nucius of Corcyra, ed. J. A. Cramer, CS, old series, 17 (1841)

Peacham, H., *The Complete Gentleman, The Truth of Our Times* and *The Art of Living in London*, ed. V. B. Heltzel (Ithaca, NY, 1962)

The Privy Purse Expences of King Henry the Eighth, ed. N. H. Nicolas (1827)

Puttenham, G., *The Arte of English Poesie*, ed. G. D. Willcock and A. Walker (Cambridge, 1970)

Ridgard, J. (ed.), *Medieval Framlingham: Select Documents 1270–1524*, Suffolk Records Society, 27 (Woodbridge, 1985)

Robinson, H. (ed.), *Original Letters relative to the English Reformation*, Parker Society (2 vols., Cambridge, 1846–7)

Rymer, T., *Foedera, Conventiones, Literae*, vol. 15 (1713)

Sackville, T., *The Complaint of Henry Duke of Buckingham Including the 'Induction', or, Thomas Sackville's Contribution to the 'Mirror for Magistrates'*, ed. M. Hearsey, Yale Studies in English, 86 (New Haven, 1936)

Sidney, P., *An Apology for Poetry*, ed. G. Shepherd (Manchester, 1973)

Smyth, J., *The Berkeley Manuscripts: The Lives of the Berkeleys*, ed. J. Maclean (2 vols., Gloucester, 1883)

The Statutes of the Realm, vol. 3, ed. T. E. Tomlins and W. E. Taunton (1817)

Stow, J., *A Survey of London*, ed. C. L. Kingsford (2 vols., Oxford, 1908)

Strype, J., *Ecclesiastical Memorials* (3 vols., Oxford, 1822)

The Register of Thetford Priory, ed. D. Dymond, Records of Social and Economic History, new series, 24, 25 (1995–6)

Third Report of the Deputy Keeper of the Public Records (1842)

Thomas, W., *The Pilgrim: A Dialogue on the Life and Actions of King Henry the Eighth*, ed., with notes from the archives at Paris and Brussels, by J. A. Froude (1861)

Tottel's Miscellany 1557–1587, ed. H. E. Rollins (2 vols., Cambridge, MA, 1928–9)

Tudor Tracts, 1532–1588, intro. A. F. Pollard (1903)

Turberville, G., *Epitaphes, Epigrams, Songs and Sonets (1567)*, intro. R. J. Panofsky (New York, 1977)

Two Early Tudor Lives, ed. R. S. Sylvester and D. P. Harding (1962)

The Anglica Historia of Polydore Vergil, AD 1485–1537, ed. D. Hay, CS, 3rd Series, 74 (1950)

Weever, J., *Ancient Funerall Monuments, London, 1631* (Amsterdam and Norwood, NJ, 1979)

Wood, M. A. E. (ed.), *Letters of Royal and Illustrious Ladies of Great Britain* (3 vols., 1846)

Wyatt, T., *The Complete Poems*, ed. R. A. Rebholz (Harmondsworth, 1997)

Secondary Works

Baker, J. H., *An Introduction to English Legal History* (1971)

Baron, H., 'Mary Fitzroy's Transcript of Surrey's Poem', and 'Mary (Howard) Fitzroy's Hand in the Devonshire Manuscript', *The Review of English Studies*, new series, 45/179 (1994)

Begent, P. J., and Chesshyre, H., *The Most Noble Order of the Garter 650 Years* (1999)

Bellamy, J., *The Tudor Law of Treason: An Introduction* (1979)

Bensly, W. T., 'St Leonard's Priory, Norwich', *Norfolk Archaeology*, 12 (1895)

Berdan, J. M., *Early Tudor Poetry, 1485–1547* (New York, 1920)

Brenan, G., and Statham, E. P., *The House of Howard* (2 vols., 1907)

Brigden, S., *London and the Reformation* (Oxford, 1989)

—'Henry Howard, Earl of Surrey and the "Conjured League"', *HJ*, 37/3 (1994)

—' "The Shadow that you Know": Sir Thomas Wyatt and Sir Francis Bryan at Court and in Embassy', *HJ*, 39/1 (1996)

—*New Worlds, Lost Worlds: The Rule of the Tudors, 1485–1603* (2000)

Burrow, C., review of W. A. Sessions, *Henry Howard, The Poet Earl of Surrey: A Life* (Oxford, 1999), in *London Review of Books*, 21/22 (11 November 1999)

Casady, E., *Henry Howard, Earl of Surrey*, The Modern Language Association of America, 8 (New York, 1938)

Cattaneo, A., 'The Italian Sources of Surrey's *Aeneid*', in *Italy and the English Renaissance*, ed. S. Rossi and D. Savoia (Milan, 1989)

Chapman, H. W., *Two Tudor Portraits: Henry Howard, Earl of Surrey and Lady Katherine Grey* (1960)

Colvin, H. M. (ed.), *The History of the King's Works* (6 vols., 1963–82)

Cruickshank, C., *Henry VIII and the Invasion of France* (Stroud, 1990)

Davies, C. S. L., 'The English People and War in the Early Sixteenth Century', in *Britain and the Netherlands*, vol. 6: *War and Society*, ed. A. C. Duke and C. A. Tamse (The Hague, 1977)

Davis, W. R., 'Contexts in Surrey's Poetry', *English Literary Renaissance*, 4/1 (1974)

Dennys, R., *Heraldry and the Heralds* (1982)

Dodds, M. H., and R., *The Pilgrimage of Grace 1536–7 and the Exeter Conspiracy 1538* (2 vols., Cambridge, 1915)

Dowling, M., *Humanism in the Age of Henry VIII* (1986)

Duncan-Jones, K., review of W. A. Sessions, *Henry Howard, The Poet Earl of Surrey: A Life* (Oxford, 1999), the *Times Literary Supplement*, 5021 (25 June 1999)

Eckert, C. W., 'The Poetry of Henry Howard, Earl of Surrey' (Washington University Ph.D., 1960)

Evans, M., *English Poetry in the Sixteenth Century* (1955)

Foley, S. M., 'The Honorable Style of Henry Howard, Earl of Surrey: A Critical Reading of Surrey's Poetry' (Yale University, Ph.D., 1979)

Fox, A., *Politics and Literature in the Reigns of Henry VII and Henry VIII* (Oxford, 1989)

Girouard, M., *Life in the English Country House: A Social and Architectural History* (1978)

Greenblatt, S., *Renaissance Self-Fashioning* (1980)

Gunn, S. J., 'The French Wars of Henry VIIII', in *The Origins of War in Early Modern Europe*, ed. J. Black (Edinburgh, 1987)

—*Early Tudor Government 1485–1558* (Basingstoke, 1995)

Guy-Bray, S., '"We Two Boys Together Clinging": The Earl of Surrey and the Duke of Richmond', *English Studies in Canada*, 21/2 (1995)

Hale, J. R., 'Armies, Navies, and the Art of War', in *The New Cambridge Modern History*, vol. 2: *The Reformation, 1520–1559*, 2nd edition, ed. G. R. Elton (Cambridge, 1990)

Hardison, O. B., *Prosody and Purpose in the English Renaissance* (1989)

Harris, B. J., 'Marriage Sixteenth-Century Style: Elizabeth Stafford and the Third Duke of Norfolk', *Journal of Social History*, 15/3 (1982)

—*Edward Stafford, Third Duke of Buckingham, 1478–1521* (Stanford, CA, 1986)

—*English Aristocratic Women, 1450–1550* (Oxford, 2002)

Head, D. M., '"Beyng Ledde and Seduced by the Devyll": The Attainder of Lord Thomas Howard and the Tudor Law of Treason', *Sixteenth Century Journal*, 13/4 (1982)

—*The Ebbs and Flows of Fortune: The Life of Thomas Howard, Third Duke of Norfolk* (1995)

Herman, P. C. (ed.), *Rethinking the Henrician Era: Essays on Early Tudor Texts and Contexts* (Urbana, IL, 1994)

Houlbrooke, R., *Death, Religion and the Family in England, 1480–1750* (Oxford, 1998)

Howard, H. of Corby, *Indications of Memorials, Monuments, Paintings and Engravings of Persons of the Howard Family etc.* (Corby Castle, 1834)

Hoyle, R. W., *The Pilgrimage of Grace and the Politics of the 1530s* (Oxford, 2001)

Ives, E. W., *Anne Boleyn* (Oxford, 1986)

James, M., *Society, Politics and Culture: Studies in Early Modern England* (Cambridge, 1986)

Jentoft, C. W., 'Surrey's Four "Orations" and the Influence of Rhetoric on Dramatic Effect', *Papers on Language and Literature*, 9/3 (1973)

—'Surrey's Five Elegies: Rhetoric, Structure, and the Poetry of Praise', *PMLA: Publications of the Modern Language Association of America*, 91/1 (1976)

—*Sir Thomas Wyatt and Henry Howard, Earl of Surrey: A Reference Guide*

(Boston, MA, 1980)

Jordan, W. K., *Edward VI* (2 vols., 1968, 1970)

Keen, M., *Chivalry* (1984)

Knecht, R. J., *Francis I* (Cambridge, 1982)

Lathrop, H. B., 'Translations from the Classics into English from Caxton to Chapman, 1477–1620', *University of Wisconsin Studies in Language and Literature*, 35 (1933)

Lehmberg, S. E., *The Later Parliaments of Henry VIII, 1536–1547* (Cambridge, 1977)

Lewis, C. S., *English Literature in the Sixteenth Century Excluding Drama* (Oxford, 1954)

Lloyd, D., *The Statesmen and Favourites of England Since the Reformation* (1665)

MacCulloch, D., *Suffolk and the Tudors: Politics and Religion in an English County 1500–1600* (Oxford, 1986)

—(ed.), *The Reign of Henry VIII: Politics, Policy and Piety* (Basingstoke, 1995)

—*Thomas Cranmer: A Life* (1996)

Malof, J., 'The Native Rhythm of English Meters', *Texas Studies in Literature and Language*, 5/4 (1964)

Manning, C. R., 'Kenninghall', *Norfolk Archaeology*, 7 (1872)

Marks, R., 'The Howard Tombs at Thetford and Framlingham: New Discoveries', *The Archaeological Journal*, 141 (1984)

Marotti, A. F., *Manuscript, Print and the English Renaissance Lyric* (1995)

Mason, H. A., *Humanism and Poetry in the Early Tudor Period* (1959)

Mertes, K., *The English Noble Household, 1250–1600: Good Governance and Politic Rule* (Oxford, 1988)

Miller, H., *Henry VIII and the English Nobility* (Oxford, 1986)

Moore, P. R., 'The Heraldic Charge Against the Earl of Surrey, 1546–47', *EHR*, 116/467 (2001)

Muir, K., 'Unpublished Poems in the Devonshire MS', *Proceedings of the Leeds Philosophical and Literary Society*, 6/4 (1947)

Murphy, B. A., *Bastard Prince: Henry VIII's Lost Son* (Stroud, 2001)

Nathan, L. 'The Course of the Particular: Surrey's Epitaph on Thomas Clere and the Fifteenth-Century Lyric Tradition', *Studies in English Literature*, 17/1 (1977)

Oras, A., 'Surrey's Technique of Phonetic Echoes: A Method and its Background', *The Journal of English and Germanic Philology*, 50/3 (1951)

Orme, N., *From Childhood to Chivalry: The Education of the English Kings and Aristocracy, 1066–1530* (1984)

Padelford, F. M., 'The Manuscript Poems of Henry Howard, Earl of Surrey', *Anglia*, 29 (1906)

—*The Poems of Henry Howard Earl of Surrey*, University of Washington

Publications: Language and Literature, 5 (Seattle, 1928)

Peck, L. L., *Northampton: Patronage and Policy at the Court of James I* (1982)

Pigman, G. W. III, *Grief and English Renaissance Elegy* (Cambridge, 1985)

Pinchbeck I., and Hewitt, M., *Children in English Society*, vol. 1: *From Tudor Times to the Eighteenth Century* (1969)

Quinn, D. B., 'Henry VIII and Ireland, 1509–34', *Irish Historical Studies*, 12/48 (1961)

Richardson, D. A., 'Humanistic Intent in Surrey's *Aeneid*', *English Literary Renaissance*, 6/2 (1976)

Richardson, G., '"Good friends and brothers"?: Francis I and Henry VIII', *History Today*, 44/9 (1994)

—*Renaissance Monarchy: The Reigns of Henry VIII, Francis I and Charles V* (2002)

Ridley, F. H. (ed.), *The Aeneid of Henry Howard Earl of Surrey*, University of California Publications, English Studies, 26 (Berkeley and Los Angeles, 1963)

Roberts, H., and Godfrey, W. H. (eds.), *Survey of London*, vol. 23: *South Bank and Vauxhall: The Parish of St Mary Lambeth, Part I* (1951)

Robinson, J. M., *The Dukes of Norfolk* (Chichester, 1995)

Scarisbrick, J. J., *Henry VIII* (1997)

Sessions, W. A., *Henry Howard, Earl of Surrey* (Boston, MA, 1986)

—'"Enough Survives": The Earl of Surrey and European Court Culture', *History Today*, 41 (1991)

—'The Earl of Surrey and Catherine Parr: A Letter and Two Portraits', *ANQ: A Quarterly Journal of Short Articles, Notes and Reviews*, new series, 5/2–3 (1992)

—'Surrey's Psalms in the Tower', in *Sacred and Profane: Secular and Devotional Interplay in Early Modern British Literature*, ed. H. Wilcox, R. Todd and A. MacDonald (Amsterdam, 1996)

Shelby, L. R., *John Rogers: Tudor Military Engineer* (Oxford, 1967)

Smith, L. B., *A Tudor Tragedy: The Life and Times of Catherine Howard* (1961)

—*Henry VIII: The Mask of Royalty* (Chicago, 1982)

Starkey, D., 'The Age of the Household: Politics, Society and the Arts, c.1350–c.1550', in *The Later Middle Ages*, ed. S. Medcalf (1981)

—*The Reign of Henry VIII: Personalities and Politics* (1985)

—(ed.), *Rivals in Power* (1990)

—*Six Wives: The Queens of Henry VIII* (2003)

Stevens, J., *Music & Poetry in the Early Tudor Court* (1961)

Stone, L., and Colvin, H., 'The Howard Tombs at Framlingham, Suffolk', *The Archaeological Journal*, 122 (1965)

Strong, R., *Tudor & Jacobean Portraits* (2 vols., 1969)

Thomas, K., *Religion and the Decline of Magic* (Harmondsworth, 1991)

Thomson, P., 'Wyatt and Surrey', in *English Poetry and Prose, 1540–1674*, ed. C. Ricks (1975)

Thurley, S., *The Royal Palaces of Tudor England: Architecture and Court Life 1460–1547* (1993)

Tromly, F. B., 'Surrey's Fidelity to Wyatt in "Wyatt Resteth Here"', *Studies in Philology*, 77/4 (1980)

Tucker, A. D., 'The Commons in the Parliament of 1545' (Oxford University D.Phil., 1966)

Tucker, M. J., *The Life of Thomas Howard, Earl of Surrey and Second Duke of Norfolk, 1443–1524* (The Hague, 1964)

Vale, M., *War and Chivalry: Warfare and Aristocratic Culture in England, France and Burgundy at the End of the Middle Ages* (1981)

Vokes, S. E., 'The Early Career of Thomas, Lord Howard, Earl of Surrey and Third Duke of Norfolk, 1474–c.1525' (University of Hull Ph.D., 1988)

Waller, G., *English Poetry of the Sixteenth Century* (1993)

Wealth and Power in Tudor England, ed. E. W. Ives, R. J. Knecht and J. J. Scarisbrick (1978)

Williams, N., *Thomas Howard Fourth Duke of Norfolk* (1964)

Wilson, D., *In the Lion's Court: Power, Ambition and Sudden Death in the Court of Henry VIII* (2001)

Woods, S., *Natural Emphasis: English Versification from Chaucer to Dryden* (San Marino, CA, 1984)

Worden, B., review of publications by T. Mayer, A. Fox, R. Warnicke and J. Stoye, in *London Review of Books*, 12/9 (1990)

Zim, R., *English Metrical Psalms: Poetry as Praise and Prayer, 1535–1601* (Cambridge, 1987)

Zitner, S. P., 'Truth and Mourning in a Sonnet by Surrey', *ELH: English Literary History* 50/3 (1983)

INDEX